Dynamics of the Party System

JAMES L. SUNDQUIST

Dynamics of the Party System

Alignment and Realignment of Political Parties
in the United States

THE BROOKINGS INSTITUTION
Washington, D.C.

Copyright © 1973 by
THE BROOKINGS INSTITUTION
1775 Massachusetts Avenue, N.W., Washington, D.C. 20036

Library of Congress Cataloging in Publication Data:

Sundquist, James L
  Dynamics of the party system.
  Includes bibliographical references.
  1. Political parties—United States—History.
I. Title.
JK2261.S9   329'.02   73-1083
ISBN 0-8157-8216-0
ISBN 0-8157-8215-2 (pbk.)

9 8 7

THE BROOKINGS INSTITUTION is an independent organization devoted to nonpartisan research, education, and publication in economics, government, foreign policy, and the social sciences generally. Its principal purposes are to aid in the development of sound public policies and to promote public understanding of issues of national importance.

The Institution was founded on December 8, 1927, to merge the activities of the Institute for Government Research, founded in 1916, the Institute of Economics, founded in 1922, and the Robert Brookings Graduate School of Economics and Government, founded in 1924.

The Board of Trustees is responsible for the general administration of the Institution, while the immediate direction of the policies, program, and staff is vested in the President, assisted by an advisory committee of the officers and staff. The by-laws of the Institution state, "It is the function of the Trustees to make possible the conduct of scientific research, and publication, under the most favorable conditions, and to safeguard the independence of the research staff in the pursuit of their studies and in the publication of the results of such studies. It is not a part of their function to determine, control, or influence the conduct of particular investigations or the conclusions reached."

The President bears final responsibility for the decision to publish a manuscript as a Brookings book or staff paper. In reaching his judgment on the competence, accuracy, and objectivity of each study, the President is advised by the director of the appropriate research program and weighs the views of a panel of expert outside readers who report to him in confidence on the quality of the work. Publication of a work signifies that it is deemed to be a competent treatment worthy of public consideration; such publication does not imply endorsement of conclusions or recommendations contained in the study.

The Institution maintains its position of neutrality on issues of public policy in order to safeguard the intellectual freedom of the staff. Hence interpretations or conclusions in Brookings publications should be understood to be solely those of the author or authors and should not be attributed to the Institution, to its trustees, officers, or other staff members, or to the organizations that support its research.

Foreword

SINCE THE FOUNDING of the Republic, except for a few brief intervals, the American political system has been based on competition between two major parties. But while the country's politics have been cast almost continuously in a two-party mold, the composition of the two parties, and sometimes even their identity, has from time to time undergone fundamental change.

During the past decade, there has been much speculation about whether the American two-party system is entering another such period of change. Some political observers and practicing politicians have found evidence, in some elections, of a realignment in favor of the Democratic party. Others have seen a shift that has created, or will create, a new Republican majority. Still others have suggested that the two-party system is going to give way to a multiparty system, or that political parties may simply disintegrate and cease to be of relevance.

The necessary basis for a judgment about where the American party system may be headed is an understanding of where it has been and how it got to where it is. This in turn requires an understanding of the dynamics of the system—how and under what circumstances the major alterations that have marked its history come about.

In this book, James L. Sundquist has analyzed three major realignments of the past—those that were identified with the critical elections of the 1850s, the 1890s, and the 1930s—as well as several minor realignments. From the historical data, he has constructed a theory of the realignment process. Finally, he has applied the theory in an analysis of recent and current trends in the party system. The findings, which will interest anyone concerned with short- or long-run prospects for decomposition of the two-party system, will bring more cheer to those who hope for a return to the pattern of party alignment characteristic of the late 1950s and the early 1960s than to those who do not.

The study was planned and carried out with the helpful interest of Gilbert Y. Steiner, director of Governmental Studies at the Brookings Institution. Gary Greenhalgh, as research assistant, assembled much of the quantitative material contained in the book and took responsibility for much of the statistical analysis. Grace Dawson compiled the initial bibliography of historical sources, and Kathryn Breen typed successive drafts and verified innumerable facts, figures, and dates. Mr. Steiner and other members of the Governmental Studies staff—Stephen Hess, Herbert Kaufman, William R. Keech, Donald R. Matthews, Daniel A. Mazmanian, and Judith H. Parris—reviewed the manuscript and offered criticism that proved unusually valuable. The manuscript was edited by Elizabeth H. Cross and indexed by Joan C. Culver.

The Brookings Institution is especially grateful to the Library of Congress for making space available for the historical research required. The Library staff, particularly those of the Stack and Reader Division and the Microfilm Reading Room, were unfailingly helpful. The Inter-University Consortium for Political Research at the University of Michigan cooperated by making available the tapes of its 1960 and 1970 election surveys, which were processed by the Social Science Computation Center at Brookings. Everett C. Ladd, Jr., of the University of Connecticut, Paul T. David of the University of Virginia, and Market Opinion Research of Detroit also contributed data.

The conclusions of the book are the responsibility of the author and should not be attributed to the trustees, the officers, or other staff members of the Brookings Institution.

KERMIT GORDON
President

March 1973
Washington, D.C.

Contents

Tables

Figures

CHAPTER ONE

Party Realignment: What?
When? How?

THE NATION "is passing through a profound political transition," concluded the *New York Times* in appraising the results of the 1970 general election. What was it transiting from? The "sound American tradition of two broadly based parties." And what was it transiting to? "It is too early to tell," hedged the *Times*. But it offered two possibilities, both of which it termed undesirable: a polarized system of two "ideologically pure conservative and liberal parties" or a fragmented system of "four or five parties on the European model."[1]

Such speculation that something fundamental was—or is—happening to the American two-party system did not begin with the 1970 election nor did it end there. One can go back to 1963, for instance, and find political scientists Roger D. Masters and Paul T. David predicting in the columns of *The Reporter* that the nomination of Barry Goldwater by the Republicans might well bring about a party realignment comparable to those that had occurred in the major transitions of American political history.[2] And after Goldwater was nominated, and defeated, came a spate of comment that permanent change had indeed been wrought in the country's politics. The dean of academic political survey analysts, Angus Campbell, asked "whether we are entering a period of party realignment which will increase the prevailing Democratic advantage in the party balance." There were indications in the survey data, he said, that such a movement might be taking place.[3]

After the 1968 election the speculation continued, but on different lines. Then, it was the division and defeat of the Democratic party that was seen as a historic turning point. Did 1968 mark "the final breakup" of the Roose-

1. *New York Times*, Nov. 5, 1970.
2. *The Reporter*, Nov. 7, 1963, pp. 23–26; Dec. 5, 1963, p. 8.
3. "Interpreting the Presidential Victory," in Milton C. Cummings, Jr. (ed.), *The National Election of 1964* (Brookings Institution, 1966), p. 281.

velt New Deal coalition, splintered by conflict over such issues as Vietnam, law and order, and the conduct of the young? Many thought so. In 1969 *U.S. News and World Report* found "signs that an era is ending"; "many professionals sense a political swing of deep significance is already well under way."[4] The veteran observer Samuel Lubell began a 1970 book with word of "the beginnings, at least, of both a voter revolution and a realignment of our parties unlike any experienced in our history."[5]

Conservatives were especially quick at that time to see, and celebrate, a realignment. "It is now apparent to most students of our politics," wrote M. Stanton Evans in 1969, "that we have entered a period of fundamental realignment. . . . political forces in this country have so obviously been getting themselves rearranged that the changes can no longer be ignored. In terms of geography, economics, and intellectual atmosphere, enormous transpositions are afoot."[6] And Kevin P. Phillips presented at book length a theory that in 1968 the nation had crossed a political divide as significant as those of 1828, 1860, 1896, and 1932. Noting that each of the previous cycles had lasted thirty-two to thirty-six years and that 1968 was exactly thirty-six years after 1932, Phillips saw Richard Nixon as "destined" to preside over the beginning of "a new cycle of Republican hegemony."[7]

As Mr. Nixon's hegemony—if not that of his party—appeared headed for a smashing confirmation in the 1972 election, pundits again saw signs of fundamental change. Columnist Joseph Alsop, for one, saw in the movement of Democratic "ethnics" to President Nixon "a permanently changing political pattern."[8] Meanwhile, to complicate matters still further, Walter Dean Burnham has assembled evidence suggesting that political parties may be losing their significance altogether.[9]

Is the United States, then, going through a period of "profound political transition," through a realignment, to use the term favored by journalists and political scientists alike? If so, what can be said about the nature of the new party system, and how will it differ from the old? To answer these questions, some other questions must be answered first. Just what is a realignment? How are realignments recognized, defined, and measured? Why

4. "Plight of the U.S. 'Liberals'—Signs that an Era is Ending" (July 14, 1969), p. 38.
5. *The Hidden Crisis in American Politics* (Norton, 1970), p. 17.
6. *The Future of Conservatism* (Doubleday, 1969), pp. xi–xii.
7. *The Emerging Republican Majority* (Arlington House, 1969), pp. 36–37, 22.
8. *Washington Post*, Sept. 15, 1972.
9. "The End of American Party Politics," *Trans-Action* (December 1969), pp. 12–22; *Critical Elections and the Mainsprings of American Politics* (Norton, 1970), esp. Chap. 5.

do they occur? Are the causes outside the party system or within it? What is the process—how does a realignment begin and end and what are the stages in between? How do parties and their leaders behave in times of realignment, and how does their behavior speed or slow the realignment process? Is there a reason for the recurrence of realignments at approximately generational intervals, or is that accidental?

To both the practical question about what is happening to the American party system in the 1970s and the theoretical questions about the nature of the realignment process, this book is addressed.

A Comparative Study of Past Realignments

If there is no consensus as to where the party system is going, even among those who agree that it is headed in a new direction, there is at least a considerable degree of consensus about where it has been. Historians agree that in the unbroken continuity of the two-party system—which dates from the 1830s, when the Whig party came into being to replace the defunct Federalists—there have been three periods of political crisis when one structure of two-party competition gave way to another. In the 1850s, the Whig party died and the Republican party was born. In the 1890s, the Populist party flared briefly, the Democratic party was radicalized, and the Republican party made significant and lasting gains. In the 1930s, millions of voters shifted their party identification from the Republicans to the Democrats. In each of these realignments, the composition of the parties (in the first case, even the identity of one) and the character of the political struggle between them was altered fundamentally, so that the country passed from one distinct "national party system" to another.[10]

To develop an understanding of the realignment process, I have undertaken to analyze as case studies these three critical periods in the American party system. I have tried in each case to identify the forces that disturbed the stability of the existing party system, to trace their origin and develop-

10. William N. Chambers, "Party Development and the American Mainstream," in Chambers and Walter Dean Burnham (eds.), *The American Party System: Stages of Political Development* (Oxford University Press, 1967), p. 3; Burnham, "Party Systems and the Political Process," in ibid., pp. 289–304. They identify five successive "national party systems" since the beginning of the republic. The first was the period of two-party competition that ended with the collapse of the Federalists about 1820. The second was the period of Whig-Democratic competition before the realignment of the 1850s. The other three were ushered in by the realignments of the 1850s, the 1890s, and the 1930s.

ment, to examine the behavior of the parties in response to them, and to follow the events of the crisis to its ultimate resolution in the establishment of a new and once again stable party system. From a comparative analysis of the case studies, I have drawn some general conclusions about the realignment process. These are presented initially in hypothetical form in Chapter 3 and in detail in Chapter 13, after the historical cases have been reviewed. In the closing chapters, the conclusions are used as the basis for analyzing the party system of the 1970s.

There are hazards, of course, in attempting to use the experience of nineteenth-century political parties, including some that are long since dead, for guidance in interpreting the politics of the present. Obviously, much has changed. In the nineteenth century, voting was wholly a masculine affair. The secret ballot was unknown. The direct primary had not been invented. United States senators were elected by state legislatures. The electorate was poorer, less well educated. Party machines built on patronage were far more powerful and pervasive. And the marketing of candidates by political parties through torchlight parades was quite a different process from today's marketing of candidates by professional advertising firms through television.

Nevertheless, there has been an extraordinary degree of institutional continuity through all the changes. The basic two-party system has prevailed with only occasional brief interruptions for fourteen decades. Whatever the factors that make for a two-party system, they appear to have lost none of their vitality during that time. The unique setting in which American parties operate—a single elected chief executive, a federal governmental structure that translates itself into a federal party structure—is basically unchanged. The institutional mechanisms of the parties themselves have evolved little from those early days: the party's governing body is still a committee at each level, and there are still conventions and caucuses and platforms, leaders and followers, contributors and campaign treasuries, systems of party rewards and discipline. More significant, for this analysis, accounts of political motivation and behavior in the nineteenth century read like accounts of these same phenomena today. Relations of leaders to one another and to their followers were much the same then as now. Coalitions took form and dissolved in the same way. Issue-oriented amateurs fought patronage-oriented professionals as they do now, and young upstarts sought to oust entrenched bosses. The same kinds of forces made for party cohesion and breakup. Minor parties played the same role. Parties and pressure groups made alliances in the same way. In short, the setting changes, but the political animal is constructed of the same genes. In any event, there is no source but history for empirical data on realignment in the American party system.[11] And since major realignments occur rarely, one must reach far back—more than a century to find even three cases, which is still a small number to provide a basis for generalization. The remoteness in time of the early cases, as well as the low total number, simply has to be recognized as an inescapable limitation on the study.

The Concept of Party Realignment

The word "realignment" has been variously used in both popular and scholarly discourse, but one element is common to all the stated or implicit definitions. A realignment is a durable change in patterns of political behavior. Every election sees some change in the distribution of the vote between parties because of transitory factors. A citizen who normally votes Democratic may vote Republican, and vice versa, because of one or another temporary influence. He may be alienated by his own party's candidate, attracted by the opposition party's candidate, or influenced by some current issue of public policy. If he crosses the party line only as a temporary matter, then he is not realigning; he is merely "deviating." Sometimes the number of deviants in a particular election is so great that the whole election can be classed as a deviation from the political norm. Campbell so identifies the presidential contest of 1916, when Democrat Woodrow Wilson was re-elected in a period when the majority of the country's voters were, and remained, Republican; and the elections of 1952 and 1956, when Republican Dwight D. Eisenhower was victorious in a period when most voters were, and remained, Democrats.[12] To these the landslides of 1964 and 1972 can be added; most of the millions of Republicans who voted for Lyndon Johnson in his year of triumph did not thereupon become converts to the Democratic

11. While understanding of the realignment process could be deepened by examination of cases from other democratic countries, that is beyond the scope of this study. Seymour M. Lipset and Stein Rokkan (eds.), *Party Systems and Voter Alignments: Cross-National Perspectives* (Free Press, 1967), have made a comparative study of alignment patterns in democratic countries, but it focuses on European systems and devotes little attention to the United States. The encyclopedic work of David Butler and Donald E. Stokes, *Political Change in Britain: Forces Shaping Electoral Choice* (St. Martin's, 1969), is a rich source of data and observations on the realignment process in twentieth-century Britain, which parallels many aspects of experience in the United States.

12. Angus Campbell, "A Classification of the Presidential Elections," in Campbell and others, *Elections and the Political Order* (Wiley, 1966), pp. 69–74.

party, nor did most of the Democrats who voted for Richard Nixon's reelection become by that act Republicans.

It is when the political norm itself changes that realignment occurs. The concept applies, then, not to voting behavior as such, but to what underlies voting behavior—to the basic party attachments of the voting citizens. "Most members of the electorate feel some degree of psychological attachment to one of the major parties," Campbell has written. "This partisan identification is remarkably resistant to passing political events and typically remains constant through the life of the individual." The voter's behavior at a particular election "derives from the interaction of his political predispositions and the short-term forces generated by the current political situation."[13] It is the pattern of those predispositions, of party identification within the electorate, that defines the alignment of the party system.[14]

Quite apart from temporary fluctuations in voting behavior, the pattern of party identification itself undergoes continuous change—sometimes rapidly, violently, and on a major scale, sometimes slowly, quietly, and on a lesser scale. Several types of change, arising from different kinds of causes, need to be distinguished conceptually.

The first distinction to be made is between the changes in relative party strength that result from *organic change in the party system* and those that do not. If the two-party system is visualized (in a somewhat oversimplified image, which will be presented more fully in the next chapter) as an electorate divided by a line of party cleavage, an organic change in the system can be defined as a relocation of the line. Any relocation, obviously, redistributes some voters across the line in one or both directions. But significant shifts in relative party strength can take place even though the line remains fixed.

Changes of the latter kind can be divided into two categories. The first is

13. "Voters and Elections: Past and Present," *Journal of Politics*, Vol. 26 (1964), p. 747.

14. In any alignment, of course, a substantial number of voters remain independent, without psychological attachment to either party. When analyzing changes in the structure of the party system, these voters have to be disregarded as being outside the system. The matter of identification is also complicated by the possibility, in a federal party system, that some voters may identify with one party at the state level and another at the national level. But survey evidence indicates that only about 1 percent of the voters admit to a split identification; another 5 percent have a conflict of identification but resolve it by thinking of themselves as partisan at one level and independent at the other; and 94 percent identify the same way at both levels. The data are from the 1958 election survey of the Survey Research Center, University of Michigan. Philip E. Converse, "On the Possibility of Major Political Realignment in the South," in Campbell and others, *Elections and the Political Order*, p. 219.

purely *demographic*, resulting from changes in the voting population. If a
newly enfranchised voting group—women half a century ago, rural southern
blacks and eighteen-year-olds more recently—prefer one party to another as
a group, the party balance alters. In the past, the Democratic party could
become the majority party in many a seaboard city without the conversion
of a single Republican voter, for every immigrant ship brought eventual
additions to the party's ranks. Voter-registration drives among politically
inactive population groups can affect the party balance without a structural
change in the system. So, over a long period, can differing birthrates.

While the line of party cleavage stays fixed, voters can also step across it,
as the result of *individual conversion*. If the party system reflects urban-rural
cleavage, the party identified with the cities may gain as the country urban-
izes. If the rationale of the party system is one of class, voters may change
party identification when they rise from the working to the middle class. In
recent years, the Republicans have perhaps gained from the movement of
city Democrats to suburban strongholds of the GOP. And so on. No population group of significant size gives its allegiance wholly to one party or the
other, but most have a measurable bias, and as the groups change in size the
balance of party strength is altered. Finally, even though neither party
changes its leadership or its programs or its image, a substantial number of
the voters of one party may decide upon mature reflection—in theory, at
least—that they have made a mistake and the other party has the better of
the political argument. Or voters of a new generation may conclude that
their parents had made the wrong choice and affiliate with the opposite party,
which is the equivalent of individual conversion even though it takes place
between rather than within generations.

The three major realignments analyzed in this book are, of course, the
most dramatic examples of the type of change that does involve an organic
alteration of the party system. In each of those three periods of political
crisis—the 1850s, the 1890s, and the 1930s—the existing rationale for the
division of voters between the parties gave way to a new one. One or both
of the major parties was radically changed in composition and character. The
voting blocs that came together as coalitions to make up the major parties
were rearranged. Thus the line of party cleavage sliced through the electorate in a new direction, shifting the party structure on its axis. When
things settled down, the changes had been so profound that in retrospect, as
noted earlier, a new party system can be seen to have replaced the old.

It was drastic upheaval of this type, naturally enough, that first attracted attention to party realignment as a field for scholarly research. A pioneering article by V. O. Key, Jr., in 1955 called attention to the significance in party history of what he termed "critical elections": "a type of election in which there occurs a sharp and durable electoral realignment between parties." Key also identified the critical election as "one in which the depth and intensity of electoral involvement are high" and "in which more or less profound readjustments occur in the relations of power within the community."[15]

Yet Key recognized that his theory of critical elections did not explain all aspects of the realignment phenomenon. Four years later, in another article, he presented a concept of "secular realignment," a long-term, rather than a sharp and sudden, redistribution of party strength—the result of processes that "operate inexorably, and almost imperceptibly, election after election, to form new party alignments and to build new party groupings." He cited examples, such as the long-term drift to the Republican party of German-Americans in a rural Ohio county and the gradual movement of Jewish voters in a Boston ward toward the Democrats.[16] Burnham, simplifying Key's terminology, speaks of "critical realignment" and "secular realignment."

The two, however, are by no means distinct phenomena. Much of what appears as secular realignment is simply a later stage, or a later series of stages, of a preceding critical realignment—the aftershocks, so to speak, as the fault lines created by the initial political earthquake settle into place. A realignment is the sum of a myriad of individual decisions, flowing from the same cause. A large proportion of the decisions may be made at the same time, during one or more "critical" elections, but others may be distributed over a long period in secular fashion, before as well as after the crisis. When the changes in party identification spring from the same cause, it confuses more than it clarifies to treat the critical and the secular as separate types of realignment rather than as phases of a single process. As will be shown in later chapters, much of the political change that has occurred since World War II is a delayed, secular phase of the realignment that reached its climax in the critical elections of the 1930s.

Other shifts in party strength that contribute to what seem to be secular

15. "A Theory of Critical Elections," *Journal of Politics*, Vol. 17 (1955), pp. 3–18. Quotations are from pp. 16 and 4.

16. "Secular Realignment and the Party System," *Journal of Politics*, Vol. 21 (1959), pp. 198–210. Quotation is from pp. 198–99.

trends differ from the "critical" realignments not in character but only in degree. If major political forces produce major upheavals on a national scale, a minor force may produce, through the same process but on a limited geographic scale or within only some population groups, a minor alteration in the patterns of party identification. A minor realignment may be as sharp and sudden for the people affected as a major one, yet be "almost imperceptible" in the aggregate election or party registration figures simply because the proportion of the electorate involved is small. It may be hidden in an election that is classed as a deviation; among the mass of voters who cross the party line in a year such as 1952 or 1964, most cross as deviants but some undoubtedly realign. Indeed, no election could pass without some degree of realignment among some population groups, from causes independent of any major realigning forces that may be at work. Each of the types of change in party strength and composition mentioned here needs to be seen as variable in scale according to the proportion of voters whose party identification is altered.

Some writers have used the term "realignment" to cover every durable, significant change in party strength, no matter what the cause. Key's definition apparently would exclude pure demographic change but cover all other changes, dividing them between "critical" elections and "secular" realignment according to the pace of change. But the question of organic change in the party system is so basic to any analysis of realignment that it is of prime importance to find a terminology that distinguishes between the shifts in relative party strength that arise from organic change and those that are independent of it. For that reason, I propose to identify as realignments only the former. The term will encompass both the "critical" and the "secular" events arising from the same realigning force. Changes in relative party strength occurring without organic change will be referred to simply as *shifts in the party balance*.[17]

17. This definition of "realignment" differs from one offered by Gerald M. Pomper. He divides elections that involve organic change into two categories, depending on whether the majority party retains its majority status or loses it, and limits the term "realigning" to the latter. The former he calls "converting" elections. *Elections in America: Control and Influence in Democratic Politics* (Dodd, Mead, 1968), p. 104. This use of terms has the great disadvantage of appropriating the common term "realignment" for a limited and somewhat specialized usage, leaving no simple term to embrace both his categories. "Realignment" is a perfectly suitable term to use for that purpose. By the structure of the word, *realignment* is the replacement of one alignment by another; its use should not be made dependent on whether, in the given instance of replacement, a particular, possibly incidental, consequence occurs. Burnham also suggests the Pomper typology may be "superfluous" (*Critical Elections*, pp. 32–33). William H. Flanigan and Nancy H.

The Partial Character of Realignments

Although each of the three major realignments of the American party system reviewed in this study replaced the existing system with one radically different, only a portion of the electorate was involved in the reshuffle. The existing pattern of party attachments was not erased and a new one drawn, even during a realignment as traumatic and violent as that of the Civil War period. This must inevitably be the case in any democratic society with a mature party system. It is hardly conceivable that any political force could arise that would be sufficiently powerful to obliterate all the reasons for attachment by members of the electorate to the existing parties.

In every new alignment of the party system, then, will be remnants of the old. Successive realignments can best be understood as new patterns drawn on transparent overlays. Each overlay defines a new line of party cleavage within the electorate (or redelineates an old line) and so distributes some elements of the voting population on either side of that line in new arrangements. But beneath the latest overlay can be seen all the lines of cleavage of the past, some more distinct than others by virtue of their recency or the strength of the colors in which they were originally drawn. Moreover, since a realignment may be a long-drawn-out process, the line of cleavage in the latest overlay may not yet be as sharp as it will ultimately become; it may still be in the process of refinement when a new one is laid down on top of it.

Even in the early nineteenth century, when this study begins, the pattern of party attachments that defined the alignment of the American party system was already a collage of successive overlays. To find the simple setting needed for a consideration of the essential process of party realignment, one must create a hypothetical society, one so simple that it has, at the outset, no political history and a totally undifferentiated social structure.

Zingale divide realigning elections into still another pair of subcategories. If the realignment is "across-the-board" in favor of one party, it is a "realigning surge"; if it involves compensating shifts in both directions, it is a "realigning interaction." "Measurement of Electoral Stability and Change, 1832 to 1968" (paper presented at annual meeting of American Political Science Association, Chicago, September 1971; processed). For the purposes of this book, I have not found it necessary to distinguish between these two types of realignment.

CHAPTER TWO

Some Hypothetical Scenarios

A COMPANY of settlers arrives in a new land. It is an isolated land, cut off from any outside influence. There the settlers set up a new community, with a democratic form of government. The families occupy tracts of land exactly equal in size and fertility. By chance, the adults of the community are identical in all the respects (except sex, of course) that political and social analysts have found significant in differentiating people—age, religion, ethnic background, wealth, education, family size, and all the rest. They are all also without previous political affiliation or identification.

A classless, partyless, ungrouped, atomized society, they begin cultivation of their land. But when the first season's crops have been gathered and the community has assembled to celebrate the harvest, one of the settlers rises to address his fellows. Let us, he says, levy a tax on each settler—in equal amounts, of course—to build an irrigation system to increase our yields. Let us lower our scale of living slightly in the short run in order to realize a greater income in future years.

Formation of a Party System

The proposal splits the community. The undifferentiated society suddenly differentiates. Some of the settlers hail the suggested irrigation system as the road to untold prosperity for the whole community. Others see in it unmitigated folly—it has never been tried, it would cost far more than anybody expects, it would not work even if it were built, and it contravenes the very laws of nature. At most, they contend, it should be attempted on an experimental scale and the tests carefully evaluated.

The advocates of the irrigation system are undaunted by the opposition. They meet to nominate for office a slate of candidates who will, if elected,

Figure 2-1. *Positions of Voting Blocs on Three Issues*[a]

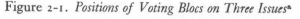

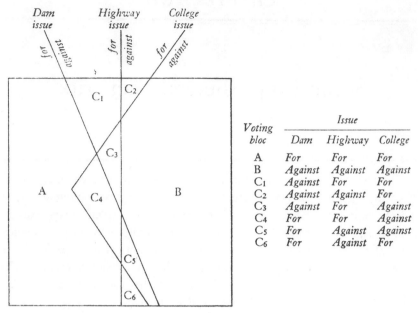

Voting	Issue		
bloc	Dam	Highway	College
A	For	For	For
B	Against	Against	Against
C_1	Against	For	For
C_2	Against	Against	For
C_3	Against	For	Against
C_4	For	For	Against
C_5	For	Against	Against
C_6	For	Against	For

a. This figure, like all the others in this chapter, is schematic rather than quantitatively precise. The size of the compartments does not measure the proportion of the electorate contained in each.

move at once to levy the tax and build the dam and the accompanying canals. Opponents then meet to nominate another slate of candidates. The election that fall revolves around the irrigation issue. The proponents win by a narrow margin and proceed to carry out their program.

Then other issues arise. The pro-dam faction, in the exuberance of victory, conceives other projects to be financed by more new taxes, including highway construction and a community college. Again the community is split. For the most part, the pro-dam people turn out to be also the pro-highway and pro-college people, and most of the opponents of the original project are also the opponents of the new ones. But a few find themselves in favor of only one or two and against the others. The lines of cleavage can be diagramed as in Figure 2-1.[1]

The preponderance of the voters, who find themselves in blocks A and B,

1. The diagraming of cleavages in the electorate and the terminology relating to them are adapted from E. E. Schattschneider, *The Semi-Sovereign People: A Realist's View of Democracy in America* (Holt, Rinehart and Winston, 1960), Chaps. 4–7.

are those who are either for or against all three projects. They recognize that the cleavage in the community is a durable one and the time has come to organize to win and hold control of the government on a continuing basis. The incumbents, in block A, call themselves the Progressive party and adopt a platform supporting all three programs. Their opponents, who occupy block B, organize the Conservative party to oppose all three. In the blocks labeled C are the voters who are not in full agreement with the policies of either party. They in turn are divided into six groups, representing the six possible combinations of advocacy of one or two of the three measures and opposition to the other one or two. As the parties organize and begin to proselyte, some of these people come to identify with one or the other political body, submerging their partial disagreement on the issues to the influence of friends, neighbors, and family. Indeed, a few who agree wholly with the program of one party may, under such influence, identify with the other party. Others in the C blocks remain genuinely independent, without psychological attachment to either party, and some of those in blocks A and B remain independent as well, because they dislike the party leaders or reject any fixed partisan commitment as a matter of principle. For purposes of analysis of party realignment, the independents can be disregarded and the party system represented as a simple rectangle divided into two cells—one containing those who think of themselves as Progressives, the other those who identify with the Conservative party.

The parties alternate in power. Whenever the Progressives overreach themselves and the tax burden becomes too onerous, the Conservatives are voted in. Then, when the voters conclude that the Conservatives are too complacent and highway construction and improvement of other public services are not proceeding fast enough, they turn to the Progressives to speed things up. Most of the voters in block A vote consistently for the Progressive party and most of those in block B for the Conservatives, and their attachment grows firmer with time. But in each election a few deviants cross the party line to support the opposition or rebuke their own leaders without shifting their basic psychological attachment. Initially the parties are evenly matched in terms of party identifiers, and the volume and direction of the net deviation and the majority support of the independents determines the election outcome. Gradually, however, the Progressive measures are accepted, particularly as children of the original settlers reach voting age, and the Progressive party achieves a somewhat larger number of adherents than the opposition—a shift in the party balance without a realignment. Nevertheless, the Conservatives are able to win elections whenever the Progressive party carries its policies too far, is tarred with patronage scandals, or commits administrative blunders, or whenever the Conservatives nominate a man of markedly superior attainment and personal appeal to head their ticket.

The difference between the Progressives and the Conservatives is more than the sum total of their differences on the specific issues of irrigation systems, highways, and public education. The members of the two parties are separated by a basic difference in attitude, outlook, and temperament, which finds expression in the positions taken on specific issues. The Progressives are united by a set of activist attitudes toward the role of government, a willingness to take risks in order to achieve quickly the kind of society they regard as good. The Conservatives are bound together by a common concern for the consequences of those risks, a suspicion that the new society will not be enough better than the old to be worth the cost. They look upon the Progressive leaders as reckless spenders of other people's money, motivated not only by the value they place on the dams and highways but also by the patronage such programs enable them to distribute. The Progressives in turn see the Conservative leaders as men without vision, enterprise, or faith, more concerned with their immediate material satisfaction than with the long-run common good. So the two parties have divergent ideologies, based on differing conceptions of what constitutes the good society.

But along comes another issue, which adds a new *moral* dimension to the community's political dispute. One of the settlers, tired of farming and not identified with either party, proposes to open a saloon at the town's main crossroads. This cleaves the community on wholly different lines. The argument is heated, and becomes more heated as time goes on. The stage is now set for a realignment of the party system.

The Prerealignment Period

Within each of the two existing parties are found both points of view on the saloon issue. Some Progressives are ready, even enthusiastic, to embrace the saloon issue as the embodiment of the idea of Progress. But other Progressives swear to oppose it to the end. Some Conservatives who oppose on principle any new departure by government see the new venture in a different light; it is, after all, private rather than public enterprise, and it would

Figure 2-2. *A New Line of Cleavage Cuts across the Old*

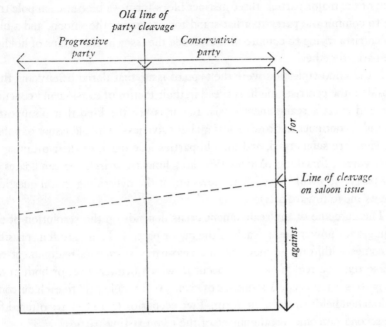

Old line of
party cleavage

Progressive   Conservative
party   party

for

against

— Line of cleavage
on saloon issue

provide refreshment after a hard day in the fields. Other Conservatives find this disturbance of the status quo as objectionable as any other. Figure 2-2 shows a new line of cleavage in the party pattern.

In each of the existing parties, a few leading spokesmen urge that the party officially endorse and sponsor the saloon proposal. At first these voices are a minority. The party leaders are hesitant. This is not the kind of issue—like a dam or a highway project—that rallies either party around the ideological position on which its unity is based. Quite the contrary. This is a cross-cutting, party-splitting issue. The party leaders recoil from it. They temporize. They evade. Would the proposed saloon be in the right location? Is the entrepreneur of good character? What restrictions and controls would have to be imposed? Does not the suggestion require further study? Should a commission be appointed to advise on the project?

As this goes on, the thirsty elements of the community begin to get impatient. Some of the more ambitious pro-saloon leaders within each party realize that here is an issue which, if exploited vigorously and skillfully, may enable them to wrest control from the established leaders. They press their case with increasing energy. The anti-saloon elements respond with a fervid counterattack. Within the community at large, opinion polarizes. And within each of the major parties, three distinct blocs form—a bloc at each pole trying to commit the party to a flat stand for or against the saloon, and a bloc of centrists trying to compromise or evade the issue as the means of holding the party together.

If the saloon question were the type of issue that flared briefly and then subsided, the centrists might succeed in their tactics of evasion and conciliation and avert a realignment crisis. But it is not the kind that disappears; instead it continues to grow in heat and divisiveness. The old issues of public spending are submerged, and the old parties lose much of their meaning as most voters, forsaking past political attachments, search for candidates of any party who will reflect their views about the overriding moral question. Events move toward a crisis.

The outcome of the realignment crisis depends on the resolution of the struggle for power within each of the major parties. There are four possible outcomes within the framework of a two-party system: a realignment can be averted or a realignment can occur in which neither, one, or both of the old parties is replaced. A sequence of events that would lead to each outcome is sketched below in scenario form. Two scenarios (2 and 3) are offered for the second outcome—realignment of the two existing parties.

Scenario 1: No Major Realignment

While the Conservative party, which happens to be in power at the time, is holding hearings, appointing study commissions, and otherwise temporizing, the pro-saloon forces stage a giant rally in the public square. As celebrants begin to arrive from all over the community, a number of influential Progressive leaders meet in hurried conclave. Emerging from their session just as the rally is concluding, they call a news conference and read a joint declaration, which says, in part: "We recognize that it is the responsibility of a political party in a democracy to respond to the will of the people. We believe that, at this time, the desire of the majority of the people in regard to the prohibition issue is unmistakably clear. They are in favor of permitting the serving of intoxicating beverages in public places under proper safeguards that will assure temperance, that will protect minors, and that will continue to preserve the Sabbath as a day of abstinence. Whatever may have been our past individual views on this issue, therefore, we now announce that we will no longer oppose the licensing of the proposed liquor-dispensing establishment, and we will urge others of the Progressive party to follow the same course." At this, the party's anti-saloon faction capitulates, the party writes a new pro-saloon platform, and its candidates set out to defeat the incumbent Conservatives who have been stalling the saloon proposal.

This development emboldens the pro-saloon wing of the Conservative party, which has been working up its own challenge to the vacillating leadership. The insurgents enter a full slate of candidates in the party's primary, and the tide is with them. They triple their voting strength, winning a clear majority in the party's central committee and almost a majority of the legislative nominations. The mandate is clear. The saloon is coming; it is only a matter of time. When the Progressives again force the issue to a vote, enough members of the Conservative majority defect to give the pro-saloon coalition its victory. In a joyous bipartisan ceremony, ground is broken for construction of the institution so long disputed, and the issue is resolved.

With that fierce, absorbing issue out of the way, the old questions of tax and spending policy become again the principal subjects of public discussion. While the community was engrossed in the struggle over the saloon, it is discovered, some farmers have been buying the land of other farmers and a new impoverished class of landless laborers has appeared. The Progressives demand a whole series of governmental actions to alleviate the poverty of the working class and provide health and welfare services for their families. Conservatives unite, as before, against the proposed expansion of the role of government. The parties become relevant again. Voters who had broken loose from their party attachments during the long saloon debate drift back. The old line of party cleavage appears in a new overlay in most of its original sharpness. Beneath can still be seen the line of cleavage on the saloon issue. It is reflected in a persistent factionalism and strained personal relations within each party, but it fades gradually as time passes.

While a major realignment was averted, some realignment on a minor scale occurred because the behavior of the two parties in relation to the new issue was not identical. The Progressives yielded to the saloon advocates first; the Conservatives later and more reluctantly. During the short interval between the parties' respective actions, some pro-saloon Conservatives cast their lot with the Progressives as the party more responsive to their overriding concern, while some irreconcilable Progressive opponents became Conservatives. Most of these defections proved to be temporary once both parties had accepted the saloon, but some shifting of allegiance remained to constitute a minor realignment.

Scenario 2 : Realignment of the Two Existing Parties

When the Progressive leaders emerge from their meeting and announce their acceptance of the saloon, an uproar arises within the party. A dozen die-hard opponents of the enterprise denounce "the little group of self-appointed, so-called leaders of the Progressive party who are willing to sacrifice the morality and health of the community for their own short-run political advantage." They vow to take the issue to the rank and file of the party at its primary elections and party conventions. But when they do, they lose. With that, the Progressive party is committed unqualifiedly to the new definition of "progressive."

Meanwhile, the Conservatives have gone in the opposite direction. Forced by events to finally resolve the issue, the incumbent Conservative administration comes off the fence, on the side of opposition. Staking the future of the party and the government on the issue, it rallies the organization, including all of the party's jobholders, behind the party position.

But in each party there remains a thoroughly aroused, disgruntled, and rebellious wing, made up of those who agree with the party's stand on the sound old issues of government spending and taxation but who cannot accept its stand on liquor. As the election approaches, these voters must make a choice. They find themselves torn between conflicting pressures. Do they stick with their party on the old issues, or do they realign with the party that expresses their convictions on the new issue? Some remain loyal. Others make the switch. Still others express their disgust by refusing to vote at all or declaring themselves independents. If the independents and the not-yet-decided are excluded, the party structure can now be diagramed as in Figure 2-3.

Voters in blocks A and D are those who have no conflict. They find themselves happily in agreement with the position of their party on both the old set of issues and the new. Blocks B and C contain the voters who are torn. Progressives in block C must either swallow their party's stand on the saloon issue or leave the party. Conservatives in block B face a similar choice. Some in each block are impelled by the force of the moral issue to cast aside old habits and enlist with the party they once opposed. They are

Figure 2-3. *Realignment of the Two Existing Parties*

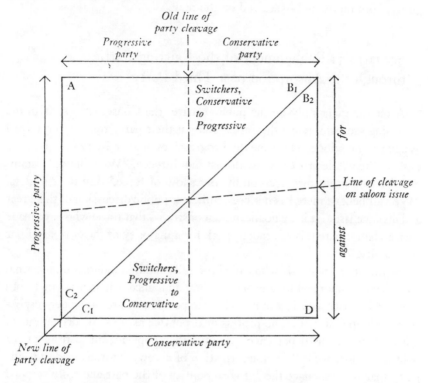

shown in blocks B_1 and C_1. But for others the ties of sentiment, of friends and family, of patronage, of party ambition, of concern for the old issues, are paramount; besides, there is always the chance that, by maintaining their party standing, they can change the decision hastily made in the heat of passion. So those voters, shown in blocks B_2 and C_2, remain loyal.

Some of the voters in blocks B and C, once they have made their party choice, are able without undue difficulty to bring their own outlook into conformity with the views of their party. But others cannot. And so there remain four identifiable minority groups, two in each party: a conservative anti-spending wing in the Progressive party (B_1), a progressive pro-spending wing in the Conservative party (C_1), a pro-saloon wing in the Conservative party (B_2), and an anti-saloon wing in the Progressive party (C_2). The old lines of cleavage that set them apart are clearly visible through the latest overlay that defines the new line of party cleavage. Within each party, the three blocs contend for control of the party's policy, and the presence of the dissenters brings about some moderation of the party's stands as the years go by, both on the old issues and on the new.

Scenario 3: Realignment of the Existing Parties through the Absorption of a Third Party

After the giant rally on the public square, the Conservatives, as in the preceding scenario, reject the appeal and put their party squarely on record as against the saloon. This time the Progressives hold no hasty session; they observe the whole proceeding with vast indifference. "We will not be stampeded into a premature decision by any show of force," say their leaders. "We still believe there has not been sufficient public discussion of this great and divisive issue. It is by no means demonstrated that those who have made such a clamor here this afternoon speak for a majority of the citizens of our community."

At this, the firebrands who called the rally hold an indignation meeting. "We have temporized long enough," they announce. "It is plain that both of the old parties have lost touch with the people and are no longer responsive to the public will. The professional politicians must be driven out of office by the aroused populace. To give that populace an instrument for political action, we call for the formation of a new, vigorous, and dynamic party that will renounce the outworn politics of the past and truly respond to the young and forward-looking citizens of this community."

A convention is held, and in a burst of mass ardor the Liberal party is launched. It is dedicated to individual freedom and to "economic expansion through diversification of the forms of retail enterprise." It elects three co-chairmen—one former Progressive, one former Conservative, and one prominent independent—and invites citizens from all three groups to affiliate. The new party quickly wins adherents and gains strength, and the party system changes, as shown in Figure 2-4.

In the Progressive party the saloon advocates are too large a minority to be suppressed, and they are a growing minority. When the Liberal party is formed, the threat to the Progressives is clear: either they yield on the saloon issue or their strength will be drained away by the energetic new organization. In the districts where the Liberals are most aggressive and successful, the Progressives find themselves forced to nominate pro-saloon candidates. The trend seems clear; one by one, the practical politicians from

Figure 2-4. *A Strong and Growing Third Party Foreshadows Realignment*

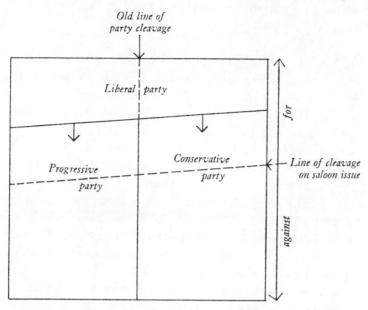

safe Progressive districts who are more concerned about the party's future than about the saloon issue in itself begin to make common cause with the pro-saloon Progressive wing. Presently, enough of the established Progressive leaders have endorsed the saloon principle to tip the balance within the party, and the rest of the practical, organization-minded Progressives join the bandwagon. At a dramatic convention, the Progressives add the Liberals' one-issue platform to their own customary progressive one. Some of the Liberal leaders who had launched their party with the hope of riding it to power cry out that the Progressives cannot be trusted and the Liberals must fight on under their own banner. But they have lost their rank and file. The third party lingers for a time, then quietly expires.

The resulting alignment is essentially the same as that shown in Figure 2-3. A few of the former Conservatives who had joined the Liberal party return home rather than join their traditional enemy, the Progressive party, but for the most part the Liberal party turns out to have been a convenient halfway house for Conservative-to-Progressive switchers. More Progressives switch than did in scenario 3, out of resentment at the "capture" of their party by the radical Liberals. But the structure of the system is the same. Within each party two blocs of dissenters can be identified, as before.

Scenario 4: Realignment through the Replacement of One Major Party

As the Liberal party begins its rapid growth, younger Progressives from pro-saloon districts, seeing their own and their party's support eroding, sound an alarm. Accept the saloon, they cry, and save the party. But this time they fail. Their party's leadership is old and out of touch; absorbed in patronage struggles with the Conservatives, it ignores all the agitation. Just be patient, say the leaders. The new party is a summer storm that in time will pass; third parties, as everybody knows, have no future. In vain the young Progressives try to move their elders.

Meanwhile, at the opposite end of the party spectrum, anti-saloon Progressives are equally aroused. They see the rising Liberal party as a social evil and political menace that must be defeated at any cost. They demand that their party cease straddling and evading and come down, like the Conservatives, in stern opposition to all things Liberal. As the issue grows in intensity and the community polarizes, the centrist leadership of the Progressive party finds its support eroding. Progressives are defecting in both directions. The Liberal party appeals to the pro-saloon voters as the dynamic, effective spokesman for their cause. And to the saloon's opponents, the Conservative party seems the fortress in which to make their stand. To hold down their losses in both directions, the Progressive leaders desperately talk of compromise. But the issue cannot be mediated; there is no way to split the difference between having a saloon and not having one. The leaders try to shift the political debate back to old ground by proposing vast new programs of public works, but no one listens. The party convention turns into a showdown between pro- and anti-saloon forces. The former win. The latter acquiesce in the decision of the convention but give the Progressive candidates no support in the election and they are crushed by a Conservative landslide. The pro-saloon Progressives now realize that the party machinery they captured is worthless by itself. What is needed, obviously, is a new party that will embrace all the pro-saloon forces of the community—Progressives, Liberals, and pro-saloon Conservatives. The initiative is taken in a few districts to create the new party, called the Action party, and presently it is organized throughout the community. The Liberals and Progressives formally dissolve. But since the Action party is made up largely of former Progressives, it adopts with some modification the old progressive ideology on taxing-spending issues.

Figure 2-5. *Realignment through the Replacement of One Party*

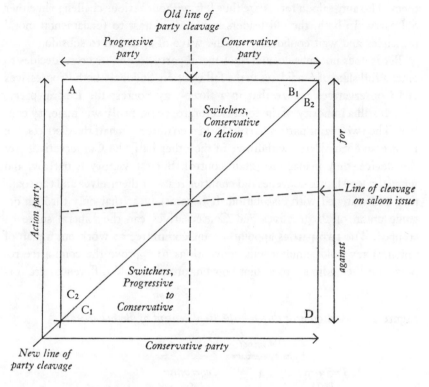

The resulting realignment (shown in Figure 2-5) is like the one in Figure 2-3, except for a change in party nomenclature.

As a variant of the above scenario, the pro-saloon Progressives and dissident Conservatives might simply have decided to join the Liberal party rather than form a new one. The result would have been the same, except for a difference in party name. In either case the Progressive party would have been replaced as one of the major parties.

Scenario 5: Realignment through the Replacement of Both Old Parties

Instead of trying to evade and compromise the issue, as in scenario 4, the Progressive party joins the Conservative party in adamant resistance. The most vocal and energetic of the saloon advocates from both major parties now desert to the new Liberal party, taking large blocs of supporters with them. The anti-saloon forces are thus left without serious challenge in either old party. In both, the old leaders remain steadfast to fundamental moral principles and wait confidently for the wave of agitation to subside.

But it does not subside, and the Liberal party, riding its crest, decides to enter a full slate of candidates in the fall election. Suddenly both Progressives and Conservatives realize that in a three-way contest the Liberal party, though still a minority of the total electorate, could easily win majority control. The two major parties hastily form a coalition; in half the districts, the Progressive candidates withdraw; in the other half, the Conservatives. By this device, they manage to retain control. But the victory is narrow, and when the legislature convenes old enmities reassert themselves and the coalition is threatened with dissolution. It becomes clear that only through organic union of Progressives and Conservatives can the Liberal surge be stopped. The two parties appoint a joint committee to work out a plan of union. They hold simultaneous conventions to approve the committee report, and then adjourn to a joint convention where old differences are for-

Figure 2-6. *Realignment through the Replacement of Both Parties*

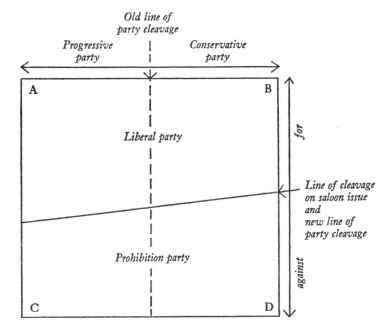

gotten in emotion-packed proceedings that bring into being the Prohibition party. Now the party structure is as shown in Figure 2-6.

Still visible is the old ideological line of cleavage, which separated former Progressives and former Conservatives on issues of government spending and taxation. But the moral issue remains uppermost, for a time at least; even when the first saloon is authorized, after the initial Liberal victory, there remain questions as to hours of operation, the kinds of beverages to be permitted, the number of additional saloons to be authorized, the extent and kind of advertising to be allowed, and the size of the tax levy to which saloons should be subjected. Moreover, related moral questions divide the electorate on the same lines. On these moral issues, which unite them, both parties are forthright and outspoken, and so they inflame the issues. When taxing and spending are debated, the parties are forced to straddle; party cohesion breaks down and Liberals and Prohibitionists of progressive sentiment (blocks A and C) collaborate across the party line, as do conservatives of both parties (blocks B and D).

CHAPTER THREE

The Realignment Process:
A Preliminary Statement

IN THE SIMPLIFIED SETTING of the hypothetical community, the process of party realignment can be seen in its essentials.

A party system that divides people into two contending political groups on the basis of their attitudes and beliefs about one set of public issues is disturbed by a new issue (or cluster of related issues). The new issue cleaves the electorate on a different line and hence divides each of the parties internally. The new issue can be of any kind, arising from any of the wide variety of dissatisfactions and grievances that can be felt by groups of citizens on matters they conceive to be the proper concern of government. Either at the outset or as it gathers momentum, the new issue comes to be of such paramount political concern to some proportion of the voters that it overrides all the considerations that form the basis of their attachment to the existing parties. In the intensity of their desire to use the machinery of politics and government to resolve the new issue, these voters are willing, if necessary, to abandon old party affiliations for new ones. The aroused citizens within each party form two hostile blocs, one at each pole. In the center of each party is a third bloc of voters who have not been polarized, who may be called centrists; while they may feel strongly about the new issue, they are not ready to sacrifice their party to the cause.

If the centrists are able to resolve the issue before the polar groups have achieved significant growth, both major parties will survive and the realignment will be minor. The scale of the realignment in that event will depend on the size of the polar forces at the time the issue is resolved and the degree of difference they perceive between the major parties. Scenario 1 of the preceding chapter described a case in which the major parties yielded on the crosscutting issue, with little difference in attitude and timing, and so averted a major realignment. Similarly, if both parties hold firm on the issue and it is the kind that wanes and disappears, a major realignment will be avoided.

But if the issue remains unresolved and public concern continues to grow, the polar forces will increase and each of the major parties will become a battleground for the three forces contending for control—the two polar blocs and the centrists who are trying to prevent the party from being torn apart. The outcome of the struggle determines the timing of the realignment, its scale, and the form it takes.

The polar groups will try, at the outset, to use the existing party machinery for their purposes. But if neither polar group can gain control of a major party—that is, of its policies and its nominations—then some elements of one or both polar groups may create a new party or parties. Other polar elements will remain within the existing parties, still striving to convert them to their ends. As long as the centrists are able to retain control of both major parties, realignment will be forestalled, and three or even four parties may compete for a time. But if the new issue becomes increasingly dominant, the polar forces will grow at the expense of the centrists, and eventually the centrists in one or both major parties either will be forced to take sides or will be overthrown. At that point, when one of the major parties comes under the control of a polar force and so moves to the polar position on the crosscutting issue, the realignment is precipitated.

The realignment will take one of the four forms described in Chapter 2 (scenarios 2 through 5). The differences among those forms, as will be seen from an examination of the diagrams accompanying the scenarios, is largely one of nomenclature, reflecting the stage of third-party development at the time of crisis. If a third party has not been formed, or if it is relatively weak, the two parties emerging from the realignment will carry the names of the old. If the leaders of one of the major parties join in organizing a third party and dissolve the old party in favor of it or if a third party has gained in strength and momentum so that its appeal exceeds that of one of the old parties, one of the major parties emerging from the realignment will bear a new name. If the two old parties join forces to combat the rising third party, then both parties may conceivably carry new names.

Whatever the names of the realigned parties, one of the major parties will have taken its stand at or near one of the poles of the crosscutting issue, and the other will be at or near the opposite pole. The voters who have made up the polar blocs then have the instruments of political action they have been endeavoring to create, and they identify accordingly. The two parties organize for a showdown on the issue that has agitated and polarized the population. A critical election turns on the issue and the voters make their choice.

If they are indecisive or if the issue is not the kind that can be quickly solved, one or more additional critical elections may follow. In any case, the party system has a new rationale, and a segment of the electorate has formed, or is in the process of forming, new party attachments on the basis of that rationale.

The question, arises: Is one possible outcome a multiparty system, in which three or even four parties vie for control through shifting coalitions? Since in the hypothetical case the existence of American political institutions and traditions has been assumed, the answer seems to be no. At no time in the history of this country has there been a sustained period of multiparty competition. Third parties have come on the scene, but only briefly; the new party has replaced an existing party as one of the major parties or it has been absorbed by an existing party or it has faded away. Some scholars have suggested that the persistence of the two-party system may be the result of a basic duality of individual attitudes in a society that is united in its basic concepts about government. Others have seen certain elements of the institutional structure as making for two-party politics: the concentration of executive power in a single rather than a plural executive, which eliminates the base for coalitions, and the winner-take-all system of electing legislators, rather than proportional representation. These theories are not mutually exclusive and may all be correct.[1] It is enough here to say that whatever the factors that have caused the American two-party system to reestablish itself after each upheaval, there is no evidence to suggest that they have lost their force. And by now the weight of tradition reinforces them. A multiparty system is not listed here among the types of realignment outcomes, therefore, but the possibility will need to be considered again in the final chapter.

Five Variables

Among the variables that determine when, in what form, and on what scale a realignment takes place, five stand out as most important. They are the breadth and depth of the underlying grievance, the capacity of the proposed remedy to provoke resistance, the motivation and capacity of party

---

1. For a recent discussion of the various explanations, see Gerald M. Pomper, *Elections in America: Control and Influence in Democratic Politics* (Dodd, Mead, 1968), pp. 44–51.

leadership, the division of the polar forces between the parties, and the strength of the ties that bind voters to the existing parties.

BREADTH AND DEPTH OF THE UNDERLYING GRIEVANCE

For an issue to shatter a party system and create a new one, it clearly must arise from a grievance that is both broad and deep, that a large number of people feel strongly about. Neither dimension is measurable or predictable. The number of voters directly affected by a grievance may be counted, perhaps—the unemployed in a depression, for instance, or the members of an aggrieved ethnic group. Yet grievances can rouse great indignation in people who are not directly affected at all; some of the most fervent abolitionists, for example, had never seen a slave. Depth of response to an issue is even less subject to measurement or prediction. An issue that is weak one year may become strong the next, or vice versa, although the underlying grievance remains essentially unchanged. Some shifts in the public mood seem inexplicable and catch even the most seasoned politicians and observers by surprise. But some can be attributed directly to the politicians who deliberately exploit a grievance, to the organizations that are formed to publicize and agitate it, and to the media that give it attention.

As awareness of a grievance spreads, sympathy and response will heighten. The duration of a grievance, then, affects both breadth and depth. Yet an issue may be a long time building. Years, even decades, may pass before the crisis is reached, and during that long period there may be intervals when the issue appears to be losing rather than gaining strength. But if a grievance is temporarily removed, then reappears (if, for instance, farm prices rise, then fall again), the depth of feeling will probably be greater the second time, and still greater each time the cycle is repeated.

The strength of an issue varies with the extent to which people look to government to redress the grievance. And on this, too, attitudes change. What may have been once considered beyond the scope of government may later be considered properly within its sphere. An economic recession in the twentieth century is a far more potent political issue than was a recession of the same relative scale in the nineteenth century, when the view of government as guarantor of prosperity had not yet become a matter of political consensus.

Above all, perhaps, the strength of an issue depends on the degree to which it is perceived as a moral issue. If a voter thinks one party right and the other wrong on, say, an economic policy, he may be in a mood to vote against his party or try to change its leadership but not to leave it altogether; after all, any group of politicians can make an honest error of judgment. But if he feels that one party is aligned with good and the other one with evil, that is another story altogether. Realignments occur when the crosscutting issue is intrinsically moral—like slavery—or when an issue that may be basically nonmoral becomes infused with moral overtones: when a debate over economic policy, for instance, is seen not as argumentation about the wisdom of opposing views, but as a struggle of honest working people against evil conspirators out to plunder and exploit them.

CAPACITY TO PROVOKE RESISTANCE

Just as the size of the polar bloc on one side of an issue is determined by the dimensions of the underlying grievance, the size of the bloc at the other pole is determined by the capacity of the issue to provoke resistance. Not all issues are of that type. Sometimes a grievance is so obviously worthy that sentiment is overwhelmingly on one side; while the country is aroused, it is not polarized. In these circumstances, both parties will be on the same side in all probability, and the incentive for voters to realign will therefore be removed.

But in other cases, proposals to remedy a grievance provoke resistance, and two polar groups come into being. Any grievance that can only be resolved by the creation of new grievances will be of such a character—proposals for the redistribution of wealth or income or opportunity, for instance, if the redistributional consequences are clear.

What was said above about the polar bloc responding to the grievance applies equally to the bloc resisting the proposed remedy. Its size will depend on the number of people affected by the remedy, the extent to which they are affected, and the depth of their feeling about the injustice of what is proposed. Theirs too becomes a grievance that can be exploited, publicized, and agitated; ultimately, it can even take the form of aggressive counter-demands. And if their position is invested with a moral quality—if, for example, they come to see themselves as defenders of the national integrity against immoral men who would dishonor it for class or partisan advantage —their polar bloc will grow accordingly.

The strength and determination of the resistance depend directly, however, not on the grievance but on the remedy proposed. And it is in the design of remedies that the next variable, that of leadership, becomes crucial.

LEADERSHIP

The power and capacity of the established party leadership are, in a sense, matched against the strength and momentum of the issue. If the leaders have the skill and motivation to handle the issue in a way that will check the growth of the polar blocs, and if the issue is the kind that allows such handling, a major realignment will not take place. If, on the other hand, they throw in their lot with one or the other polar group, the realignment becomes inevitable. The historic realignments of the American party system occurred because the leaders either did not try to mediate and compromise the issue or tried and failed.

In examining some episodes of history, it is easy to construct alternative scenarios in which the leaders acted differently and realignment did not occur. Usually the alternatives relate to the conduct of the one preeminent leader, the president. An issue that was not compromised might have been, if the president had been willing. A grievance might have been ameliorated, if the president had understood it and admitted its validity. A realignment would have been prevented, if the president had not positively promoted it by aligning himself, out of personal conviction, with one of the polar groups. A different man in the seat of power would have done different things at the crucial time.

Yet not all grievances are of a type that government can quickly remove, whatever its will and capability, and sometimes even compromise becomes impossible. For a powerful polarizing issue, as observed earlier, is one that comes to be perceived in moral terms, as a contest between good and evil; then compromise itself becomes reprehensible, for good men do not go halfway with evil. A concession to one polar group, in these circumstances, may lead only to the expansion of the other. A compromise that embodies concessions to both groups may infuriate more than it conciliates.

Then there are other leaders on the scene—men outside the White House seeking to get in. A strong issue produces strong leaders at the poles; they may be the match of the moderate centrists in skill and eloquence, and they are committed to positively seeking realignment as their road to power. The centrist leaders of the out-party have a stake in the existing party system, but since they also have a stake in discrediting the centrist leaders of the in-party, particularly the president, they may be ambivalent. At least some of their leaders are likely to give aid and comfort to the agitators at both poles, for the out-party during three and a half of each four years is not much more than the arena for a power struggle, and throughout that time even its centrist bloc speaks with the voices of various leaders of contending factions. In the American governmental system, power is dispersed, and many rivals are in a position to block a president. Then it is the strength of the issue that determines which leaders will ultimately prevail. In some episodes of history events appear inexorable; leadership could influence only the timing and form of the inevitable upheaval.

DIVISION OF THE POLAR FORCES BETWEEN PARTIES

In the hypothetical case in Chapter 2, it was assumed that the proposed saloon appealed almost equally to the members of the two existing parties, with only slightly more strength among Progressives than among Conservatives. The issue was shown as slicing through the existing party alignment nearly at right angles. That, of course, need not be the case. A polar bloc created by a new issue may be divided between the parties in any proportion —60-40, 75-25, 80-20, or any other. And the opposing polar bloc does not necessarily divide between the parties in the opposite proportion; it is entirely possible that one party will have the larger share of each.

If the opposing blocs find themselves preponderantly on opposite sides of the existing alignment—if 80 percent of one is in party A, say, and 80 percent of the other in party B—the crisis will be reached and resolved relatively quickly, for the pressure within each party moving it toward one of the poles will heavily outweigh the resistance. The realignment will in all likelihood take the form of scenario 2, without the appearance of a third party, and its scale will be relatively minor, for only 20 percent of each polar bloc will feel impelled even to consider changing parties. Indeed, its significance may be more in what it does to reinforce and reinvigorate the existing alignment, since those who make up the 80 percent of each bloc will have found new reason to value and support their party.

If, on the other hand, the blocs are about evenly balanced within each party, the realignment will be delayed. The centrists, caught between nearly equal pressures, will find it far more difficult to make a choice. The polar blocs will have more time to grow, and third parties time to form and flourish. The tension within the system will heighten, and when the disruption comes it will be more drastic. More people will be affected, the scale of realignment will be greater, and the likelihood of a realignment in the form of scenario 3, 4, or 5 rather than of one taking place within the existing parties will be increased.

STRENGTH OF EXISTING PARTY ATTACHMENTS

The variable of party attachment must be considered in both individual and group terms. To the individual, the political party system has its greatest meaning at a time of realignment. Voters who are polarized by the realigning issue and who find at that time that a political party has made itself their instrument to achieve their ends are likely to develop a strong and direct identification with the party. It belongs to them, to be used for this all-important purpose, and so they belong to it. The party is like a band of brothers, crusading together for righteousness and against evil. The brothers identify, and attachments so formed are those that last a lifetime.

But after a realignment, as time passes, persons who did not live through the original experience enter the electorate. The party's reason for being— its distinctive outlook and spirit, its fundamental meaning—is not so clear to them. They may perceive no great difference between the parties, and in that they may not be wholly wrong. For as the realignment crisis is surmounted and the issue that gave rise to the crisis is resolved, passions cool and the polar groups dwindle and dissolve. The parties then move back from the poles toward the center on the issue that divided them (which may drop from public discussion entirely), and on other issues, which now cut across the new alignment, they tend to straddle and to muffle rather than to sharpen the party conflict. Not finding the party system pertinent to the resolution of current issues that may concern him deeply, a new voter is less likely than the voters of the preceding generation to develop a strong direct identification with a party as an institution. With each year, in the absence of a new polarizing and realigning issue, strong party identifiers will pass from the electorate and weak party identifiers will enter it. Granted that party identification grows gradually stronger with age,[2] the ties between the electorate as a whole and the parties will weaken. The weaker the party bonds, the

2. For a summary of evidence that partisan attachments grow stronger the longer a voter is identified with his party, see Angus Campbell and others, *The American Voter* (Wiley, 1960), pp. 161–65 and 497–98. Also Philip E. Converse, "Of Time and Partisan Stability," *Comparative Political Studies*, Vol. 2 (1969), pp. 139–67.

more easily they can be severed and the voters realigned. Hence an electorate that could be realigned at one time only by the most powerful of polarizing issues may be realigned in later years by one much weaker. This lends an element of credence to the generational theory propounded by writers such as Kevin Phillips; realignments have occurred at intervals of thirty-six years or so, about the length of time required for a generation that was too young to be politically aware at the time of a realignment crisis to become a majority of the electorate.

A second factor influencing the strength of a voter's attachment to his party is the strength of his identification with various groups which are in turn identified with one or another party. Most groups in society have some degree of partisan bias, sometimes deeply embedded in the group's tradition, and most people identify, more or less closely, with one or more such groups. Through these groups—called "reference groups"—they absorb the partisan coloration of their fellows.[3] If such ties weaken or shift, changes in party identification may be made more readily.

In the almost endless range of groups that influence the political identification of the individual, the most important is, of course, the family. Parents influence children; in politically active families, party identification may be considered almost as inherited, along with the family name and the family heirlooms. Husbands influence wives, and vice versa.

Beyond the family are the larger aggregates with which persons, or families, identify. An aggregate may be a racial, religious, or ethnic group; a person may be a Democrat because he is black or a Republican because that is the preponderant affiliation of the members of his church. The aggregate may be regional; a voter may think of himself as a southerner and of the Democratic party as the party of the South, or he may be a Republican because he is a northerner. He may be a Republican because he lives in upstate New York or suburban Cook County and thinks of the GOP as being the party of the rural areas or the suburbs and the Democrats as the party of

3. The ways in which a "reference group," or "solidary group," influences a person's political behavior are discussed in Eugene Burdick and Arthur J. Brodbeck (eds.), *American Voting Behavior* (Free Press, 1959); see particularly Talcott Parsons, " 'Voting' and the Equilibrium of the American Political System," pp. 91–92 and 96–97; Henry W. Riecken, "Primary Groups and Political Party Choice"; and R. Duncan Luce, "Analyzing the Social Process Underlying Group Voting Patterns." See also Campbell and others, *American Voter*, Chaps. 12 and 13; and Herbert McClosky and Harold E. Dahlgren, "Primary Group Influence on Party Loyalty," *American Political Science Review*, Vol. 53 (1959), pp. 757–76. Reference groups are both "positive" and "negative"; in the latter case, one identifies with a party because he sees the opposition party as the party of a group he dislikes or fears.

corrupt big-city machines. Or the aggregate may be an economic class or group; the voter may think of himself as a workingman and the Democrats as the party of his class. A businessman may think of the Republican party as the party of business. A young voter may think of a party as the party of youth; an older voter may identify with the other party, for the same reason. It was noted in Chapter 1 that significant shifts in the party balance can occur because some groups, biased toward one party, grow at the expense of groups that lean toward the other party.

Within many of these aggregates are organizations that serve as a channel through which the partisan bias of the aggregate is communicated to the individuals and families who compose it. Such communication has often been overt, deliberate, and direct. Farm and labor organizations have affiliated with parties, quite openly if not officially; some still do. Business organizations have influenced their employees or even coerced them outright; again, some still do. Clergymen have mixed politics with religion. Ethnic civic groups and lay religious bodies have developed partisan identities. Through publications, through the partisan activities of organization leaders, and through a variety of other means, the organizations within an aggregate convey to the members of that aggregate the suggestion that a particular party is the party of *their* kind of people that can be relied on to reflect *their* group interest. For their part, the political parties cooperate with the allied organizations to impart the same message. They nominate balanced tickets. They give recognition to the major voting groups identified with them in apportioning their patronage. As soon as a young person becomes politically aware, he learns that if he accepts the partisan attitudes of his group he too will be eligible someday for his share of recognition and tangible reward. And in its policies and program, the party reflects the political philosophy and sponsors the specific measures of its constituent voting groups, mediating among them as may be necessary when they conflict.

So the bonds between a voter and his party are compounded of links of group identity, patronage, and philosophy and program; they are emotional, intellectual, and financial, and they tend to grow stronger, or "settle in," as time passes. If they are all mutually reinforcing, the voter is likely to be bound closely to his party. Often, of course, they conflict; a voter may belong to two aggregates who identify with different parties. A Catholic businessman, for instance, may be drawn to the Democratic party by the tradition of his religious group and to the Republican party by the identity of his economic associates. A married voter may be pulled in one direction by the position of his own family and in another by that of his in-laws. Such a voter is said to be "cross-pressured"; his party attachment is likely to be weaker than that of the voter subject to no such conflict, and he may become an independent.

The strength of the indirect attachment of a person to his party, through his reference groups, will vary as the strength of his attachments to these groups varies over the course of his lifetime. For current political analysis, the most significant factor may be a long-term trend toward a general loosening of the attachments of voters to certain of the reference groups that have been most influential politically in the past. These include churches and ethnic groups, in particular, as the country becomes more secular and homogenized. The influence of labor unions has probably also declined with the increase of affluence and economic independence. As these attachments weaken, the ties of voters to the parties are correspondingly weakened, and it becomes easier for polar groups to form and grow and for third parties to arise. Thus with the passage of time after a realignment and the weakening of the influence of reference groups, any realignment process that is set in motion will encounter less resistance.

As all these variables interact, realignments seem essentially accidental phenomena. There is nothing inevitable about them. Only the last of the five variables has a cyclical element—the gradual weakening of party attachments after a realignment period—but that in itself does not bring about a new realignment. No cycle controls the rise of crosscutting issues or determines what kind of leaders will be in power at the time or how they, and their opponents, will behave. Those who attribute the regularity of past major realignments to cyclical factors rather than coincidence simply read too much precision into history.

Searching the Past

As it happens, each of the three major political transitions examined in this study illustrates a different outcome of the realignment process. The first realignment occurred when a third party, the Republicans, supplanted an existing party (scenario 4 of the preceding chapter). The second was marked by the absorption of an important third party, the Populists, by one of the existing parties (scenario 3). The third realigned the two existing major parties (scenario 2).

In each of these cases, the realignment process took place not in one or two critical elections, or even in the course of a few years, but over a period of decades. In the first two realignments, polar groups made their appearance and began to gather momentum a full generation before the realignment crisis. The third realignment had no such buildup; it was the response to a sudden cataclysmic event, but it took decades afterward to work its way through the decentralized American party system. To tell the story of these three realignments is to cover most of the span of American party history since the 1830s. The decades that were not marked as prerealignment or realignment periods are of interest too in a study of the realignment process. The Progressive Era of the early twentieth century, as one such period, exemplifies a period of ferment arising from crosscutting issues when realignment was averted (scenario 1). And the late 1910s and early 1920s saw a reshuffling of party loyalties that amounted to a distinct though minor realignment in one region—the upper Midwest.

The next nine chapters therefore contain an almost continuous history of the American party system as a structure of political competition from the pre–Civil War to the post–New Deal years. The major organic changes in the system are identified through election returns and other data and analyzed in terms of the realignment process. Some of the minor changes are also examined, while others are simply noted. The whole effort is imprecise, of course, for conclusions about party realignment rest on judgments about causation of political behavior, and such judgments must rely heavily on inference. First, realignments must be distinguished from simple deviations in voting behavior, which cannot be done with precision. Then each realignment must be attributed to a cause, and that can be uncertain if several realigning forces are simultaneously at work. Judgments must depend on analysis of the quantitative data, which tell *what* happened, and of nonquantitative information, which may suggest *why* it happened. In this study I have tried to blend the findings of the quantitative analysts of voter behavior with those of the students of institutional party behavior—the activities of party leaders and the conventions, caucuses, and campaigns that make up organized party activity.

In the chapters that follow, the reader will be led at times into the remote byways of the American party system. National parties in this country are not unified bodies but federations of state parties, each of which responds to national and local forces in its own way. State parties are in turn made up of local party organizations, which often act with a high degree of autonomy.

So the course and extent of a realignment are determined by the course and extent of the myriad semi-independent state and local realignments that may be set in motion by a common circumstance or single series of events. The process can be traced only by examining the pieces of the mosaic that is the party system.

The body of information available to the analyst of party dynamics has grown rapidly in recent years, as students have undertaken the meticulous examination of newspapers, diaries, correspondence, memoirs, and election data (supplemented, in studies of recent events, by interviews) and prepared the detailed narratives of what happened in the party system in, say, Massachusetts in 1846, Kansas in 1890, or North Dakota in 1922. Much of their scholarship is contained in unpublished doctoral dissertations, perfectly designed in some cases for the kind of synthesis attempted here. Many gaps, of course, are still unfilled; no one researcher can fill many of them, and I do not pretend to have done so. Newspaper and manuscript sources were consulted in a few cases where the gaps were particularly critical to the analysis, but with these occasional exceptions the pattern of events in individual states and localities has had to be constructed from what has been produced by the labor of other scholars.

Why, then, did the major realignments of the past take place? Which were the crucial variables? How did the political parties—the leaders, followers, and organizations that make up the institutional structure—respond to the forces that threatened to disrupt them? How did voter behavior influence party behavior, and how did party behavior impel great segments of the electorate to seek and form new political allegiances? After examining the cases, the preliminary statement of the realignment process with which this chapter began can be amplified. Then what may be happening to the American party system in the 1970s can be considered.

CHAPTER FOUR

Slavery Polarizes the Nation

THERE HAD BEEN agitation against slavery since before the founding of the republic, but the rise of the militant abolitionist movement is usually dated from 1831, when William Lloyd Garrison founded the *Liberator*. On that basis, the prerealignment period that preceded the first of the three great political upheavals analyzed in this book—the realignment of the 1850s—lasted almost a quarter of a century. The slavery issue cut squarely across the two major parties that existed at the time, the Democrats and the Whigs. Indeed, the schism could be plotted geographically, along the Mason-Dixon line and the Ohio River, which separated the slave states from the free. At each pole, in each region, a political force dedicated above all else to the resolution of the slavery issue took form and grew. For two decades and more, the politics of the nation centered around the struggle between the two polar forces and the moderate centrists who, straddling the Mason-Dixon line and the slavery issue, struggled to hold the parties and the nation together.

The prerealignment period, the subject of this chapter, can be described in three stages. In the first stage, the centrists were in full control of both parties; the antislavery forces, while struggling as a minority in the major parties, also found expression in a new Liberty party. Then the minority began to disrupt the major parties with determined attacks on the centrist leaders, and a more powerful third party, the Free-Soilers, came into being. Finally, in the third stage, the centrists in the Whig party were overwhelmed and the party was literally pulled apart. The realignment was then precipitated.

Ascendancy of the Compromisers

"I am in earnest; I will not equivocate; I will not retreat a single inch, and I will be heard," wrote Garrison in the first issue of the *Liberator*. There

39

followed a wave of organization. Local abolitionist societies that had been quiescent in the North since that region had outlawed slavery were revived to concern themselves with slavery in other regions. Petitions, directed primarily at slavery in the District of Columbia, deluged the Congress, and literature flowed into the southern states. The South at once demanded that abolitionist agitation be suppressed.

For a few years the South had the preponderant support of northern sentiment. In 1835, northern leaders of both parties organized antiabolition rallies throughout the region. The meetings adopted resolutions decrying the abolitionist activities but generally stopped short of supporting the southern demands for legislation that would interfere with the agitators' freedom of speech and press. The newspapers were all but unanimous in condemning the abolitionists. So were the churches. The Methodist General Conference in 1836 pronounced its opposition to abolitionism and wholly disclaimed "any right, wish, or intention, to interfere in the civil and political relation between master and slave as it exists in the slaveholding states of the union."[1] The American Baptist Convention protested that abolitionist agitation could split the church. Even the Quakers ostracized the publisher of an antislavery pamphlet and denied the abolitionists the use of their meeting houses.[2] Often the antiabolitionist sentiment spilled over into violence: Garrison was dragged through the streets of Boston, Elijah P. Lovejoy was murdered in Alton, Illinois, an antiabolitionist mob rioted in New York, and an abolitionist meeting hall in Philadelphia was burned.

THE MONOLITHIC DEMOCRATS

The Democratic party, then the majority party of the nation, was troubled by no irresolution in responding to the South's demands. The party had been formed originally as an alliance of southern planters and New Yorkers and had always spanned both regions. Northern men of abolitionist sympathies were accustomed to sitting with slaveholders in presidential cabinets and collaborating with them in the halls of Congress—and to joining with them to divert attention from the slavery issue whenever it arose. Martin Van Buren, the architect of the new Jacksonian party, had been quite explicit. Writing to Thomas Ritchie of Richmond in 1827, he had argued that

---

1. Lorman Ratner, *Powder Keg: Northern Opposition to the Anti-Slavery Movement, 1831–1840* (Basic Books, 1968), p. 107.
2. Ibid., pp. 122–23.

national parties were the means of keeping the slavery issue quiet. Only when the party system broke down under President Monroe had "the clamor against the Southern Influence and African Slavery" made headway in the North, he noted.[3]

So President Jackson, himself a slaveholder, denounced the "unconstitutional wicked" activities of the abolitionists and asked Congress in 1835 for legislation closing the mails in the southern states to "incendiary publications intended to instigate the slaves to insurrections."[4] The legislation was not enacted, but Jackson's postmaster general authorized southern postmasters to use their own discretion in confiscating such materials.

Van Buren, as the prospective candidate of his party to succeed Jackson in 1836, took pains both directly and through his spokesmen to reassure the South that he opposed both the methods and the objectives of the abolitionists. Thus Senator Silas Wright, Jr., of New York wrote that Van Buren would consider it "impolitic" for Congress to abolish slavery in the District of Columbia. The Albany *Argus*, edited by a Van Buren ally, described the candidate as a "Northern man with Southern principles." Van Buren's friends, with some Whig support, organized the Albany antiabolitionist rally of 1835, which "deprecated" the conduct of the abolitionists as "disloyal to the union," and Van Buren personally sent copies of the proceedings to southern Democrats. Six months later, Van Buren promised in a letter to a group of North Carolinians that he would be the "uncompromising opponent" of any bill abolishing slavery in the District of Columbia.[5]

In the Congress, similarly, northern Democrats dissociated their party from the abolitionists. Senator Wright proudly related to the Senate how the citizens of Utica broke up a statewide abolitionist meeting in 1835 and sacked an abolitionist printing plant. Senator Isaac Hill, New Hampshire Democrat, agreed that "never were the people of the North so entirely united" on any subject as they were against the "weak or wicked" abolitionists. "The good sense of the community has utterly prostrated the fanatical party," he assured the South. Senator James Buchanan, Pennsylvania Democrat later to be President, said the reaction of his constituents to

3. Cited by Robert V. Remini, *Martin Van Buren and the Making of the Democratic Party* (Columbia University Press, 1959), pp. 131–32.
4. Seventh Annual Message, Dec. 7, 1835, *A Compilation of the Messages and Papers of the Presidents* (1789–1897), Vol. 4 (Bureau of National Literature, 1897), pp. 1366–96.
5. Richard Williams Smith, "The Career of Martin Van Buren in Connection with the Slavery Controversy through the Election of 1840" (Ph.D. dissertation, Ohio State University, 1959), pp. 113–14, 145, 157–60, 204–06.

his speech defending slavery in the District of Columbia was one of "general approbation." And in the House, another future Democratic President, Franklin Pierce of New Hampshire, agreed that the abolitionists, in their "misguided and fanatical zeal . . . received no more sanction among the great mass of people of the North, than they did at the South."[6]

In the Senate, northern Democrats joined with their southern colleagues, with only two dissents, in adopting a Buchanan motion to reject the petitions being generated by the abolitionist crusade. In 1836, northern Democrats in the House voted 61–14 with their southern colleagues against even receiving the petitions—the so-called gag rule.[7] And on a resolution declaring that the Congress "ought not to interfere in any way with slavery in the District of Columbia," northern Democrats voted 75–5 in the affirmative.[8]

THE LESS-THAN-MONOLITHIC WHIGS

Although the Whigs as a national party faced the same problem as the Democrats in holding North and South together, the northern Whigs nevertheless found a party position somewhat less hostile to abolitionism. On the 1836 petition vote that had united House Democrats, the Whigs split on regional lines, with northerners voting 43–1 to receive the pleas. Though, like the Democrats, they might disagree with most of what the petitioners demanded, they could rally—with former President John Quincy Adams as their conscience and leader—around the "sacred right of petition itself."

The two major parties in the North, then, assumed somewhat different postures toward the antislavery movement from the beginning. Why? Either Whiggery and sympathy with abolitionism had a common root cause, presumably in some basic set of attitudes toward life and politics, or the coincidence of the two positions was the product of the dynamics of the political system itself, or both.

As abolitionism grew, it flourished primarily in New England and in the westward path of New England migration—from upstate New York and northern Pennsylvania through Ohio's Western Reserve to Michigan and those parts of Indiana and Illinois lying north of the 41st parallel.[9] That was

6. *Register of Debates in Congress*, 24 Cong. 1 sess. (Jan. 19, 1836), pp. 203–05; (Feb. 12, 1836), pp. 484–87; (March 2, 1836), p. 679; (Dec. 28, 1835), p. 33.

7. *Congressional Globe*, 24 Cong. 1 sess. (Dec. 16, 1835), p. 24. The North is defined as the free states—those north of the Mason-Dixon line and the Ohio River.

8. Ibid. (Feb. 8, 1836), p. 155.

9. Of the twenty-five counties that cast more than 10 percent of their vote for the Liberty (abolitionist) party candidate for president in 1844, twenty-three were north of the 41st parallel, one was astride the line, and one was half a degree south of it.

Whig territory. But more significant, when the abolitionists entered politics it was from the Whigs rather than the Democrats *within* that territory (as will be shown later) that they drew most of their votes. Who were the Whigs and who were the Democrats? The traditional view is that the distinction was one of class, with the Whigs representing the more prosperous groups. If that is the case, it suggests class status as a common cause for both Whiggery and sympathy for abolitionists, since abolitionism was an upper-class movement; laborers, especially urban laborers, saw in abolition the specter of hordes of black workingmen flowing north to compete for jobs. Other historians, particularly Lee Benson and Ronald P. Formisano, contend that the cleavage between the parties corresponded more closely to religious and ethnic than to class lines. Abolition was a church-centered movement, and it was centered, moreover, in particular sects; evidently those were the Whig sects and the common root cause would be found in the doctrine and philosophy of those particular New England churches.[10]

Even if both these interpretations are credited, they do not provide the whole, or even a major part of, the explanation for the mutual sympathy of Whigs and abolitionists. One need only look at the adjacent Yankee states of New Hampshire and Vermont, which were settled by people of the same stock, were comparable in economic structure, and shared a common intellectual and religious tradition. Yet through some accident of development, New Hampshire became a Democratic state and Vermont a Whig state, not by narrow margins but by overwhelming ones. In the 1830s the Whig leaders of Vermont were among major party politicians closest to the abolitionists while their Democratic counterparts in New Hampshire, who belonged to the same social class and the same churches and made their livings in the same way, were among the most faithful northern apologists for the southern slaveholders. One could make a similar comparison between Whig and Democratic congressmen who represented adjacent districts in upstate New York. Clearly something in the dynamics of party politics caused the parties to take opposing positions on antislavery issues.

One factor seems to be the difference in political position between the

10. Benson, *The Concept of Jacksonian Democracy: New York as a Test Case* (Princeton University Press, 1961), esp. pp. 140–207. Formisano reports that in Michigan Presbyterian Whigs led in founding the state's antislavery society, and that when the Liberty party was formed it was "a splinter group of the Whig-Presbyterian-evangelical subculture." *The Birth of Mass Political Parties: Michigan, 1827–1861* (Princeton University Press, 1971), p. 120. He also documents in great detail the religious basis of partisanship in Michigan in the prewar period (Chap. 8).

in-party and the out-party. The Democrats had long enjoyed the fruits of party unity. Jackson had introduced the "spoils system"; loyal party henchmen occupied the post offices and the customs houses and took their ideological cue from the President. Some northern Democrats, looking to the future, saw John C. Calhoun of South Carolina as a coming president, and new alliances were being formed across the Mason-Dixon line.[11] It was easy for Democrats to perceive abolitionism as a threat not only to the Union but to the national party that had rewarded, and would continue to reward, them.

The Whigs, on the other hand, were a new party looking for issues with which to challenge the incumbents. The antislavery cause was a promising one, especially if pressed in the context of the right to petition. They could be against slavery, which most northerners disliked or even detested in the abstract, and for freedom of speech but still avoid the stigma of abolitionism.

There is nothing to compel an out-party to be consistent. Southern Whigs could at the same time try to build the party in their region by criticizing the ruling Democratic party for its concessions to the North. The recurrent debate over the right to petition, or "gag rule," found Whigs taking the lead on both sides on some occasions.[12] In national campaigns, of course, southern and northern Whigs, like their Democratic opponents, did their best to talk of other subjects and suppress discussion of the issue that divided them.

THE LIBERTY PARTY

As Henry Clay had predicted,[13] the gag rule of the House of Representatives only enabled the abolitionists "greatly to increase their numerical strength." So did such outrages as the mobbing of Garrison and the martyrdom of Lovejoy—"In the track of every mob [abolitionist] societies sprang up like mushrooms."[14] So, of course, did the incessant pamphleteering and the lecturing and preaching of itinerant representatives of the antislavery societies. By 1841, the abolitionists claimed two hundred societies with 200,000 members, plus uncounted thousands of sympathizers who joined in

11. The Massachusetts Democratic organization, for example, was split between Calhounites and Van Burenites, with the former dominant for a time. Arthur Darling, *Political Changes in Massachusetts, 1824–1848* (Yale University Press, 1925), esp. pp. 339–42.

12. R. W. Smith, "Career of Martin Van Buren," pp. 220–24.

13. *Congressional Globe*, 25 Cong. 3 sess. (Feb. 7, 1839), p. 177.

14. Theodore Clarke Smith, *The Liberty and Free Soil Parties in the Northwest* (Russell and Russell, 1897), p. 17.

the petitions that deluged the Congress. It was inevitable that the abolitionists would consider other forms of political action.

In 1837, the New York Anti-Slavery Society interrogated candidates to get their views on record. The next year, societies in several states went a step further by formally pledging their members not to vote for candidates who did not pass the interrogation tests. In Massachusetts, they succeeded in defeating an antiabolition Whig congressman, Samuel Hoar, and electing his Democratic opponent.[15] In Ohio, they were credited with defeating the Whig governor, Joseph Vance.[16] A year later, abolitionists of Geauga County, Ohio, found legislative candidates of both major parties unsatisfactory and nominated their own independent candidate, who received 12 percent of the vote.[17] Independent abolitionist candidates also ran that year in New England and upstate New York.[18]

Looking ahead to the 1840 national election, one wing of the abolitionist movement argued that the Geauga County course was the only one open to it. The candidates of both national parties would have been chosen through compromise with the "slave power," and how could an abolitionist acquiesce in compromise? State and county antislavery societies began adopting resolutions demanding their own independent abolitionist candidates, and in November 1839 a convention of the radical wing of the movement in Warsaw, New York, nominated as its presidential candidate James G. Birney, a former Kentucky slaveholder turned abolitionist. Birney declined, but after the Whigs nominated a slaveholder, William Henry Harrison, as their presidential candidate, Birney was nominated again by a more broadly representative gathering and agreed to run. But in November, with his Liberty party not on the ballot everywhere, he received only 7,000 votes —about one-tenth the number of voters belonging to the antislavery societies. Too many abolitionists believed in moral suasion rather than political activity, or sought to achieve their goals through the established parties.

15. Ralph Waldo Emerson condemned the abolitionists for defeating "an affectionate, honest, able gentleman because, as the lovely philanthropists say, the only question they ask is 'What is his relation to the slave?'" Darling, *Political Changes in Massachusetts*, p. 249.
16. Governor Vance had arrested and delivered to Kentucky just before the election a fugitive wanted in that state for assisting a runaway slave.
17. T. C. Smith, *Liberty and Free Soil Parties*, p. 32.
18. Margaret Louise Plunkett, "A History of the Liberty Party with Emphasis upon Its Activities in the Northeastern States" (Ph.D. dissertation, Cornell University, 1930), pp. 69–70.

The Liberty party grew steadily, if slowly. In 1842, it elected five state legislators in Massachusetts[19] and two in Maine. In 1844, Birney received 62,000 votes—almost nine times as many as four years earlier. His share exceeded 8 percent in Massachusetts, New Hampshire, and Vermont.

Yet the gains of 1844 were deeply disappointing to the Liberty party leaders. The issue had been sharp enough: both major parties had nominated for president southern slaveholders, James K. Polk and Henry Clay, who were sworn enemies of the abolitionists.[20] But the inherent difficulties of third-party movements could not be overcome. Those who voted for Liberty party candidate Birney would renounce their chance to influence the choice the country was about to make between Polk and Clay. Indeed, as the Whigs incessantly pointed out, the Birney vote could only help to elect Polk, the candidate most strongly committed to the proslavery position. Moreover, there were other issues that, unlike slavery, directly affected northern voters —the tariff, banking, internal improvements—on which the Liberty party had no position; even among voters who were avowed abolitionists slavery was not a single-minded obsession. And for those with political ambition, opportunity appeared to lie in the major parties, not in a third-party movement made up of political extremists.[21]

The Liberty party had made a profound impression, nevertheless. Contemporary analysts gave it the credit—or the blame—for defeating Clay. Its vote in New York was more than twice the margin by which Polk carried the state, and New York gave Polk his national victory. Without the Liberty party, it was assumed, abolitionists would have supported Clay as the lesser of the evils. The New York *Tribune* estimated that 90 percent of the Liberty

19. Darling, *Political Changes in Massachusetts*, pp. 289–91.

20. Clay, the Whig candidate, was, in the tradition of Jefferson, a strong advocate of voluntary emancipation. But he repeatedly denounced the abolitionists' aims and their methods. In a two-hour Senate speech in 1839, for example, he had accused them of seeking "the destruction of property [in slaves] to the amount of twelve hundred millions of dollars" and said their real aim was amalgamation of the races, which he called "vile and loathsome." *Congressional Globe*, 25 Cong. 3 sess. (Feb. 7, 1839), p. 117. He was a champion of the southern position on slavery in the District of Columbia. And during the 1844 campaign, he made clear that he did not rule out the ultimate annexation of Texas as a slave state, which was the key antislavery issue of the time. As for the Democrats, Polk was marked as a southerner who had been chosen over Van Buren largely because of the latter's opposition to immediate annexation of Texas.

21. The Liberty party was also the victim of an indiscretion by Birney: in October, the Whigs dramatically exposed the fact that he had accepted a Democratic nomination for the state legislature in his home county in Michigan the month before, and his explanation was drowned out in the Whig outcry that his supposedly independent candidacy was nothing more than a Democratic plot to defeat Clay. T. C. Smith, *Liberty and Free Soil Parties*, pp. 76–80.

vote in New York came from former Whigs.[22] Secretary of War John C. Spencer put his estimate at 75 percent.[23]

To many northern Whigs the message was clear: if compromise with the South on slavery questions meant losing the presidency in any case, they might as well protect and enhance their position in their own states by keeping pace with public opinion there. And in sections where the Liberty vote was substantial and rising—it exceeded 10 percent in twenty-four counties—the Democrats had to take notice too. For it was their hegemony that was threatened in New Hampshire, some sections of upstate New York, and elsewhere.

So the major party politicians in the North moved as far toward the abolitionist pole as necessary to absorb most of the movement, to the frustration of the third-party politicians. Salmon P. Chase, a young Cincinnati lawyer who of all Liberty party men was to go farthest in national politics, wrote of their dilemma: "As fast as we can bring public sentiment right the other parties will approach our ground and keep sufficiently close to it to prevent any great accession to our numbers. If this be so, the Liberty party can never hope to accomplish anything as such, but only through its indirect action upon the other parties."[24]

At the other pole, southern politics tended to mirror those of the North throughout the prerealignment period. As abolitionist societies grew in the North, so did "Southern rights" societies below the Mason-Dixon line. As the former developed the moral case against slavery, the latter found biblical passages that, they contended, showed the institution to be the fulfillment of God's purposes. The abolitionist political movement had its counterpart in the disunion movement, led by Calhoun and centered in the cotton belt, which called for secession if and when the North gained enough supremacy in the national government to impose its will.

22. Benson, *Concept of Jacksonian Democracy*, p. 208.
23. George Poage, *Henry Clay and the Whig Party* (Peter Smith, 1965), p. 151. The contemporary judgment is borne out by analysis of the election returns. In eleven northern states as a group and in each of them except Maine and New Hampshire the counties of greatest Liberty party strength were also those of disproportionate Whig loss. Following are the correlations of Liberty strength, by counties, with Whig and Democratic losses between 1840 and 1844: Maine, correlation with Whig losses, 0.493, with Democratic losses, 0.711; New Hampshire, −0.104 and 0.657; Vermont, 0.892 and 0.644; Massachusetts, 0.781 and −0.160; Connecticut, 0.608 and 0.026; New York, 0.617 and 0.412; Pennsylvania, 0.851 and −0.355; Ohio, 0.716 and 0.146; Illinois, 0.654 and 0.347; Indiana, 0.821 and 0.104; Michigan, 0.597 and 0.183; the eleven states, 0.707 and 0.247. (Computations by Gary Greenhalgh.)
24. Letter to John P. Hale, May 12, 1847, cited in T. C. Smith, *Liberty and Free Soil Parties*, p. 111.

The Disruption of the Old Parties

The indirect effects of the Liberty party on the other parties, to which Chase referred, were quick to appear. By 1848, the tensions created by the antislavery issue within those parties in several northern states could no longer be contained. The parties burst, and the beleaguered third-party abolitionists suddenly found their numbers increased fivefold.

THE HALE REVOLT IN NEW HAMPSHIRE

The earliest spectacular split came, appropriately, in the state with the greatest relative Liberty party strength—New Hampshire, where Birney polled 8.5 percent of the vote in 1844. Two months after the election a freshman Democratic congressman, John P. Hale, who had earlier split from his delegation to vote against the "gag rule," announced his intention to defy the instructions of the New Hampshire legislature and oppose the annexation of Texas as a slave state. He acted, he said, from "an imperious sense of duty" and appealed over the heads of the party leadership to "a committee of the whole people of the state" to sustain him at the polls.[25] To Franklin Pierce, then state party chairman, Hale's deliberate betrayal of the party that had supported him sprang not from duty but from ambition—a selfish exploitation of the slavery issue to foster his own ends—and Pierce forthwith convened a special convention to replace Hale as the party's nominee for reelection. Anti-Texas Democrats hastily organized as "Independent Democrats" and Hale drew just enough votes in the election (held in March in the state at large) to prevent the Democratic convention's candidate from winning the majority that was then required. Two further elections produced the same result, and the seat remained vacant. But out of the campaign grew an antislavery coalition of Whigs, Liberty party men, and Independent Democrats that won control of the legislature in 1846. New Hampshire then declared itself. The legislature chose the Whig candidate as governor[26] and Hale as U.S. senator and adopted resolutions opposing slavery in the District

25. Richard H. Sewell, *John P. Hale and the Politics of Abolition* (Harvard University Press, 1965), p. 52.
26. The New Hampshire constitution provided that when no candidate for state office obtained a majority of the popular vote the decision would be made by the legislature.

of Columbia and in territories and the admission of any new slave states. Resolutions endorsing the Mexican war and Polk's conduct of it were defeated.

THE CONSCIENCE WHIGS

Meanwhile, a corresponding tension developed in the neighboring abolitionist stronghold of Massachusetts within that state's dominant party, the Whigs. Early in 1845 a group of young Whigs openly demanded that the party's entrenched elders turn their party on a more militant antislavery course. The young Whigs had nothing to lose politically, for their way to the top of the party was blocked in any case, and they had much to gain by taking advantage of the rising antislavery sentiment. Expressing their antislavery feelings freely and emotionally, they took the position, and assumed the name, of Conscience Whigs.[27]

The split developed on the Texas annexation issue. Both blocs were opposed to annexation, but differences grew over attitude and tactics. The Conscience bloc appealed to antislavery sentiment by making its case largely one of opposition to slavery itself. The Cotton Whigs, as the ruling conservative group came to be called, chose not to antagonize their southern allies by denouncing slavery but presented constitutional arguments against annexation instead. After Congress voted to admit Texas, the rift widened. The Cotton Whigs, in their eagerness to suppress the slavery issue, accepted the congressional decision as final while the Conscience bloc, in alliance with the abolitionists, strove to mobilize Massachusetts against the actual admission of Texas when the prospective state presented its draft constitution for congressional approval. From there the Conscience Whigs moved to a position

27. Kinley J. Brauer has emphasized the social and economic roots of the Massachusetts struggle. The conservative Whig leaders were, in the modern usage of the term, an establishment, dominating the state socially and economically as well as politically. Their economic base was cotton manufacture, and that determined their politics: the industry depended on a protective tariff; the Whigs were the party of protection; the necessity of electing a Whig president and Congress compelled the maintenance of a strong party uniting North and South; antislavery agitation could only destroy that unity; ergo, the agitation should be suppressed. Their challengers, on the other hand, did not earn their livelihood in cotton manufacture and so felt no compelling economic stake in the national Whig party. Many came from families that had been displaced in social and political leadership by the new cotton lords. *Cotton Versus Conscience: Massachusetts Whig Politics and Southwestern Expansion 1843–1848* (University of Kentucky Press, 1967). See also Frank Otto Gatell, "Palfrey's Vote, the Conscience Whigs, and the Election of Speaker Winthrop," *New England Quarterly*, Vol. 31 (June 1958), p. 220.

of all-out opposition to the Mexican war—even to the point of opposing supplies for the United States army—and then to an attack on the constitutional
compromise itself by demanding that the Massachusetts Whig party oppose
slavery *within the southern states*. Finally, they swore not to support for president a slave owner, and when the national Whig convention in 1848 nominated such a man in Zachary Taylor, who had the preconvention backing of
the Cotton bloc, the time had come for the Conscience Whigs to leave the
party.

THE BARNBURNERS

The next explosion came in New York. There for more than a decade the
majority Democratic party had been in the process of splitting, for reasons
quite separate from the slavery issue. The conflict arose over state policies
on canal development, spread to issues of banking regulation, and was sharpened and solidified in incessant factional quarrels over state patronage. The
Whigs, a cohesive minority, skillfully used their votes in the legislature to
widen the split between the Democratic factions, popularly known as the
Barnburners—who were the reformers in the state conflicts—and the
Hunkers. By 1847, it was clear that "the two elements hated and feared each
other more than they hated and feared the common enemy, the Whigs."[28]

Into this caldron was thrown the newest antislavery issue—a proposal by
David Wilmot, young Democratic congressman from the Pennsylvania
mountains, to forbid slavery in any territory (that is, New Mexico and California) that might be acquired from Mexico. After an initial period in which
members of both factions generally supported the Wilmot Proviso they
moved to opposite sides. The Hunkers rallied behind Polk and opposed the
proviso; the Barnburners joined with Wilmot. Since there was no inherent
reason that the issue of slavery, which had not entered into the original party
split, would fit so exactly the existing line of cleavage, the explanation must
lie in considerations of factional politics. Van Buren's closest political
friends were Barnburners. They had remained unreconciled when Polk defeated their leader in the 1844 convention, and when he appointed a Hunker
to his cabinet they were infuriated. Now the Barnburners found in the proviso an opportunity to take a high moral position on slavery and at the same

28. Herbert D. A. Donovan, *The Barnburners* (New York University Press, 1925),
p. 97.

time vent their resentment against Polk and the northerners who had betrayed Van Buren in 1844.

The Hunkers (whose name derived from their alleged "hunkering" after patronage) had a direct pecuniary interest in maintaining and strengthening their ties with Polk and, equally important, with the prospective 1848 Democratic presidential nominee, Senator Lewis Cass of Michigan, one of the five northern senators who had voted against the proviso. As for the principle involved, the Hunker could contend that the proviso was an inflammatory scheme that threatened to dissolve the Union while the alternative approach—"squatter sovereignty," which would leave the decision to the settlers of the new states—would have the same practical effect of excluding slavery from New Mexico and California without exciting the South.

The Hunkers, then, had political ties to the South—analogous to the political and economic ties of the Cotton Whigs—that impelled them, like the latter, to seek to suppress the rising slavery issue. But the Barnburners, like the Conscience Whigs, had little stake in the national party and reason to provoke the issue as a means to political supremacy at home. Again, expediency supported principle; they could express fervent views about slavery without the same concern for practical considerations that would inhibit a Hunker with equally deep convictions. One comes away from a study of the period with a feeling, however, that the Barnburners took the more extreme position against slavery as a matter, in some measure, of conviction. Perhaps this is because of a difference in temperament between reformers and patronage-oriented politicians; the Barnburners were the reform faction in matters of public finance and of government-business relations, and to become the reform party in regard to the institution of slavery as well appears a natural progression. It seems natural also that the Hunkers, enjoying and anticipating the fruits of patronage and lacking zeal to change the moral order in their own state, should be more complacent about the moral order in a distant region.

At the state convention at Syracuse in 1847, the Hunkers used their narrow margin of control to defeat endorsement of the proviso, to commend the Polk administration, to nominate their own man to replace the Barnburner state comptroller, Azariah C. Flagg, and to reorganize the party's state committee. Defeated at every turn and claiming that the seizure of the state committee was illegal, the "hotspurs" among the Barnburners, as Flagg called them, denounced the convention and called their own assembly to meet at Herkimer. There they poured forth at length their views on slavery and on the Hunker convention. On election day, they and their supporters either voted Whig or stayed at home, and the Whig candidate for comptroller, Millard Fillmore, was elected handily.

Both factions held conventions in 1848 and sent delegates to the Democratic national convention in Baltimore. That body, knowing well that a Barnburner defection could elect a Whig president, tried to heal the split by dividing New York's votes equally between the delegations. This the Barnburners refused, and they promptly left Baltimore in the same dudgeon they had displayed at Syracuse.

THE FREE-SOIL PARTY

The polar political force that had been centered in the tiny Liberty party was now augmented by two large, well-organized groups—the New York Barnburners and the Massachusetts Conscience Whigs—which had chosen, whatever their motives, to put their concern about slavery ahead of considerations of party loyalty and which found themselves, as a result, politically homeless. Coalescence with each other and with the Liberty party was inevitable. The Barnburners took the lead. They called a state convention for June and nominated for president on a free-soil ticket a reluctant Martin Van Buren, the original "Northern man with Southern principles," who as late as the Baltimore convention had counseled his party to nominate candidates "who have not committed themselves to either side of this important and delicate question" (the slavery issue)[29] but who in May of 1848 had finally gone on record for free-soil principles. Then, acting simultaneously with an "Ohio Free Territory Convention" composed of antislavery men of all parties, they summoned a national convention to meet in Buffalo.

The Conscience Whigs came. The Liberty party came, after some internal resistance from purists who saw in any alliance with men like Van Buren a compromise of principle. From other states came the counterparts of the Massachusetts Whigs—men like Congressman Joshua Giddings of Ohio's Western Reserve, where "people's meetings" in each county had been demanding the formation of a new party.[30] And there came the counterparts of New York's Barnburners, like Hale of New Hampshire and the

---

29. In a memorandum of May 3, 1848, carried to the convention by his son, John. Van Buren papers (Library of Congress, microfilm reel 30).
30. T. C. Smith, *Liberty and Free Soil Parties*, p. 128.

nascent Free-Soil party of Vermont.[31] In a convention so fervent that it rang in men's memories for a generation afterward, the Free-Soil party—the party of "Free Democracy"—came into being. It adopted a platform pledging "no more slave states, no slave territory," and abolition in the District of Columbia, plus planks on other issues, written by Salmon P. Chase, that were more Democratic than Whig in tone. Then, recognizing the Barnburners as the most powerful single element at the convention and attracted by the idea of having as their presidential candidate someone with the prestige of a former president, it nominated Van Buren over the more obscure Hale, who had been the Liberty party's nominee. Charles Francis Adams of the Conscience Whigs was chosen to run for vice-president.

That fall the Free-Soil party outpolled the Hunker Democrats in New York and finished second to the Whigs in Massachusetts and Vermont. It won majorities in six counties and pluralities in forty-four more, all in the same abolitionist belt extending from New England through central New York along the routes of New England migration to northern Illinois and Wisconsin. Its total vote was nearly 300,000, almost five times the Liberty vote of four years before. Thirteen Free-Soilers were elected to Congress, including Wilmot and Giddings. Unlike the Liberty party, the Free-Soil party drew heavily from the Democrats.[32] The party split made this result

31. The origin of the Vermont Free-Soil party was charmingly described forty-five years later in the memoirs of the party's first state chairman, L. E. Chittenden, *Personal Reminiscences, 1840–1890* (Richmond, Croscup, 1893), pp. 7–8. As the Vermont Democratic state convention of 1848 met, Chittenden (who was twenty-four that day) and five other delegates were incensed at the apparent readiness of Vermont Democrats, like those of other states, to reject the Wilmot Proviso and go along with squatter sovereignty. The six dissenters were "treated with contempt" but carried their fight to the convention floor. But when Chittenden finished his appeal to the convention on behalf of the six against the proposed platform planks,

> an ancient Democrat, whose mind was impervious to argument, then arose and observed that as "the boy had spoken his piece, we might as well proceed to the business of the convention." No one else spoke. There was a subdued affirmative vote and a sharp "No" from the six to the resolutions. . . . the opposition party of six walked out of the convention. There was an effort to raise a hiss. It failed, and we took our departure in a profound and unbroken silence.
> We crossed the street to the Pavilion Hotel . . . and the first Free Soil party formed in this republic . . . was organized.

32. Following are correlations, by counties, of the Free-Soil presidential vote of 1848 with Democratic and Whig losses between 1844 and 1848: Maine, correlation with Democratic losses, −0.151, with Whig losses, 0.811; New Hampshire, 0.356 and 0.705; Vermont, 0.736 and 0.373; Massachusetts, 0.183 and 0.832; Connecticut, 0.577 and 0.868; New York, 0.809 and 0.376; Pennsylvania, 0.813 and 0.469; Ohio, 0.428 and 0.962; Illinois, 0.795 and 0.757; Indiana, 0.411 and 0.791; Michigan, 0.211 and 0.546; the eleven states, 0.540 and 0.688. (Computations by Gary Greenhalgh.) As a curious aspect of coalition politics, in several strong Free-Soil counties in Ohio, the Whigs and Democrats united against the third party. T. C. Smith, *Liberty and Free Soil Parties*, p. 182.

predictable in New York, of course, but elsewhere too the nomination of so conspicuous a partisan as Van Buren under the banner of "Free Democracy" gave the new party a flavor that attracted Jacksonian Democrats while making it unacceptable to Whigs of free-soil sympathy. Moreover, the Whig party in large areas of the North had become thoroughly identified with free-soil principles—the Cotton Whigs of Massachusetts and their counterparts in other centers of trade with the South were the exception. While the Democrats were compromising, northern Whigs in Congress had voted unanimously for the Wilmot Proviso. True, the party had nominated a slaveholder in Zachary Taylor, but its northern spokesmen contended that Taylor did not believe in the presidential veto and so would let the proviso become law. Whig orators and newspapers in 1848 could argue that the new party, in the words of the Detroit *Advertiser*, "can say nothing in favor of free soil, free men, or free speech that is not said daily by the Whig party. . . . The Whig party is the true anti-slavery party of the country"; [33] and Whig votes for the third-party candidate would only serve to elect Cass as they had elected Polk four years earlier. This time the arguments were effective. Enough Whigs were held in line to put Taylor in the White House.

COALITION AND REGROUPING

Political events in 1849 illustrate vividly the inherent instability of a three-party structure in American politics. Van Buren and his Free-Soil party had not carried a single state, but they had finished second in New York, Massachusetts, and Vermont and had attracted enough support in most other northern states to hold a balance-of-power position between the older parties. With that much strength already, could not the new party occupying the polar position be expected to gain adherents steadily and automatically as the country polarized? Many of those who had formed the party at the Buffalo convention saw such a future. But after its first election, the party went into swift decline.

A polar bloc, by definition, puts principle above party, but for that very reason its allegiance will be no firmer to a new party than to the old ones. Its purpose is to choose the political mechanism that will best serve its principles. A major party, if it can be captured—that is, if it can be brought to

33. Aug. 4, 1848, quoted in ibid., p. 149. Formisano observes that from 1843 to 1852 Whig platforms in Michigan "emitted almost as much anti-southernism as did Liberty declarations." *Birth of Mass Political Parties*, p. 206.

adopt the principles of the polar bloc—is likely to be the superior mechanism, for it offers the prize of its large body of traditional adherents while a new party must start from the beginning. The northern components of the major parties in 1849 were especially vulnerable to capture. Drawn by the allure of those 300,000 Free-Soil votes toward the third party's pole, they were inhibited little by internal resistance, for an issue that splits a party geographically cleaves the national party but not most of its state and local constituents. Whigs throughout the North had generally embraced free-soil principles, and when in 1849 local Democrats were freed of the discipline of national patronage, no great obstacle prevented their doing the same.

Moreover, not all the 300,000 Free-Soil voters were genuinely members of a zealous, issue-oriented polar bloc. Many were simply deviants, who had crossed the party line temporarily, impelled by factional politics. That was conspicuously the case with the Barnburners of New York. They were, in the eyes of their leaders, the "regular" Democratic party that had been denied its legacy by the corrupt and illegal manipulations of its factional opponents. To the Barnburners the 1848 election was basically a contest for control of the Democratic party in New York rather than a crusade for free-soil principles, although those principles were a convenient asset to capitalize on in the intraparty struggle. Van Buren in his campaign never uttered the words free soil "in earnest," according to one biographer,[34] and in 1849 he was referring to the Barnburners and Hunkers as "two sections" of the Democratic party.[35]

Even so, it took two years for the sections to reunite. In 1849 the Hunkers' refusal to accept the Wilmot Proviso prevented fusion, but a deal was made whereby each faction, meeting separately, nominated four of the eight candidates for state office. "The day of compromise [on principles] is past, but in regards to candidates of state offices, we are still a commercial people," John Van Buren, son of the former president, was reported as saying.[36] Of the eight, four—three Hunkers and one Barnburner—were elected. Next year the Barnburners stopped insisting on the free-soil platform, there was only one Democratic convention, and all its nominees except the gubernatorial candidate were successful.

Democrats in Vermont were reunited almost painlessly. In May, negotia-

34. William Allen Butler, *Martin Van Buren: Lawyer, Statesman and Man* (Appleton, 1862), pp. 33–34, cited by Donovan, *The Barnburners*, p. 112.

35. Alto Lee Whitehurst, "Martin Van Buren and the Free Soil Movement" (Ph.D. dissertation, University of Chicago, 1932), p. 191.

36. Charles Buxton Going, *David Wilmot, Free-Soiler* (Appleton, 1924), pp. 354–55.

tors agreed on a state ticket and a set of resolutions embodying the Free-Soil platform of 1848, and the agreement was ratified by a single convention.[37] The Barnburners of the Chicago area "marched back into the old ranks" in 1850 after the Democratic congressional candidate committed himself to free-soil principles.[38] Similar "reunions" took place in Rhode Island, Indiana, and other states. But in Michigan, Senator Cass could not repudiate his 1848 position by endorsing the Wilmot Proviso, and the free-soil wing of the Democratic party formed an uneasy coalition—and in many counties fused outright—with the Whigs. Democrats opposed to the proviso forced a similar Whig–Free-Soil coalition in Iowa.

Free-Soil purists like Charles Francis Adams, who regarded both major parties as hopelessly compromised on slavery, could only watch in dismay as their party eroded. Even in Adams's own Massachusetts, local coalitions were formed in 1849, generally with the Democrats. The next year the talk was of a deal with the Democrats patterned after one in Ohio that had exchanged a Democratic governor for a Free-Soil senator (Chase). That proposition struck Adams as "a renunciation of all moral character which will ultimately lead to our annihilation as a party," for a Democratic governor could only "promote the ascendancy of General Cass." But Charles Sumner saw it differently. Sumner "considers the possession of a Senator's place by one of our friends as more important than the whole State government in the hands of traitors or opponents," Adams recorded in his diary.[39] But Adams began to find himself leading a minority at party meetings, and after the 1850 election the deal was consummated: a Democratic–Free-Soil coalition in the legislature elected a Democrat as governor and Sumner to the Senate. The deal "must infallibly carry us all into the jaws of a proslavery democracy in Massachusetts," wrote the last of the Free-Soil purists.[40]

So the whole third-party edifice crumbled. The Free-Soilers in 1852 polled barely half their 1848 popular vote (although outside New York it fell by less than a quarter): they could claim two senators, but only as the result of coalition maneuvering, and as a continuing political organization the party consisted of nothing much beyond the original "philanthropists" who had made up the Liberty party.

37. T. C. Smith, *Liberty and Free Soil Parties*, pp. 180, 185; Whitehurst, "Martin Van Buren," pp. 210–11.

38. T. C. Smith, *Liberty and Free Soil Parties*, p. 196.

39. Charles Francis Adams, diary, Aug. 10, Aug. 24, 1850 (Library of Congress, mss. division, microfilm reel 71).

40. Adams diary, Nov. 16, 1850 (microfilm reel 72).

Division of the Whig Party

But while the Free-Soil party went into decline after the enthusiasm of 1848, the forces that had produced it did not. As the party ruptures of 1848 were being healed, a wave of declarations supporting free-soil principles came from party conventions and legislatures throughout the North. It was time for the moderate centrists of both parties to make one last heroic attempt to avert the polarization of the country.

THE COMPROMISE OF 1850

Henry Clay of Kentucky took the Senate floor on February 5 and 6, 1850, to decry the "intemperance of party spirit" that led Whigs and Democrats of the North to woo for local advantage the votes of "a small party called Abolitionists," and called upon his colleagues "to pause—solemnly to pause—at the edge of the precipice." He urged upon them a five-point compromise scheme he had introduced a few days earlier to dispose of all pending questions pertaining to slavery.[41] Clay's plan was bound to offend the militants of both North and South—those of the North because it did not apply the Wilmot Proviso in organizing the New Mexico and Utah territories[42] and because it embodied a strong fugitive slave law; those of the South because it failed to guarantee the right of slaveholding in the territories, admitted California as a free state, reduced the size of Texas in favor of New Mexico, and abolished the slave trade (though not slavery itself) in the District of Columbia. But it was artful in apparently offending both sides about equally, and it succeeded in bringing together leading senators of both parties who desired to suppress the slavery issue.

The titular head of the Democratic party, Senator Cass, and all Cass's rivals for national party leadership fell in behind the seventy-three-year-old Kentuckian. So did the other great Senate elder of the Whigs, Daniel Webster. But two other Whigs, significantly, did not. One was President Taylor, the other his close adviser and principal spokesman in the Senate, William H. Seward of New York. Taylor held that the various questions embraced in the compromise should be considered separately and he "hotly resented"

41. Appendix to *Congressional Globe*, 31 Cong. 1 sess., pp. 115–27.
42. Clay's position was that the territories were already free under Mexican law. In the final Compromise of 1850, the question was left to popular sovereignty—Cass's position in the 1848 campaign.

being upstaged by Clay's dramatic seizure of party and national leadership.[43] Seward denounced Clay's plan—in its particulars, as well as on the general ground that its components should be dealt with separately—and he remarked that "there is a higher law than the Constitution, which regulates our authority."[44] The fate of the party was sealed when the main body of northern Whigs chose to follow him rather than Clay and Webster. When Fillmore acceded to the presidency on Taylor's death in July and endorsed the compromise, he found his party had slipped from under him. The northern Whigs abandoned their southern colleagues in favor of free-soil principles and votes at home, and it was the northern Democrats led by Stephen A. Douglas of Illinois, along with southern moderates of both parties, who made possible the Compromise of 1850.[45]

President Fillmore saw "a final settlement of the dangerous and exciting subjects" once the legislation was enacted.[46] But Hale's verdict was different. "Let not gentlemen deceive themselves . . . there is no peace to those who think they have successfully dug the grave in which the hopes, the rights, and the interests of freedom have been buried. No, sir, that peace will be short."[47] Fillmore's prediction seemed borne out in the period that fol-

---

43. Frank H. Hodder, "The Authorship of the Compromise of 1850," *Mississippi Valley Historical Review*, Vol. 22 (March 1936), p. 527.

44. Appendix to *Congressional Globe*, 31 Cong. 1 sess. (March 11, 1850), pp. 262–65. Seward's biographer, Edward Everett Hale, Jr., in *William H. Seward* (George W. Jacobs, 1910), pp. 192–93, argues convincingly that Seward's famous appeal to "higher law" was spoken in support of the Constitution rather than in defiance of it but the other interpretation was given to it in the South, where Seward became a symbol of Northern intransigence.

45. On the Senate bill to organize the New Mexico territory without the Wilmot Proviso, northern Democrats voted 10–3 in the affirmative, northern Whigs, 6–1 in the negative. Northern Democrats voted for the corresponding Utah bill, 11–3, northern Whigs against it, 11–0. This vote was on engrossment for third reading rather than on final passage, which was accomplished without a roll call. In the House, northern Democrats voted for the New Mexico bill, 32–14, and the Utah bill, 30–14, while northern Whigs voted against both, 42–23 and 44–11, respectively. An even more critical test came on the hated fugitive slave law. There were no northern Whig votes for it in the Senate, 8 voted against it, and 5 were absent. Northern Whigs voted 47–3 against in the House. But northern Democrats loyally went down the line for it, 26–16, in the House, and provided the necessary margin in the Senate either with their votes or their absences (3 voted for it, 3 against it, and 9 were absent). For an analysis of party and individual roles in the Compromise of 1850, see Holman Hamilton, "Democratic Senate Leadership and the Compromise of 1850," *Mississippi Historical Review*, Vol. 41 (December 1954), pp. 403–08, 410; and Hamilton, "The 'Cave of the Winds' and the Compromise of 1850," *Journal of Southern History*, Vol. 23 (August 1957), pp. 331–53, esp. pp. 348–50. See also Hodder, "The Authorship of the Compromise of 1850," pp. 525–36.

46. First Annual Message, Dec. 2, 1850, *A Compilation of the Messages and Papers of the Presidents* (1789–1897), Vol. 6 (Bureau of National Literature, 1897), p. 2629.

47. *Congressional Globe*, 31 Cong. 1 sess. (Sept. 18, 1850), p. 1860.

lowed. After the months of arduous maneuvering and intense debate that produced the compromise, "People . . . desired never to hear the words 'Free Soil' or 'Wilmot Proviso' again; all they wanted was peace, and this the Compromise offered."[48] In New York, the Barnburners gave up the fight for their free-soil platform in reuniting with the Hunkers. Newspapers that had backed the free-soil cause now supported the compromise and called for an end to agitation.

REJECTION IN MASSACHUSETTS

Only in Massachusetts did events seem to bear out Hale's prophecy that the peace would be a short one. One element of the compromise, the fugitive slave law, carried dynamite for the North that could explode at any time, and it was detonated that very fall in Massachusetts. For two weeks in October the state was in "a ferment" when southern slave catchers came to Boston to seize an escaped Negro couple who had been living there in freedom. The couple was hidden and the pursuers were harassed by the city's vigilance committee until they were driven out of town.[49] The Democratic–Free-Soil coalition press denounced Webster and the Whig administration of President Fillmore, who had supported the law, as the proslavery party. And in November came a stunning coalition victory—the one that added Sumner to the uncompromising antislavery minority in the Senate. The Boston *Atlas*, a Whig paper, offered a reason for the party's reversal after its impressive 1848 victory: in the former year "we did not outrage the consciences of our people."[50]

ACCEPTANCE IN THE SOUTH

Each party was split in the South, as in the North, between militants and moderates, but the schism was deeper in the Democratic party. Calhoun had carried most Whig states' rights zealots into the Democratic party with him when he had bolted the Whigs a dozen years before, in a move that followed the pattern and can be considered a precursor of the realignment of the

48. T. C. Smith, *Liberty and Free Soil Parties*, p. 226.
49. Lawrence Lader, *The Bold Brahmins: New England's War Against Slavery, 1831–1863* (Dutton, 1961), pp. 139–43.
50. Nov. 14, 1850.

1850s. That shift had left the Whigs predominantly on the side of moderation and preservation of the Union.[51]

To the militants in the South, as in the North, the Compromise of 1850 was surrender; Calhoun had denounced it before he died. It was also a springboard for an effort by the proslavery polar bloc to seize unchallenged leadership in the individual states and in the region. But in this it failed. When Georgia called a convention to decide the state's course, Speaker Howell Cobb and other Georgia members of Congress who had supported the compromise came home to stump the state. A majority of procompromise, or Union, delegates was elected, and the convention endorsed the compromise in language that carried a "thus far but no farther" tone.

At the Georgia convention, the moderates saw the necessity for a new political vehicle that would embrace the union forces of both old parties, and they formed the Constitutional Union party, which succeeded in electing Cobb governor. Similar parties were formed in Alabama and Mississippi, and each was successful in its initial election. But all three were short-lived. Their Democratic members saw them as single-purpose vehicles, and when they had accomplished their task the Democrats returned to their old allegiance to prepare for the 1852 election. The Whigs of these states had no choice but to do the same, for the idea of a national Union party developed no support elsewhere.[52]

REJECTION BY THE NORTHERN WHIGS

But the national Whig party found that its pre-1850 cohesion was not again attainable. Having repudiated their centrist President (Fillmore) in Washington with virtual unanimity, the northern free-soil Whigs had no course but to pursue their victory at home. New York, as the state of both Fillmore and Seward, was crucial, and there the Seward forces won decisively. The state Whig convention rejected a pro-Fillmore report of its resolutions committee and adopted an alternative full of praise for Seward, whereupon the Fillmore men (who became the "Silver Greys") walked out and held a separate convention, which duly commended Fillmore. Seward

51. They participated to only a limited extent, for example, in the regionwide Nashville convention of 1850 called by the disunionists. Arthur Charles Cole, *The Whig Party in the South* (American Historical Association, 1914), pp. 163–73 and 181.

52. Ibid., pp. 212–15, 240–41. Clay had reportedly given his blessing to such a party, but Cass and other northern Democratic centrists rejected it. Roy F. Nichols, *The Democratic Machine 1850–1854* (Columbia University Press, 1923), p. 28.

then enlisted behind the candidacy for president of General Winfield Scott, the conqueror of Mexico, who had announced he was against the extension of slavery. Whig leaders and party conventions in most other northern states also came out for Scott, coupling their endorsement of him with antislavery resolutions, which included demands for repeal of the fugitive slave law.[53] In April northern Whigs in the House voted two-to-one against a resolution acknowledging the Compromise of 1850 as a "permanent solution" of the issues it dealt with (while northern Democrats approved it by a similar margin), and two weeks later a Whig congressional caucus split on the same issue, with most of the southerners walking out of the meeting.[54] At the Whig national convention Fillmore, the New Yorker, was the candidate of the South and the Silver Greys; Scott, originally a Virginian, was the candidate of most of the North. The northern Whigs accepted a platform plank "acquiescing" in the Compromise of 1850, but when Scott was nominated, control passed finally and decisively from the centrists who had tried to hold the party together.

The polar bloc had at last captured a major party, but it was not a party that could win—not in 1852, at any rate. In the South, Whig leaders could emphasize the party's procompromise platform and Scott's endorsement of it, but they could not repair their candidate's image as "Seward's lackey."[55] In the North, the mood was procompromise, and "Franklin Pierce rode confidently to the White House on the magic carpet of the most important letter of his life, in which he pronounced himself a Compromise Democrat."[56]

The bonds uniting northern and southern Whigs were now dissolved. Southern leaders tried to hold their organizations together around local issues. In Georgia and Mississippi they reestablished the coalition Union parties of 1851 but this time were defeated. Gradually they lost strength to the Democrats, as well as to the Native American, or "Know-Nothing," party just forming, while their leaders waited for the opportunity to reestablish a national party in which they would ally themselves with northern conservatives dedicated to preservation of the Union.

The division of the Whig party had been ordained more than a decade earlier, almost at its birth, when the northern Whigs had aligned themselves behind John Quincy Adams and his fight against the "gag rule." From that

53. Cole, *Whig Party in the South*, pp. 224–27.
54. Ibid., pp. 236–38.
55. Carlton Luther Jackson, "A History of the Whig Party in Alabama, 1823–60" (Ph.D. dissertation, University of Georgia, 1962), pp. 221–30.
56. Hamilton, "Democratic Senate Leadership," p. 414.

time forward, they had steadfastly bent their doctrines to appeal to the abolitionists, first on the gag rule, then on the Texas question, then on the Mexican war, then on the Wilmot Proviso, and finally, in defiance of their most eminent leaders, on the Compromise of 1850. This had been a matter of political necessity as well as conviction. For in the North the Whigs were the party in the middle: the northern Democrats, led for years by compromisers, had preempted the prosouthern position while at the other extreme the Liberty party and then the Free-Soil party were appealing to the growing body of antislavery militants. As sentiment polarized on the slavery issue, the party in the middle was inevitably the one that was torn. It was caught between the requirement for survival as a national party, which was to accept compromise, and the requirement for survival in the northern states, which was to reject it. The local compulsions were overriding, for the party's leaders had to protect their local power bases before they could even think of national supremacy. To put it another way, the rising antislavery sentiment of the North was bound to have its political vehicle; if the Whigs declined to be that vehicle, the Free-Soil party would be, and the Whigs would find themselves supplanted.

So as the worn links between northern and southern Whigs finally parted, the former were set free to stir the moral fervor of the North against slavery and rise to power on its crest. They were free to unite with the men who had already rejected centrism and its compromises—the men of the Free Democracy, still waging their single-minded crusade—and with Democrats of like mind who had deserted the free-soil coalition after 1848 but might be won back. The realignment was under way.

CHAPTER FIVE

The Realignment of the 1850s

"I FERVENTLY HOPE that the question is at rest," Franklin Pierce said in his inaugural address. But the rest was broken within a year, and by the very man who had been the floor leader in Senate passage of the Compromise of 1850, Stephen A. Douglas.

In January 1854, Senator Douglas reported from his Committee on Territories a bill to organize the territories of Kansas and Nebraska, and in doing so to abrogate the provisions of the Missouri Compromise of 1820 that had excluded slavery from those territories. He proposed to apply instead the doctrine of popular sovereignty that had been adopted in 1850 for New Mexico and Utah.

Allan Nevins has called Douglas's course "one of the most arresting enigmas in all American history,"[1] because it was likely that a Kansas-Nebraska bill, based on the Missouri Compromise, that had come close to enactment in 1853 could have passed. But southern senators had become adamant against any organization of the territories that forbade southerners to migrate there with their human property; and Douglas could contend that the territories would be free in any case, for even if popular sovereignty were approved the South could not people Kansas and Nebraska with slaveholders. If the Democratic party were to be preserved from the same kind of schism that had by then all but destroyed the Whigs, compromise was once more necessary—and what principle of compromise could be more appealing than the one so strenuously hammered out in 1850 and since then so widely accepted? Douglas's own presidential ambitions depended on a unified Democratic party dedicated to the spirit of compromise with which he had become identified.

1. Allan Nevins, *Ordeal of the Union*, Vol. 2, *A House Dividing, 1852–1857* (Scribner's, 1947), p. 91.

Political opponents seized at once on the last of these concerns: the proposal was a crass bargain to make Douglas president with southern votes.
"Will the people permit their dearest interests to be thus made the mere
hazards of a presidential game?" cried Salmon P. Chase, Charles Sumner,
and four House Free-Soilers in an "Appeal to the People" issued when the
bill was reported. At least one Douglas biographer adopts that view: "It
seems not too much to assert that the new proposal was intended to open a
road to the presidency which was to be purchased at the heavy cost of renewed sectional warfare."[2] Nevins rejects any such simple explanation,
points to "a multiplicity of motives," and emphasizes Douglas's propensity
for "rapid decisions and headlong action" and his "pronounced love of combat."[3] Students of the period agree that Douglas badly underestimated the
northern reaction to repeal of the Missouri Compromise; feeling no moral
outrage himself at the institution of slavery,[4] he lacked sensitivity to the
depth of that feeling in others, a feeling that had been steadily deepening.
That winter, some half a million copies of *Uncle Tom's Cabin* were being
read by firesides throughout the North. Every northern excursion by southern Legrees seeking to recapture fugitive slaves created a local crisis, and
many blacks were protected or rescued by mob action.

Douglas and his southern allies had obtained Pierce's promise of support
and with the help of presidential patronage and in endless hours of caucuses
they held the Senate Democrats together through five weeks of debate.
Northern Democrats voted for the final Kansas-Nebraska bill 14 to 4. Defection in the House was more serious, but 44 of 86 northern Democrats
finally voted for the measure and it was passed. Meanwhile the northern
Whigs eagerly seized the occasion to create a party issue: not a single northern Whig voted for the bill in either house.

That vote cut whatever tenuous ties still remained between northern and
southern Whigs. The former were now a regional party united on free-soil
principles. So, of course, were the Free-Soil remnants, and no barriers of
party organization or principle now stood in the way of a fusion of the two
organizations. Men had been talking more and more since 1852 of a great

2. Henry Parker Willis, *Stephen A. Douglas* (George W. Jacobs, 1910), p. 191. This
is also the interpretation of T. C. Smith, *Parties and Slavery 1850–1859* (Harper, 1906),
p. 96.

3. Nevins, *Ordeal of the Union*, Vol. 2, p. 106.

4. Douglas had married into a North Carolina slaveholding family, and his wife (who
died in 1853) and children had inherited slaves. For an analysis of his "want of sensitive-
ness to the force of ethical convictions stirring the masses," see Allen Johnson, *Stephen A.
Douglas: A Study in American Politics* (Macmillan, 1908), pp. 270–72.

new party that would not only unite Whigs and Free-Soilers but bring in the half or more of the northern Democrats who could not stomach their party's constant compromises with slavery. In the wave of indignation that swept the North over passage of the Kansas-Nebraska Act, the new party took form.

A New Major Party: The Republicans

It began with mass meetings throughout the North, which were called by anti-Nebraska Democrats as well as by Whigs and Free-Soilers. The meetings featured speakers from all three groups. In Cincinnati, a thousand "unquestioned and adamantine" Democrats joined in calling an anti-Nebraska meeting; a Chicago gathering was led by Democrats who had previously supported Douglas.[5] Democratic newspapers defected.[6] The legislatures of Maine, Massachusetts, Rhode Island, New York, and Wisconsin passed resolutions of opposition by overwhelming bipartisan majorities; only Illinois expressed support. Connecticut Democrats at their state convention resolved against the bill; Pennsylvania Democrats refused to support it. In a spring election, the Democrats lost the Detroit mayoralty. German-Americans appeared to be cutting loose from their traditional Democratic loyalties.

One of the anti-Nebraska mass meetings, held in Ripon, Wisconsin, in February 1854, is generally credited with being the first to call explicitly for the foundation of a new party. At a second meeting in Ripon on March 20, the new party was born. "We went into the little meeting held in a schoolhouse Whigs, Free Soilers, and Democrats. We came out of it Republicans," wrote Alvan E. Bovay some years later.[7] After the Kansas-Nebraska bill was enacted, its enemies in Michigan called a state convention, held in July, and nominated a fusion ticket on a platform devoted wholly to that "relic of barbarism," slavery. The new fusion party expressly postponed consideration of the matters of "political economy or administrative policy" that had traditionally divided Whigs from Democrats. The Free-Soil party of Michigan dissolved the day the fusion party (which afterward took the name Re-

5. Nevins, *Ordeal of the Union*, Vol. 2, p. 126.
6. Among them were the New York *Evening Post*, the Buffalo *Republic*, the Detroit *Times*, and the Chicago *Democrat*. Ibid., p. 131.
7. Quoted by William Starr Myers, *The Republican Party: A History* (Century, 1928), p. 44.

publican) was formed, and the Whigs did the same three months later. The fusion candidates were victorious in November.

Throughout the Northwest, corresponding steps were being taken. Within days after Michigan had acted, a Republican party was formed in Wisconsin, an anti-Nebraska party in Ohio, and a People's party in Indiana. In Illinois the Republican party was formed in the northern districts whose center was Chicago (where Douglas was howled down by a hostile crowd in September), but downstate the Whigs, including Abraham Lincoln, insisted on maintaining their party identity, and the consequence in 1854 was a joint ticket of Whigs and Republicans rather than a merger.

To the east, where the Whigs were stronger, they could hope to be the beneficiaries of anti-Nebraska sentiment without the need for allies, and they resisted any move that would force them to share the rewards of victory. So while the Republican party was organized in some eastern states in 1854, it was made up mostly of Free-Soilers, and the Whigs remained in existence throughout that region. In the East, however, the Whigs found powerful competition from a new source—the American, or "Know-Nothing," party, a group built on anti-Catholic, anti-immigrant sentiment that had won a few local elections (often in fusion with the Whigs).[8] Appealing to Democrats alienated by the party's Kansas-Nebraska stand, as well as to Whigs who foresaw the death of their own party and were looking for the party of the future, the Know-Nothings were converted almost overnight from a fringe group to a major political force. On the slavery issue, they reflected the mood of their respective states—strongly antislavery in New England, conciliatory in the border states.

THE ANTI-NEBRASKA TIDE

The opposition to the Democrats—whether Whig, Republican, Know-Nothing, or fusion—won smashing victories in the elections of 1854 and the spring of 1855. The new Republican party swept Michigan for the first Democratic defeat in more than a decade, and won in Wisconsin, while the anti-Nebraska candidates carried Ohio and the People's party was victorious in Indiana. Fusionists elected a majority of the legislature in Douglas's home state of Illinois. A coalition of free-soilers and prohibitionists elected a gov-

8. Including a mayor of New York City and several congressmen from New York City and Philadelphia.

ernor in Maine. Know-Nothings were victorious in New Hampshire, Massachusetts, Rhode Island, and Connecticut.

When legislatures met in 1855, three of the Senate Democratic compromisers—from Indiana, Illinois, and Iowa—were beaten or stepped aside, and were replaced with staunch anti-Nebraska men.[9] Two New Hampshire seats held in 1854 by Douglas supporters were filled by free-soilers, one of them John P. Hale. Northern Democratic ranks in the House were decimated. Their number had fallen from ninety-one in the preceding Congress to seventeen, as measured by the vote for the Democratic caucus candidate for Speaker.[10]

In the wake of the Democratic collapse, the Republican party moved eastward in 1855, though with little immediate success. In Ohio it was created in July from the anti-Nebraska organization of the previous year and that fall elected Salmon P. Chase as Ohio's first Republican governor.[11] The Pennsylvania party was formed in September with David Wilmot as chairman of its state committee but was unsuccessful that year. A new Massachusetts Republican party finished second to the Know-Nothings as the votes received by the two old parties, the Whigs and the Democrats, fell respectively to 10 and 25 percent of the total. The New York party, formed in September, also lost to the Know-Nothings.

Within the space of only a few months, however, the Know-Nothing party was to collapse for the same reason that the Whigs had failed. The slavery issue that had split the older party into sectional blocs now prevented the newer party from congealing its sectional elements into a national entity. United only on their nativism, the Know-Nothings tried to sidestep the question of slavery; to that end their second national conference, held in Philadelphia in June 1855, simply endorsed the status quo. But the status quo included the Kansas-Nebraska Act, and that issue was too explosive to be evaded. A group of delegates from New England and the Northwest walked out. The northern wing of the American party then found itself split three ways. Some, including leaders of the walkout, urged their fellow Know-

9. The Indiana senator-designate was not seated by the Senate, however, and the seat remained vacant until 1857.

10. In the confusion of party labels in 1855, the *Congressional Globe* abandoned for the Thirty-fourth Congress its practice of listing members by party affiliation. Of the seventeen who voted for the Democratic candidate for Speaker (W. A. Richardson of Illinois), at least two were on record as anti-Nebraska Democrats.

11. Know-Nothings were given the other eight places on the state ticket. Joe Hoover Bindley, "An Analysis of Voting Behavior in Ohio" (Ph.D. dissertation, University of Pittsburgh, 1959), p. 43.

Nothings to become Republicans; some accepted the Philadelphia platform and refused to abandon the concept of a national party; still others, who called themselves "North Americans," looked to an all-northern party based on anti-Nebraska principles but under their, rather than Republican, leadership. [12] The following year the scene was repeated; North American delegates walked out after another status quo platform was adopted and Fillmore nominated for president. But the North Americans were no more than a remnant of a party compared with the flourishing Republicans. [13]

THE REPUBLICAN PARTIES FEDERATE

The Republicans, having no aspirations to become a national party, had no difficulty federating in the North. As in Michigan, they tried in other states to be as nearly as possible a single-issue party.

What constitutes a crosscutting issue depends on the rationale of the original alignment. To the Democrats and the Whigs, who had been unified around their respective positions on domestic economic policy, slavery was a crosscutting issue that threatened party unity, and so when it arose the parties' established leaders did their best to straddle it. Leaders of the Know-Nothing party, formed on nativism, also sought to straddle slavery. The Republican party, however, had been brought into being on the slavery issue; so to it the other issues—economic questions, nativism, prohibition—were crosscutting. And the Republican leaders, who were a polar force on the one issue, acted as moderate centrists on the others, striving in the accustomed way of centrist leaders to straddle and suppress them.

So temperance delegates had to be voted down by a Republican convention in Iowa and nativists by the party's gathering in Massachusetts. "We require no conformity of opinion on other subjects of National or State policy [than extension of slavery]," declared the Massachusetts Republican platform of 1855. "We all recognize the duty of making the question of Freedom paramount. To secure uniformity of action here, we attempt no uniformity of action elsewhere."[14] Some Republican conventions were un-

---

12. Andrew Wallace Crandall, *The Early History of the Republican Party, 1854–1856* (first published, 1930; Peter Smith, 1960), pp. 28–31, 38–40.
13. Ibid., pp. 135–42. As for what remained of the northern Whig party, it could do no better than endorse Fillmore and then disband.
14. Godfrey Tryggve Anderson, "The Slavery Issue as a Factor in Massachusetts Politics, from the Compromise of 1850 to the Outbreak of the Civil War" (Ph.D. dissertation, University of Chicago, 1947), p. 149.

able to limit themselves quite so severely. In Indiana, Republicans were compelled by the temperance advocates to incorporate a statement on the subject in their first platform but, with an eye to the German vote, managed to straddle with a "judiciously worded resolution."[15] In Illinois, German leaders won a plank repudiating the basic legislative proposals of the Know-Nothings.[16]

As the state Republican parties convened in 1856 to form a national party and nominate a presidential ticket, they were faced with the same necessity. To form a popular majority in the North they would have to appeal to the nativists yet not alienate the immigrants, particularly the Germans, who they believed could be lured into the Republican party as a bloc on the free-soil issue. And having the free-soil vote of the upper North assured, they also needed to appeal to the more moderate sentiment of the border North—New Jersey, Pennsylvania, and the southern sections of the Ohio River states. The most conspicuous leaders of the new party, Chase and William H. Seward, stood too far from its center on both issues. Both were too closely identified with the radicals on slavery; as for nativism, Chase had associated himself with the Know-Nothings in Ohio and Seward had denounced them in New York.[17] The practical politicians and editors developed a consensus that a "new man," unburdened by enemies from past campaigns, was needed, and in the familiar Whig manner they found him in a popular hero—not a general this time but a colonel, the "Pathfinder of the Rockies," John C. Frémont. The platform was devoted chiefly to Kansas-Nebraska and related safe and established antislavery issues but included planks on a few matters with strong regional appeal on which the North was agreed—a central railroad to the Pacific and river and harbor improvements.[18]

15. Mildred C. Stoler, "Insurgent Democrats of Indiana and Illinois in 1854," *Indiana Magazine of History,* Vol. 33 (March 1937), p. 20.

16. Mildred C. Stoler, "The Democratic Element in the New Republican Party in Illinois, 1856–1860," *Papers in Illinois History* (1942), p. 8.

17. Crandall, *Early History of Republican Party*, p. 155.

18. Some general language in the 1856 platform supporting "liberty of conscience and equality of rights among citizens" was also included, suggesting disapproval of Know-Nothing principles. Ibid., p. 198. Yet where necessary the Republicans were not above cooperating with the American party. In Massachusetts they refrained from nominating a candidate for governor and supported the incumbent American for reelection. In Connecticut the Republicans and Know-Nothings joined as a fusion party against the Democrats and then merged in 1857 as the Union party; but the party split the following year after a quarrel over a nativist resolution (which was defeated) at the state convention. Carroll John Noonan, *Nativism in Connecticut, 1829–1860* (Catholic University of America Press, 1938), pp. 294–311. Jarlath Robert Lane, *A Political History of Connecticut during the Civil War* (Catholic University of America Press, 1941), pp. 80–96.

The Kansas-Nebraska issue, which had precipitated the Republican party, continued to propel it. The new party's papers carried an endless stream of exciting news from the new Kansas territory as free-state and slave-state settlers waged virtual civil war. Then in May 1856, after delivering a speech entitled "The Crime Against Kansas," Senator Sumner was caned on the Senate floor by Congressman Preston Brooks of South Carolina and incapacitated. As northern indignation grew—and was ceaselessly fanned by Republican politicians—the regional antislavery party grew with it.

In November it was clearly established as the major party of the North. Frémont carried eleven states in that region; the winning Democratic candidate, James Buchanan, five. The election was so close that only two things would be required to give the country's first exclusively regional party control of the national government—the final disappearance of the Know-Nothing party in the North, and a swing in public sentiment against the Buchanan administration sufficient to give the Republicans Pennsylvania and one or two of the other free states carried by the Democrats in 1856.

REPUBLICANS TRIUMPHANT

The first came naturally enough. In Pennsylvania, Republicans and some Know-Nothing leaders formed a Union party in 1857, which absorbed most of the Know-Nothings.[19] Next year the consolidation of a single opposition party was completed, and by 1860 the name Republican was restored to it. Elsewhere the Know-Nothing party died a similar death.

And events brought about the necessary shift of northern sentiment against the Democratic administration. The panic of 1857 closed banks and factories throughout the North and sent railroads into backruptcy (the South's economy somehow escaping any corresponding damage). Republicans blamed Democratic low-tariff policies and gained a potent new issue, especially in Pennsylvania, where politicians of both parties had long been committed to tariff protection. Meanwhile, the Supreme Court with its southern majority had rendered the Dred Scott decision, so hateful to the North, and the situation in Kansas continued to deteriorate. In the 1858 election, the Democrats lost 40 percent of their northern seats in the House

19. The only concessions in the platform to nativist principles were two minor planks condemning abuse of the naturalization laws for partisan purposes and advocating deportation of "foreign criminals." Theophane Geary, *A History of Third Parties in Pennsylvania, 1840–1860* (Catholic University of America Press, 1938), pp. 207–28.

—twenty-one seats in all, eleven of them in Pennsylvania. Northern Republicans (or union or fusion representatives) outnumbered northern Democrats by more than three to one.

By 1858 the new alignment was firmly in place throughout the North. The revulsion against the Buchanan administration continued, a North-South schism further weakened the Democrats, the Republicans solidified their position by embracing the protective tariff and the homestead issues, and in 1860 Abraham Lincoln carried every free state except New Jersey. Then followed secession and civil war.

Substance of the Realignment

With the reestablishment of the two-party system, the American political structure had turned on its axis. The realignment had followed the pattern of scenario 4 of Chapter 2—replacement of one of the old major parties by a new one.

To recapitulate, in the prerealignment period the slavery issue had cut across the existing alignment, and polar forces had formed at either end. As of 1848, the party system was as diagramed in Figure 5-1. Pressing from the antislavery pole was the Free-Soil party, made up of the former Liberty party and the former Whigs and Democrats who had joined it. The Whig party was a battleground where three groups contested for control: the antislavery zealots, of whom Seward was the leader, in block 1; a small (compared to the Democrats) group of southern disunionists in block 5; and the moderate centrists—Clay, Webster, Fillmore, the Cotton Whigs, and their allies—who came from both sides of the line of cleavage, in blocks 3. Their counterparts were three contending groups within the Democratic party—the abolitionist sympathizers in block 2; the southern disunionists led by Calhoun in block 6; and in blocks 4 the centrists, who included all the party's presidential candidates from 1844 to 1860—Polk, Cass, Pierce, Buchanan, and Douglas—procompromise factions like the New York Hunkers, and southerners like Cobb of Georgia.

When the Whig centrists failed and the party split, the two blocks 3 were absorbed, respectively, in blocks 1 and 5. The Republican party was then formed from the Free-Soil party and the two old-party polar elements, blocks 1 and 2. The picture that emerged is shown in Figure 5-2 (the blocks are lettered to correspond to those for Figure 2-5).

Figure 5-1. *The Realignment of the 1850s: The Prerealignment Period*

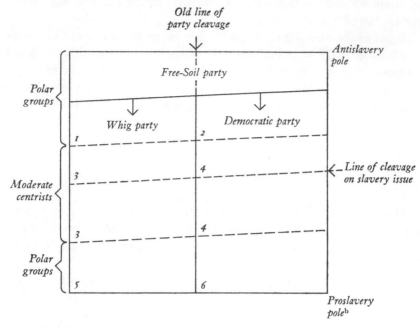

a. This figure and others like it in this chapter are schematic rather than quantitatively precise. The size of the compartments does not measure the proportion of the electorate contained in each.

b. The term "proslavery" is not fully satisfactory to describe all members of the polar group at this end of the spectrum, for some were against slavery as an institution but also against government action to interfere with it. "Antiabolition" or "anti-antislavery" might more accurately describe that segment of the polar group.

THE DEMOCRATS-TURNED-REPUBLICANS

The body of voters in block B_1—the Democrats who switched to the Republican party—proved to be of sufficient number to make the new party the majority party in the North. They represented all strata of political activity—top leaders, intermediate leaders, party workers, and supporters. Among the former Democrats who emerged as early Republican leaders were the party's first presidential candidate, Frémont; its second vice-presidential nominee, Hannibal Hamlin of Maine; the president of the 1856 national convention, Francis P. Blair, Sr., of Maryland; at least nine Republican senators of the Thirty-seventh Congress that convened in 1861 (Hale of New Hampshire, Preston King of New York, Wilmot and Simon

Figure 5-2. *The Realignment of the 1850s*

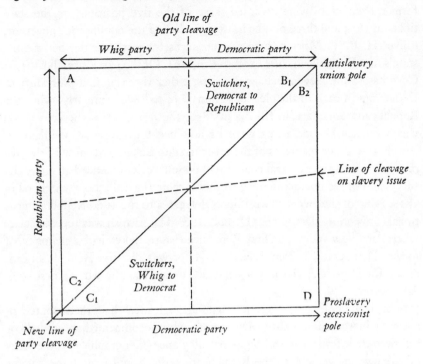

Cameron of Pennsylvania, Chase of Ohio,[20] Kingsley Scott Bingham of Michigan, J. R. Doolittle of Wisconsin, Lyman Trumbull of Illinois, and James Henry Lane of Kansas), and four of the seven members of Lincoln's cabinet (Cameron, Chase, Gideon Welles of Connecticut, and Montgomery Blair of Maryland).

After carefully tracing the way in which insurgent Democrats were absorbed into the new Republican party in Indiana and Illinois, Mildred C. Stoler concluded that the former Democrats were prominent in leadership positions far out of proportion to the voting strength they brought the party at the outset. Their elevation was a deliberate stratagem on the part of the preponderant Whigs, who reasoned that the prominence of former Democrats as candidates and leaders was the means of attracting the decisive mar-

20. Chase is not easily classified. He began his career as a Whig, switched to the Liberty party, and moved from there to the Free-Soil party; but he identified himself as a Democrat in his private correspondence in 1851 and is so identified in the *Congressional Globe* of the Thirty-second Congress (1851–53).

gin of Democratic rank-and-file voters into the party. Thus in Indiana former Democrats were awarded three of the five positions on the state ticket in 1854 and three of nine in 1856, including the nominee for governor, Oliver H. P. T. Morton, who was unsuccessful that year but became the state's first Republican chief executive in 1861. Of the party's candidates for Congress in the eleven Indiana districts, either three or four were former Democrats in each of the elections from 1854 to 1860. Similarly, when the Republicans organized in Illinois in 1856, the president of the convention was a former Democrat, as were its nominee for governor, William H. Bissell, two other members of the six-man state ticket, and three of the five members of the state central committee. Bissell's election ended an unbroken succession of Democrats in the governor's chair since Illinois's statehood in 1818. Nine of the twenty-two Illinois delegates to the 1860 Republican national convention were former Democrats.[21] The pattern was repeated elsewhere: in New York the first Republican state ticket had a majority of former Democrats; in Pennsylvania Wilmot was the first Republican candidate for governor; and in Connecticut Welles was the party's first standard-bearer.

The Democrats who became Republican leaders had their source of strength in the rank-and-file Democrats who accompanied, preceded, or followed their leaders in shifting party allegiance. Geographically, the areas of large *net* movement to the Republicans were heavily rural; except for Chicago, no large cities showed dramatic shifts. The net volume of switching varied with latitude: stronger to the North, weaker toward the Mason-Dixon line and the Ohio River.

The greatest Republican gains occurred, then, in the abolitionist belt. Indeed, even though the new party absorbed almost the whole of the northern Whig party (block A in Figure 5-2), the distribution of Republican party strength correlated most closely not with the pattern of basic Whig strength but with that of the Free-Soil party. Correlation of the Republican presidential vote of 1860 and 1864 (averaging the two years) with the vote of the three parties in 1848 discloses only one state—New Hampshire—in which the Republican and Whig votes were closely related. In most of the other states, the association of Republican strength with Free-Soil strength is

21. Stoler, "The Democratic Element in the New Republican Party in Indiana," *Indiana Magazine of History*, Vol. 36 (September 1940); Stoler, "Insurgent Democrats of Indiana and Illinois"; Stoler, "Democratic Element in the New Republican Party in Illinois." The new party in Indiana was officially the People's party until the name Republican came into usage during the 1856 campaign.

striking. Following are the results of the correlations, by counties, for eleven states:[22]

	Democratic	*Whig*	*Free-Soil*
Maine	−0.283	0.053	0.326
New Hampshire	−0.910	0.932	−0.051
Vermont	−0.754	0.387	0.345
Massachusetts	−0.515	0.184	0.183
Connecticut	−0.072	−0.843	0.831
New York	−0.560	−0.039	0.507
Pennsylvania	−0.635	−0.039	0.691
Ohio	−0.862	−0.017	0.718
Indiana	−0.460	0.088	0.601
Illinois	−0.704	−0.240	0.706
Michigan	−0.357	−0.022	0.375

How the Republican party flourished in the path of the Free-Soil movement is further shown in Figures 5-3 and 5-4.

"A SINGLE CAUSE, SLAVERY"

These correlations lend quantitative support to those who have attributed the party realignment and the Civil War primarily to the slavery issue, as I have done. That was the traditional interpretation. "Of the American Civil War it may safely be asserted that there was a single cause, slavery," wrote James Ford Rhodes in 1913.[23] But later, after Charles A. Beard had reinterpreted the Constitution in economic terms and particularly after the depression of the 1930s had riveted national attention on economic matters, scholars (including Beard) began to question the purity of their forebears' motives regarding slavery and to find that hard economic considerations underlay the sectional rivalry and hostility. Thus John R. Commons called the Republicans not an antislavery party but "a homestead party";[24] Wilfred E. Binkley considered the slavery issue "merely incidental" to the homestead issue;[25] and William G. Carleton identified the Democratic defectors who joined in creating the Republican party as its "liberal capitalist

22. Computations by Gary Greenhalgh.
23. "Lectures on the American Civil War" in Kenneth M. Stampp, *The Causes of the Civil War* (Prentice-Hall, 1959), p. 107.
24. Quoted by Don E. Fehrenbacher, "The Republican Decision at Chicago," in Norman A. Graebner (ed.), *Politics and the Crisis of 1860* (University of Illinois Press, 1961), p. 35.
25. *American Political Parties: Their Natural History* (3d ed., Knopf, 1958), p. 213.

Figure 5-3. *Free-Soil Strength in the North, 1848 Presidential Vote*

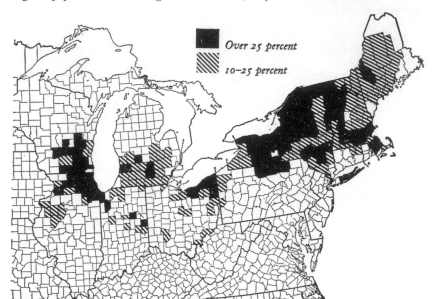

wing," not its antislavery wing. "The slavery question has been too much emphasized as a force bringing these groups together," Carleton contended; "liberal capitalism has been stressed too little as a cohesive force."[26] Even so, the weight of historical opinion appears still to be on the side of Rhodes rather than on that of Beard and his successors. "The first item one can generalize about with safety is that the canvass for Lincoln involved a moral crusade," wrote Joseph Schafer, and he cited a passage from the *Reminiscences* of Carl Schurz:

> There has never been in the history of this Republic a political movement in which the moral motive was so strong—indeed, so dominant and decisive. . . . I have been active in many political campaigns, but in none in which the best impulses of human nature were so forceful and effective and aroused the masses to so high a pitch of almost religious fervor.[27]

26. "Political Aspects of the Van Buren Era," *South Atlantic Quarterly*, Vol. 50 (April 1951), pp. 184–85. An extreme example of the economic interpretation is the explanation given by an Ohio politician of the time for the bolt of the northeastern Ohio Whigs to the Free-Soil party in 1848 after the nomination of Zachary Taylor, the Louisiana slaveholder, for president. The action was attributed by the unnamed politician to the concern of a maple-sugar area at the prospect of a cane-sugar planter in the White House. Binkley, *American Political Parties*, p. 187.

27. Schafer, "Who Elected Lincoln?" *American Historical Review*, Vol. 47 (October 1941), p. 56.

Figure 5-4. *Republican Strength in Eleven Northern States, Average of 1860 and 1864 Republican Presidential Vote*

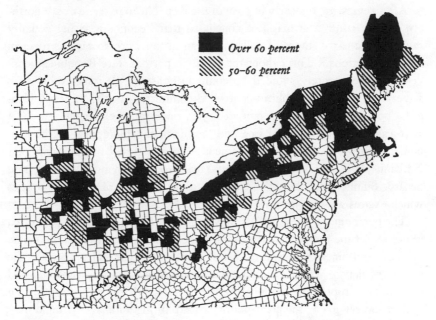

Over 60 percent

50–60 percent

Norman A. Graebner asserted flatly: "Slavery accounted for the vast revolution in American politics during the fifties. . . . The success of the anti-slavery movement in Northern politics . . . resulted from the fear engendered by the notion that a slave power threatened to overrun the nation and destroy the free institutions of the North. . . . The nation, in Lincoln's words, could not exist half slave and half free. Eventually one would triumph over the other."[28] Lawrence Lader argued that the economic differences between the sections could have been adjusted through the normal processes of politics, as nullification was adjusted by the compromise tariff of 1833, but "it was the genius of the abolitionists that they saw from the start that every significant economic and political grievance sprang from the slave system itself and that nothing could be *really* solved apart from the central, inescapable issue."[29] Other writers have pointed out that economic considerations alone would tend to knit North and South together rather than to divide

28. Graebner, *Politics and the Crisis of 1860*, p. ix.
29. Lader, *The Bold Brahmins: New England's War Against Slavery 1831–1863* (Dutton, 1961), p. 273.

them, for southern cotton was sold in northern markets and northern manufacture benefited from southern raw materials and markets.

After reviewing the early history of the Republican party in every northern state, Arthur Matthias Lee concluded that "economic issues actually raised in the early stages of political organization were so rare as to seem like indiscretions." Throughout the 1854–56 period, state Republican conventions "deliberately avoided by common consent" all issues other than slavery. From the Republican-controlled committees in the 1855–56 Congress no economic program emerged. Just once in an extensive search of 1856 campaign material did Lee find "an unmistakable appeal to the economic interest of the business element"—in a speech by House Speaker Nathaniel P. Banks before the New York Stock Exchange. Slavery, said Senator Sumner, "is the only subject within the field of national politics which excites any real interest."[30]

The contemporary civil rights movement has dramatically demonstrated in our own time the power of a moral issue to disrupt political alignments. So in the mid-nineteenth century, it was morals, not economics, that was the subject of debate whenever political tempers rose and party meetings and conventions erupted in emotional frenzy. It is true that, as northern feeling against slavery grew, the polar politicians exploiting antislavery found they could embellish the issue to give it broader appeal. Thus the attack on slavery as an institution became an attack on the "slave power," and the slave power was portrayed not merely as evil but as economically threatening—as unfair competition to free labor and as a threat to settlement of the West by free farmers. Issues like the tariff and internal improvements became aspects of the struggle of the free North against the slave power. Antislavery sentiment was transformed into a generalized antisouthern sentiment, but it was the moral issue, not the economic ones, that placed the sectional conflict beyond the capacity of centrist politicians to resolve.[31]

PROHIBITIONISTS-NATIVISTS-ABOLITIONISTS

While the realignment had its basis in the reformist response to the evil of human slavery, two other reformist movements, mentioned earlier, en-

30. Arthur Matthias Lee, "The Development of an Economic Policy in the Early Republican Party" (Ph.D. dissertation, Syracuse University, 1953). Quotations are from pp. 22, 24, 44, 23.

31. For an analysis of the interrelationship between antislavery sentiment and other antisouthern attitudes, see particularly Roy F. Nichols, *The Disruption of American Democracy* (Macmillan, 1948), pp. 21–40; also Fehrenbacher, "Republican Decision at Chicago," pp. 35–37.

tered into the realignment and influenced the character of the Republican party in particular localities. These were temperance and nativism, both of which flourished in the 1850s. Prohibitionists, like the abolitionists a decade earlier, were disappointed in the two major parties and began to turn to independent political action, though only sporadically and on a local scale. The temperance movement appealed to the same reformist mentality that had been aroused by slavery, and as the Republican party took form as a reformist organization, the temperance forces moved into it in strength. So did the nativists after the collapse of the American party; their strength is evidenced by the Massachusetts constitutional amendment of 1859, adopted under Republican auspices, prohibiting naturalized citizens from voting until two years after their naturalization. Temperance and nativism were allied too, for prohibitionists directed their fire especially at the Irishman's whiskey and the German's beer. National Republican leaders resisted the intrusion of both issues; they avoided any official identification with prohibition, and in their 1860 platform they decisively repudiated nativism,[32] yet the two movements left a stamp on the Republican party in its formative years that had a decisive influence on political alignments long after the slavery issue had passed into history.

Recent research has further identified the extent to which these reformist movements—and hence the Republican party as well—were centered in certain church denominations. These were the revivalist, or "pietist," denominations, which demanded "that the government actively support the cause of Christianity by abolishing the sinful institutions that stood in the way of revivals."[33] The pietists' theological rivals and opponents, the orthodox or "liturgical" groups, looked upon the church rather than the government as the enforcer of morality and denounced the pietists as "fanatics." Characteristically, according to Richard Jensen, the pietist denominations split into northern and southern organizations over the slavery issue before the Civil War, while the liturgical sects did not discipline their slaveholding members and remained intact as national organizations. Jensen's studies of party and church affiliation in several midwestern communities in the 1870s, based on local directories, show a very close relation between church and party—the Roman Catholics were Democratic by overwhelming margins and such pietist denominations (in the Midwest, at least) as the Methodists,

32. Specifically, they opposed both any change in the naturalization laws and state legislation abridging the rights of naturalized citizens.

33. Richard Jensen, "The Historical Roots of Party Identification" (paper delivered to the annual meeting of the American Political Science Association, September 1969).

Congregationalists, Disciples of Christ, Quakers, and Unitarians were Republican by equally large majorities.[34] Paul Kleppner, in his exhaustive study of post–Civil War politics in three midwestern states (Ohio, Michigan, and Wisconsin), based on analysis of election data by minor civil divisions, found that the difference between Republicans and Democrats was explained mainly by religious and ethnic identity, not by class or occupation. Again, he found that Catholics were heavily Democratic and that that party had majorities also among the liturgical German Lutheran groups, while some pietist denominations—Methodists, Congregationalists, and Free-Will Baptists—could be considered 90 percent or more Republican.[35]

These studies of the religious-ethnic basis of postwar Republicanism are consistent with the less intensive examinations of the original Republican movement of the 1850s. The difference in political behavior between "Yankees" and "Yorkers" that was noted by Lee Benson in his study of New York politics in the 1840s (see page 43, note 10, above) continued into the 1850s, when the Yankee counties of northern and western New York went decisively Republican while the Dutch counties of the Hudson valley remained Democratic. The German Protestant sects of Pennsylvania, like the Dutch Protestants, were also relatively unmoved by the antislavery agitation; the Republicans failed in Pennsylvania in 1856, and not until they later successfully exploited the tariff issue and the panic of 1857 did they carry the day in that state. Further west, Joseph Schafer and others have noted, Catholics remained solidly Democratic in the 1850s. "Lincoln was elected through an upsurge of moral enthusiasm and determination on the part of the distinctly American folk," Schafer concluded.[36]

MAGNITUDE AND TIMING OF THE REALIGNMENT

In absorbing the main body of northern Whigs (block A of Figure 5-2) as well as the antislavery Democrats (B_1), the Republican party emerged from

34. Ibid.

35. *The Cross of Culture: A Social Analysis of Midwestern Politics, 1850–1900* (Free Press, 1970), Chap. 2, esp. table on p. 70.

36. Schafer, "Who Elected Lincoln?" pp. 56–57. Hildegard Binder Johnson, "The Election of 1860 and the Germans in Minnesota," *Minnesota History*, Vol. 28 (March 1947); Jay Monoghan, "Did Abraham Lincoln Receive the Illinois German Vote?" *Illinois State Historical Society Journal*, Vol. 35 (June 1942); Bernard Mandel, *Labor, Free and Slave: Workingmen and the Anti-Slavery Movement in the United States* (Associated Authors, 1955), pp. 165–67; Andreas Dorpalen, "The German Element and the Issues of the Civil War," *Mississippi Valley Historical Review*, Vol. 29 (June 1942), pp. 73–76; Morton Mervin Rosenberg, "The Democratic Party of Iowa 1850–1860" (Ph.D. dissertation, State University of Iowa, 1957), pp. 232–34.

the realignment much stronger than the Whigs had been. It displaced the Democrats as the dominant party in Pennsylvania, in New Hampshire, in parts of upstate New York, and in states of the Northwest where the Whigs had been notably weak. Figure 5-5 shows the magnitude, as well as the timing, of the swing to the Republicans in presidential voting, state by state. The upper panel shows the states of the northernmost tier—New England (except Connecticut), Michigan, and Wisconsin—where the Republican vote in 1856 exceeded the Whig level of 1852 by from 13 to 27 percentage points and was sustained at the new higher level. The second panel shows the realignment in four other states that became predominantly Republican in the 1850s but with a less spectacular shift in voting strength. The apparent delay until 1860 of the realignment in Illinois can probably be attributed to the brief career of the Know-Nothing party. Since Fillmore, the former President who ran as the Know-Nothing candidate in 1856, had been a Whig and drew much of his support from Old-Line Whigs, it might be logical to look upon the Know-Nothing vote as essentially part of the Whig-Republican stream. In that case, the realignment in Illinois, and in Ohio as well, would appear in 1856 rather than later. For Pennsylvania, however, the shift to the Republicans would still be charted in 1860—in part, at least, because James Buchanan, the Democratic standard-bearer in 1856, was a Pennsylvanian. Lines are added for Cook County (Chicago) and Bradford County, Pennsylvania (Wilmot's home), to show that in the northern sections of these states the realignment came in 1856, as in upper New England and Michigan. Of the older northern states, only Indiana, New York, and New Jersey showed no substantial net Republican gain from the realignment of the 1850s, but a county-by-county, or precinct-by-precinct, analysis would undoubtedly show significant though offsetting movement of voters across the party line in both directions.

The issue-oriented voters who switched parties were augmented, of course, by others influenced little by the reformist urge. Any realignment creates its own bandwagon, and political hangers-on and patronage-seekers moved to the new party as they saw greater opportunity there, embracing its principles as they went; Democratic newspapers were prone to condemn all defectors as "disappointed office-seekers." And one cannot examine the election data without noting a large element of chance. Neighboring counties essentially the same in economics, ethnic and religious composition, and tradition may show sharp differences in the degree of party-switching that seem attributable only to differences in the attitude and effectiveness of the respective counties' political leaders and other local influential persons.

Figure 5-5. *The Realignment of the 1850s in the North, as Shown by the Rise in the Whig-Republican Percentage of the Presidential Vote in Selected Areas, 1836–76*[a]

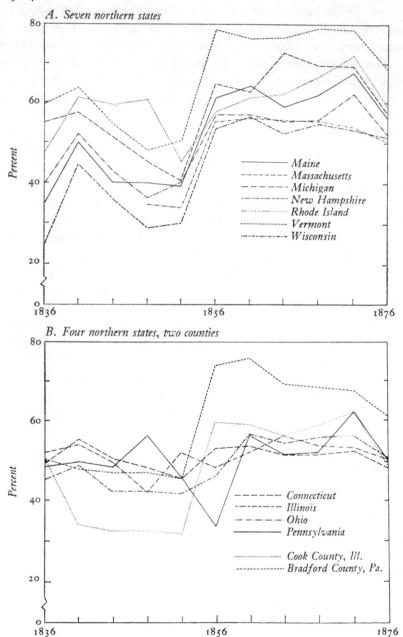

A. *Seven northern states*

Maine
Massachusetts
Michigan
New Hampshire
Rhode Island
Vermont
Wisconsin

B. *Four northern states, two counties*

Connecticut
Illinois
Ohio
Pennsylvania

Cook County, Ill.
Bradford County, Pa.

Sources: Walter Dean Burnham, *Presidential Ballots, 1836–1892* (Johns Hopkins Press, 1955); Svend Petersen, *A Statistical History of the American Presidential Elections* (Frederick Ungar, 1963).

a. Whig vote, 1836–52; Republican vote, 1856–76.

THE COUNTERFLOW TO THE DEMOCRATS

As for the reverse flow of Whigs into the Democratic ranks (block C_1 in Figure 5-2), pro-Democratic switching in the North appears to have been concentrated geographically, as might be expected, in the bigger cities having commercial ties with the South and along the borders, especially in counties that had been largely settled by southerners. Figure 5-6 shows a pro-Democratic realignment in four northern counties: Franklin County, Ohio (which includes the city of Columbus), a rural county that adjoins Franklin to the south, a county lying on Pennsylvania's southern border, and a southern Indiana county.

Cincinnati and Philadelphia, as examples of cities with southern ties, emerged from the realignment with Republican strength roughly equal to the Whig strength of the earlier period; since they were surely not immune to the forces that were making Republicans of former Democrats, there must have been an offsetting movement of former Whigs into the Democratic ranks. Andrew Crandall reported that the Democrats made inroads into the "conservative business interests" of Philadelphia, especially the "cottonocracy" of Old-Line Whig families.[37] Henry R. Mueller too stated that in Pennsylvania "the Democrats absorbed a large number of Whigs who were alarmed at the radicalism of the new parties," and added that the Democratic party also absorbed much of the American party leadership in Philadelphia when that party collapsed.[38] But it seems likely that in more places the Democrats made their gains from just the opposite group, from foreignborn voters who had supported the Whigs but were alienated by the nativist flavor the new Republican party had taken from the Know-Nothings.

In the South, the bulk of the Whig party was ultimately absorbed by the Democratic party in the areas that were to become the Democratic Solid South, but the movement was not concurrent with the northern realignment, and so is discussed in a later section.

37. *Early History of the Republican Party*, p. 265. That the movement of businessmen from the Whigs to the Democrats was not confined to cities with close links to the South is indicated by Alexandra McCoy's study of Detroit. She found much more Whig-to-Democrat switching among the economic elite than Democrat-to-Republican switching. "Political Affiliations of American Economic Elites: Wayne County, Michigan, 1844, 1860, as a Test Case" (Ph.D. dissertation, Wayne State University, 1965), Chap. 6; cited by Ronald P. Formisano, *The Birth of Mass Political Parties: Michigan, 1827–1861* (Princeton University Press, 1971), p. 275.

38. *The Whig Party in Pennsylvania* (Columbia University Press, 1922), pp. 219, 221, 246.

Figure 5-6. *Pro-Democratic Realignment, as Shown by the Democratic Percentage of the Presidential Vote in Four Northern Counties, 1836–76*

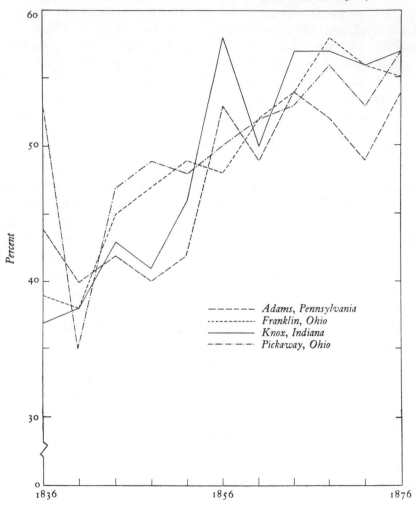

Source: Burnham, *Presidential Ballots.*

Solidification of the New Alignment

With the secession of the southern states and the firing on Fort Sumter, the original crosscutting moral issue of slavery was absorbed into a broader issue that involved attitudes not only about slavery but about the constitutional right of secession, the preservation of the Union, and war itself. So what had appeared initially as a relatively simple single issue now became a cluster of related issues—slavery–secession–war—and once the shooting began the combined issue had far more polarizing power than the original issue alone had had. After the war, a new set of issues arose, and the cluster became slavery–secession–war–reconstruction–Negro rights.

THE POLARIZATION INTENSIFIES

The divergent and consistently polarized positions of the two parties on the cluster of related issues illustrates the manner in which the newer elements of the cluster reinforced the original alignment. As events moved from secession to war to reconstruction, each party went naturally and confidently down the road that the prewar struggles had marked for it. The Republicans, as the party founded to combat an aggressive "slave power," claimed vindication: it was the slaveholders, not the friends of freedom, who had dissolved the Union—unconstitutionally and without provocation, it was argued, for Lincoln had not even been inaugurated yet. The new party supported the war wholeheartedly as a righteous cause; and after the war, they remained a polar political force under radical leadership, intent on advancing the rights of Negroes and penalizing their former masters.

But those who had been loyal to the compromise policies of Pierce and Buchanan and Douglas could also claim vindication as war began, for they had warned that the victory of a radical, sectional party would inevitably be followed by disunion and then by bloodshed. The crisis, said Pennsylvania Democrats in January 1861, had been brought on by "the teachings of an anti-constitutional party"; they opposed any "armed aggression" by the North until "the rights of the South" were secured.[39] At the extreme was the party's "Copperhead" wing, which was openly prosouthern and unconditionally opposed to the war. Its strength was not inconsiderable. When Clement L. Vallandigham, a former congressman, was convicted by a military tribunal of seditious utterances and banished by President Lincoln, Ohio Democrats promptly nominated him for governor. He won 40 percent of the vote and carried eighteen counties in the 1863 election, even though he had to conduct his campaign from Canada.

39. Address by the Democratic state executive committee of Pennsylvania, quoted by Erwin Stanley Bradley, *The Triumph of Militant Republicanism: A Study of Pennsylvania and Presidential Politics, 1860–1872* (University of Pennsylvania Press, 1964), pp. 111–12.

On the other hand, a Democratic voter did not have to become a Republican to support the war. Many Democrats rallied to the Republican President and the flag and called themselves War Democrats (block B_2 of Figure 5-2). Douglas was their most conspicuous leader until his death in June 1861, and their ranks included most Democratic members of the Congress and such party leaders as the wartime governors of New York and New Jersey, Horatio Seymour and Joel Parker.

War Democrats and Copperheads could unite on many questions related to the conduct of the war: suppression of civil liberties by the Lincoln administration, military inefficiency and corruption, inequities of conscription. And they came together when Lincoln issued his Emancipation Proclamation. Here the party could stand on resolutions adopted almost unanimously by both houses of Congress in July 1861 that rejected as a purpose of the war any interference with the rights or "established institutions" of the rebel states. "Slavery as an institution should not be disturbed in the prosecution of the war," declared the New Hampshire Democratic platform of 1862. "We unqualifiedly condemn the late proclamation of the President relative to emancipation."[40] "We denounce the abolition of slavery in the District of Columbia at the cost of the United States as unconstitutional," said the Wisconsin Democrats' 1862 "address to the people," as platforms were then called.[41] Massachusetts Democrats were more restrained: "We respectfully but earnestly protest against the emancipation proclamation." The United States government was established "exclusively for the white man," asserted Pennsylvania Democrats in denouncing emancipation; "for white men," echoed Iowa Democrats in a similar resolution a few days later. "While we fight secessionism in the field, we must fight abolitionism and radicals at the ballot box," declared New Jersey's Democratic state central committee, and the state assembly, controlled by Democrats, passed a bill barring Negroes from the state. Two years later, Democrats in the New Jersey legislature in a solid party vote rejected the Thirteenth Amendment, which abolished slavery, and it became part of the Constitution without New Jersey's vote.[42]

40. James O. Lyford, *Life of Edward H. Rollings* (Dana Estes, 1906), p. 146.
41. Ralph G. Plumb, *Badger Politics 1836–1930* (Brandt Printing and Binding, 1930), p. 48.
42. Resolution of Massachusetts Democratic state convention, October 1862, quoted by Edith Ellen Ware, "Political Opinion in Massachusetts during Civil War and Reconstruction" (Ph.D. dissertation, Columbia University, 1916), p. 119. Pennsylvania state platform of 1862, quoted by Bradley, *Triumph of Militant Republicanism*, p. 152. Iowa state Democratic platform, quoted by Olynthus B. Clark, *The Politics of Iowa during the*

FURTHER SHIFTS IN PARTY STRENGTH

The heightened polarization of the war years etched the slavery–secession–war–reconstruction–Negro-rights line of cleavage more deeply into the political pattern until old lines dividing the electorate were all but obliterated. More and more voters made their party choices on the basis of the new line of cleavage rather than the old (blocks B_1 and C_1 in Figure 5-2 grew at the expense of B_2 and C_2), especially the new generation of voters just coming to political maturity. The army was heavily Republican. Republican politicians were among the generals and colonels who raised and led the blue-clad regiments, and they took pains (corruptly, the Democrats alleged) to make sure that the soldiers understood which party supported their cause and which opposed it. Horace Greeley estimated the Republican share of the soldier vote in 1864 as 75 percent,[43] an estimate that was confirmed in some state elections where the soldier vote was tallied separately.[44] After the war, the veterans' organization, the Grand Army of the Republic, became a virtual adjunct of the Republican party. Allen G. Thurman, a former Democratic senator and governor of Ohio, angrily walked out of a GAR encampment because, he said, it was "nothing but a damned Republican mass meeting."[45]

To win over the War Democrats, the Republicans in some states as early as 1861 formed Union parties in which Democrats were given conspicuous roles,[46] and in 1864 Lincoln followed that tactic on a national scale. The Republican party was rechristened the Union party, and Lincoln took Andrew Johnson, a Union Democrat from Tennessee, as his running mate. Through this coalition process, at least some Democrats made their way into the

---

Civil War and Reconstruction (Clio Press, 1911), p. 147. Address to the people by the New Jersey Democratic party, October 1862, quoted in Charles Merriam Knapp, *New Jersey Politics during the Period of the Civil War and Reconstruction* (Humphrey, 1924), pp. 73,164.

43. Harold M. Dudley, "The Election of 1864," *Mississippi Valley Historical Review*, Vol. 18 (March 1932), p. 517.

44. The soldier vote in New Hampshire went for Lincoln, 2,018 to 671, while the regular vote was split almost evenly, 34,382 to 32,200. Lyford, *Life of Edward Rollins*, p. 173. In Wisconsin, the soldier vote was Republican by 5 to 1, while the home vote gave Lincoln a majority of only 3,000. Plumb, *Badger Politics*, p. 53. In Connecticut in 1863, the division of the soldier vote was estimated at 9 to 1. Lane, *Political History of Connecticut*, p. 237.

45. Edward Noyes, "The Ohio G.A.R. and Politics from 1866–1900," *Ohio State Political Quarterly*, Vol. 4 (1946), pp. 86, 96.

46. Two War Democrats were elected to the Ohio governorship as Union candidates: David Tod in 1861 and John Brough in 1863.

Republican party, for prominent political figures who made the switch can be identified in almost every state.[47]

Yet there is little indication of any significant *net* accretion of relative strength to the Republicans after 1860. If the Republicans gained from the indoctrination of the young voters during the war and from the drift of War Democrats to their party (movement from block B_2 to B_1 of Figure 5-2), their gains must have been offset by a countermovement of antiwar voters to the Democrats (C_2 to C_1). Moreover, the Democrats struggled, successfully for the most part, to suppress their Copperhead wing and nominate only War Democrats, so that antislavery, prowar northern Democrats could in good conscience remain within their party. General George B. McClellan, the 1864 presidential nominee, could be criticized for military blunders but hardly for lack of patriotism. In 1868, the nominee was another Democrat of impeccable wartime credentials, former Governor Horatio Seymour. And so it went throughout the postwar period—not only in national but in state politics. If there was a shift in the party balance toward the Republicans as young voters replaced older ones, immigration in the postwar years continued to help the Democrats. Finally, some potent causes of discontent of the period—dissatisfaction with the way the war was prosecuted, the excesses of reconstruction, agitation for and adoption of Negro suffrage,[48] the scandals of the Grant administration,[49] and new economic issues (the subject of the next chapter)—would all work in favor of the Democrats, since the Republicans were in power.

In any case, while the North as a whole settled down after the war as

47. Among the more prominent were John White Geary, Democratic governor of territorial Kansas, who became a postwar Republican governor of Pennsylvania; and John A. Logan, Civil War general who became a Republican senator from Illinois and the party's nominee for vice-president.

48. Negro suffrage was rejected by popular vote by Ohio, Michigan, Minnesota, and Kansas in 1867; by Michigan and Missouri in 1868. The issue was also the major factor in the Democratic sweep of New Jersey legislative elections in 1867. Knapp, *New Jersey Politics*, pp. 169–70, 183.

49. In 1872 "Grantism" produced a schism in the GOP, and liberal Republicans and Democrats joined forces unsuccessfully behind Horace Greeley, a coalition that resulted in some permanent crossing of party lines in what may be considered a minor realignment. Among prominent prewar and wartime Republicans who ended their political careers as Democrats, as the result of the 1872 schism or earlier conflict over reconstruction policy, were Senators Lyman Trumbull of Illinois, James R. Doolittle of Wisconsin, and James Dixon of Connecticut; Pennsylvania's war governor, Andrew G. Curtin, and former Speaker Nathaniel P. Banks of Massachusetts. Since some of these were originally Democrats, their return might be considered the end of a period of deviance rather than a realignment. The last of the Cotton Whigs of Massachusetts, former Senator Robert C. Winthrop, who had never declared himself a Republican, also finally joined the Democratic party.

"normally Republican," the Democrats remained a vital competitive force, centered in urban strongholds where they could count on the growing Irish vote as a solid core. They were dominant in one state, New Jersey, and enjoyed an even balance with the Republicans in several others—New York, Connecticut, Indiana, California, Oregon, and Nevada. Moreover, in still other states, the Republican majorities were so tenuous that the Democrats could win statewide elections whenever the Republicans were weakened at the state level by internal division, scandal, ineffective leadership, or excessive zeal on reformist issues such as prohibition, or whenever economic depression or scandal at the national level lost them voter confidence.

THE SOUTH AND THE BORDER

The realignment in the South was more drastic than in the North, for the South, not only defeated in war but subjected afterward to Negro and carpet-bagger rule, was even more polarized. This expressed itself in the emergence of a Democratic Solid South, based on an antipathy for the Republicans felt by the white voters in areas of Confederate sympathy that is still the dominant political sentiment in many places. Conversely, the mountain strongholds that had opposed secession emerged after the war as among the staunchest Republican regions in the country.

In the four slaveholding states that did not secede—Delaware, Maryland, Kentucky, and Missouri—plus West Virginia after it was formed from Virginia in 1863, the Republicans had a stronger foothold. There unionist sentiment had been strong enough to prevent secession, and unionists, in alliance with military commanders, governed during the war, but they did not all become Republicans afterward. They split into radical and conservative factions, and the latter—although some dreamed for a time of a restored Whig party—eventually coalesced with the Democratic party as it revived after the war. The Republicans, identified with military rule, denial of civil liberties, and "ultraproscriptive" measures in the treatment of former Confederates, sank into minority status throughout the border states as in the deeper South.

A LATITUDINAL POLITICAL PATTERN

As the political system stabilized after the end of reconstruction, the country's politics congealed on a latitudinal pattern: the northernmost tier of states a reliable Republican belt; the northern border states (as well as

New York and Connecticut) usually Republican but with strong two-party competition in some of them; the southern border states (and Tennessee) predominantly Democratic but with a weak potential for two-party competition; and the deep southern states a one-party Democratic region. When the northern wing of the Whig party moved almost intact into the Republican ranks, it brought with it the nationalistic economic policies that had characterized Whiggery when Henry Clay was its leader. The new party, like the Whigs, stood for aggressive action by the national government to develop manufacturing and commerce through a protective tariff, expansionist banking policies, and internal improvements—logically extended to include a transcontinental railroad and homestead legislation (which Democratic President Buchanan had vetoed) to promote the settlement of the West. During the war, the major elements of the program were enacted. The new moral reformist movements—prohibition and nativism—found their home, for the most part, in the party that had embodied the great reformist crusade of the mid-century.

The departure of its antislavery polar bloc significantly altered the composition of the Democratic party in the North. Having lost its rural base in the northernmost states, it became an urban party there. More significant, having lost so much of its old-stock American base, it became even more than before the party of the immigrants and their descendants, and increasingly so as immigration swelled; and a political line of cleavage on ethnic and religious lines that had long existed—old-stock Protestants in one party and new-stock Catholics in the other—was sharpened. Having lost its reform element, the Democratic party became the party of the professional politician—for the "hunkers" remained loyal to the discredited Democratic administrations of Pierce and Buchanan to the end. Still faithful on economic matters to its Jacksonian antecedents, it tended to resist the popular Whig-Republican expansionist measures while having no alternative activist program of its own. It had little sympathy, obviously, for nativism or prohibition.

The new alignment, then, was governed by some of the same principles that ordered the party system in the Jacksonian era but to a greater degree by new ones. And this political alignment, indurated by the passions of war, was to be for decades immutable. For a generation political orators in both regions would stir their followers with "bloody shirt" appeals to wartime emotion, identifying northern Republicanism and southern Democracy with patriotism, family loyalty, and regional pride, making of them not mere parties but political churches, the secular expression of the moral life.

Brand Whitlock recalled the Republicanism of his Ohio youth during that era:

in the Ohio of those days it was natural to be a Republican; it was more than that, it was inevitable that one should be a Republican; it was not a matter of intellectual choice, it was a process of biological selection. The Republican party was not a faction, not a group, not a wing, it was an institution like those Emerson speaks of in his essay on Politics, rooted like oak-trees in the center around which men group themselves as best they can. It was a fundamental and self-evident thing, like life, and liberty, and the pursuit of happiness, or like the flag, or the federal judiciary. It was elemental, like gravity, the sun, the stars, the ocean. It was merely a synonym for patriotism, another name for the nation. One became, in Urbana and in Ohio for many years, a Republican just as the Eskimo dons fur clothes. It was inconceivable that any self-respecting person should be a Democrat. There were, perhaps, Democrats in Lighttown; but then there were rebels in Alabama, and in the Ku-Klux-Klan, about which we read in the evening, in the *Cincinnati Gazette*.[50]

With a substitution of party and place names, the same could have been written of Democracy in the South.

50. Whitlock, *Forty Years of It* (Appleton, 1914), p. 27.

CHAPTER SIX

The Agrarian Revolt and
the Rise of Populism

EVEN BEFORE the end of the Reconstruction Era, a party system aligned primarily on a slavery–secession–war–reconstruction–Negro-rights cluster of issues began to become irrelevant. To be sure, important matters relating to those issues remained to be settled—the readmission of the Southern states, restoration of citizenship to the "rebels," raising the Negro to full citizenship not only in the South but in the North as well. But the working-man of the East was more directly interested in his hours of work, his rate of pay, and the security of his employment. And the western farmer was more deeply concerned about the prices of wheat or corn and of farm supplies and equipment. On these economic matters, neither party offered the farmer or the workingman a program. The party platforms contained only plati-tudes about labor and no word at all on agriculture.

It has been customary to explain that both parties, but particularly the dominant Republican party, came out of the war under the control of the emerging class of industrialists and financiers and remained under its control during the postwar period of rampant capitalist expansion.[1] Yet the parties did not have much of a program for the capitalists, either. Once the Republi-can protective tariff and the national banking system were established during the war, the industrialists and bankers only wanted the government to stand aside and let them conduct their enterprises as they pleased.

So, as the burning issues of the 1850s and 1860s faded and disappeared, the parties lost their sense of mission altogether. The Republicans of Ohio, wrote Eugene H. Roseboom, "pointed with pride to the party's past but had

[1]. The Republican party, wrote Arthur M. Schlesinger, Jr., was "captured during and after the war by a boarding party of bankers and industrialists." *The Age of Jackson* (Little, Brown, 1945), p. 503. By 1870, the Republican party "had become the party of industrial capitalism. . . . But so, too, had the Democratic," according to a standard textbook by Louis M. Hacker and Benjamin B. Kendrick, *The United States Since 1865* (Appleton-Century-Crofts, 1949), p. 61.

no program for the new problems that loomed ahead. . . . Organization, patronage, and party discipline had taken the place of zeal for a cause." And the Democratic party, "dropping its vaunted devotion to the common man . . . had become, after the revolution of 1854, a conservative, anti-Negro, compromising element."[2] Concluding his study of postwar Connecticut, William John Niven, Jr., observed: "Neither party was able to offer a challenging program or indeed seemed aware of any social needs which it might fulfill." Under these circumstances, "the two parties drew closer in outlook" and "political morals continued to degenerate."[3] The same could be said of the northern states in general. Patronage, rather than program, became the object of politics. Businessmen saw to it that politicians shared in the opportunities for enrichment offered by the conquest of a continent. The politicians rode on free railroad passes, bought stock at preferential prices, and moved freely from the halls of Congress to corporation presidencies and back again. It was the period of the Crédit Mobilier and the Tweed Ring, of Jay Gould and Jim Fisk, and of the corruption and spoilsmanship that made up "Grantism."

But it was not the best of all possible worlds, and men had grievances against the political and economic order, or thought they had. In the newer states of the West, in particular, tens of thousands of farmers were developing an intense class consciousness and an acute hostility toward the powerful class of financiers and entrepreneurs that appeared to control not only the economy but the polity as well. For three postwar decades, the clamor for the resolution of the farmers' grievances mounted, not steadily but in spurts that reflected economic cycles, until it dominated the national political debate.

The farmers found neither major party responsive to their interests— consistently and reliably, at any rate—and this was inevitable, for the party system that emerged from the Civil War was not organized to reflect class interests. The major parties reflected the national policy cleavage on the issues arising from the slavery controversy, and a geographical cleavage between North and South. But they could not reflect these cleavages and at the same time express new ones that cut across the electorate in quite a dif-

2. *The Civil War Era 1850–1873*, Vol. 4 in Carl Wittke (ed.), *The History of the State of Ohio* (Ohio State Archaeological and Historical Society, 1944), p. 484.
3. "The Time of the Whirlwind: A Study in the Political, Social, and Economic History of Connecticut, 1861–1875" (Ph.D. dissertation, Columbia University, 1954), p. 390.

ferent direction, dividing voters *within* the North, *within* the South, *within* groups supporting Negro suffrage, and *within* those opposing it.

The postwar parties responded to new divisive, crosscutting issues just as the prewar parties had—defensively. They evaded and straddled and post-poned, just as prewar Whigs and Democrats had evaded the demands of abolitionists. And so the farmers in their zeal for a redress of grievances were driven to the recourse the abolitionists had found—third-party action. The economic issues that became the dominant conflicts of society in the 1870s were fought for two more decades not between the major parties, but between them, on one side, and a series of minor parties on the other. But tensions within one of the major parties—this time the Democrats—even-tually reached the breaking point. Then the long prerealignment period came to an end and a major rearrangement of party loyalties took place.

The Farmers Enter Politics

Responding to the Homestead Act and the coming of the railroads, the farmers by 1873 had pushed the frontier of settlement well beyond the Missouri River. Wheatland had been increased by more than a million acres a year since 1866, and output had almost doubled. With the surge of produc-tion, the average price to the farmer for a bushel of wheat fell from $2.06 in 1866 to $1.17 in 1873.[4] The heavily mortgaged farmers of the West found themselves overwhelmed by debt. Detached observers might place the blame on the farmers themselves, for defying the law of supply and demand; but the farmers were not detached. They saw a host of other factors, mostly in the form of corporate power arrayed against them. They were at the mercy of the grain elevators, which graded their wheat and set its price, indepen-dent of any regulation. They were at the mercy of the railroads, which were free to charge whatever the traffic would bear, to discriminate among ship-ping points, and to make up from small farmers the rebates they gave to larger shippers. They were at the mercy of the moneylenders, who charged interest rates up to 20 percent,[5] and of the farm suppliers. They sold at prices determined by the buyers and bought at prices determined by the sellers. Moreover, the corporate bodies with whom they dealt could com-bine to rig prices and restrain trade, while the scattered farmers were in no

4. U.S. Bureau of the Census, *Historical Statistics of the United States, Colonial Times to 1957*, Series K269-71 (1960), p. 297.
5. Allan Nevins, *The Emergence of Modern America* (Macmillan, 1935), p. 166.

position to act collectively. As the farmer saw it, the prices of what he bought rose constantly, returns from his own production went down and down, and speculators made fortunes dealing in the commodities that brought him only poverty. To him, all these impersonal corporations run from the eastern seaboard seemed like a giant conspiracy for the exploitation of his arduous labor—a conspiracy of the "monopolies" and the middlemen against the producer, a conspiracy of the East against the West.[6] The central villains in the conspiracy were the railroads, now merging into noncompetitive giants, and it was against them that the farmers' ire was initially directed.

THE FARMERS' INDEPENDENT PARTIES

In those days, the farmers looked not to Washington but to the state capitals for action, and when their pressure was strong enough, the dominant Republican party in the western states was not unresponsive. In Illinois, then the leading producer of both wheat and corn, a constitutional convention under the pressure of farmers' clubs in 1870 directed the legislature to set maximum railroad rates, and the legislature responded at its next session by creating a railroad commission with the necessary authority. When that law was declared unconstitutional by the Illinois supreme court in January 1873, the legislature enacted an even stronger one.

But the battle for influence within the Republican party was a never-ending one, for the railroads and their allies sought also to make the party their political instrument. Prominent in the Republican party in every state were the railroad representatives, and they were lavish with their contributions, beginning with the free passes. At best, the farmers could only share power in the party with their enemies, the railroads; they could not control it. The party, confronting a crosscutting issue, could not cope with it decisively, and this situation could only continue unless the agrarian zealots could somehow realign the party system.

In the spring of 1873, an organized polar force came into being with that as its explicit aim. This was the time when the first great effort in the country's history to organize the farmers, the Granger movement, was approach-

---

6. The economic plight of the western farmers and their grievances are summarized in Solon J. Buck, *The Granger Movement: A Study of Agricultural Organization and Its Political, Economic and Social Manifestations, 1870–1880* (Harvard University Press, 1913), Chap. 1; and John D. Hicks, *The Populist Revolt: A History of the Farmers' Alliance and the People's Party* (University of Minnesota Press, 1931), Chap. 3.

ing its peak of success. Conceived in 1867, the Patrons of Husbandry had by 1873 organized 7,325 local granges. Of these, 676 were in Illinois.[7] The granges were pledged by their charters to stay out of politics, but as they met to talk of their economic ills they were bound to talk of political and governmental remedies. If the grange itself could not engage in political action, the members could still meet "outside the gates" of the grange hall and do so. Moreover, farmers' clubs outside the grange structure had long been organized for the express purpose of political action; more were formed at this time, and from these clubs and the granges the State Farmers' Association of Illinois was born. In April 1873, while the legislature was considering a measure that would avoid the faults the state supreme court had found in the 1871 railroad law, farmers from throughout the state convened in Springfield and adopted a dozen strongly worded resolutions on railroad questions. It was under this pressure that the legislature enacted the new regulatory law stronger than the one that had been invalidated.

Then the farmers moved into politics en masse as an independent force and put the Republican party to rout. Farmers' conventions nominated judicial candidates in the state's thirty-one circuits, and the Republicans offered competition in only four of them. "The Republican party does not feel disposed to get into a conflict with the Granges, in which conflict it would certainly come out second best," observed the Chicago *Tribune*. "The farmers' movement has paralyzed the Republican party of Illinois."[8] In a district judicial election, the farmers decisively defeated the state's chief justice, who had rendered the despised opinion voiding the 1871 railroad law. Then they prepared to move into the county elections throughout the state in the fall. Read at meetings held on Independence Day (called that year the "Farmers' Fourth of July") was a "Farmers' Declaration of Independence," which committed the farmers to "declare ourselves absolutely free and independent of all past political connections."[9]

The *Tribune* set out the rationale for party realignment:

The Republican party had for its purpose the overthrow of slavery; the war became a part of this work, and reconstruction was a necessary sequence of the war. The party's mission was then performed. It had nothing else to do, and since then has done nothing else but divide offices and public plunder among its chiefs.

7. Buck, *Granger Movement*, pp. 58ff. In 1875, the first year for which Buck was able to report membership figures, granges averaged thirty-seven members each, so the Illinois membership in 1873 may have been about twenty-five thousand.

8. May 24, 1873.

9. Buck, *Granger Movement*, pp. 86–87.

Why should the majority of the American people, the owners and cultivators of the soil, the great bodies of producers and consumers, stand year after year in chains, absolutely slaves to protected monopolies that rule them and the Governments,—municipal, State, and National,—and piteously ask a comparatively small squad of professional office-holders and office-seekers to intervene in their behalf, when by one firm and united blow they can emancipate themselves?

Special wrongs need special organizations to remedy them. For forty years people waited for the Whig and Democratic parties to apply the corrective to the aggressions of the slave-owners. For ten years the experiment was tried of electing free-soil Whigs and free-soil Democrats; but there was no relief until the people, leaving these old parties, formed a new one for the special purpose of extirpating slavery. Then the work that was needed was done. And so it will be in this case. The farmers are now asked to elect "Democratic Grangers" or "Republican Grangers". Let them have nothing to do with either.[10]

In the fall elections, the farmers ran what were loosely termed "antimonopoly" candidates in 66 of the state's 102 counties, and won in 53 of them.[11] In the 66 counties, they obtained 54 percent of the vote.

Meanwhile, the Illinois model was being copied throughout the newer states of the Northwest. Where statewide elections were scheduled, county organizations coalesced into a state party carrying a "Reform" or "Anti-Monopoly" label. The Democrats, as the proprietors of an opposition party too discredited to oppose effectively, gave way gracefully, either endorsing the Anti-Monopoly candidates or agreeing on a slate of nominees. "Political partisanship has almost ceased to exist, especially in the agricultural regions," President Grant observed in his annual message to the Congress in December.[12]

The farmers' hastily built organizations fell short of sweeping everything before them, but the results were still spectacular for a political movement less than a year old. The entire fusion slate was elected in Wisconsin, helped by reaction against a Republican-sponsored state liquor law. Two state officers were elected in Minnesota. The new parties captured the lower house of the Kansas legislature, attained a tie in the Iowa house, and won a balance of power between Republicans and Democrats in California. The first of the western agrarian reformers whose views and activities were to inspirit the U.S. Senate for more than half a century, John S. Hager and Newton Booth of California and James M. Harvey of Kansas, took their seats in that body.

10. Excerpts from a Chicago *Tribune* editorial, June 7, 1873.
11. Buck, *Granger Movement*, p. 88. The account that follows relies on his chronology of events, pp. 89–102, and on *Appleton's Annual Cyclopedia*, Vol. 13 (1873) and Vol. 14 (1874).
12. *A Compilation of the Messages and Papers of the Presidents (1789–1897)*, Vol. 10 (Bureau of National Literature, 1897), p. 4189.

The legislatures of Wisconsin, Iowa, and Minnesota passed "Granger" railroad regulatory laws in 1874.

The movement continued its surge in the political season of that year. In Illinois, the Independent Reform party elected its candidate for state superintendent of public instruction, who carried Democratic endorsement, and won the balance of power in both houses of the legislature. Independents or third-party men were elected to Congress from Illinois, Wisconsin, and Iowa. Independents also won the balance of power in the Indiana state senate, with five members, and in both houses of the Oregon legislature, with twenty-eight.

In 1875, however, the Republicans rebounded. There were no electoral gains for the reformers anywhere that year, and by 1876 the Granger phase of the farmers' revolt had burned itself out. The railroad regulatory laws of Wisconsin, Iowa, and Minnesota were repealed.

Railroad regulation had proved too narrow an issue on which to build a party. In the four states where regulatory laws were passed, once the state parties appeared to have accomplished their mission, interest slackened. They suffered further because the laws did not work well. In the states toward the frontier, where people still wanted more railroads, an antirailroad party was particularly vulnerable. The parties were never organized effectively at the state level or adequately financed. As the presidential campaign of 1876 approached, the farmers' movement found itself with no political role to play, and local leaders and followers alike were attracted back to the major national parties where the action lay.

THE GREENBACK PARTY

A few dedicated believers in independent political action, however, had already taken steps to extend their organization on a national scale. On the initiative of the Indiana Independent party (which had been organized in 1874 following the farmers' successes in Illinois), a National Independent (or Greenback, as it was popularly known) party was organized, incorporating urban as well as rural reform elements and placing its emphasis on currency reform rather than railroad regulation.

The new party's campaign for the presidency in 1876 was abortive (in only three states did the party poll more than 3 percent of the vote), but after its defeat it gained rather than lost momentum. A deepening depression and falling wages gave rise to the most extensive and bloodiest strikes the country had yet experienced. As the powers of government at all levels were used against the strikers, workingmen's political organizations sprang into being,[13] and the Greenback party seized the opportunity to embrace the workers' cause and call for joint action under the greenback banner. By this time, too, the currency issue itself had taken a new turn; a drop in the price of silver compared to that of gold had led to a proposal that the former metal —demonetized in 1873 by an act that was almost unopposed—be restored to the currency to permit payment of the public debt in cheaper dollars. Within a year the idea of relieving the money stringency with silver had swept the West and South and even rural sections of the East.

Propelled by the labor unrest, the continued hard times, the new silver issue, and the old greenback issue, the Greenback and Greenback-Labor fusion tickets fared well in 1877 and 1878. In both Wisconsin and Iowa, the third-party candidates for governor captured nearly 15 percent of the vote.[14] In Pennsylvania, the Greenback-Labor candidates for state offices polled nearly 10 percent, and the party elected its local ticket in the anthracite county of Luzerne (Wilkes-Barre) and three mayors, including Terence V. Powderly, who would next year become Grand Master Workman of the Knights of Labor, as mayor of Scranton.[15] The new party also defeated both old parties in Toledo.

The 1878 elections, however, turned out to be the Greenback party's peak. The end of the long depression of the seventies took some of the force out of the protest movement, while the Republicans could gleefully claim a cause-and-effect relationship and boast the vindication of their hard-money philosophy. Internally, the Greenback party suffered from a chronic inability to merge its eastern labor and western agrarian elements into any true unity.[16] And finally, in most states the new party had been lured down the path of fusion.

The party's national committee had forbidden its state and local officials

13. Edward Topping James, "American Labor and Political Action, 1865–1896: The Knights of Labor and Its Predecessors" (Ph.D. dissertation, Harvard University, 1954), pp. 127–28.

14. *Appleton's Annual Cyclopedia*, Vol. 17 (1877), pp. 769, 400.

15. Ralph R. Ricker, *The Greenback-Labor Movement in Pennsylvania* (Pennsylvania Heritage, 1966), p. 39.

16. The emerging labor leaders found the old Greenbackers conservative on issues of direct interest to labor and preoccupied with their single panacean solution to all the country's economic ills, while some of the currency reformers saw the labor leaders as extremists inclined to violence and dangerously imbued with European socialistic doctrines. See, for example, statement of Edward P. Allis, Milwaukee businessman and Greenback leader, dated Feb. 24, 1878, in Ellis B. Usher, *The Greenback Movement of 1875–84 and Wisconsin's Part in It* (Ellis B. Usher, 1911), pp. 54–55. See also comments of Powderly, quoted by James, "American Labor and Political Action," p. 190, and James's narrative and discussion, pp. 161–66, 174, 180, 190.

to form alliances with other parties. By remaining independent, it argued, the Greenbackers could supersede the Democrats as the country's major opposition party—just as the Republicans had superseded the Whigs. But its advice went unheeded. To the ambitious local candidate the national policy reflected only a remote and long-term hope while alliance with the Democrats (or, in a few places, with the Republicans) promised immediate reward. The Democrats reasoned similarly; where they were a hopeless minority, as in the newer states of the Northwest, they had nothing to lose by proposing generous terms for fusion. And fusion did bring quick results. In Pennsylvania, several congressmen were elected on fusion tickets. In Iowa, the Democratic-Greenback fusion ticket made the best opposition showing since the founding of the Republican party in the state, with more than 48 percent of the vote, and two prominent Greenbackers were elected to Congress. By counting all the votes cast for fusion candidates, the party could claim more than a million votes, which was twelve times the number of 1876 and nearly 15 percent of the total vote in the country.[17] Only one Greenbacker (in Maine) was elected to Congress over both Republican and Democratic opposition, but some two dozen were elected on fusion tickets or with official Greenback support. In the election of the Speaker of the House in 1879, fourteen members cast their ballots for the Greenback candidate. But fusion inevitably weakened attachment of voters to a new political group that lacked tradition, organization, experience, newspapers, patronage, and financial support.

As the presidential campaign approached, many who had supported the Greenback party in state and local campaigns were inevitably attracted back to the major parties that would contest for the national prize. Even with the dynamic General James B. Weaver (one of the new Iowa congressmen) as their candidate, the Greenbackers could poll only 308,000 presidential votes in 1880. The party remained a force in several states—notably Massachusetts, where it joined with the Democrats in electing Benjamin F. Butler governor in 1882, and in Iowa and Michigan—but on the national scene it had been superseded by the time of the 1884 campaign.

As the Greenback party declined, its adherents apparently went back to the parties from which they had come. Despite the Democratic adoption of "soft money" policies and despite the willingness of the Democrats to join

17. *Appleton's Annual Cyclopedia* (Vol. 18 [1878], p. 808) tabulates 1,000,365 votes cast in thirty-seven states in 1878. The percentage of the total vote is calculated from Murray S. Stedman, Jr., and Susan W. Stedman, *Discontent at the Polls: A Study of Farmer and Labor Parties 1827–1948* (Columbia University Press, 1950), p. 173.

in organizing fusion tickets, the rise and fall of the Greenback party left almost no perceptible increase in Democratic strength. Republican green-backers had shown themselves willing to leave their party at least tempo-rarily—like Republican Grangers in 1873–74—but only under a third-party banner. When the choice was to continue their fight for greenback principles as Democrats or return to the Republican fold and give up the fight, they chose the latter, even in states where they had enough strength to take over the Democratic party and mold it to their liking.

What repelled them, clearly, was the Democratic label itself; they were willing to ally themselves with the Democratic party but unwilling to be called Democrats. The party's stigma was still vivid, and its political ene-mies were devoting themselves to seeing that it remained so.[18] Until a new generation of voters and politicians whose partisanship had not been hard-ened in battle arose, an alignment of parties around the crucial new issues of a new age would not be possible.

Tensions within the Old Parties

The protest from the West that powered the third-party movements of the 1870s also inevitably created strains within the major parties. Within each party, a western wing took form, reflecting the soft-money, anti-monopoly views of the farmers and their allies, while an eastern wing de-fended hard-money orthodoxy and the interests of industrialists and finan-ciers.

THE OHIO IDEA CLEAVES BOTH PARTIES

As early as 1868, the Democratic party, so recently sundered on North-South lines, was cleft between East and West. What was called the "Ohio Idea," a scheme for paying the war debt in depreciated greenbacks rather than in gold, was sweeping the West, and former Congressman George H. Pendleton of Cincinnati entered the party's convention with solid sectional support as the candidate of the Ohio plan's backers. On the first ballot, Pendleton received 72 of the 95 delegate votes of the northern states from

18. The Republican platform of 1876 had declared: "We charge the Democratic party with being the same in character and spirit as when it sympathized with treason . . . with reasserting and applauding in the National Capitol the sentiments of unrepentent rebellion; with sending Union soldiers to the rear and promoting Confederate soldiers to the front." It would be a long time before Republican "bloody shirt" orators would cease painting the Democratic party in such a hue.

Ohio westward and 28½ from the border states, but only 4½ from the rest of the country. The result was a classic major-party compromise on a cross-cutting issue: the convention accepted a greenback platform plank but rejected Pendleton in favor of a hard-money candidate—Governor Horatio Seymour of New York—who thereupon endorsed the platform and took the offensive on the issue. In the end, Seymour concluded, it contributed to his defeat.[19]

To a lesser degree, the Ohio Idea had split the Republican party also. Ohio Republicans in particular, including Senator John Sherman, had found themselves compelled to line up almost solidly behind it, and in the nation the idea was seen as the state's bipartisan proposal.[20] But the Republican national convention of 1868 saw no need to make concessions to the West. "We denounce all forms of repudiation as a national crime," proclaimed its platform. After the victory it settled the question with a congressional resolution pledging eventual redemption of the bonds in gold. Three-fourths of the Republicans in each house supported the measure; all but six of the dissenters were from the West and South, but even there most Republicans, including Sherman, went with the party leadership. Democrats, conversely, voted heavily against the measure, 25–11 in the House and 6–0 in the Senate. Nine of the eleven hard-money House Democrats were from the East.

SO DOES THE INFLATION BILL OF 1874

The currency question would not stay settled. During the economic depression that followed the panic of 1873, currency theorists of every stripe advanced their nostrums. The Grant administration vacillated,[21] but in the

19. Not only the bondholders but "all creditors and business men" were alarmed, he wrote. "Instead of looking to a return to the standard of the world, we were charged with the purpose of putting out to sea and sailing away from land. . . . It was like Satan's flight into Chaos." Letter to George L. Miller of Omaha, quoted by Charles H. Coleman, *The Election of 1868: The Democratic Effort to Regain Control* (Columbia University Press, 1933), p. 373.

20. Clifford H. Moore, "Ohio in National Politics, 1865–1869," *Ohio Archaeological and Historical Quarterly*, Vol. 37 (April–July, 1928), p. 351.

21. In his annual message, President Grant urged the Congress to provide for more elasticity in the currency, so that the volume might rise or fall with business needs, but he left the question of the means to the Congress. "The difference of opinion on this subject is so great," said Treasury Secretary William A. Richardson in his annual report, that he could only "earnestly commend to the wisdom of Congress a careful and thorough consideration" of "the multitude of plans." "Annual Report of the Secretary of the Treasury, Dec. 1, 1873," in *Message from the President of the United States to the Two Houses of Congress . . . with the Reports of the Heads of Departments* (1873), pp. 39–40.

Senate the expansionists took control and wrote what came to be called the Inflation Bill. On that hotly contested measure (which proposed to expand the currency by $18 million in addition to legalizing an earlier action by the Grant administration that released $26 million in greenbacks from the Treasury reserve), the battle line was drawn not between the two major parties but between two bipartisan sectional coalitions, as shown by the vote breakdown in Table 6-1.

Table 6-1. *Congressional Votes on the Passage of the Inflation Bill of 1874, by Region and Party*

Region[a]	Republican		Democrat		Other		Total	
	Yea	Nay	Yea	Nay	Yea	Nay	Yea	Nay
				Senate				
East	2	12	0	4	0	0	2	16
Midwest	14	4	1	1	0	0	15	5
South	11	2	6	3	1	0	18	5
Pacific	1	3	0	2	0	0	1	5
Total	28	21	7	10	1	0	36	31
				House				
East	15	50	1	17	0	1	16	68
Midwest	61	9	11	8	0	0	72	17
South	28	3	23	11	0	0	51	14
Pacific	1	2	0	1	0	0	1	3
Total	105	64	35	37	0	1	140	102

Sources: The Senate vote was on April 6. *Congressional Record*, 43 Cong. 1 sess., p. 2835. The totals include ten paired senators whose positions were announced in addition to those actually voting. The House vote was on April 14. Ibid., p. 3075. The figures are taken from Irwin Unger, *The Greenback Era: A Social and Political History of American Finance, 1865–1879* (Princeton University Press, 1964), App. C, p. 410.

a. Regions are defined in this chapter so as to best reflect voting configurations. In this table, Delaware and Maryland are included in the East, Missouri in the Midwest, and West Virginia in the South.

Easterners of both parties voted overwhelmingly against the bill in both houses; large majorities of both parties from the Midwest and the South supported it. The sectional nature of the vote becomes even more striking when it is observed that thirteen of the fifteen expansionist votes by eastern Republicans in the House were from Pennsylvania, whose western counties, where the iron industry was concentrated, responded like the Midwest to the money issue. In all of New England, New York, and New Jersey, only three of seventy-two congressmen (of both parties) voted for the bill.

Interestingly, the Democrats, who had made their progreenback stance a major issue of the 1868 campaign, emerged as the party most strongly in favor of hard money in 1874, casting a slight majority in both houses against the bill. One factor was that at that time the western farmers' movement had not yet embraced soft money, unlike a substantial segment of the business community, whose expansionist sentiment was reflected in the Republican vote.[22] The resolutions of the granges and other farm organizations at that time were generally conservative on the money question (except in Indiana and Illinois), reflecting the old Jacksonian antipathy to paper money. The same agrarian tradition probably accounts also for the relatively high percentage of anti-inflation votes in the reemerging Democratic party of the South.

When the bill was passed, the pressures that had been directed at the Congress focused in all their intensity on President Grant. Besides the economic argument there was the political one: in the interest of his party, the Republican President should approve the handiwork of his GOP colleagues in the Congress. But after a struggle with his conscience, Grant rose above politics and acted on his inner convictions. The veto was "a brave and noble act," says historian James Ford Rhodes, expressing the moralism of "sound money" men that has continued into this century. "It . . . atones for a multitude of errors."[23] The quarrel continued for two more months while the Congress framed a substitute measure conservative enough for the President to sign. In the fall, the Republicans lost nearly half their seats in the House of Representatives—electing 109 of the 292 members as against 198 two years before—and control of the House passed to the Democrats for the first time since prewar days. The Republicans also lost three northern governorships and seven northern and border Senate seats. There were many reasons for the setback (the depression was undoubtedly the paramount factor), but the Democrats capitalized heavily on the veto of the Inflation Bill, as they forced each Republican candidate to repudiate either his party's record in the Congress or his President.

22. A second influence was the Democrats' alliance with the liberal Republicans, carried over from the Horace Greeley campaign of 1872. The liberals, as reformers, were hard-money fundamentalists, and the 1872 Democratic-Liberal campaign had been faithful to those principles.

23. *History of the United States, from the Compromise of 1850 to the Final Restoration of Home Rule in the South in 1877* (Macmillan, 1906), p. 128. Rhodes's account of Grant's internal struggle is on pp. 126–27.

CONSERVATISM CONTROLS BOTH PARTIES

As the Republicans of the "lame duck" Congress returned to Washington after their defeat, they found it imperative to forge a unified position on the money question, a miracle they accomplished under the leadership of John Sherman of Ohio as chairman of a Senate Republican caucus committee that represented all shades of party opinion. Sherman obtained his consensus in the manner of the original great compromiser, Henry Clay, by incorporating in a single measure some of the demands of both sides. The hard-money men were given a fixed date, January 1, 1879, when repayment of bonds in gold would begin, and the expansionists of the West and South were granted their long-standing demand for "free banking"—that is, removal of the $300 million limit on national bank notes contained in the original national banking act of 1862. As bank notes were issued, greenbacks would be withdrawn but at a rate that would permit increase in the volume of currency in circulation. Republican party discipline was invoked in the Senate and debate cut short in the House, and the Resumption Act of 1875 became law.

Whatever may have been the intent of its sponsors, the Resumption Act turned out to be a deflationary measure. In the depressed business conditions of the time, the national banks issued few new notes, and Treasury Secretary Benjamin H. Bristow used his authority under the law to retire greenbacks and bring about a net contraction of $13 million in the currency.[24]

Western Democrats denounced the deflation, and in Ohio the party turned the 1875 gubernatorial election into a referendum on the Resumption Act and Bristow's administration of it. The Republicans responded with a resounding defense of their return to Christian virtue.[25] Inflation was equated with sin and with communism. The "immorality" of Democrats on the money question was subtly—or not so subtly—linked with their abandonment of moral principle during the Civil War. The Protestant clergy dealt with the ethics of currency from the pulpit and in the religious press. Hard-money advocate Rutherford B. Hayes was elected governor, a victory that vindicated the hard-money wing of the GOP and clinched the position of the party, from that time forward, as squarely on the side of monetary virtue.

The Democrats, if not united, were chastened. After the decision in Ohio, the anti–Resumption Act campaign of the Democrats in Pennsylvania

---

24. Irwin Unger, *The Greenback Era: A Social and Political History of American Finance, 1865–1879* (Princeton University Press, 1964), pp. 264–65.
25. See quotations from Republican campaigners in ibid., pp. 276–79.

(where the election was a month later) collapsed. In the new Democrat-controlled House of Representatives, the hard-money men were able to elect their candidate for Speaker—by a 30-vote margin in the caucus—and he in turn organized the key committees with men of like principle who could be counted on to bottle up any inflationary measures. Samuel J. Tilden of New York was nominated for president on a platform that was essentially conservative. For the time being, at least, both parties were secure against radicalism on the money issue.

The Protest Forces Regather

With the Greenback party in decline and both major parties under conservative domination, the forces of protest had to forge new political instruments. The farmers found theirs in an organization called the Farmers' Alliance, which, unlike the Grange, was to engage directly and openly in political action. Texas farmers formed an Alliance in 1878, a county organization with the same name was established in 1880 in Cook County, Illinois, and from these beginnings the idea spread to neighboring states. Momentum gathered slowly, but as the Granger movement of the previous decade had demonstrated, the potential political power of organized farmers in the agricultural regions was limitless. An early successful test came in Nebraska in 1882. There Alliancemen, Greenbackers, dissident Republicans, and independents, angered by a Republican proposal to reduce taxes on railroads, formed an Anti-Monopoly party, which received 19 percent of the vote for governor and, in fusion with the Democrats, elected a state treasurer and won control of the state senate.[26]

Antimonopolist leagues and parties were being formed in New York, Illinois, Wisconsin, and New Jersey, and the antimonopoly concept appeared a likely successor to the narrower greenback idea as the basis for third-party activity. But when a national Anti-Monopoly party ran Governor Benjamin Butler of Massachusetts for president in 1884, he made a poorer showing than had General Weaver four years earlier, receiving even fewer votes than the new Prohibition party.

26. James C. Olson, *History of Nebraska* (University of Nebraska Press, 1955), pp. 223–26. The 1882 success was short-lived: in 1884, Democrats and Anti-Monopolists joined in nominating a candidate for governor but failed to elect him. *Appleton's Annual Cyclopedia*, Vol. 22 (1882), p. 587.

In the next four years, the protest movement was to rise, crest, and fall once more. This time it was predominantly an urban uprising with organized labor—specifically, the Knights of Labor—as its base. When the economy turned down in 1883 and employers responded to falling prices by ordering wage reductions, the Knights found thousands of new recruits, and after the organization won a series of victories in 1884 in negotiations with the railroads, the country's workingmen entered its ranks in a "virtual stampede." In one twelve-month period in 1885–86 over 4,000 new assemblies were organized and 600,000 members added.[27] Terence Powderly and his associates in the Knights of Labor national leadership, profiting from the experience of the Greenback party, chose not to try to throw the order's entire strength into partisan politics; they had been going down a different, nonpartisan path —trying to influence the platforms of the major parties at all levels, to bring about the nomination by those parties of prolabor candidates, to exact commitments from all candidates on labor issues, and then to support the friends of labor and punish its enemies. This approach had won some successes in federal and state legislation.

But the leaders of the Knights of Labor had no control over the vast accretion of new members. As the 1886 election approached, assemblies everywhere were organizing to run their own slates of candidates or enter into fusion deals with Democrats or Republicans. All Powderly and his associates could do was forbid the member assemblies to call their third parties "Knights of Labor" parties, and even that rule they could not enforce. Independent labor parties fielded candidates for one or another office in at least twenty-six states. There was usually no time to organize for statewide campaigns, so the victories were local. Labor candidates were elected to local office in Milwaukee, Fort Worth, Richmond, Lynn (Massachusetts), Leadville (Colorado), and Key West (Florida); to some fifty legislative seats in a dozen states and to Congress from the districts embracing Milwaukee, Raleigh (North Carolina), and Lynchburg-Roanoke (Virginia). In the spring, labor tickets won local elections in Seattle, Dubuque, Kansas City (Kansas), Mobile, and many smaller cities. In Chicago and Milwaukee, the labor parties forced the two old parties to combine behind a single candidate, and even then the laborites were able to carry the city of Milwaukee (though not the county as a whole).[28]

It was inevitable that someone would try to organize a national party

27. James, "American Labor and Political Action," pp. 269–70.
28. Ibid., p. 339.

from this massive demonstration of political strength, and the Union Labor party was formed to contest the election of 1888. But the crest of the protest wave had passed once more, and the new party found itself on the downhill slope. Like the Granger parties after 1874 and the Greenback party after 1878, the Knights of Labor and allied local parties collapsed quickly after the spring of 1887. Edward Topping James has suggested four reasons: ideological dissension within the labor movement, particularly between socialists and moderates (or, in the case of New York, single-taxers), but also between laborers and intellectuals and between the Knights' assemblies and the craft unions that were then banding together to form what became the American Federation of Labor; personality conflicts; effective counter-attacks by the opposition, including in some cases the buying off of independent party politicians; and the inevitable decline in enthusiasm following the fever pitch of the 1886–87 campaigns.[29] By 1888, the country was engrossed in the great controversy between the major parties over the tariff, and the Union Labor party polled even fewer votes in the presidential election than the Anti-Monopoly party had received in 1884.

With each rise and fall of the protest tide, however, new ideas were added to the agenda of reform. As platform builders, the third parties of the years between 1876 and 1888 were extraordinarily productive. They originated many of the progressive proposals that later became the proud achievements of the major parties, in some cases a quarter-century or a half-century later. The original Greenback party of 1876 was a one-issue, one-solution party, which was among its weaknesses. Monetary policy remained the center of its platform four years later, but ten planks were added on other subjects. The Greenbackers reached out for labor support with a series of specific measures, including inspection of factories and mines, abolition of the use of convict labor under contract, establishment of a bureau of labor statistics (created in 1884), prohibition of employment of children under fourteen, a requirement that wages be paid in cash, and an end to the importation of Chinese labor. It denounced monopoly, called for regulation of railroad and

29. To an even greater degree than the farmer, the urban laborer saw the politicians in whom he had placed his faith, including some of his own leaders, prove faithless once they came close to the emoluments of power. The records of the Knights of Labor are full of complaints about self-seeking politicians who had lost interest in the cause that elected them. James, "American Labor and Political Action," pp. 356–57. James relates that even Terence Powderly was almost seduced in 1888 when Republicans offered to finance the publication of his book of memoirs (which eventually appeared as *Thirty Years of Labor*). Powderly finally called off the transaction because, in his words, he was "beginning to feel like a thief" (pp. 437–40).

telegraph rates, demanded the forfeiture of undeveloped railroad land grants, and urged a graduated income tax.[30] The Anti-Monopolists four years later put their emphasis on railroad legislation but picked up most of the earlier ideas and added some new ones: a postal savings system, a postal telegraph, direct election of U.S. senators, and women's suffrage. In 1888 the demand for regulation of railroads, having been met by the passage of the Interstate Commerce Act, was supplanted by a proposal for government ownership.

The Major Parties Respond Slowly

The massive voting power of the farm organizations as early as the 1870s and of the Knights of Labor in the next decade might have been expected to mark them as blocs to be courted by the major parties. The Grangers at their peak numbered nearly a million members (even though perhaps close to half were nonvoting women), and the Knights at their height approached that figure. In an electorate that cast 6.5 million votes for president in 1872 and 11 million in 1888, well over a million organized potential voters would seem a not insignificant prize.

Yet the national leadership of the two parties undertook nothing that can be called a courtship. In the presidential year of 1880, neither major party had a word to say about monopoly or railroad regulation, even though a bill to regulate railroads had passed the House in the previous Congress with the support of a majority of both parties. The party platforms were empty, backward-looking documents. The Democrats put their greatest emphasis on a denunciation of the "great fraud of 1876–77" that elected Hayes, while the Republicans waved the "bloody shirt" (the Democrats "have advocated the principles and sought the favor of the Rebellion against the Nation"). Both offered labor the restriction of Chinese immigration, and both promised the farmers to reserve the public lands for actual settlers. This was their total response to agrarian and urban protest, and on these and other matters their platforms were almost indistinguishable. Only on the tariff was there a difference, but even that was obliterated when the Democratic candidate, General Winfield S. Hancock, disavowed his party's "tariff for revenue only" plank with the comment that the tariff was "a local question." The

30. *Appleton's Annual Cyclopedia*, Vol. 20 (1880), pp. 696–97. The major parties also had planks on importation of Chinese labor.

campaign was "barren of issues and devoid of drama."[31] The parties were not seeking issues; they were avoiding them.

In 1884 the platform rhetoric improved but otherwise the situation was unchanged. In the intervening years, neither party had developed a program. President Arthur in 1883 had endorsed federal regulation of railroads, but legislation was easily blocked in Congress. He had recommended repeal of the statutory requirement that $2 million in silver dollars be minted monthly, but Congress did not act. The Democrats, in control of the House during the last two years of the Arthur administration, had struggled endlessly with the tariff, but with each member in fact treating it as "a local question" the House could pass no legislation. Chinese immigration was restricted for ten years, and a bureau of labor was created in the Department of the Interior. But none of these became a strong party issue; the struggle between the parties had become "more and more merely a struggle for office," with a sharp party division "only on those questions that affected the parties themselves, such as the control of elections or the distribution of patronage."[32]

So when the Democrats under Grover Cleveland recaptured the White House in 1884 after a twenty-four-year absence, the shift in control brought no change to economic policy. Cleveland had been presented in the campaign as the ruggedly independent governor of New York who had dared to veto bills that favored Tammany and who would, in contrast to the tainted James G. Blaine, bring to the White House an unimpeachable integrity and a penchant for curbing administrative waste. That image elected him, as the Mugwump Republicans deserted Blaine.[33] And it was to administrative efficiency and governmental economy that he devoted himself after his inauguration. He wrote scores of veto messages on private pension bills, but he proposed no major new departures in domestic policy. He did not even recommend railroad regulation, as had Arthur, although he signed the Interstate Com-

31. Eugene H. Roseboom, *A History of Presidential Elections from George Washington to Richard M. Nixon* (3d ed., Macmillan, 1970), p. 258.

32. Harrison Cook Thomas, *The Return of the Democratic Party to Power in 1884* (Columbia University Press, 1919), p. 26. Thomas applied this generalization not just to the year 1884 but to the whole postreconstruction period.

33. A severe economic slump in 1884 no doubt contributed something to the Democratic victory, but since Cleveland did not make the depression an issue or promise in any way to do anything about it, it is probably correct to accept the standard interpretation that the swing to the Democrats was a reaction primarily against the corruption of the patronage-oriented political machines at all levels. Thomas (ibid., pp. 228–31) lists the depression as only one of the secondary factors influencing the election outcome. Such a traditional historian as Rhodes does not even mention it (*History of the United States, from Hayes to McKinley 1877–1896* [Macmillan, 1919], p. 231).

merce Act when it was passed in 1887. He pursued the same fiscal and monetary policies as his Republican predecessors and, like them, asked for repeal
of the requirement that the Treasury purchase $2 million of silver monthly.
As his cabinet member from the agrarian West he chose a railroad attorney,
William F. Vilas of Wisconsin, and made him, as postmaster general, the
administration's chief patronage dispenser. In short, he made no gesture
whatever toward either the farm or the labor protest movement. He adopted
none of their demands, and on the silver issue he opposed them outright.

Back in the hinterland, however, his party was not so placidly unresponsive to the pressures from the left. On the two major issues that bubbled up
from the agrarian ferment, railroad regulation and currency expansion, the
farmers found champions in the major parties, and most of them were Democrats. The result was a sharpening of party cleavage in spite of the national
leaders. Table 6-2, which compares two votes on the interstate commerce
bill offered by Representative John H. Reagan, Texas Democrat, shows how
Republicans from the agricultural West shifted from a position of support in
1878 to one of almost solid opposition in 1884, while Democrats in every
region were moving to a position of stronger support. While the circumstances were not strictly comparable,[34] the two votes show that the parties
in the House (presumably reflecting the parties in their districts) polarized
on the railroad issue during the intervening six years of agitation and debate.
In 1878 the issue was more a regional than a party matter. Republicans and
Democrats backed the bill to about the same degree; within each party representatives from the East (except Pennsylvania) were overwhelmingly
against the measure while those from the rest of the country were markedly
favorable. In 1884, regional differences were obliterated within the Republican party and nearly so within the Democratic party; the Democrats voted

---

34. The railroads were divided on the issue in 1878 and united in 1884. Moreover,
the 1878 vote shown in the table is on passage of the bill (there were no roll call votes on
amendments), while the 1884 vote is on substitution of the Reagan bill for a much milder,
committee-approved measure that incorporated modifications insisted on by the railroads.
(The Reagan bill was described by a backer of the committee bill as a "list of bristling
and fulminating prohibitions and penalties and nothing more." Representative John D.
Long [R., Mass.], *Congressional Record*, 48 Cong. 1 sess. [Dec. 3, 1884], p. 44.) The vote
on the substitution is more revealing of party and regional attitudes than the vote on final
passage, because once the Reagan bill was accepted as a substitute it picked up support
from those who recognized that some form of federal railroad regulation was essential—
and demanded by their constituents—while the Republican Senate could be counted on to
modify the House measure. The vote on final passage was 161–75. The Senate passed a
weaker bill and Congress adjourned without reconciling the differences. In 1887, House
and Senate versions were finally compromised and the Interstate Commerce Act became
law.

Table 6-2. *Votes in the House of Representatives on Railroad and Silver Legislation, 1878–86, by Region and Party*

Region	Democrats			Republicans			Other			Total		
	Yea	Nay	Not vot- ing	Yea	Nay	Not vot- ing	Yea	Nay	Not vot- ing	Yea	Nay	Not vot- ing
Vote on passage of Reagan interstate commerce bill, Dec. 11, 1878												
East[a]	2	18	12	8	28	7	0	0	0	10	46	19
Pennsylvania[a]	6	2	1	15	1	1	0	0	0	21	3	2
West[b]	23	9	7	39	26	4	0	0	0	62	35	11
South	40	20	14	6	0	2	0	0	0	46	20	16
Total	71	49	34	68	55	14	0	0	0	139	104	48
Vote on substitution of Reagan interstate commerce bill for committee bill, Dec. 16, 1884												
East[c]	12	12	19	7	33	16	0	1	1	19	46	36
West[b]	47	10	16	6	35	11	2	0	0	55	45	27
South	65	3	13	3	3	4	0	1	3	68	7	20
Total	124	25	48	16	71	31	2	2	4	142	98	83
Vote on passage of Bland bill for unlimited silver coinage, April 8, 1886												
East[c]	1	34	3	3	52	9	0	0	0	4	86	12
West[b]	38	13	7	23	39	6	1	0	0	62	52	13
South	56	23	7	4	2	2	0	0	0	60	25	9
Total	95	70	17	30	93	17	1	0	0	126	163	34

Sources: *Congressional Record*, 45 Cong. 3 sess. (1878), pp. 101–02; ibid., 48 Cong. 2 sess. (1884), p. 295; ibid., 49 Cong. 1 sess. (1886), pp. 3300–01.

a. Includes Delaware and Maryland. Pennsylvania is shown separately because it diverged sharply from the pattern in the rest of the East. Comments during congressional debate suggested this was due to the influence of the Pennsylvania Railroad, which as an intrastate line at that time apparently favored federal regulation of interstate carriers.

b. Includes Missouri and West Virginia.

c. Includes Delaware, Maryland, and Pennsylvania. By 1884, Pennsylvania had reverted to the eastern pattern of opposition to federal regulation, Democrats voting in opposition, 7–1, and Republicans, 14–2.

five to one in favor of the bill preferred by the agrarian reformers—and, more important at this time, many manufacturers and shippers—and the Republicans almost as overwhelmingly in favor of the amendments instigated by the railroads.

Regional differences were fading within the Republican party on the silver question too, as western representatives moved to a conservative position comparable to that of their eastern colleagues. When the bill for free and unlimited coinage of silver offered by Representative Richard P. Bland, Missouri Democrat, came to a vote in 1886, Republicans voted against it, 93–30, with western Republicans opposed 39–23, as shown in Table 6-2.

But within the Democratic party the regional division of the previous decade (see Table 6-1) had lost none of its sharpness. Eastern Democrats voted 34–1 against the bill, while those of the West and South supported it by votes of 38–13 and 56–23, respectively.

Democrats from the agricultural regions were frank as to the class and regional basis of the silver legislation. Representative Samuel W. T. Lanham of Texas saw the issue as one between "the monetary centers, the national banks, the owners of fixed incomes, the syndicates of wealth, the possessors of gold, almost every organized association of capital," the "money kings," the "bondholders and plutocrats," on one side, and "men of small means and limited transactions . . . debtors . . . laborers . . . the varied and multiplied sons of toil . . . those who eat bread by the sweat of their brows," on the other.[35] Representative Charles F. Crisp of Georgia put it simply: "The East is the creditor and the South and West the debtor, the East is the money-lender and the South and the West the money borrower. . . . Their interests are not the same. . . . In the South it is hardly too much to say that nine-tenths of the people are in debt."[36]

Grover Cleveland identified himself wholly with the eastern creditors. He was not a man to compromise; his public standing rested on his reputation as an upholder of right and morality regardless of the odds against him, whether the conflict was with Tammany Hall grafters or inflationary heretics from the West. So he made no move—could make none consistent with his public character and self-image—to conciliate the western and southern Democrats who made up a large majority of the party. Unlike Democratic presidents of the prewar generation—centrists and compromisers all—Cleveland himself became in a time of national polarization a polarizing force. This fatally weakened the party's centrist bloc and hastened realignment.

The Prairie State Parties of 1890

In the winter of 1887–88 the boom on the western prairies collapsed. The immediate cause was a change in the weather. After almost a decade of abundant rainfall and bountiful harvests, the cycle of wet years ended in 1886 and the next year brought drought. Suddenly the land could not support

35. *Congressional Record*, 49 Cong. 1 sess. (March 20, 1886), pp. 2139–40.
36. Ibid. (April 7, 1886), pp. 3221–22.

its mortgage burden. Land values plummeted. Farms were foreclosed. Loan companies failed. Cities became insolvent. The speculators returned to the East. Boom towns disappeared from the map. Rural western Kansas, more of it occupied by speculators than by bona fide farmers, lost half its population.[37] The zone of greatest desperation was the frontier zone of genuine agriculture, where settlers were tied to the land. There the mortgage burden was higher than in the older settlements farther east, and there, where normal rainfall was barely enough to support agriculture, the drought had greater impact.[38] Eleven thousand farm mortgages were foreclosed in Kansas in four years.[39] In 1888 the whole national economy entered a period of depression, but the farmer could see none whose plight compared with his. The prices of what he bought had fallen relatively little. His resentment turned, as it always had in hard times, toward the railroads, the middlemen, and the monopolies, but this time it turned, above all, toward the creditors who were foreclosing on his land. The chief enemy was a vague but malignant "money power."[40] It had to be combated through political action, for it was the government, controlled by the creditors and their allies, who had eliminated the greenback, demonetized silver, and otherwise constricted the currency to bring about a price deflation—and an increase in the real value of gold and of gold instruments—that had been almost continuous since the end of the Civil War.

Into this breach stepped the Farmers' Alliance with its monetary radicalism inherited from the Greenback party. Farmers who had been apathetic

37. Raymond Curtis Miller, "The Background of Populism in Kansas," *Mississippi Valley Historical Review*, Vol. 11 (March 1925), p. 477. See also Hallie Farmer, "The Economic Background of Frontier Populism," *Mississippi Valley Historical Review*, Vol. 10 (March 1924).

38. John D. Barnhart, "Rainfall and the Populist Party in Nebraska," *American Political Science Review*, Vol. 19 (1925), pp. 527–40, esp. p. 538.

39. Hicks, *Populist Revolt*, p. 84. Elizabeth N. Barr says that of the 441,406 mortgages written on Kansas property between 1880 and 1890, 150,000 were foreclosed or deeded to the holder without legal proceedings. "The Populist Uprising," in William E. Connelley (ed.), *History of Kansas* (American Historical Society, 1928), Vol. 2, p. 1157. Statistics on the latter type of transaction are not compiled, and Mrs. Barr gives no basis for her estimate.

40. Richard Hofstadter has emphasized the conspiratorial conception of history that ran through Populist thought, the "unusually strong tendency to account for relatively impersonal events in highly personal terms." "In Populist thought," he wrote, "the farmer is not a speculating businessman, victimized by the risk economy of which he is a part, but rather a wounded yeoman, preyed upon by those who are alien to the life of folkish culture." He quotes the preamble to the 1892 Populist platform: "A vast conspiracy against mankind has been organized on two continents, and it is rapidly taking possession of the world." *The Age of Reform: From Bryan to F.D.R.* (Knopf, 1955), pp. 72–74.

toward the organization in good times now flocked to it. By the end of 1889 the Kansas alliance claimed 70,000 members in 1,200 local organizations. "They say," wrote the correspondent of the Republican *Weekly Capital* (Topeka) on December 19, 1889, "that money trusts, corporations, and monopolies are sucking the life-blood from the agricultural interests, and it is time to call a halt." A year later the organization reported 130,000 members.[41]

The political path for the rising organization had already been blazed in rural Cowley County, Kansas. There the Alliance joined with the Democrats and some disgruntled Republicans to call a "people's convention" in the county and create what became, according to a local Republican newspaper, "a very compact and orderly political machine."[42] When its candidates defeated the entrenched Republican organization by a wide margin in the local elections in 1889, farmers throughout Kansas looked to the Cowley party as their model. The state Alliance then resolved to launch a People's party for the 1890 state and congressional campaigns, and the Knights of Labor and other farm organizations joined with the Alliance in June to create the new party. To the radical program were added three new demands —government loans to farmers at 4 percent, a reduction of mortgage debt in proportion to the shrinkage of land values, and exemption of homesteads from taxation.

Relations with the Democrats were not as easily resolved as they had been in Cowley County, for the Democrats were hardly ready to dissolve throughout the state in favor of their upstart rival. A partial fusion was all that could be arranged in contests for state office,[43] but in four of the seven congressional districts and in most state legislative races, the Democrats either made no nominations or formally endorsed the Farmers' Alliance or People's party candidate.

The campaign, wrote Elizabeth N. Barr, was "a religious revival, a crusade, a pentecost of politics in which a tongue of flame sat upon every man."[44] Mary Elizabeth Lease, a thirty-seven-year-old Wichita lawyer who became the premier prairie orator, could lash out in a single speech at

41. Barr, "The Populist Uprising," p. 1159.

42. The Winfield (Kansas) *Courier*, quoted in ibid., p. 1161.

43. The Democrats nominated their own state ticket except for the office of attorney general, the one post for which the Populists had named a former Democrat. William Frank Zornow, *Kansas: A History of the Jayhawk State* (University of Oklahoma Press, 1957), p. 198.

44. "The Populist Uprising," p. 1165.

eight-cent corn, two-cent beef, the Santa Fe railroad, the "loan-shark companies," the "blood-hounds of money," "white wage slavery," the old political parties, and "government of Wall Street, by Wall Street and for Wall
Street," and called on farmers to oppose the "accursed foreclosure system"
by force if necessary.[45]

The Republicans succeeded in electing their governor, but by only 39
percent of the vote, as the People's candidate polled 36 percent and the Democrats finished a poor third. The fusion candidate for attorney general won
with 58 percent. Only two Republican congressmen survived, and in each
case only because the Democrats and the Populists split the opposition vote.
In the four fusion districts, the People's or Farmers' Alliance candidates
were elected, and in one district the Populists won a majority in a three-way
race. The lower house of the new legislature consisted of ninety Alliancemen, twenty-seven Republicans, and eight Democrats. Of the ninety Alliance legislators, sixty-two had been Republicans.[46] An immediate result
was the election to the U.S. Senate of its first Populist, William A. Peffer,
editor of a farm journal and former Republican presidential elector.

North along the frontier to the Canadian border the political turmoil was
much the same. In Nebraska, Republicans were defeated—for the first time
since Nebraska became a state—as their candidate for governor finished
third in a narrow three-way race, 2,500 votes behind the victorious Democrat and 1,300 behind the nominee of an Independent party formed on the
initiative of the Farmers' Alliance.[47] Independents elected two congressmen
and obtained clear majorities in both houses of the legislature.

In South Dakota, the Independents became the second largest party in the
legislature and combined with the Democrats to send an Independent, James
H. Kyle, to the U.S. Senate. An Alliance party elected a congressman in
Minnesota, and a fusion candidate for state auditor won easily. The Farmers' Alliance also participated in the formation of new parties in North
Dakota, Colorado, Indiana, and Michigan, but they were formed late in the
campaign season and fared poorly.

The campaigns of 1890 confirmed what the elections of the preceding two
decades had shown. When the farmers organized as an independent party

45. Quoted in ibid., p. 1167.
46. *Appleton's Annual Cyclopedia*, Vol. 30 (1890), p. 472.
47. The Democratic plurality over the Independents was credited to the party's forthright stand against a prohibition amendment that was decisively defeated in the same election; Republicans and Independents had refused to take a position on the issue. Olson,
History of Nebraska, p. 235.

they had a difficult uphill struggle; in three-way races they could claim three congressmen but no governors or other state officials. But when they succeeded in fusing with the Democrats they elected state candidates with ease. Then what prevented outright merger? In other words, since the Farmers' Alliance had the strength of numbers to do so, why did they not take over the weak Democratic party in those states and make it their instrument, as they were doing in the South?

James C. Olson, speaking of Nebraska, has offered four reasons: "The Democrats were still the party of rebellion; they were dominated by Catholics and opposed to prohibition, which many of the Protestant farmers favored; the intransigent conservatism of their leaders made cooperation with the Democratic party seem impossible."[48] Olson's first three points (which add up to "rum, Romanism, and rebellion," in reverse order) are no doubt accurate in their description of the Democratic image in the whole region. Alliancemen in the Northwest were overwhelmingly Republican by background; they could join an organization that asked them to disregard their previous party affiliation and vote their economic interest if that meant a new party of their own or even fusion arrangements with the Democrats. But to cross the threshold to actual affiliation with the party they had been rejecting at every election for thirty years was quite another thing. Whenever fusion relations with the Democrats became too intimate, the Republicans in the farmers' movement began drifting back to the GOP.

Olson's final point—the conservatism of Democratic leadership—is surely of general applicability also. In every state the party had its share of corporation lawyers, bankers, and railroad executives among its leaders; the corporations and their lobbyists were accustomed to working both sides of the political street. At the national level the domination of the Democratic party by men close to the monopolies and the "money power" was even more pronounced. Each of the first seven postwar Democratic conventions— from 1868 to 1892—turned to the East for its presidential candidate. Six of its candidates came from New York, the citadel of the new capitalism, where the Democratic party had consistently vied with the Republicans in demonstrating economic "soundness" to the bankers, industrialists, and political contributors of downtown Manhattan. Among its leaders were not only the Tildens and the Clevelands (corporation lawyers both), but also men like August Belmont, the long-time national chairman who was the

48. Ibid., p. 227.

New York representative of the Rothschilds; Senator Arthur P. Gorman of Maryland, Democratic floor leader, who was the partner of the Republican Senate leader, Nelson W. Aldrich of Rhode Island, in business ventures; Senator Henry B. Payne of Ohio, former railroad president whose son was treasurer of Standard Oil; and railroad magnate James J. Hill. These men had no trouble working with the patronage-oriented machine politicians who formed another major element of the party. Small wonder that currency expansion had been blocked and the Interstate Commerce Act stalled for a decade and so weakened by railroad influence by the time it passed that it was of dubious effectiveness. To a Mary Elizabeth Lease or a group like the Nebraska Farmers' Alliance, which called for a "war on capital,"[49] the Democratic party could only seem a useless vehicle.

So the agrarian reformers dreamed instead of a party of their own that they would not have to share with anyone who lacked their own moral intensity, that would be ideologically pristine, that would faithfully reflect their views and interests free of the corrupting influence of professional politicians or the "money power" and free of the taint of rum, Romanism, or rebellion. When the crusade of 1890 drew to its successful close, they thought that perhaps such a party had been born.

Democratic Radicalism in the South

The Democratic party in the South, by contrast, was the party of regional pride and patriotism, the party that had "redeemed" the South from Republican–carpetbagger–Negro rule. "Independentism" carried a stigma there, for anything that would divide Democratic voters might enable the blacks and the Republicans to play the factions against each other and regain control. So the agrarian protest movement in the South took a different political course from that of its western counterpart. Its object was capture of the dominant Democratic party.

The agrarian revolt centered in the Farmers' Alliance crested in the South in 1890 too, and its victories there were even more spectacular than those in the West. Benjamin R. Tillman, a farmer, overthrew the Democratic establishment to win the governorship of South Carolina. The president of the Tennessee Alliance, John P. Buchanan, was elected governor of that state. James S. Hogg was chosen governor of Texas with Alliance endorsement

49. Olson, *History of Nebraska*, p. 226.

on a platform promising railroad regulation. The Alliance claimed a majority of the Florida legislature and most of the Alabama assemblymen. It won strong representation in the constitutional conventions elected in Mississippi and Kentucky. [50] Countless other non-Alliance politicans survived only by accepting the organization's platform; in all, more than fifty congressmen were so pledged.[51] In Georgia, said the Atlanta *Constitution*, "the Farmers' Alliance *is* the Democratic party."[52] It "controlled the state convention, chose the governor, wrote the platform, named three-fourths of the senators and four-fifths of the representatives."[53] Six Bourbon congressmen were replaced by Alliancemen.[54] Only in Arkansas had the Alliance taken the third-party route, casting its lot there with the Union Labor party.

Nevertheless, a large proportion of the southern radicals formed a political bloc as truly polar as that of their kindred spirits in the West. They were in politics not for patronage but to advance a cause. Their interest was not to preserve the Democratic party as an institution but to use it. If it was not useful for their purposes, they would scrap it willingly in favor of something more effective. Western radicals had learned through experience that their region's majority party—in which they could do no better, over the long run, than share power with their enemies—was an uncertain vessel to entrust with the farmers' hopes. Once the southern radicals, through a corresponding experience, had learned the same lesson, the polar forces would be able to merge in a national oragnization and pursue a common strategy.

50. C. Vann Woodward, *Origins of the New South, 1877–1913* (Louisiana State University Press, 1951), p. 203.
51. Ibid., p. 235. Hicks puts the figure at "perhaps as many as forty-four" (*Populist Revolt*, p. 178).
52. July 4, 1890; quoted by Alex M. Arnett, *The Populist Movement in Georgia: A View of the "Agrarian Crusade" in the Light of Solid-South Politics* (Columbia University Press, 1922), p. 107.
53. Ibid., p. 116.
54. Hicks, *Populist Revolt*, p. 176.

CHAPTER SEVEN

The Realignment of the 1890s

THE PRAIRIE FIRE that swept the frontier states in 1890 was bound to move eastward. As third-party politicians began their quadrennial efforts to organize for the presidential election two years away, they had a solid regional foundation to build on—by far the strongest political base any off-year election had had since the Civil War. The western victories energized and inspired reformers everywhere. The men and women who had been catapulted into national prominence by these victories found themselves in the vanguard of national third-party politics. And they assumed that role with missionary zeal.

Creation of the People's Party

To the West, the lesson was obvious: convert the whole Farmers' Alliance into a People's party, as had been successfully done in Kansas. The annual meeting of the Southern Alliance was scheduled for December 1890 in Ocala, Florida, and exultant Kansas Alliancemen entrained for Ocala determined to lead their southern brethren down the road they had followed. The delegates from Cowley County brought with them the draft of a call for a national convention to be held in Cincinnati in February 1891.[1]

At Ocala they met powerful resistance from southern Alliancemen who were fresh from their own series of victories, all within the Democratic party. The South's successful Alliancemen were now the proprietors (or co-proprietors at least) of the majority party's machinery and had little interest in third-party adventures. But eventually they accepted compromise with the firebrand Kansans. Let a committee join with similar committees from other

1. Elizabeth N. Barr, "The Populist Uprising," in William E. Connelley (ed.), *History of Kansas* (American Historical Society, 1928), Vol. 2, p. 1174.

farm groups and from the Knights of Labor to call a great conference of producer groups in February 1892, with delegates to be newly chosen by the members. If the conference concluded that a third party was necessary, one could then be formed. This compromise the Ocala meeting adopted. The Kansans went ahead with their call for a national convention in 1891 (in May rather than February), but while this convention created a People's party, with a chairman and national executive committee, it deferred all plans for nominations and campaigns until after the conference scheduled for February 1892.

In the meantime, southern Alliancemen were coming to appreciate the problems of trying to pursue a radical course through a party that spanned the whole spectrum of economic views. In Texas, Governor James S. Hogg and the legislature created the state railway commission, as promised, but the governor and the Alliance promptly fell out when he refused to appoint to the commission the Alliance nominee.[2] In Georgia, the Alliance-dominated legislature elected to the U.S. Senate not someone identified with the Alliance but a Bourbon former governor, former senator, and railroad promoter, General John B. Gordon (who, however, had uttered the necessary words about the "great, growing, grasping Money Power"), and enacted a legislative program that seemed to the more radical Alliancemen "merely a weak compromise on the major issues."[3] Governor Benjamin R. Tillman of South Carolina "recommended only moderate changes once in power," failed to achieve some of these, and rejected the idea of political alliance with the West; in 1891 the state Alliance formally and unanimously repudiated him.[4] The Democratic legislatures of Virginia and Kentucky failed to enact the railroad regulation promised by the party leaders. Governor John P. Buchanan of Tennessee provided no sharp break with the conservatism of his Democratic predecessors.[5] And on the national scene, the Alliance discovered that its control over the forty or fifty Alliance-pledged or -supported congressmen was just as tenuous. Few Democratic congressmen appeared to take the Alliance platform seriously.

2. Roscoe C. Martin, *The People's Party in Texas: A Study in Third Party Politics* (University of Texas, Bulletin No. 3308, Feb. 22, 1933), pp. 26–27; C. Vann Woodward, *Origins of the New South, 1877–1913* (Louisiana State University Press, 1951), pp. 238–39.

3. Alex M. Arnett, *The Populist Movement in Georgia: A View of the "Agrarian Crusade" in the Light of Solid-South Politics* (Columbia University Press, 1922), pp. 120–22.

4. Woodward, *Origins of the New South*, pp. 237–38; Francis B. Simkins, *The Tillman Movement in South Carolina* (Duke University Press, 1926), pp. 149–57.

5. Woodward, *Origins of the New South*, p. 237.

As for the national Democratic party, it appeared to have taken no cognizance at all of the farmers' revolt. As the 1892 convention approached, it was clear that the front runner was Grover Cleveland and his principal challenger was another New Yorker, Governor David B. Hill, a machine politician ardently supported by Tammany Hall. While some southerners thought Hill might be acceptable on the silver issue, he had little appeal to Alliance radicals. Cleveland had none at all. Colonel L. L. Polk of North Carolina, the Alliance president, called Cleveland "a true and consistent friend of the money power" and branded him unacceptable to the Alliance.[6]

By the time of the February 1892 conference in St. Louis, then, the die was cast. Enough southern Alliancemen had been won over to third-party action—among them Colonel Polk, who had presidential ambitions himself —to ensure that the most powerful of protest organizations, with a membership estimated at about three million, would be officially committed to the cause. Those present at St. Louis, including the executive committee of the People's party formed the previous year, called a nominating convention for July. Just before the convention, Colonel Polk died, and the new party turned to the Greenback presidential candidate of 1880, General James B. Weaver of Iowa, as its nominee. The platform included all the familiar agrarian demands—free silver, currency expansion by the government through the subtreasury plan[7] "or a better system," a graduated income tax, government ownership of railroads, telegraph, and telephone systems, forfeiture of undeveloped railroad land grants, direct election of senators—plus some planks on labor issues, including restriction of "undesirable immigration." The tariff question was called "a sham battle" between the old parties and otherwise not mentioned.[8]

6. Ibid., p. 242.
7. Under the plan, government warehouses would accept and store the farmer's produce and issue money to him based on its value.
8. "The tariff was a capitalistic device which the western farmers seem to have regarded with a surprising degree of indifference," wrote Hallie Farmer in "The Economic Background of Frontier Populism," *Mississippi Valley Historical Review*, Vol. 10 (March 1924), pp. 425–26. "In so far as the farmers of the states under discussion thought about the tariff they were probably opposed to protection, but it is hard to know what they really thought for they said little about the subject. The problems of low prices, railroad rates, and expansion of the currency were the subjects in which they were interested and upon which they expressed themselves."

"Some papers wonder why the western farmer does not kick on the tariff," wrote the editor of the Kansas City (Kansas) *Gazette* in 1889. It is because "the few cents more he may have to pay for an article does not affect the question of what he ought to get and does get for what he produces." Quoted by the Atchison *Champion*, Dec. 26, 1889.

"While our two great parties split hairs on the tariff, people starve," a Populist organizer says in a Hamlin Garland story. "The time has come for rebellion." From "A Spoil of Office," *The Arena*, Vol. 6 (June 1892), p. 118.

In polling over a million popular votes (more than 8 percent of the total cast in 1892), the People's party won a plurality in five states—Kansas, North Dakota, Colorado, Idaho, and Nevada. Their electoral votes were the first won by a third party in thirty-two years.[9] The Populists supplanted the Democrats as the principal opposition to the Republicans in Nebraska (where they polled more than three times the Democratic vote), South Dakota (almost three times), and Oregon (almost double). A Populist-Democratic fusion state ticket carried Wyoming. In the South the new party finished second to the Democrats in Texas, Mississippi, and Alabama, and made respectable showings in Georgia and North Carolina, even though, in Vann Woodward's language, "changing one's party in the South of the nineties. . . . might involve a falling-off of clients, the loss of a job, of credit at the store, or of one's welcome at church. . . . could split families, and . . . might even call in question one's loyalty to his race and his people."[10] The Populist candidate for governor of Alabama was probably elected but deprived of the office by a dishonest count of the ballots, and elsewhere in the South Democratic victories were won only by fraud and intimidation.[11] Populist strength in the new Congress was three senators and eleven House members, all from the Northwest. Populist governors were elected in Kansas, Colorado, and North Dakota.

The People's party was still almost wholly a regional movement; General Weaver's campaign was scarcely organized at all in most northern states east of the Mississippi River. But clearly it had gained a momentum that the major parties could no longer ignore.

Polarization of the Democratic Party

William Jennings Bryan defined the Democrats' dilemma:

To-day the Democratic party stands between two great forces, each inviting its support. On the one side stand the corporate interests of the nation, its moneyed institutions, its aggregations of wealth and capital, imperious, arrogant, compassionless. They demand special legislation, favors, privileges, and immunities. They can subscribe magnificently to campaign funds; they can strike down opposition with their all-pervading influence, and, to those who fawn and flatter, bring

9. In Kansas, the Democrats fused with the Populists in support of Weaver. In North Dakota, Democrats endorsed the Populist ticket but the electoral votes were divided. In addition, Weaver received one electoral vote from an Oregon Populist nominated also by the Democrats. The total electoral vote for the People's candidates was 22 out of 444.

10. *Origins of the New South*, p. 244.

11. Ibid., pp. 259–62; John D. Hicks, *The Populist Revolt: A History of the Farmers' Alliance and the People's Party* (University of Minnesota Press, 1931), pp. 250–54.

ease and plenty. They demand that the Democratic party become their agent to execute their merciless decrees.

On the other side stands that unnumbered throng which gave a name to the Democratic party and for which it has assumed to speak. Work-worn and dust-begrimed, they make their sad appeal. . . .

This army, vast and daily vaster growing, begs the party to be its champion in the present conflict.[12]

The young congressman described a country that had polarized. From the Pacific Coast to the Plains and across the South to the Atlantic, the "work-worn and dust-begrimed" had risen in bitterness against the economic order. Something was wrong with the system, it seemed obvious to them. "There's no money in the country," Hamlin Garland's father told him in 1889. "I can't get money enough to pay my taxes. Look at my clothes! I haven't had a new suit in three years. Your mother is in the same fix. I wanted to bring her down [to St. Louis], but she had no clothes to wear." Garland joined the Populist crusade. "He had come a long way," he wrote of his father, "from the buoyant faith of '66, and the change in him was typical of the change in the west—in America—and it produced in me a sense of dismay, of rebellious bitterness. Why should our great new land fall into this slough of discouragement? . . . Why should children cry for food in our cities whilst fruits rotted on the vines and wheat had no value to the harvester?"[13]

THE EAST AGAINST THE WEST

Not until 1893 did anyone have an accurate measure of what was happening to the farmers. In that year a Senate committee published the first historical series of price indexes, and they confirmed what the farmers and all who dealt in commodities knew—that prices had declined steadily, almost without interruption, since the Civil War. This is shown in Figure 7-1.

One commodity, of course, rose in value as much as other commodities declined. This was the commodity in which the value of all others was measured—gold. Even silver, which had once served with gold as a monetary standard, fell rapidly in price, to the distress of the silver-mining states of the West. Farmers did not have to be experts on the quantity theory of money to understand that the value of money too was governed by the law of supply and demand—a greater supply of money would depress its value and correspondingly raise the price of every good and service. To them, it

12. *Congressional Record*, 53 Cong. 1 sess. (Aug. 16, 1893), pp. 410–11.
13. Hamlin Garland, *A Son of the Middle Border* (first published, 1917; Macmillan, 1962), pp. 360–62.

Figure 7-1. *Long-term Price Decline after the Civil War*

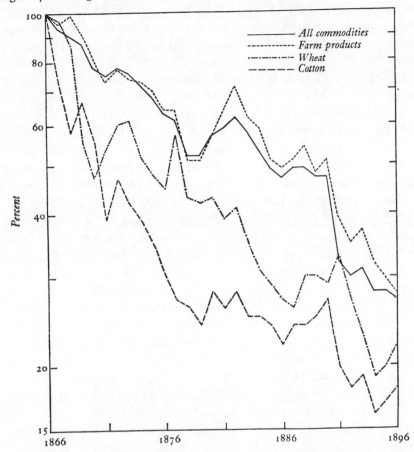

Sources: U.S. Bureau of the Census, *Historical Statistics of the United States: Colonial Times to 1957* (1960). Wholesale price index data from Series E1–12, p. 115, and E13–24, p. 117, converted to 1890 base index. Wheat index computed from prices per bushel in Series E101–112, pp. 123–24 (New York price to 1880, Chicago price thereafter). The series covers three different varieties of wheat, one to 1880, one from 1880 to 1890, a third from 1890 to 1896. The 1891–95 index is reduced by two points based on the price differential between the two varieties in 1890. Cotton index computed from prices per pound in Series E101–112, pp. 123–24.

The weaknesses of the data, particularly for the earlier years, are discussed in the introduction to the series.

In all indexes, 1866 = 100.

was clear that the government, which controlled the money supply, had not increased that supply to keep pace with the volume of business; otherwise, why would prices have declined for three long decades? The monetary policies of both parties had been determined by the East, administered by secretaries of the treasury who listened not to the nation's debtors but to the New York bankers, and heavily influenced by campaign contributors whose offices were in downtown Manhattan. "We feel," said Populist senator William V. Allen of Nebraska, speaking for the West, "that, through the operation of a shrinking volume of money, which has been caused by Eastern votes and influences for purely selfish purposes, the East has placed its hands on the throat of the West and refused to afford us that measure of justice which we, as citizens of a common country, are entitled to receive."[14]

But the East saw the issue in a wholly different light. The value of gold *did* have to be defended at all costs, for the very reason that it *was* the monetary standard. If the price of a particular commodity—say, wheat—declined, or if people lost confidence in the future of the wheat market, then according to classic economic theory they would shift their investment to something else in greater demand, the economy as a whole would benefit from the shift, and wheat itself would benefit as prices rose again. But if people lost confidence in the value of gold because of any sustained decline, the whole system would collapse. Gold would be hoarded, foreign creditors would demand gold payments, the reserves of the banks and of the U.S. Treasury itself would be depleted, and panic would ensue. What had happened to the price of farm commodities (which was only dimly understood in the East anyway) could be dismissed as one of the normal vicissitudes of the free enterprise system. But under no circumstances could anything comparable be permitted to happen to the value of gold.

As had been the case ever since the Civil War, the currency argument transcended economics and became one of honor, of national integrity, of public morals. Free silver was condemned in terms of ethical symbolism— "repudiation," "dishonor," "debasement." "I would plant high up on our altars, so that all mankind could read it, the inscription that we cherish our honor as much as our liberty," declaimed Representative Isidor Rayner, Baltimore Democrat, in opening the silver debate of 1893, "and that we would sooner fall and perish than dishonor any of the obligations upon which we have imprinted or emblazoned the emblem of the Republic."[15] Profes-

14. William V. Allen, "Western Feeling Toward the East," *North American Review*, Vol. 162 (May 1896), p. 590.

15. *Congressional Record*, 53 Cong. 1 sess. (Aug. 11, 1893), p. 247.

sional defenders of the public morals—the clergy, the press, the Mugwump political reformers—took up the cause, as they had done in earlier currency debates; currency inflation was equated with the grosser forms of political corruption, like graft in public contracts, the open buying of votes, and the patronage system. The Populist frenzy was painted as a Jacobin uprising against the very foundations of society, based on an ignorance of economic principles, embodying an immoral disregard for the rights of property, and led by demagogues.

THE REPUBLICAN "DOUGHFACES"

When the country was aroused a generation earlier on another great emotional issue, it had been the role of the national leaders of both parties—Clay and Webster, Cass and Pierce and Buchanan and Douglas—to seek lines of compromise that would forestall polarization within the two parties and so preserve them as mediating influences in the national conflict. Webster was reviled in Boston, and the Democratic "doughfaces" have been disparaged by later generations as men deficient in moral sensitivity, but their compromises did preserve the Union, for a time, at a cost few then thought too high. In the late 1880s and early 1890s, the Republicans showed a touch of the same genius for finding the middle course that might satisfy both sides. They had their own equivalent of the doughfaces—"western men with eastern principles," as they have inevitably been called, like Senators John Sherman of Ohio, William B. Allison of Iowa, and Shelby M. Cullom of Illinois, and President Benjamin Harrison (of Indiana). Cullom piloted through the Senate the Interstate Commerce Act, after making sure that its provisions would not affect the railroads too adversely. In 1890 Sherman initiated what became the nation's first antitrust law, although it was greatly weakened in the course of passage. And in the same year the Republicans accepted a compromise silver purchase measure, which also bore Sherman's name, increasing monthly purchases from $2 million worth of silver to 4.5 million ounces (roughly the equivalent of total U.S. production).

The silver purchase measure had dual tactical objectives. The first was to head off a free coinage measure that appeared likely to pass both houses with the support of western Republicans. The second was to win western Republican support for the protectionist tariff bill that was the party's top legislative objective. One scholar has described the goal of Republican leaders in the Senate (referring to the antitrust act as well as the silver measure) as one of "gaining, with the fewest possible concessions to agrarian demands, the acceptance in the mid-West of a party program whose basic features reflected the dominant influence of an essentially Eastern industrialism."[16] Even those concessions were distasteful to men of principle. "I voted for it," said John Sherman of his Silver Purchase Act, "but the day it became law I was ready to repeal it, if repeal could be had without substituting in its place absolutely free coinage."[17] Nevertheless, through the processes of compromise the purpose of holding the party together in the enactment of a party program was achieved.

That the program itself turned out to be a political disaster is another matter. The reaction against the McKinley tariff act was so severe that it contributed mightily to the Democratic, or Democratic-Populist, landslide in the 1890 congressional elections that reduced the Republicans to barely 25 percent of the membership of the House. At the same time, the concessions contained in the Silver Purchase Act did not suit the polarized mood of the time. While not satisfying the South and West, they were too much for many of the Republicans' usual supporters in the business and financial world of the East. The kingmakers of Manhattan began to look to Grover Cleveland as an alternative to Harrison in 1892, a man who would be solid as a rock where Harrison had wavered. As the convention approached, "the great banking interests" of New York and "a large part of Wall Street" were in Cleveland's corner, and his campaign manager was William C. Whitney, long recognized as "a representative of corporate finance in politics."[18]

GROVER CLEVELAND: A STUDY IN RIGIDITY

Cleveland had established his reliability on the money question in his first term, when he defied the majority of his party. The party, however, had grown steadily less reliable; and during Harrison's administration, free from Cleveland's restraining hand, it went all the way. Under party discipline and bent on embarrassing the Republican administration, Democrats in Congress voted almost unanimously for free silver in 1890 and early 1891. State Democratic conventions throughout the South and from Ohio west-

16. Clarence Ames Stern, "Leadership and Formation of Policy within the Republican Party, 1889–1901" (Ph.D. dissertation, University of Nebraska, 1959), p. xxiv.

17. John Sherman, *Recollections of Forty Years in the House, Senate and Cabinet* (Werner, 1895), p. 830.

18. Allan Nevins, *Grover Cleveland: A Study in Courage* (Dodd, Mead, 1933), pp. 481, 195.

ward endorsed free silver in 1890. But that did not deter Cleveland, as he looked, from his Manhattan vantage point, toward the next presidential contest. "I am supposed to be a leader in my party," he told those who counseled compromise. "If any word of mine can check these dangerous fallacies, it is my duty to give that word, whatever the cost may be to me."[19] In February 1891 he took his public stand, in a letter to the Reform Club of New York, against "the dangerous and reckless experiment" of free silver.

Cleveland was at times quite capable of compromise, as his detractors have emphasized. But he was neither agile nor happy as a political maneuverer. His political and intellectual base was in the moral reform movement of the Mugwumps and the early progressives, and he was never happier than when he took an unflinching stand on some issue of public morals. "A weight has been lifted and a cloud removed," he wrote to a friend after he had made his public declaration against free silver.[20] "One of the most dramatic and fearless acts of Cleveland's career" was the judgment of Allan Nevins, who subtitled his biography of Cleveland *A Study in Courage*.[21] Yet Cleveland's moral stands had never proved politically disadvantageous. Quite the contrary. They had propelled him in three short years from anonymity to the presidency, and made him, even after his defeat for reelection, still his party's leading prospect for that office. When he told his friends he was against free silver "whatever the cost may be to me," he must have at least suspected that the cost of losing his image as an uncompromising reformer would have been far greater. Such a political professional as Senator William F. Vilas of Wisconsin called the Cleveland letter "*great, big, sound, wise politics*." And Democratic Governor William E. Russell of Massachusetts advocated what today would be called an "eastern strategy": to deliberately abandon the West in exchange for the support of the eastern Mugwump reformers.[22] In many respects, it would have taken more personal courage for Cleveland to defy his social, professional, and political associates in the Wall Street circle than to challenge the distant West.

In any event, Cleveland chose to become a polarizing force himself. Instead of trying to reconcile the polar forces in his party, as a Clay or a Sherman would have, he placed himself at the head of one of them. The congressional free-silver leaders, among them Bryan and Richard P. (Silver Dick)

19. Ibid., p. 467.
20. Ibid., p. 468.
21. Ibid., p. 466.
22. Ibid., p. 469.

Bland of Missouri, commanded the other. The moderate centrists, deserted by the White House, could not hold.

The variable of leadership seems singularly important in the realignment of the 1890s. To be sure, Cleveland was at once a cause and a result. The country was headed for a showdown; the polar groups were rapidly gaining strength, and they were bound to have their leaders. Those at the hard-money pole would have accepted as their leader only a man committed to defend the gold standard at any cost, as Benjamin Harrison learned. Cleveland himself was not their man until he made his stand on silver clear beyond all doubt. Yet in the exigencies of politics they might have failed to find a leader with the political standing and skill to win the nomination, and a more moderate politician like New York's Hill (now a senator) might have been the Democratic choice. As president, either Hill or Harrison would presumably at least have tried to check the polarization of the country instead of— as Cleveland did—accelerating it. And in this case, a delayed realignment might have been an averted one, for (as will be noted later) the money issue was to fade within a few years for reasons quite independent of governmental action.

Within the Democratic party, the practical politicians who occupied the party's center made one last try at compromise. If they could not persuade Cleveland to take a middle course, at least they could give him a platform that did. The platform of 1892 was specific in its endorsement of bimetalism —"the use of both gold and silver as the standard money of the country"— but this stopped far short of the free-silver policy that the Democratic party in the Congress had supported almost unanimously only a few months earlier. Indeed, it promised nothing more than had been provided by the Silver Purchase Act of 1890 and the Bland-Allison Act of 1878. Yet it clearly ruled out the abandonment of silver altogether and the return to gold as a single standard.

Cleveland's high sense of morality did not extend to the sanctity of party platforms—not, at least, in the circumstances of 1893. Toward the end of 1892 the dire predictions that had been uttered by the conservatives ever since passage of the Sherman Silver Purchase Act seemed to be coming true. Gold had been flowing out of the country, and the $100 million Treasury reserve that had been considered the minimum safe level was being sustained only by an emergency loan from New York bankers. A run on gold seemed a real possibility. The stock market was uneasy. Cleveland assembled his cabinet designees to hear railroad magnate Henry Villard argue for an immediate special session of Congress to repeal the Silver Purchase Act.[23] On February 26, 1893, came the first of a series of spectacular business failures, that of the Reading Railroad. While this could be blamed on mismanagement, others followed. In April the Treasury's gold reserve fell below $100 million. In May came the failure of the National Cordage Company. The stock market collapsed, and panic ensued. As factories and mines shut down, as creditors demanded gold and banks closed their doors, Cleveland took his stand as upholder of the gold standard. He called the Congress into session to reverse "a financial policy . . . embodied in unwise laws." From that time forward, the President was the leader of only a segment of his party.

To Cleveland it was palpable that the Sherman act was at the bottom of the nation's difficulty, but that was by no means clear to the agrarians of the West and South. Hard times for them had long antedated the panic. They had been victimized for years by the "money power," as they saw it, and that money power was now using the business crisis to demand further contraction of the currency and thus further penalize the agricultural regions. It is not necessary, in a study of party realignment, to decide which side of a dispute is right. Political movements flow from the *perceptions* that people hold, whether accurate or not. Yet the irreconcilability of the conflict of the 1890s may well have been because, under the monetary system of the time, both sides saw the facts quite accurately. The East may have been right in its contention that the gold dollar must be protected at all costs, for the whole structure of investment and employment rested on the intangible called "confidence," and confidence was heightened by any rise in the value of the gold dollar but quickly eroded by any significant, sustained loss or, as in 1893, any threat that the gold dollar might be replaced by one of lesser value. But the West and South were surely just as correct in their view that any system dependent on a steadily rising gold value tilted the scales in favor of the creditor against the debtor. Under these circumstances, neither side could yield. The economic conflict was as "irrepressible" as the moral conflict a generation earlier.

From the agrarian point of view, a demand by New York bankers that their confidence be restored by currency contraction was the equivalent of blackmail. Cleveland, far from a leader of courage, was seen as a weakling or a tool. The beneficiaries of the monetary system—not only Wall Street but Lombard Street as well—set the terms under which they would resume

---

23. Ibid., p. 524.

investment and employment, and the government of the United States was compelled to accept, as Bryan put it, "their merciless decrees."[24]

During 1893, one-sixth of the nation's railroads, more than six hundred banks and other financial institutions, and some thirty-two iron and steel companies failed.[25] But by August, when Congress met, the worst seemed over. The economy, though not yet recovering, appeared to have struck bottom. The gold outflow had been reversed, bank reserves were rising, and some of the plants that had closed were resuming operation. The revival of confidence might be attributed to the assurance that a majority in the Congress was ready to support Cleveland, but in any case the congressional debate did not take place in an atmosphere of panic. The agrarians tried to focus the discussion on the long-term, fundamental grievances of their regions rather than on the immediate crisis, and to a large extent they succeeded.

"HE WILL DESTROY HIS PARTY . . ."

To a surprising degree, for those who view party platforms cynically, the debate centered on the Democratic silver plank of 1892. The silverites invoked it constantly, interpreted it specifically, and stressed its binding character. "Does anyone believe that Mr. Cleveland could have been elected president upon a platform declaring in favor of the unconditional repeal of the Sherman law?" asked Bryan.[26] Administration supporters stressed the platform's ambiguities, particularly its reference to the need for international agreement to establish silver as a monetary standard. Or they just dismissed it: "I am not in the slightest degree disturbed or intimidated by the glittering catchwords of political conventions. I am guided by a purer and a higher faith," said Isidor Rayner in the opening speech of the silver debate,

24. For a dispassionate analysis of the economic aspects of the panic of 1893, see Rendigs Fels, *American Business Cycles—1865–1897* (University of North Carolina Press, 1959), pp. 183–88. He blames the beginning of the depression on a decline in exports caused by business contraction abroad and a return to normal crop yields from earlier exceptional harvests. The subsequent business failures and ensuing panic he attributes to the underlying business situation and the weak banking structure as well as to the silver law. The threat to the gold standard implicit in that law brought about a money stringency that resulted in a sharper, deeper contraction than would otherwise have been the case, Fels concludes, but even if there had been no silver problem the other factors operative at the time might have been sufficient to produce a panic and severe depression.

25. Ibid., p. 187.

26. *Congressional Record*, 53 Cong. 1 sess. (Aug. 16, 1893), p. 410.

in words reminiscent of Seward's "higher law."[27] But the westerners too could put principle above party. Like Silver Dick Bland, who had practiced law in the silver state of Nevada before entering Missouri politics:

> Speaking as a Democrat . . . I am yet an American above Democracy. I do not intend, we do not intend, that any party shall survive, if we can help it, that will lay the confiscating hand upon Americans in the interest of England or of Europe. Now, mark it. This may be strong language, but heed it. The people mean it, and my friends of Eastern Democracy, we bid farewell when you do that thing. . . . You may pass your bill and do these things; but if you do we are going to cut loose from you.[28]

On the left, the People's party beckoned—a magnet, a weapon against the East, a potential refuge. Its existence and growing strength encouraged men like Bland to talk, almost literally, of rule or ruin.

The vote on the repeal of the Sherman Silver Purchase Act once more laid bare the chasm that divided Democrats. Through the ruthless use of patronage,[29] Cleveland was able to whip back into line most of the Democrats from the East and the older industrializing midwestern states who had swung over to free silver, but he lost a majority of his party from the newer western states and from the South (see Table 7-1). He had a chance to compromise the issue when, during the Senate filibuster, 37 of the 44 Democratic senators sent him a letter proposing that the silver purchases be continued through June 1894 and that the Treasury's seigniorage on silver coined up to that time, amounting to $55 million, also be minted into coin. That sagacious old compromiser, John Sherman, who supported the proposal, predicted that if Cleveland did not accept it, "he will destroy his party, and his administration will be broken down."[30] But the President was more alert to political pressures from the other side. If he failed to support unconditional repeal of the Silver Purchase Act, he wrote, "there is a great danger of our friends the enemy gaining more credit with the country than we."[31] Caught in the middle between Populists and Republicans, he would try to seize the latter's ground. So whether he rationalized his political judgment to match his principles or vice versa, they coincided. Characteristically, he "smote the table with his fist and declared that he would not yield an inch."[32] This stand and

27. Ibid. (Aug. 11, 1893), p. 247.
28. Ibid., p. 252.
29. Nevins, *Grover Cleveland*, pp. 541–43; James Ford Rhodes, *History of the United States, from Hayes to McKinley 1877–1896* (Macmillan, 1919), pp. 403, 412–13.
30. Cited by Horace S. Merrill, *Bourbon Leader: Grover Cleveland and the Democratic Party* (Little, Brown, 1957), p. 180.
31. Communication to Senator William F. Vilas, cited in ibid., p. 181.
32. Nevins, *Grover Cleveland*, p. 546.

Table 7-1. *Congressional Votes in 1893 on Repeal of the Silver Purchase Act, by Region and Party*

Region[a]	Democrats			Republicans			Independents and Populists			Totals		
	Yea	Nay	Not voting	Yea	Nay	Not voting	Yea	Nay	Not voting	Yea	Nay	Not voting
House of Representatives, August 28												
East	52	1	2	53	0	0	0	0	0	105	1	2
Old Northwest	39	4	0	28	5	1	0	0	0	67	9	1
Trans-Mississippi West	6	17	0	18	17	0	0	10	0	24	44	0
South	40	51	3	3	3	0	0	0	0	43	54	3
Total	137	73	5	102	25	1	0	10	0	239	108	6
Senate, October 30												
East	8	0	0	15	1	0	0	0	0	23	1	0
Old Northwest	6	0	0	4	0	0	0	0	0	10	0	0
Trans-Mississippi West	0	5	0	6	11	2	0	3	0	6	19	2
South	7	16	1	0	0	0	0	0	0	7	16	1
Total	21	21	1	25	12	2	0	3	0	46	36	3

Source: *Congressional Record*, 53 Cong. 1 sess., pp. 1008, 2958. Seven absent senators whose positions were announced are tabulated as voting.

a. The East includes Delaware, Maryland, West Virginia; the Old Northwest includes Ohio, Indiana, Illinois, Michigan, Wisconsin; the Trans-Mississippi West includes Missouri.

the favorable public response to it broke the filibuster. But when repeal came to a vote in the Senate, the regional split within the Democratic party was even sharper than in the earlier House tally.

During the ensuing months, Sherman's prediction came true as event after event served to heighten class and sectional antagonisms and further polarize the country—and the Democrats. The Democratic party, broken by the silver issue, was reduced to wreckage by the tariff. A protectionist Democratic bloc in Congress deserted the party platform and Cleveland charged them with "party perfidy and party dishonor." The President once more infuriated the agrarians when he vetoed a bill to add the seigniorage to the money supply. And in 1894 he outraged organized labor and its sympathizers by using troops and federal court injunctions to break the Pullman strike and jail its leaders, including Eugene V. Debs.[33]

33. Attorney General Richard Olney, himself a railroad lawyer and executive before assuming his office, declared his objective to be to "make it [the strike] a failure everywhere"; he appointed as special U.S. attorney in Chicago the general counsel of the rail-

Repeal of the Silver Purchase Act, it turned out, not only failed to revive the economy, but did not even halt the slide. The depression wore on into the summer of 1894, intensified by the coal and railroad strikes, and as the Democratic party degenerated into a leaderless shambles, the voters turned en masse to the Republicans in the fall elections. A House of Representatives that had been 62 percent Democratic became 69 percent Republican, a net gain for the Republicans of 117 seats, or about one-third of the total membership. The Democrats were reduced to a mere dozen seats from the entire North and West, half of them from New York City. The Populists only held their own in the Congress, with four senators and eight representatives (exclusive of Populist-supported fusionists), but their total vote rose to about 1,500,000 from the 1,030,000 cast for General Weaver in the presidential election two years before.[34] Hopeful Populists had reason to forecast that the Democratic party, caught in the middle as the country polarized, would be pulled apart—just as the Whigs had been split by another polarization forty years before—and the country would be left with two parties, Populists and Republicans, representing the two extremes.

Silver Democrats Capture the Party

The silver Democrats, of course, saw the situation differently. All the Democratic party had to do to win over the Populists and again become the dominant party was to wrest control from Cleveland and his coterie of New York bankers and corporation lawyers. Bryan lost no time in casting down the gauntlet. In opposing a Cleveland banking bill, he told the House to the loud applause of his fellow silverites:

---

road General Managers' Association and together the government and the association devised the legal measures to crush the union. Harold U. Faulkner, *Politics, Reform and Expansion, 1890–1900* (Harper, 1959), pp. 174–76.

34. They lost their three governorships—Kansas, Colorado, and North Dakota—but elected a governor in Nebraska and a majority of the state senate in North Carolina, while the Silver party carried Nevada. In each of the states where governorships were lost, the Populist administration had been beset with difficulties, which are detailed in Hicks, *Populist Revolt*, Chap. 10. Without undivided control of the legislatures of their states, the Populists were in some cases blocked from enacting their radical measures; they were hamstrung also by an adverse judiciary; and some of the inexperienced party officials proved inept. "Generally speaking, the experiments with Populism in the West had done little to engender confidence in the ability of the new party to rule," observed the generally sympathetic Hicks. "Evidently their genius lay in protest rather than in performance." He added, however, that two years of divided control of state government was not a conclusive test (pp. 299–300).

We are sometimes asked why we are not willing to compromise. Our answer is that principles cannot be compromised. . . . Gentlemen plead for harmony, but there can be no harmony between those who adhere to the financial views of Mr. Cleveland and those who adhere to the financial views of Thomas Jefferson. . . .

It is useless to shut our eyes to the division in the Democratic party . . . but who is to blame? Did not the President ignore the silver Democrats in making up his Cabinet? Has he not ignored them in the distribution of patronage? Has he not refused to counsel with or consider those Democrats who stand by the traditions of the party? Did he not press through Congress with all the power at his command the unconditional repeal of the Sherman law, in spite of the earnest protests of nearly half the Democratic members of the two Houses? . . .

Did he not oppose the income tax, which a large majority of the Democratic party favored? Has he not in fact joined with the Democrats of the Northeast time and again to defeat the wishes of the Democrats of the South and West? We desire harmony, but we can not purchase it at a sacrifice of principle. . . . If the party is rent in twain let the responsibility rest upon the President and his followers. . . . Let the fight go on.[35]

The fight went on. Bryan, defeated for the Senate in the Republican sweep, embarked on a series of "lecture" tours of the South and West, financed by western mining interests. Bland, also defeated, went lecturing in the same areas. Those who sought to calm the crisis were without influence. "Such men as Arthur Pue Gorman, who had premised his career upon compromise, could find almost no one who cared to negotiate," Robert H. Wiebe has written. "As the Democratic party fell apart, Gorman and a few others hurried helplessly to and fro, frustrated, angry, and now obsolete in a time that could no longer use their skills."[36] And every event seemed designed to strengthen the silver wing of the party in its attacks on Cleveland and the "New York hegemony." Gold withdrawals continued despite the party-wrecking repeal of the Silver Purchase Act, and early in 1895, the President negotiated secretly on unfavorable terms a $65 million gold loan from a syndicate headed by J. P. Morgan and August Belmont, the Rothschild representative.[37] The silverites depicted the American government in all its majesty as being brought to heel by a little group of international "Shylocks." Then came a series of Supreme Court decisions favoring the corporations and the rich—one upholding labor injunctions in the Debs case, another dismissing an antitrust suit against the sugar trust (to the gratifica-

35. *Congressional Record*, 53 Cong. 3 sess. (Dec. 22, 1894), App., pp. 154–55. According to Nevins, Cleveland favored the income tax on principle but objected to attaching it to the tariff bill (*Grover Cleveland*, p. 667).

36. *The Search for Order 1877–1920* (Hill and Wang, 1967), p. 97.

37. Sold to the syndicate at 104½, the bonds were offered immediately at 112½, netting the bankers overnight a minimum profit of $5 million, were promptly oversubscribed, and rose quickly to 119. Even Nevins calls the Morgan-Rothschild demands "a hard bargain" (*Grover Cleveland*, p. 664).

tion of Attorney General Olney, who had branded the law "no good"), and a third declaring unconstitutional by a five to four decision the income tax that had been appended by the agrarians to the tariff act. And the silver movement was even given its *Uncle Tom's Cabin* in a tract called *Coin's Financial School*, by W. H. Harvey, which sold over a million copies and was widely reprinted in newspapers.

As 1896 approached, silver sentiment welled up in the rural sections of the South and West, and politicians both nourished the sentiment and capitalized on it. Everywhere but in the Northeast, Democratic conventions resolved for silver, and even New York could produce only a weak gold plank. It was clear that the silverites would write the national platform for the 1896 campaign; the only question was whether the gold bloc had enough strength to veto the choice of a candidate under the rule then in effect requiring a two-thirds vote to nominate.

That question was settled as soon as the convention met. The silver bloc carried almost two-thirds of the delegates in overturning the national committee's nomination of Senator Hill of New York as temporary chairman, and more than two-thirds in adopting a platform calling for free and unlimited coinage of silver. Most astonishing, a resolution commending the Democratic administration of Grover Cleveland was defeated, 564 to 357. When the time came for selecting a candidate, most of the gold Democrats abstained from voting, even though one of their number—former Governor Robert E. Pattison of Pennsylvania—had been nominated. Bryan, who had crystallized the defiant mood of the convention with his "Cross of Gold" speech, was chosen over Bland on the fifth ballot. The party split was on the regional lines foreshadowed through all the preceding years: on the platform, the gold Democrats had a solid bloc of states running from Maine to Maryland and Pennsylvania, but in the vast reaches of the country beyond they had only Michigan, Wisconsin, Minnesota, and South Dakota, and among these only the Wisconsin delegation had a majority that held out to the end against endorsing Bryan.[38]

If the silverites could put principle above party by repudiating Cleveland and the gold standard, the gold Democrats were men of principle too. Cleveland himself, just before the convention, had called the proposed free-silver plank "foolish and unpatriotic." The more ardent of his followers had made clear at the convention that they had no intention of putting patriotism aside

38. Richard C. Bain and Judith H. Parris, *Convention Decisions and Voting Records* (2d ed., Brookings Institution, 1973), pp. 154–56 and App. C.

and swallowing the insults heaped on Cleveland. The "Gold Bugs" immediately called their own convention and put into the field a ticket headed by seventy-eight-year-old Senator John M. Palmer of Illinois. The Cleveland administration, demoralized and disintegrating, threw its remaining prestige and what patronage forces it could muster behind Palmer, while other gold Democrats remained, as Senator Hill described himself, "Democrats still—very still."[39] But the silver Democrats were not alarmed. There were far more silver Republicans than gold Democrats, they believed; Governor John P. Altgeld of Illinois observed that half the Republicans of his state were silver Republicans. Realignment of the parties on the money issue would surely give the Democrats a clear and reliable national majority, for "the people" had the strength of numbers against "the interests."

The silver Democrats were encouraged by the schism that had occurred at the Republican convention three weeks earlier. When the GOP adopted the inevitable gold plank (tempered with a reference to bimetalism under international agreement), thirty-four delegates from the mountain states led by Senator Henry M. Teller of Colorado left the convention, and their party, amid shouts of "Go! Go!" Teller was one of the presidential contenders at the subsequent Democratic convention and received eight votes.

The Populists Are Absorbed

The Populists had seen the realignment coming and had divided, naturally, between those who were willing to be swallowed up in a Democratic party committed to silver and those who held out for a continued independent course. The latter had strong arguments on their side; silver, after all, was not their entire platform or even the most important element of it, and the southern Populists, in particular, saw fusion with the Democrats as leading straight to their own submergence and a return to Bourbonism in their re-

---

39. As an indication of the extent of Democratic defections in the East, Bryan failed to receive the support in Connecticut of the party's state chairman, its national committeeman, at least twelve of the twenty-four-man central committee, two former governors, and most former officeholders. Frederick Morrison Heath, "Politics and Steady Habits: Issues and Elections in Connecticut, 1894–1914" (Ph.D. dissertation, Columbia University, 1965), pp. 67–68. The party dwindled to not much more than its solid Catholic base. In Massachusetts, the Democratic nominee for governor refused to support Bryan and "almost every Democrat with a check book left the party that year," according to Michael E. Hennessy in *Four Decades of Massachusetts Politics, 1890–1935* (Norwood Press, 1935), p. 45.

gion. "If we fuse, we are sunk," wrote Henry Demarest Lloyd. "If we don't fuse, all the silver men we have will leave us for the more powerful Democrats."[40] But practical politicians like General Weaver, Senator William V. Allen of Nebraska, and National Chairman H. E. Taubeneck saw the prospects of an immediate great national victory through the merger of silver Democrats, silver Republicans, and Populists. Better to seize that opportunity than to continue down the long and tortuous third-party road to power.

When the Democratic convention adjourned, the Populists advocating fusion quickly gained the upper hand. Bryan was a Populist in all but name, and the Democratic platform had a Populist ring not only in its silver plank but throughout. It condemned "trafficking with banking syndicates," suggested reconstitution of the Supreme Court to reverse its income tax decision, urged stricter control over railroads to "protect the people from robbery and oppression" and over trusts to prevent the "absorption of wealth by the few," and denounced "government by injunction" as "a new and highly dangerous form of oppression." The Populists at their own convention went further, particularly in demanding government ownership of railroads and telegraph systems, but the two platforms were kindred in spirit. Populists could not accept the Democratic vice-presidential nominee, Sumner Sewall of Maine, who while a free-silver man was also an easterner, a rich man, a banker, and a railroad executive, so they nominated their own candidate for vice-president, Thomas Watson of Georgia. But in the presidential balloting, those who wanted an independent Populist candidate were handicapped by lack of any outstanding prospect, and Bryan won, 1,042–333, on the first tally. "The fear ruled that unless the reform forces united this time they would never again have the opportunity to unite," wrote Lloyd, who resigned from the Populist party and voted the Socialist Labor ticket. "It was in the air that there must be union. The footfall for the hour of action was heard approaching."[41] Democratic-Populist fusion slates of electors—"Popocrats" or "Demopops," as the Republican press liked to refer to them—were arranged in twenty-eight states, and state and congressional tickets were similarly fused, with the Democrats generally the senior partner.[42]

40. Letter of July 10, 1896, quoted by Norman Pollack, *The Populist Response to Industrial America: Midwestern Populist Thought* (Harvard University Press, 1962), p. 140.
41. *Review of Reviews*, September 1896; quoted by Pollack, *Populist Response*, p. 105.
42. Hicks, *Populist Revolt*, Chap. 13.

Finally, then, what had been foreshadowed by the Ohio Idea and the Granger movement and a long series of later protest efforts had come to pass. The economic rationale for the party system that had been displaced in midcentury by the issues of slavery, war, and reconstruction had re-emerged at last. The major parties were again aligned on opposite sides of the genuine and crucial conflict of the day. In a country rent by economic depression, they appealed to the polarized electorate from opposing poles.

The Critical Election of 1896

With the nomination of Bryan, the tone of party competition changed. For twenty years, the contests between Democrats and Republicans had been little more than sham battles that decided no consequential issues (except the tariff) but ordained mainly who would gain and allocate the spoils of office. The major parties had waged essentially empty campaigns. They appealed to wartime loyalties, they exposed each other's corruption and claimed moral superiority, and they magnified out of proportion the few real issues, like the tariff, that divided them. But on the fundamental question of the time—the role of government in a modern industrial society—the two national parties had no quarrel. Both saw an identity of interest between the government and the great banking, manufacturing, and railroad corporations that had come into being, or whose assets had skyrocketed, in the postwar decades. Both took for granted the merger of economic and political power, so dramatically symbolized in the partnership between the railroads and the Cleveland administration that had crushed the railroad strike of 1894. Republicans and Democrats had left it to third parties to argue that the combination of economic and political power should be dissolved and that the powers of government should be used not to abet the monopolies and the "money power," but rather to control them on behalf of the public.

As long as this radical proposition was the exclusive political property of Greenbackers, Anti-Monopolists, and other fringe elements of the party system, it could be ignored by those whose economic interests were challenged and its advocates could be dismissed with ridicule. The Populists were more alarming than the earlier third parties, for they had elected governors and taken over entire states. But those states were far away, on the frontier or in the Deep South, and in settled, urbanizing America the Populists were nonexistent. Now one of the major parties itself had succumbed to frontier radicalism. Not since the days of Andrew Jackson had the country's economic power structure been so challenged.

A NATION POLARIZED

Bryan set out deliberately to press the challenge and heighten the polarization of the country. This was not only true to the spirit of both conventions that had selected him as standard bearer; it was also dictated by necessity. To win, Bryan had to complete the realignment that had been set in motion by his nomination; to offset his lost Democratic support, he had to jar loose a substantial bloc of Republican voters from the anti-Democratic fixation in which they had been frozen since the days of slavery and civil war, and to do that he had to make the economic issue paramount and compelling. So he appealed for a coalition of what he called the "toiling masses" —farmers and urban workingmen, organized as an avowed class party against the interests that had exploited them.

To one who reviews the period from a post–New Deal perspective, the program he offered hardly seems radical. He and his party had abjured the more extreme ideas of the Farmers' Alliance and the Populists, such as the subtreasury plan and government ownership of railroads and telegraph. Far from threatening the free enterprise system, the message of his "Cross of Gold" speech was that the concept of business was not extended far enough —farmers and laborers too were simply businessmen who deserved the same protection from the government that was tendered corporations. Even his central proposition—currency inflation through silver—had been supported, from time to time and to some degree, by such pillars of conservatism as John Sherman and William McKinley.

Yet Bryan and his program were greeted by the country's conservatives with something akin to terror. "The Chicago platform is in league with Hell," proclaimed the New York *Tribune*.[43] The Democratic party had been taken over by "demagogues," "anarchists," "socialists," "communists," "agitators," "Jacobins," was the outcry of other journals. Theodore Roosevelt foresaw "a red government of lawlessness and dishonesty as phantastic and vicious as the Paris Commune itself." To the Reverend Charles H. Parkhurst, Bryan represented the "yawning depths of lying lawlessness and obstreperous anarchy."[44] All this vituperation did rest on a solid fact, about

43. Quoted by Wayne C. Williams, *William Jennings Bryan: A Study in Political Vindication* (Putnam's, 1936), p. 152.
44. Ibid., p. 187.

which the Democrats themselves boasted: the Democratic party had been reborn, with new leaders and a new economic program. That program, however exaggerated by its opponents, was still far more radical than any presented to the people by a major party within the memory of any but the oldest living men (if, indeed, the Jackson program had been in fact as radical). And if it was not the immediate platform that terrified the conservatives, it was the prospect of what might happen if the "toiling masses" really did succeed in organizing against them, of what might follow a shift of the control of government, in the polarized country, to the opposite pole. If Bryan was no extremist, Altgeld, Watson, Debs, and the prairie Populists were (or appeared to be), and Bryan would be beholden to his radical supporters. Such a prospect warranted a massive and crushing counterattack. As it happened, the genius to organize the counterattack was on the scene, in the person of Marcus A. Hanna, manager of the Republican candidate, William McKinley.

In those days before corporate contributions to political campaigns were outlawed, Hanna raised unprecedented sums by the simple expedient of assessing major corporations at the rate of one-fourth of one percent of capital.[45] Banks cheerfully contributed. So did insurance companies. The Republicans admitted to spending $3.5 million, while unofficial estimates ran to several times that amount. Hanna matched his systematic money-raising with the most thorough and methodical political organization the country had yet seen. At the end, organization merged into coercion, as employers threatened their employees, creditors their borrowers, buyers their suppliers. Coercion was "bold, unashamed, and effective," wrote Republican William Allen White.[46] The press enlisted in the crusade; Democratic papers went over to McKinley en masse.[47] So did the academic community; Bryan was howled down by Yale students on the New Haven green.[48] The clergy joined in the struggle. "No pulpit can keep silent when this country is threatened and the political situation casts a dark cloud over this great

---

45. So Standard Oil gave $250,000 on a valuation of $100 million, the Beef Trust $400,000. Matthew Josephson, *The Politicos, 1865–1896* (Harcourt, Brace, 1938), p. 699.

46. *Autobiography*, p. 285, quoted by Harold U. Faulkner, *Politics, Reform and Expansion 1890–1900* (Harper, 1959), p. 209. Illustrations of coercive tactics are in Robert F. Durden, *The Climax of Populism: The Election of 1896* (University of Kentucky Press, 1965), pp. 138–40; Heath, "Politics and Steady Habits," pp. 89–90.

47. For lists of Democratic papers that deserted Bryan, see Joseph Rogers Hollingsworth, *The Whirligig of Politics: The Democracy of Cleveland and Bryan* (University of Chicago Press, 1963), p. 70.

48. Heath, "Politics and Steady Habits," pp. 84–85.

Republic," New York Baptists heard their preacher say.[49] The Chicago *Tribune* took occasion to praise ministers "who have started to impress upon their congregations the infamous project of immorality which Bryan is seeking to impose on the people as a national financial principle. . . . It is in no respect a question of politics, but of moral principle. It is taking the commandment, 'Thou Shalt Not Steal,' which is a common text, and applying it to the Nation."[50] On the Sunday before election, every Protestant minister in New Haven except one preached an anti-Bryan sermon.[51] To counter the concentrated Republican economic power and campaign resources, Bryan could travel 18,000 miles and address from three to five million people but he could raise for his "righteous cause" a campaign chest of only $650,000.

McKinley's plurality was 600,000 in an extraordinarily high turnout of 13.9 million votes.[52] But the vote was distributed in a wholly new configuration. Superimposed on the latitudinal pattern that had marked the party system since the 1850s was a longitudinal, East-West division resembling the schism expressed in so many congressional roll calls in the postwar decades. McKinley won because he carried solidly the country's industrial Northeast and Midwest and most of the states bordering on the industrial heartland as well—from Delaware and Maryland through West Virginia and Kentucky to Iowa and Minnesota. Everything beyond except North Dakota, Oregon, and California was Bryan's.

Most accounts of the 1896 campaign, especially those written by Bryan partisans, accept William Allen White's "bold . . . effective" coercion as the explanation for McKinley's victory. Wayne C. Williams, a Bryan biographer, flatly attributes the McKinley sweep of the Northeast and old Midwest to "the power of money and industrial coercion." But these were one-time factors that applied to the 1896 campaign alone. As such, they could produce electoral deviations. But the election of 1896 was a *realigning*, not simply a deviating, election. A major shift in party allegiance remained, after Republican campaign methods returned to normal and after the Democrats had modified their extremist image of the 1896 campaign. Most of the

49. *New York Times* report quoted by Pollack, *Populist Response*, p. 148. The *Times* quoted other sermons and concurred editorially that the issues were "distinctively moral" (pp. 148–49).
50. Quoted by Stanley L. Jones, *The Presidential Election of 1896* (University of Wisconsin Press, 1964), p. 337. Jones offers excerpts from various sermons on pp. 337–38, 340.
51. Heath, "Politics and Steady Habits," p. 90.
52. The candidate of the gold Democrats, John Palmer, polled a negligible 135,000.

switching voters were not coerced into voting for McKinley; they were *converted.*[53]

The 1896 election was the first to be fought out along the new line of cleavage that had been developing in American politics since the 1860s, cutting across the line established on the issues of slavery, war, and reconstruction. (Whether the line should be looked on as an essentially "new" one or as an old line of Whig-Democratic cleavage that had been temporarily overshadowed but reappeared is for purposes of this analysis unimportant.) For twenty years the two-party system had been based on dead issues of the past. It had offered the voters no means of expressing a choice on the crucial issues of domestic economic policy around which the country had been polarizing—slowly at first, but beginning in the late 1880s at a headlong pace. Then suddenly, with the nomination of Bryan in 1896, the party system took on meaning once again. Each major party now had a position, and a program, that was relevant on economic matters. Each reflected one of the polar positions in the polarized society. The day of political unresponsiveness, of evasion and straddling on fundamental, burning questions, was over. To each polar group, its party embodied sanity and righteousness and the other represented immorality and intellectual error. The party became, again, something like a church—a militant, crusading church, to whose holy aims the true believer could give no less than full devotion. Political bonds formed at such a time prove durable.

1896 AS THE DECISIVE YEAR

This chapter and the preceding one have traced a causal chain for the realignment of the 1890s—the decades of agrarian unrest that culminated in the Populist movement, the nomination of Bryan, and the election of 1896. However, other factors influenced voting behavior in the 1890s, and they should be weighed in an interpretation of the realignment outcome.

The central partisan issue of the pre-1896 period had been the tariff. The popularity of the Republican stand in favor of protection probably accounts for at least some of the shift to the GOP in Pennsylvania industrial communities that could be seen in the election returns of the 1880s. Some drift to the Republicans in the North could be expected as the long-term effect of

53. Paul Kleppner also takes exception, on the same grounds, to the traditional emphasis placed by "liberal historians" on coercion. He observes that "a series of percentage point declines *over time* cannot be explained by the intrusion of coercive elements at *one point in time.*" *The Cross of Culture: A Social Analysis of Midwestern Politics, 1895–1900* (Free Press, 1970), p. 297.

the realignment of the 1850s, as older voters attached to the Jacksonian Democratic party died and younger voters who came to political maturity in the prewar and war years of regional patriotism took their place. This drift might be offset in part or wholly by a pro-Democratic shift in the party balance resulting from an increase in the proportion of the electorate made up of Catholics and other pro-Democratic ethnic-religious groups. But some of the pro-Republican drift, where it can be identified, can probably be attributed to the Republican tariff and other probusiness policies. Nevertheless, the Republican gains represented at most a minor and localized realignment, for there was no massive movement across party lines during the years the tariff issue was preeminent.

Not until the panic of 1893 did a sharp and decisive shift of voters to the Republicans take place. But that still leaves an important question: To what extent was the realignment of the 1890s really the result of the agrarian revolt, Bryan, Democratic radicalism, and the scare campaign of 1896, and to what extent was it simply the consequence of a depression visited upon the country when a Democratic administration was in power? The experience of the 1930s is enough to tell us that depression can be an overwhelming political force, quite apart from any other factor.

The most thorough study with direct bearing on this point is the one by Kleppner, which covers the states of Ohio, Michigan, and Wisconsin. His findings are that the voter movements of the 1892–94 period and those of the next two years were distinct and different, and that it was the second of the movements that had the most to do with defining the new configuration. Correlations of party percentages by counties showed a high degree of association between 1892 and 1894, despite the heavy voting swing to the Republicans the latter year, and a high degree of association also between 1896 and 1900. But the correlation between 1894 and 1896 was in every case lower and in some cases much lower, indicating that the essential break in voting habits and redistribution of party loyalties took place in that interval rather than the earlier one, and can be attributed more to the circumstances of 1896 than to the depression, whose effect was felt primarily in 1894.[54]

Analysis of these and other election data suggests that the voters' response to the depression, in and of itself, was more deviating than realigning. In 1893 and 1894, a general and uniform swing to the Republicans took place throughout the North, clearly a rebuke to the incumbent party. In 1896, the

54. Ibid., pp. 273–79, esp. Table 34. Kleppner's figures also show how stable the voting pattern was between 1860 and 1892. "Despite extensive population changes and the emergence of minor parties, the distribution of the Democratic vote in 1860 and 1892 in Michigan and Ohio correlates at +.772, and in Wisconsin at +.762" (p. 13).

Democrats recovered from their low point and the pendulum swung partway back, but the return movement was not uniform. Some voters returned to the Democratic party, marking them as deviants (most of them, anyway, for the possibility exists of twice-realigned voters). But others remained Republicans. The sorting out of the 1894 switchers, which was the essential realignment, occurred in 1896, on the basis of the factors of that year's election. The 1894 election can therefore be seen as primarily a deviation, and the realignment was mainly the product of factors newly operative in 1896—specifically, the transformation and radicalization of the Democratic party.

Substance of the Realignment

The realignment of the 1890s followed the pattern of scenario 3 in Chapter 2—realignment through absorption of a third party. The process and the result are diagrammed in Figure 7-2.

Figure 7-2. *The Realignment of the 1890s*[a]

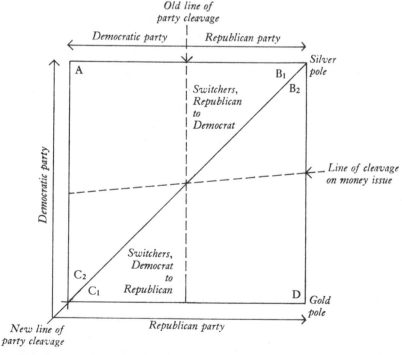

a. This figure is schematic rather than quantitatively precise. The size of the compartments does not measure the proportion of the electorate contained in each.

The voters making up block C_1 so heavily outnumbered those in B_1 that they transformed a nation that had been closely balanced politically into one with a normal Republican majority. Between the realignment of the 1890s and that of the 1930s, the Democrats elected only one president, Woodrow Wilson, and he gained office in 1912 only because the Republican party split. After 1896, states that had been evenly divided between the parties—Connecticut, New York, New Jersey, Indiana, California—and even the Democratic states of Delaware and West Virginia now became predominantly Republican. Others that had already leaned to the Republican side but had occasional Democratic victories—Pennsylvania, Michigan, Illinois, Wisconsin, Iowa—became virtual one-party domains. Former Democratic strongholds along the border—Kentucky and Missouri—became doubtful states. Only in the silver states of the Rocky Mountains did the Democratic party gain.

THE CITIES GO REPUBLICAN

The massive swing to the Republicans in the North was predominantly urban.[55] In rural counties in the Midwest and even in the East, the Democrats showed relatively slight losses from their strength of 1892. But in the urban centers the shift was decisive and lasting, and it was reflected in state as well as national elections. Table 7-2 measures this shift in major metropolitan centers and compares it with the movement in the states containing those centers. The table also indicates how much of the 1896 swing proved to be deviation and how much realignment. In Boston, almost all the switchers returned in 1900, but only half returned in New York City, and none at all (on a net basis) in Philadelphia and Pittsburgh.

It is clear that Bryan failed disastrously to win over the urban element of his "toiling masses" coalition. "The simple fact which shines out from the election returns is that Bryan failed to win the support of labor," concluded Faulkner.[56] That objective may have been hopeless from the outset. Among

55. Bryan captured 40.6 percent of the national urban vote, 48.3 of the rural. Paul W. Glad, *McKinley, Bryan and the People* (Lippincott, 1964), p. 203. Walter Dean Burnham has calculated a direct relation between the degree of urbanization of Pennsylvania's counties and the extent of their pro-Republican shift in 1896 compared with 1892. The shift ranges from 4.4 percentage points in the eleven wholly rural counties to 13.9 percentage points (or one-third of the 1892 Democratic strength) in the two metropolitan counties, Philadelphia and Allegheny. *Critical Elections and the Mainsprings of American Politics* (Norton, 1970), p. 40.

56. Faulkner, *Politics, Reform and Expansion*, p. 210. Kleppner demonstrates that in Ohio, Michigan, and Wisconsin the 1896 election returns show no evidence that Bryan exercised a class appeal in either urban or rural areas. Democratic gains or losses, unlike those of 1892 and 1894, were not concentrated in poorer areas but were spread evenly across economic classes (*Cross of Culture*, pp. 288–97).

Table 7-2. *Democratic Losses in Selected Urban Centers in 1896*

State and urban center[a]	Democratic percentage of presidential vote					Gain or loss in percentage points, 1892–96	Gain or loss as a percentage of 1892 proportion
	1888	*1892*	*1896*	*1900*	*1904*		
Massachusetts							
Suffolk (Boston)	55	54	35	52	52	−19	−35
Rest of state	41	43	24	34	33	−19	−44
New York							
New York City	57	59	42	51	50	−17	−29
Rest of state	43	43	37	39	37	−6	−14
Pennsylvania							
Philadelphia	45	42	26	25	17	−16	−38
Allegheny (Pittsburgh)	35	39	27	27	18	−12	−31
Rest of state	46	47	40	41	32	−7	−15
Maryland							
Baltimore (city)	52	57	38	46	49	−19	−33
Rest of state	49	51	44	46	49	−7	−14
Ohio							
Cuyahoga (Cleveland)	47	51	46	47	27	−5	−10
Hamilton (Cincinnati)	47	47	40	41	25	−7	−15
Rest of state	47	47	48	46	36	1	2
Michigan							
Wayne (Detroit)	54	50	41	43	28	−9	−18
Rest of state	44	43	44	38	25	1	2
Illinois							
Cook (Chicago)	49	55	40	47	26	−15	−27
Rest of state	46	46	44	44	33	−2	−4
Kentucky							
Jefferson (Louisville)	57	59	35	45	50	−24	−41
Rest of state	55	51	51	51	50	0	0
Indiana							
Marion (Indianapolis)	50	50	42	44	37	−8	−16
Rest of state	49	47	48	47	41	1	2

Sources: Walter Dean Burnham, *Presidential Ballots 1836–1892* (Johns Hopkins Press, 1955); Edgar E. Robinson, *The Presidential Vote 1896–1932* (Octagon Books, 1970).

a. The centers are indicated by both county and city designations except for New York City, which includes five counties; Philadelphia, which is both a city and a county; and Baltimore, which is an independent city. Where the county is named, the figures are for the county.

the organized workingmen, only the Knights of Labor had been sympathetic to a united farmer-labor protest party, and by 1896 the Knights had almost ceased to be. Samuel Gompers, head of the American Federation of Labor, had steered his followers in quite the opposite direction. The Populists, he said in 1892, were "employing farmers," and "cooperation or amalgamation of the wage-workers' organizations with the People's Party" was "impossible, because it is unnatural."[57] Nor did he share the Bryan-Populist views on monopoly. He had opposed the antitrust law on grounds that it could be used against labor; rather than interfere with the new industrial giants, his aim was to match them with giant labor organizations. Basically, he opposed any organized partisan political activity by labor as inimical to its long-run economic objectives. Of the AFL leaders who were more interested in electoral politics than was Gompers, many were looking for their model to the British Labour party or to Continental proletarian movements with socialist rather than agrarian programs.[58]

But even if labor had been more receptive, Bryan's appeal was too narrow. The Democratic platform contained a labor plank, but Bryan made little effort to amplify it. He talked silver to the urban as well as to the rural masses. As Kleppner points out, however, that represented a "jarringly anachronistic perception" of the role and attitudes of wage earners. Urban laborers suffering the privations of a major depression were interested in "the job supply," not the money supply. They were "producers," yes, but not entrepreneurs who owned what they produced.[59] So free silver scared rather than attracted them; among the dollars that would fall in value were those in the worker's pay envelope—"wages paid in fifty-three-cent dollars" was the Republican cry. Bryan's campaign polarized sentiment on what, for his purposes, was the wrong basis. He did not set class against class; he set rural against urban. When in his "Cross of Gold" speech he spoke of "*your* cities" and "*our* farms," he cast out of his circle not just urban capital but urban labor too.

The Republicans, on the other hand, offered the urban workingman a program that was much more clearly job-related—the tariff. Even before the climactic 1896 campaign, large blocs of workingmen in the iron and steel and other heavy industries had become convinced that the liberal tariff stance of the Democratic party was against their interests. Lewis Rathgeber, in his study of the Democratic party of Pennsylvania in the late nineteenth

57. "Organized Labor in the Campaign," *North American Review*, July 1892; quoted by Chester McArthur Destler, *American Radicalism 1865–1901* (Connecticut College, 1946), p. 29.

58. Arthur Power Dudden, "The Historical Background and Intellectual Origins of the Antitrust Movement in the United States" (Ph.D. dissertation, University of Michigan, 1950), pp. 287–91; Irving Bernstein (ed.), "Samuel Gompers and Free Silver, 1896," in *Mississippi Valley Historical Review*, Vol. 29 (December 1942), pp. 394–400; Destler, *American Radicalism*, Chaps. 9 and 11; Nathan Fine, *Labor and Farmer Parties in the United States 1828–1928* (first published, 1928; Russell and Russell, 1961), pp. 137–44.

59. *Cross of Culture*, pp. 303–04.

century, found that the long-term Democratic decline began in the 1880s and suggests that the tariff may have been the basic reason.[60] The tariff may well account for Cleveland's loss of Pennsylvania, and perhaps of Ohio as well, in 1892. The Democratic strength elsewhere in the North generally held up through 1892 despite Cleveland's low-tariff crusade, but with the onset of depression in 1893, the issue became far more potent.

Moreover, McKinley and Hanna could not be portrayed as antilabor devils. Both had established themselves as sympathetic to the aims of organized labor,[61] while from labor's standpoint the Democratic administration of Grover Cleveland was full of devils.

Finally, the Republican campaign of 1896 and the events on which it was based undoubtedly painted in the minds of many urban voters a new image of the Democratic party. Bryan enthusiasts may denounce the campaign as built on "scare" tactics that drastically distorted the facts. Be that as it may, the campaign succeeded. Many voters were in fact scared. To the image of the Democrats as the party of rum, Romanism, rebellion, and economic recession was added another R—radicalism.

As if to solidify the GOP's association with the "full dinner pail" McKinley had promised, the economy turned upward almost coincidentally with his election. Employment, wages, and earnings began to climb again, and trade unions recouped their lost vigor. Farm prices also rose. By 1900 the country had come all the way out of the Democratic depression to the Republican boom. The Bryan Democrats might contend that the economic upturn affirmed their policy position rather than that of the Republicans, for it directly followed an increase in the world money supply brought about by gold discoveries in South Africa and Alaska.[62] But inevitably the incumbent party was the beneficiary. To the urban workingman of the North, the Republicans were the party not only of moral respectability but of protection and prosperity as well.

NO COUNTERMOVEMENT AMONG THE FARMERS

While Bryan was losing in the cities, he made no appreciable net gains among the farmers. The anticipated defection of silver Republicans of the

60. Lewis Wesley Rathgeber, "The Democratic Party in Pennsylvania, 1880–1896" (Ph.D. dissertation, University of Pittsburgh, 1956), pp. 322, 355. Rathgeber also cites rising Catholic influence in the Democratic party as a factor driving Protestants into Republican ranks (pp. 315–21).

61. Hollingsworth, *Whirligig of Politics*, p. 93.

62. Their judgment is at least in part confirmed by modern economists. See, for example, Fels, *American Business Cycles*, pp. 209–12.

agrarian West did not materialize; if they believed in silver, they believed still more deeply in "the party of Abraham Lincoln, the Union, and the Homestead Act."[63] In the East and older Midwest, in fact, farmers, like urban workingmen, had begun to believe in the Republican tariff as a solution to their problems.[64] And McKinley had affirmed the Republican platform pledge to seek an international silver agreement. Not a single county in Illinois, Indiana, Iowa, or Wisconsin showed a gain in its Democratic percentage over the combined Democratic-Populist strength of 1892. Bryan carried only three counties in all of Wisconsin. He lost ground in North Dakota and even in his home state of Nebraska as against the 1892 showing of the two parties combined and gained only slightly in Kansas.[65] In short, the Republican farmers who could be lured away from the Grand Old Party by free-silver notions had joined the Populist revolt already, and when the Populists became an adjunct of the Democrats, there were few additional recruits; in fact, some of the Populists returned to the Republicans rather than accept a Democratic label. General Weaver could become a Democrat for the rest of his life, but Populist Senator William A. Peffer of Kansas became an ardent supporter of Republicans McKinley and Roosevelt after he left the Senate in 1897.[66] The Populist prairie heartland shortly joined the rest of the North as predominantly Republican. The silver Republicans recruited to the Democracy in 1896 turned out to be very few beyond the mine owners (like Senator Teller, whose holdings were estimated at $2 million), the mine workers, and other residents of states where silver was a basic industry.

63. Elwyn B. Robinson, *The History of North Dakota* (University of Nebraska Press, 1966), p. 230.

64. Kleppner, *Cross of Culture*, p. 310.

65. These net county figures necessarily conceal some pro-Democratic movement that was offset by pro-Republican crossing of party lines in the same counties. Kleppner has identified many small communities in the rural Midwest, including Wisconsin, that showed a significant rise in the Democratic percentage of the vote in 1896 from that in 1892, and it is clear that in some of these cases the Democratic percentage in the latter year was higher than the combined Democratic-Populist proportion in 1892. *Cross of Culture*, pp. 325–38.

66. Solon J. Buck, *The Agrarian Crusade: A Chronicle of the Farmer in Politics* (Yale University Press, 1921), p. 195. The Populist faction that had opposed fusion in 1896 tried to revive the party as an independent force but could only fail. When the depression ended, shortly after McKinley took office, Populism "could retain neither its militancy nor its membership without the sharp prodding of massive poverty." Durden, *Climax of Populism*, p. 163. The diminished force of party loyalists in 1900 nominated an independent ticket of old third-party stalwarts that cut no figure in the election. The People's party lingered through two more presidential campaigns and then faded into history.

PIETISTS AND LITURGICALS

The shift to the Republicans was disproportionately made up of voters belonging to Catholic, German Lutheran, and other liturgical religious communities that had been predominantly Democratic, according to Kleppner's analyses. Conversely, Democratic gains, where they occurred, were in pietist communities that had been originally Republican (but had been showing in some cases Populist or Prohibition party strength). Both of these movements could be expected in a realignment based on economic issues, since economic attitudes presumably cut more or less evenly across religious denominations, and the cross-pressures would tend to pull the majority party in most communities toward the mean (or sometimes even beyond it). But Kleppner put heavy emphasis on the reversal in 1896 of the traditional Democratic and Republican appeals to religious attitudes. Bryan, the Democrat, appeared as an evangelical crusader in a moral cause and thus appealed to the pietists who had supported abolition, temperance, nativism—and Republicanism. And his campaign was directed not at reinforcing traditional loyalties among Democratic liturgical groups, but at converting reform-minded Republicans and Prohibitionists while retaining the Populist zealots. At the same time, McKinley, who represented the branch of Ohio Republicanism that had courted the Catholics and German Lutherans and rejected prohibition and nativism, appeared to many in those groups as more conciliatory and sympathetic to their views—more "culturally safe"—than Bryan. Kleppner found a surprisingly high correlation between the distribution of the Bryan vote in 1896 in Michigan and Ohio and the pattern of the "dry" vote in other years on prohibition questions.[67]

Burnham's analysis of the 1896 realignment in Pennsylvania confirms Kleppner's findings. The counties of northern Pennsylvania that were in the path of New England and upstate New York migration had been the most responsive in the state to the Free-Soil party and to early Republicanism; they also had the strongest Prohibition party support and were the most resistant to the Republican trend in 1896. But the resistance turned out to be temporary. After 1896, when the Democratic party was rebounding in the more urban sections of the state from its low point, it continued to lose ground in the northern counties. The realignment in that region was simply delayed. The lag may have been partly due, Burnham has suggested, to the

67. Kleppner, *Cross of Culture*, Chap. 8.

relative isolation of the rural counties from the political currents of the time, but in the main it would appear to be the equivalent of a deviation, the pietist communities having temporarily resisted the general pro-Republican trend in the North because of the particular appeal of Bryan as a moral crusader (and McKinley's lack of appeal as a compromiser on moral issues).[68]

Probably such pro-Democratic movement as appeared in 1896 among pietists in the Midwest turned out to be essentially a deviation also; certainly one has difficulty finding, in the gross analysis of election returns, any permanent shift of a significant number of pietist voters to the Democratic party as a result of the peculiar reversal of roles in 1896.[69] By the second and third decades of the twentieth century, the Republican party had clearly established itself as more sympathetic to prohibition and to such nativist causes as immigration restriction, and as the preferred party of northern Protestants of pietist denominations. The Democratic party was as firmly identified, throughout the North, as the party of the Catholics, the "wets," and the immigrants.

The Catholics, particularly the Irish, consolidated their domination of the Democratic party even more solidly in that region upon the departure of the Mugwump reformers of the Protestant upper class who had been one of the bases of Cleveland's support. Thus the religious and ethnic character of the party division throughout the North became even more pronounced than previously.[70]

Persistence of the Civil War Alignment

The return of the Populist belt to its original Republican loyalties suggests the persistent potency of the Civil War alignment. Despite the heat and passion of the most polarizing campaign since 1860, the new line of cleavage established in 1896 by no means supplanted the old. Of the voters who found themselves cross-pressured in 1896 (blocks B and C in Figure 7-2), more stayed with their original attachment (B2 and C2) than made the party switch (B1 and C1). Those who did change their party loyalty were for the most part voters whose shift in attachment was *in the direction of conformity with the regional party system established before and during the Civil War.* So

68. Burnham, *Critical Elections*, pp. 41–50.
69. Kleppner's analysis does not extend beyond 1896, so it is not known whether the pro-Democratic movement in the communities he studied was temporary or permanent.
70. Hollingsworth, *Whirligig of Politics*, pp. 99–100; Wiebe, *Search for Order*, p. 106.

that system, rather than being weakened by the new upheaval, was reinforced.

This was especially apparent in the South, where the Civil War pattern was hardly disturbed at all. The Republicans gained in the border states as in the North, but the Solid Democratic South of the former Confederacy was as solid after 1896 as before. Even the most conservative of the southern Gold Bugs did not necessarily join the party of William McKinley, for it was also the party of Lincoln while the Democrats were the party of white supremacy, which was the overriding consideration. Secretary of the Interior Hoke Smith of Atlanta resigned his office rather than go with the rest of the Cleveland administration in supporting the Gold Bug candidate, John M. Palmer—not, he made clear, because he agreed with Bryan's silver policy but because of the "local situation" in Georgia.[71]

Similarly, the persistence of the Civil War attachments made the realignment in the North largely a one-way movement—pro-Republican. Northern Democrats could become Republicans without too great an emotional and psychological strain, but silver Republicans could not bring themselves to become Democrats. So the Democratic party was unable, even a generation after the Civil War, to absorb, become the vehicle of, and be rejuvenated by the massive forces of agrarian protest that had been building for three long decades of economic squeeze. Voters could freely cross the party line *into* the party of regional patriotism and respectability, but the barrier to crossing in the other direction remained all but impassable. The alignment of the party system forged in war was greatly modified in 1896, but it was simply too strong to be superseded.

71. Nevins, *Grover Cleveland*, p. 710. The ferment of the 1890s did have a profound and lasting effect, however, on the character of the Democratic party in the South, and hence on the course of regional and national politics. Alarmed by the threat to white supremacy of the brief revival of two-party politics in the Populist era, the white South moved to put an end, once and for all, to Negro political power. During the next decade this was accomplished by deliberate legal steps. By constitutional conventions, constitutional amendments, and legislative acts, a dozen states adopted poll taxes, literacy tests, property qualifications, and the "grandfather" clauses that eliminated all but token Negro voting in most rural areas and sharply reduced it in the cities. Negro registration in Louisiana fell from 130,000 in 1897 to 1,342 in 1904. The poll taxes and property qualifications served to bar from the ballot box many poor whites as well. While this turn in southern politics served the outcome of conservative as well as white supremacy (and was described by some as a deliberate conservative tactic to this end), it was by no means the product of conservatives alone. Radical whites—Ben Tillman, for example—joined wholeheartedly in the move to disfranchise the blacks, and in some cases took the initiative. Woodward, *Origins of the New South*, Chap. 12.

CHAPTER EIGHT

Realignment Averted:
The Progressive Era

THE PERIOD between the Spanish-American War and the First World War was a time of great political turmoil. One of the most dynamic reform movements of the country's history, the progressive movement, took form, gained strength, accomplished fundamental change in many of the country's basic institutions, then declined as national attention turned to preparedness and war. During that period, the strongest third party the nation had known, the Theodore Roosevelt Progressive party, had its brief career. Reform movements, third parties, turmoil these in the nineteenth century had been the heralds of major party realignments. Yet the Progressive Era came and went without any such upheaval. The distribution of party strength when the era closed did not differ radically from the pattern established in the 1890s.

Examination of the reasons for a nonevent, it has been frequently remarked, can sometimes be as informative as analysis of an event. So a powerful and effective protest movement that did not result in significant realignment deserves at least a brief consideration.

If the Progressive Era is examined from the standpoint of the propositions set forth in Chapter 3, it seems clear that realignment was averted because (1) the major parties responded to the demands for reform, and (2) they responded at about the same time and to about the same degree, so that no sharp distinction could be drawn between them. Events thus followed the course of scenario 1 in Chapter 2, in which realignment did not occur. The Progressive Era has no parallel in American history in the extent to which the two parties vied with one another as agents of reform—not at all times and in all places and on all matters, to be sure, and often better in rhetoric than in performance, but nevertheless responding to the grievances of the time rather than resisting change.

The nonevent can be analyzed in terms of several of the variables listed in Chapter 3—the nature of the grievances and the remedies and their capacity to polarize the country, the division of the forces of reform between the major parties, and the motivation and capacity of party leadership.

Diffuse Character of the Progressive Movement

Progressivism was a singular diffuse reform movement, particularly at the outset. It did not appear as a single dramatic issue, like extension of slavery in the 1840s and 1850s and free coinage of silver in 1896, but was concerned with a myriad of legislative and administrative reforms in a multitude of places. A community could polarize over a specific local question, but clearly defined polar forces, either supporting progressivism at all costs or resisting it with determination, were slow to coalesce on a national scale.

The progressive movement grew from the convergence of three distinct reform movements, each with its own base, its own leaders, and its own preoccupations. One was what remained of the Populist-Bryan crusade, with its program of agrarian legislation. The second was the urban political reform movement represented earlier by the Liberal Republicans and the Mugwumps, a group that had been diametrically opposed to the agrarians in 1896. Among their aims was regulation of monopoly, but the monopolies they were most concerned about were local ones—transit companies and other municipal utilities that, in friendly alliance with the political bosses, were milking the citizenry. The third current that made up progressivism was also of urban origin. This was the movement for social legislation to ameliorate the conditions of the millions of poor who had flooded into the city slums from Europe, a group whose problems were far removed from those of the farmers, and even from those of the political reformers. No central organization brought these three streams of reformist thought and action into complete unity or developed a concerted strategy for all progressives. The movement retained sharp regional differences.[1]

Nevertheless, if progressives were not bound together by a common origin and a single program, they were united in the intangibles of mood and

---

1. These differences in turn have led to differing definitions of progressivism and interpretations of its essential character. A recent symposium, for example, juxtaposes three essays by three historians, each of which, in the words of the editor, singles out a different social group as being the most important originator of the Progressive program: radical farmers, the urban elite, the big-city masses. John D. Hicks, "Populist Origins"; George E. Mowry, "The Urban Gentry on the Defensive"; and J. Joseph Huthmacher, "The Urban Masses on the Move"; all in Arthur Mann (ed.), *The Progressive Era: Liberal Renaissance or Liberal Failure?* (Holt, Rinehart and Winston, 1963), pp. 17–47.

manner. They were dissatisfied. They saw evils that demanded change. They were optimistic and combative. This reformist mood became the prevailing public mood during the Progressive Era, a national consensus in favor of reform as overwhelming as the consensus against reform had been in the preceding two decades.[2] The muckrakers crystallized the public mood. Ida Tarbell told the story of Standard Oil, Ray Stannard Baker of railroad malpractices, Upton Sinclair of the meatpacking "jungle," Lincoln Steffens of the corrupt alliances of businessmen and bosses, all feeding the circulation wars of a new group of ten-cent, mass-circulation magazines. Theodore Roosevelt became the movement's articulator. Together they brought about a group awareness among progressives and coalesced a series of diverse and localized reform efforts into a single dominant national impulse.

A common theme of progressivism in all regions was its emphasis on the reform of political and governmental processes. Whatever the substantive reform that was being sought, it could not be achieved without a seizure of political and governmental power by those who were in favor of change. In other words, reform required dethroning the political bosses who in alliance with the holders of concentrated economic power defended the status quo. The aggrieved and the exploited had the power of numbers, and had only to use that power to topple the monopolists and the boodlers alike and then reform society. "I had then, and have had ever since, absolute confidence in the people," Robert M. La Follette, Sr., wrote in his autobiography,[3] echoing the declaration of the Populists at their Sioux Falls convention: "A majority of the people can never be corruptly influenced."[4]

Then why had not the majority, which had been aroused from time to time, already prevailed? The answer, the progressives believed (and the agrarian crusaders had believed earlier), lay in flaws in the mechanics of government: indirect processes of election and of legislation that placed too many intermediaries between the citizen and the policy output of the government. The remedy was to eliminate the intermediate points, where the public will was corrupted, and restore power to the people. This was the reform

2. Later generations have become familiar with the almost cyclical regularity of such alternations of the public mood. For a theoretical analysis of the inevitability of alternation between periods of activism and periods of complacency, see James L. Sundquist, *Politics and Policy: The Eisenhower, Kennedy, and Johnson Years* (Brookings Institution, 1968), pp. 499–505.

3. Robert M. La Follette, *Autobiography* (first published, 1911; University of Wisconsin Press, 1960), p. 96.

4. Cited by Hicks, "Populist Origins," p. 19.

objective that gave progressivism its universal theme and distinctive character.

Foremost were electoral reforms transferring power to the voting public —power to legislate directly through the initiative and the referendum, power to elect U.S. senators directly, power to nominate candidates for office through the direct primary, power to elect judges, power to recall unfaithful elected officials. Corporate power would be curbed through measures to control lobbying at state capitals and to regulate corporate spending in elections. Party bosses would be weakened by the extension of civil service systems and by the introduction of nonpartisan elections, at least at the municipal level. Women's suffrage not only was just in itself but also would infuse purity of motive into the political system.

If power was to be exercised effectively by the people, moreover, administrative machinery had to be improved. So progressives sought to consolidate local governments, strengthen chief executives, introduce city commission and city manager forms of government, establish unified executive budget systems, and make administration more professional through city managers and civil service systems and higher standards for government employment.

In its political and administrative reforms, the targets of progressivism were primarily state and local. The same was true, particularly in the early stages, of its drive for child labor laws, housing codes, factory laws, and other social legislation. Even in the antimonopoly elements of their program, the progressives looked chiefly to state regulatory bodies. This was the period when state governments assumed their modern form and role, transformed from passive to active instruments of government, a revolution that the national government would not undergo until the New Deal era. So the battles of progressivism were fought in scattered arenas, at different times, over a diverse array of specific propositions; and whatever their intrinsic polarizing power singly and collectively, they did not thrust the whole nation at once into the kind of fierce political conflict over deep and genuine issues of public policy from which realignments stem.

A Bipartisan Responsiveness

So diffuse a movement inevitably encountered an equally diffuse opposition. The major parties took no monolithic stands nationally. State and local progressives could therefore play Democrats and Republicans against one another; if one party resisted reform proposals, the other could see the advantage of conciliating the reformers, and so one or both of the old organizations often fell in line with popular sentiment and sought candidates who would bring a progressive image to their parties. Where the bosses did not respond, they could be toppled by well-organized, well-led, and determined insurgent movements. The early successes of La Follette and Albert Cummins in seizing control of the Republican parties of Wisconsin and Iowa, respectively, and winning the governorships of those states (La Follette in 1900 and Cummins in 1901) showed the way to others of their party; presently (1906) New York, the most notorious center of bossism and cynical corruption, fell to Charles Evans Hughes when President Roosevelt forced him on the state GOP leadership.[5] Meanwhile, on the Democratic side, the crusading St. Louis prosecutor, Joseph W. Folk, had ridden the reform movement to the governorship of Missouri (1904).

In no state did groups striving for reform in the early years of the Progressive Era find it necessary to go outside the two-party structure. Mayor Samuel L. "Golden Rule" Jones of Toledo (1897–1904) did seek the governorship of Ohio as an independent in 1899, but when he finished a weak third the movement died and the banner of reform was picked up by the major parties. Mayor Tom L. Johnson of Cleveland (1902–09), if anything more radical than Jones, was the Democratic nominee for governor of Ohio four years later. Local independent parties, like that of the Citizens' Union in New York City, were of course formed, but their ambitions did not extend beyond municipal boundaries. In Milwaukee, Bridgeport, and a few other cities Socialist mayors were elected, but the Socialists never broadened their appeal sufficiently to become a force in state politics anywhere.

In the states and cities, the reform movement found expression through the major parties in somewhat equal balance. This may seem an anomaly, since the 1896 election had been fought on lines of radicalism against conservatism and had realigned the party system on that basis. But one consequence of the realignment was to right the balance of reform sentiment by driving out of the Democratic party a major element of the reform movement. This was the Democratic, or "Mugwump," wing of the "urban gentry," the men of substance and of lineage who had deserted Blaine for Cleveland in 1884, had supported Cleveland for the dozen years thereafter, but could have no further use for a party that had fallen into the hands of a leveler like Bryan. Their return to the Republican ranks not only severely weak-

5. Robert F. Wesser, *Charles Evans Hughes: Politics and Reform in New York 1905–1910* (Cornell University Press, 1967), pp. 56–67.

ened the Democratic party as an instrument of reform, but also made the Republican party far more receptive to new ideas. Some of the younger switchers of 1896, like George L. Record of New Jersey, went on to become leaders of progressivism as Republicans (although Record himself later joined Democratic Governor Woodrow Wilson in Trenton). And the urban Democratic machines that were left to dominate the Democratic party in many states—though not nationally—were the very antithesis of reform.

So the urban political and governmental reform sector of the progressive movement was largely Republican-led. The first of the reform mayors of the progressive tradition, Hazen S. Pingree of Detroit (1890–97), who went on to the governorship of Michigan (1897–1901), was a Republican, as was Seth Low of New York City (1902–03). Golden Rule Jones of Toledo was first elected mayor as a Republican (but was reelected as an independent when his party refused to renominate him). Yet some were Democrats, like Mayor Johnson of Cleveland and Governor Folk of Missouri. To the east, the reform movement of New Jersey began with the election of a reform Republican mayor of Jersey City in 1901, gained impetus as a reform wing of the Republican party but reached fruition under a Democratic governor, Woodrow Wilson (1911–13). In New York, the outstanding progressive governor was Republican Hughes (1907–10); in Ohio, Democrat James M. Cox (1913–15). As the progressive movement in the cities turned increasingly from its negative emphasis on municipal corruption to a positive concern for social legislation, the outstanding progressive figures were the ethnic political leaders who rose directly out of the urban immigrant milieu, like Alfred E. Smith and Robert F. Wagner in the New York legislature and Governor David I. Walsh in Massachusetts (1914–16), and they bore the label, usually Democratic, of the groups from which they came. The progressives of the South, as well as their opponents, were of course Democrats.

In the rural areas too, a reform stream flowed into the Republican party. When the Populists returned to their original Republican allegiance, they carried their ideological baggage with them, and at once joined forces as an insurgent wing with the Republicans who, though Populist in sympathy, had remained behind in the old party when the more daring had bolted.[6] The

6. Orval G. Clanton, "The Kansas Populists: A Study of the Leadership and Ideology of the Kansas People's Party" (Ph.D. dissertation, University of Kansas, 1967), pp. 315, 312. Michael Rogin points out, however, that some of the radical protest movement that made up Populism and Bryanism did not flow anywhere, but simply became alienated and uninvolved when the political "system of 1896" proved irrelevant "to the concerns of many rural residents and urban poor" ("California Populism and the 'System of 1896,' "

most renowned governors of the agrarian brand of progressivism in the West—La Follette of Wisconsin, Cummins of Iowa, and Hiram Johnson of California (1911–17)—were Republicans, as were a host of lesser lights, although occasionally a Democratic governor, like John A. Johnson of Minnesota (1905–09) or John Burke of North Dakota (1907–12), became his state's instrument of reform.

The displacement of conservative by progressive party leadership was to a large extent a generational phenomenon. The typical conservative leader was of the generation that had come to political maturity in a simpler age, before the Industrial Revolution and an exploding urbanization had transformed America. He had outlived the passionate issues of the midcentury but had not grasped the issues of a later day. His politics were devoid of substance, built around appeals to tradition and old loyalties and aimed at patronage. The typical progressive was of a newer generation, drawn into politics by concern about the problems arising from industrialization and urbanization. He was young and issue-oriented. Patronage might be a means to the end, for the progressive, but it was not itself the goal of politics.

When La Follette was nominated for governor in 1900, a veteran Wisconsin politician wrote, "A new cult has arisen and has forced its way to the front. Never before were so many new faces seen in a republican state convention in Wisconsin. The majority are young men whose enthusiasm has taken the place of experience."[7] La Follette was almost forty years younger than the Republican party boss, Senator Philetus Sawyer, whom he overthrew. "The average age of the important progressive leaders who upset the Southern Pacific Railroad machine in California," George Mowry found, "was a little over thirty-eight."[8] The men who led the successful revolt against the "czar" of the House of Representatives, seventy-one-year-old Speaker Joseph G. Cannon, were, on the average, thirty years his junior.

Just as both major parties shared in the achievements of progressivism in the states and cities, so they did on the national scene. Each party had its

---

Western Political Quarterly, Vol. 22 [March 1969], p. 181). Further illustrating the link between Populism and insurgent Republicanism in the former strongholds of the People's party, Clanton notes that Victor Murdock of Wichita, who became a leader of the band of insurgent Republicans in the House of Representatives, delivered the oration at the funeral of former Populist Congressman Jerry Simpson in 1905 ("Kansas Populists," p. 315).

7. Quoted by Albert O. Barton, *La Follette's Winning of Wisconsin (1894–1904)* (Homestead, 1922), p. 160.

8. George E. Mowry, *The Era of Theodore Roosevelt 1900–1912* (Harper and Row, 1958), p. 85.

activist President: Theodore Roosevelt for the Republicans and Woodrow Wilson for the Democrats. In the Congress, Republican insurgents, mostly from the West, collaborated with Democratic progressives from the urban centers. And the responsiveness of the parties is measured by the fact that when the Progressive Era ended, virtually the entire agenda of national reform legislation that had been accumulating for decades had been enacted.

A constitutional amendment authorized the income tax, and one was written into law. Another constitutional amendment provided for the direct election of senators, and another gave the franchise to women. New legislation made the impotent railroad regulation and antitrust legislation of earlier years more effective. Child labor was outlawed (although the legislation was later ruled unconstitutional). Pure-food and meat-inspection laws were enacted. The demand of the West and South for a banking and monetary system adjusted to their needs was finally met through a new federal reserve system and a new and separate government-sponsored system of agricultural credit. Immigration was restricted. A model workmen's compensation law covered federal employees. Federal aid was granted for highways, vocational education, and agricultural extension. Even tariff reduction came at last. Some of this legislation was enacted under Roosevelt, some under Taft, but it reached its climax in the first Wilson administration when a coalition of Democrats and insurgent Republicans responded to presidential leadership and the clear progressive mandate of the 1912 election.

The Accidents of Leadership

Of the variables that contributed to the nonrealignment outcome, the one that appears to have been crucial was leadership. That the Democrats should have remained under progressive dominance after the realignment of the 1890s has an air of inevitability about it. But one might have expected just the opposite of the Republicans. True, the flow of Mugwump political reformers and of ex-Populist agrarian reformers into the Republican party in 1896 and afterward made it more receptive to progressive ideas, but that alone would not have assured the emergence of progressive leadership. That the GOP became progressive at the crucial time was entirely accidental. The story of how Theodore Roosevelt was "kicked upstairs" to the vice-presidency by Thomas C. Platt, the New York Republican boss, to get him out of the New York governorship has been often told. His accession to the presidency was the consequence of an assassin's bullet. Even in 1904, he might have had a struggle to win the nomination in his own right if Mark Hanna, the natural rallying point of the conservative opposition and its prospective candidate against Roosevelt, had not died early that year.

One may speculate that even if McKinley had lived out his presidency, the forces of progressivism within the party would have been sufficient by 1904 to nominate a progressive—Roosevelt, La Follette, or someone else—but it seems more likely that McKinley and Hanna would have kept the party under sufficiently tight control to have steered the nomination to a conservative. Even Taft, who in 1912 was seen as a conservative, and an unpopular one, was able to control his party's convention and win renomination over the redoubtable opposition of T.R. If the McKinleys, the Hannas, and the Nelson Aldriches had maintained control of the GOP, events would probably have moved in a completely different direction—toward interparty polarization, as in 1896. In that event, a major realignment, which would have consolidated the progressive movement in the Democratic party, would have been at least a possibility, despite the many disabilities suffered by the party as it emerged from the realignment of the 1890s.

As it was, the Republican party came by accident under the control of a gifted and magnetic leader who gave support and encouragement to the progressive wing of the party throughout the country. Among other things, he made the GOP attractive to the former Populists of the Midwest and consolidated their support. Mary Elizabeth Lease by 1904 had found Theodore Roosevelt to be "a man of destiny, an instrument in God's hands."[9] John D. Hicks ends his narrative of the Populist party with a quotation from an unnamed delegate to the People's party convention of 1908: "Roosevelt's messages read like the preamble to the Populist platform."[10] The accident of Roosevelt's leadership thus attracted into the GOP progressive elements that in turn strengthened T.R.'s hold on the party.[11]

---

9. Clanton, "The Kansas Populists," p. 315.
10. *The Populist Revolt: A History of the Farmers' Alliance and the People's Party* (University of Minnesota Press, 1931), p. 403.
11. This interpretation of Roosevelt as a preeminent progressive figure is based on the assessment made by the country at the time. Some historians have questioned whether his progressivism was genuine, basing their critique on his record as distinguished from his rhetoric. They cite his continued close political association with many of the staunchest conservatives of the party, the financial support the Republican party continued to receive from the centers of corporate power, and Roosevelt's limited achievements in "trust busting," which on the national level was the preeminent progressive issue of the day. "Whether or not Roosevelt was really a progressive during his two terms as Presi-

In the absence of a realignment that would have brought an influx of progressives into the Democratic party, it was also something of an accident that the party remained progressive after Bryan ceased to be its candidate. The progressive Woodrow Wilson came to the top in 1912 only because of the fortuitous circumstance that the Democratic party, many years before, had adopted a rule unusual for political bodies, requiring a two-thirds vote for party nominations. Had the Democrats nominated by a simple majority, as they do now and as the Republicans did then, their candidate in 1912 would have been Speaker Champ Clark of Missouri, who had a majority of the convention votes on the tenth ballot. Again, one may speculate that, given the temper of the party and the country in that year, Clark as a candidate would have run as a progressive. He had supported Bryan and made a reputation as a progressive, and the party's platform was progressive, but in the preconvention campaign he had sought conservative support, and at the convention his backing was from that wing of the party.[12] Had Clark as a Democratic nominee in 1912 kept faith with those to whom he owed the nomination, it is at least plausible to speculate that enough Bryan-Wilson progressives would have crossed the party line to have elected Roosevelt on his Bull Moose ticket. "If Governor Wilson had not been nominated at Baltimore," wrote Brand Whitlock at the time, "we should have had a new liberal party and the alignment at last would have been clear."[13]

---

dent is an open question," wrote Russell B. Nye. "It was not until after he had retired from the Presidency that he developed, under the influence of Eastern intellectuals like Herbert Croly, a larger and more distinctly progressive political philosophy." *Midwestern Progressive Politics: A Historical Study of Its Origins and Development 1870–1950* (Michigan State University Press, 1951), p. 248. But there can be no doubt about how his contemporaries saw him. George Mowry has written of Roosevelt's relation to the California progressive movement: "Of all the outside personal forces operating to inspire progressive rebellion in California, Theodore Roosevelt was by far the greatest. His name and his doctrines were grafted into the very origins of the movement. . . . But Theodore Roosevelt was not venerated simply for the advantage his position afforded them. To a great degree, the President's moral and political doctrines struck close to the California progressive ideal. He was a source of inspiration, a symbol of progressive virtues, and a protector at the highest court" ("The Urban Gentry on the Defensive," pp. 30–31). Roosevelt became "the nation's focal point for progressivism," concludes J. Rogers Hollingsworth, in *The Whirligig of Politics: The Democracy of Cleveland and Bryan* (University of Chicago Press, 1963), p. 195. In his own state of New York, Roosevelt carried on a continuous feud with the party's Old Guard, as evidenced in the use of his influence to gain the nomination of the progressive Charles Evans Hughes for governor in 1906.

12. Richard C. Bain and Judith H. Parris, *Convention Decisions and Voting Records* (2d ed., Brookings Institution, 1973), pp. 184–91.

13. Quoted by Matthew Josephson, *The President Makers 1896–1919* (first published, 1940; Frederick Ungar, 1964), p. 456.

The Deviation of 1912

When Theodore Roosevelt bolted the Republican party in 1912, however, two major progressive parties were pitted against the conservative Republicans. Together the two progressives plus Socialist Eugene V. Debs polled three-quarters of the popular vote (Wilson 42 percent, Roosevelt 27, Debs 6), while President Taft as the symbol of conservatism (yet by no means unresponsive to progressive forces, as his record of antitrust prosecutions shows) received less than one-quarter.

Yet even so powerful a third party—actually the second party in both electoral and popular votes—produced no realignment. The four million voters who supported Roosevelt in 1912 did not make up a true polar force as had the Populists and Free-Soilers. They were no committed ideological bloc whose political course was dictated by what was necessary to advance a program; they merely followed their leader where he led. Roosevelt's Progressive party remained in being, but when, in the 1914 midterm election, the Wilson administration showed a loss of support, it was the Republicans rather than the Progressives who benefited. It was evident that the public support given the Progressive party in 1912 had been Roosevelt's personal following, which did not attach automatically to other candidates running as Progressives. The country was clearly headed back to two-party normalcy. In 1916, the Republican and Progressive parties scheduled simultaneous conventions, and leaders entered into formal negotiations to find a basis for reunion. Looking for a candidate who would not be anathema to the Progressives, the Republicans found one in Charles Evans Hughes, the former progressive governor of New York who as a Supreme Court justice had been sheltered from the acrimony of 1912. The Progressives nominated Roosevelt, but when he withdrew in favor of Hughes the schism was ended.

Wilson's percentage of the popular vote rose from 42 to 49 percent, while the Republican vote climbed from 23 to 46. Most of the Progressives, clearly, had returned to the GOP. Even the seven-point Democratic gain appears only as a deviation—an expression of confidence in an incumbent president who had kept the country out of war—for later election returns show no evidence of significant permanent party switching.[14]

14. To the extent that the Wilson gain of 1916 constituted a minor realignment, the party switching was more than offset four years later by another minor realignment of voters alienated from the Democrats during and after the war. This is clear from the fact

By 1920 the two-party system had essentially returned to the pattern of 1896, with Republican hegemony throughout the North and West and a normal Republican majority nationally. So a decade and a half of great political, social, and institutional change proved, in the end, to be a period of stability in the party system.

---

that the Republican party was stronger throughout the 1920s than it was in 1916, not only in presidential voting but in voting for Republican candidates for governor, U.S. senator, and U.S. representative, which is a better measure of basic party strength. Paul T. David, *Party Strength in the United States 1872–1970* (University Press of Virginia, 1972), p. 303.

CHAPTER NINE

Minor Realignments of the 1920s

IN THE COMPLACENT 1920s, the Roosevelt strain of progressivism became increasingly submerged within the Republican party, which thus became less and less promising as an instrument of reform. The country was generally prosperous; the public had reacted against the foreign, if not the domestic, adventurism of Woodrow Wilson and given the Republicans a mandate under President Warren G. Harding to return to what he called "normalcy." Harding, and even more emphatically his successor, Calvin Coolidge ("the business of America is business"), had no intention of leading an assault on the status quo.

But the Democrats, as the decade opened, were not a party of reform either. Wilson had been unable, like Bryan before him, to consolidate the country's progressive forces in the Democratic party. The accident of Roosevelt's sojourn as head of the Republican party had prevented that. And the failure of Wilson's leadership in his later years weakened progressive influence in Democratic ranks and laid the ground for a resurgence of the party's conservative element. So John W. Davis, counsel to J. P. Morgan, was nominated as the Democratic presidential candidate in 1924, and the party's national committee fell under the control of men who were as much a part of the world of big business and high finance as were the Republican leaders themselves.

Frustrated and restless, progressives met to argue strategy and tactics, pushed and probed and experimented. Their efforts produced no major realignment. But they did create minor alterations in the party system that resembled in character, and even seemed to anticipate, the changes that were to come on a grand scale a decade later. These alterations are worth analysis not only as examples of the realignment process on a limited scale, but also as indicators of some of the forces that went into the political revolution of the 1930s.

The Minnesota Farmer-Labor Party

One of the most distinct and dramatic of the minor realignments of the period took place within the confines of a single state, Minnesota. Its origin, however, was elsewhere—in Bismarck, North Dakota, in February 1915.

The North Dakota state legislature had once again rejected the farmers' plea for a state-owned grain terminal elevator, and one legislator, in the course of the debate, was reported to have told the angry farmers to "go home and slop the hogs." Without even waiting for spring thaws to clear the country roads, thirty-five-year-old Arthur C. Townley, who had been an organizer in rural areas for the Socialist party, set out by bobsled to form a new and independent organization of farmers that would have enough power to force its demands on the politicians of the major parties. Convinced that the Socialist third-party route was one of futility, his aim was to use the state's newly established direct primary to capture the majority Republican party. His farmers would be bound together in a tightly organized party-within-a-party. The name of the new organization—the Farmers' Nonpartisan Political League—reflected its tactics.[1]

Townley was able to build his organization with astonishing speed. In 1916 the league's candidates swept both the Republican primary and the fall election, and Lynn J. Frazier, a farmer not previously in politics, became governor.

Even before that triumph, Townley had moved on to larger fields. From North Dakota he sent organizers into the wheatlands of neighboring states, among them Minnesota. He himself moved to St. Paul to set up offices of the National Nonpartisan League (NPL) and take a direct hand in the Minnesota campaign. But Minnesota, unlike North Dakota, was not one vast expanse of wheatland. It had cities too, and political success depended on perfecting an alliance of the rural with the urban discontented, the objective at which Bryan had so conspicuously failed. Labor leaders of the Twin Cities and the Iron Range were ready for such an alliance, and once the league had shown its strength among the wheat farmers of the northwest counties, labor created a committee to cooperate with the farmers in political action.

1. Robert L. Morlan, *Political Prairie Fire: The Nonpartisan League, 1915–22* (University of Minnesota Press, 1955), pp. 18–28; Elwyn B. Robinson, *The History of North Dakota* (University of Nebraska Press, 1966), pp. 328–31; Theodore Saloutos and John D. Hicks, *Agricultural Discontent in the Middle West 1900–1939* (University of Wisconsin Press, 1951), pp. 150–58, 190–205.

Successes in Minnesota were less immediate and decisive than those in North Dakota. In 1918, the NPL voted to back former Congressman Charles A. Lindbergh for governor in the Republican primary, but this proved to be an unfortunate choice in wartime, for Lindbergh had cast antipreparedness votes in Congress and had subsequently written a book attacking the United States' entry into the war. Bipartisan antileague organizations sprang into being to save the state not just from socialism but from "seditionists" and "traitors" as well, and enough Democrats crossed party lines to defeat Lindbergh in the Republican primary.[2] Some Leaguers then decided to try again in the fall with a slate of independents, who took the name Farmer-Labor party, but again they were defeated. In 1920 NPL candidates, who were also the candidates of a counterpart labor organization known as the Working People's Nonpartisan Political League, organized in 1919,[3] were defeated twice, narrowly in the Republican primary (again by Democratic votes) and decisively in the fall.

The series of defeats brought a change in tactics; over Townley's objections, the leagues voted to drop nonpartisanship and put all their energies into third-party organization. The Farmer-Labor party came into being as a loose-knit but full-fledged party, and at once became the chief competition for the majority Republicans as the Democratic party went into limbo. Then came a partial success. The new party in 1922 elected a senator, Henrik Shipstead, and two wheatland congressmen, and workers' organizations captured twelve of twenty-six Minneapolis city council seats. Next year, in a special election, Farmer-Laborite Magnus Johnson was sent to the Senate. Johnson was subsequently defeated in a regular election, but Shipstead was reelected twice as a Farmer-Laborite. Finally, in 1930, the Farmer-Labor party broke through as a clear majority with the election of its candidate for governor, Floyd B. Olson.[4]

The Nonpartisan League, like the Farmers' Alliance a generation earlier, was the prototype of a polar political force, organized around a cluster of issues that cut across the existing party structure, with a loyalty to its program that transcended any established Democratic or Republican attach-

2. Arthur Naftalin, "The Farmer-Labor Party in Minnesota" (Ph.D. dissertation, University of Minnesota, 1948), p. 54.
3. In its first year, 300 labor unions with 45,000 members joined the new organization. Ibid., p. 58.
4. Leslie Gene Rude, "A Rhetorical Analysis of the Minnesota Farmer-Labor Movement" (Ph.D. dissertation, University of Illinois, 1962), pp. 69–78; Morlan, *Political Prairie Fire*, pp. 187–201, 279–84, 301, 345–46; Saloutos and Hicks, *Agricultural Discontent*, pp. 177–81, 186–88, 197–98.

ments. To gain power, the polar politicians would work within the existing two-party system or they would set out to realign it, whichever appeared to serve their purpose better. In North Dakota and Wisconsin they saw the opportunity to capture the Republican label and tradition, and succeeded (in Wisconsin in alliance with the La Follette wing of the GOP). In Idaho, Colorado, and Montana—all silver states where the Democratic party had been strengthened in 1896—they set out to control that party and, again with allies, succeeded, for a time at least. In Minnesota and Washington they organized an independent party, and in South Dakota ran independent candidates in two elections. In all these states, the Nonpartisan campaigns polarized politics between radicals and conservatives, often forcing Republican and Democratic conservatives into temporary coalition. No doubt some permanent shifts in party allegiance took place, but except in Minnesota the results appear essentially as deviation.

The contrast between the careers of the Farmer-Labor parties in Minnesota and Washington is instructive. In Washington, the third party reached a peak of 31 percent of the vote in the race for governor in 1920, pulling its strength wholly from the Democratic party. But it could only divide the opposition with the Democrats; it was unable to supplant that party, and within a few years it disappeared and an unbalanced two-party competition between Republicans and Democrats was restored. The Farmer-Labor excursion added no net strength to the Democrats, and the whole episode appears (to judge from the aggregate election returns) to have been a deviation. In Minnesota, on the other hand, almost the whole of the Democratic party was absorbed in the Farmer-Labor uprising. As Democratic ranks dwindled to 3.2 percent of the vote for senator in 1926 and 5.4 percent of the vote for governor, the Farmer-Laborites replaced them as the state's second party, much as the Republicans had replaced the Whigs in the realignment of the 1850s.

As the second party in Minnesota, the Farmer-Laborites gave the Republicans stronger competition in that state than the Democrats were able to give the GOP in Washington and in most of the other northwestern states. The difference in competitive strength seemed to reaffirm the lesson learned in the 1890s and earlier decades: aggrieved Protestant Republicans could be lured away from their traditional attachment by a *new* party made up of, and led by, people like themselves who shared their political background. But except in a few silver states they could not bring themselves to shift to the Democratic party, with its different tradition and multiple disabilities carried over from the nineteenth century, and so it could not create a competitive balance in the region.

La Follette, McNary-Haugenism, and Al Smith

After 1920, the Nonpartisan League disintegrated rapidly as an organization,[5] but the radical political groups that it had spawned throughout the Northwest remained as so many building blocks to be brought together to create a national structure. Some were well-organized factions within the Republican party, like the North Dakota NPL and the La Follette branch of the Wisconsin GOP (which branch, of course, predated the league but was strengthened by it). Some were Democratic groups, like Burton K. Wheeler's Montana Democratic party and the Washington Democrats who as defectors had made up that state's short-lived Farmer-Labor party. Strongest of all was the Minnesota Farmer-Labor organization.

Discontent had not yet been politically organized in the urban states, but by 1924 it was well developed, particularly among the railroad brotherhoods, whose strike had been broken by a federal court injunction obtained by Harding's attorney general.[6] On the initiative of the rail unions, a Conference for Progressive Political Action had been formed in 1922. The CPPA contained many advocates of third-party action, who were citing the Labour party of Great Britain and the National Progressive party of Canada as successful models. Once the Democrats had nominated Davis in 1924 and La Follette had indicated his availability as an independent candidate, progressives were unanimous. They fell in enthusiastically behind La Follette.

La Follette received 4.8 million votes, 16.6 percent of the total, but this was far short of the total strength of the country's progressive forces. Handicapped by lack of funds (he spent only $222,000, according to the official report), by the difficulty of getting on the ballot, and by lack of organization,

5. Discredited by a jail sentence for conspiring to discourage enlistments during the war and embroiled in a dispute between factions of the North Dakota NPL, Townley resigned in 1922 as president of the national league; Morlan, *Political Prairie Fire*, pp. 255–61. The state organizations, already going their independent ways, gave less and less support to the national body and in 1923, beset with financial difficulties, it crumbled. One by one the state leagues disintegrated, too, except for the original North Dakota body. It recovered to elect Frazier to the Senate in 1922 and recapture the governorship and the lower house of the legislature two years later, and lived on as a political force for four more decades.

6. Both parties used this tactic. An injunction had been obtained by the Wilson administration to break a coal strike in 1919.

he could make a serious contest only in places where the building blocks of a radical political party were already in place—in other words, in the Northwest.[7] In many states there, the Democrats merely went through the motions of a campaign and threw their strength to La Follette. Even so, he could carry only one state, his own Wisconsin. In the Nonpartisan League's North Dakota, he received 45 percent of the vote; in Farmer-Labor Minnesota, 42 percent; in Wheeler's Montana and in Washington, 38 percent; in South Dakota, 37 percent; in California, 35 percent. In five other states he received more votes than the Democrats, who were reduced to 7 percent of the vote in Minnesota and North Dakota, 8 percent in Wisconsin and California, and less than 25 percent in each of the others. The states in which La Follette ran second formed a solid belt from the Wisconsin border through the northern wheat and mining states to Washington, Oregon, and California.

But in the East, organized labor made a similar showing for La Follette in only a few areas. Kenneth Mackay has estimated that, of La Follette's 4.8 million votes, 2.5 million came from the agrarians, 1 million from the Socialists, and the rest from nonsocialist union members and independent progressives.[8] But among the farmers at least, the protest vote was still organized as a polar bloc, ready for realignment whenever a truly progressive party emerged.

In the next four years, the Republicans did little to conciliate the farmers. The depression that had so affected agriculture in the early 1920s continued, long after manufacturing industries had revived. "Well, farmers never have made money," remarked Coolidge. "I don't believe we can do much about it."[9]

For those who thought that something could be done, a bill first offered in 1924 by Senator Charles L. McNary of Oregon and Representative Gilbert N. Haugen of Iowa, both Republicans, became the rallying point. It

7. Kenneth Campbell Mackay, *The Progressive Movement of 1924* (Columbia University Press, 1947), Chap. 2. La Follette was forced in some states to run under the label of an established party, which in many cases meant that of either the Socialists or another left-wing party that alienated moderate progressives. In a few states he failed to get on the ballot at all.

8. Ibid., p. 221. La Follette finished second to Coolidge in the counties containing Cleveland and Toledo, Ohio; Pittsburgh, Pennsylvania; Rochester, New York; and Passaic, New Jersey. But generally the coalition simply did not coalesce. Many labor leaders were lukewarm or hostile toward the independent candidate, even though he carried official endorsement. As in 1896, employers intimidated their employees, threatening layoffs if Coolidge was defeated, but prosperity was undoubtedly a more important factor in labor's support of the status quo.

9. William Allen White, *A Puritan in Babylon: The Story of Calvin Coolidge* (Capricorn Books, 1965), p. 344.

introduced the concept of parity prices for farm products (that is, the same ratio between farm prices and the general price index as had prevailed in pre-war years) and authorized the government to support basic farm commodity prices at parity by buying price-depressing surpluses. The surpluses would be sold on the world market, and the losses would be recouped through an "equalization fee" levied on the units sold domestically.

In the first year, the McNary-Haugen bill was endorsed by more than two hundred farm organizations, including the American Farm Bureau Federation and the National Grange, and by many business and banking organizations in the West. More than ten thousand endorsements were received by the House Committee on Agriculture. It failed to pass in 1924—opposed by the representatives of the cotton South as well as by the ad-ministration—but that was only the signal for a militant organizational and educational effort. A Corn Belt Committee was formed, whose chairman saw in the measure "enough dynamite . . . to change the political map for the next fifty years."[10]

By 1927, the cotton belt had swung into line with the corn and wheat belts, and that was enough to get the bill, in amended form, through Con-gress. But Coolidge vetoed it. In 1928 it passed again, and once more the President killed it. The severity of the farm depression must not be under-estimated, he acknowledged, but this bill would "poison the very wellsprings of our national spirit." It embodied, he said, "a formidable array of perils for agriculture . . . in a maze of ponderously futile bureaucratic paraphernalia . . . a nation-wide system of . . . intolerable espionage. . . . bureaucracy gone mad. . . . an intolerable tyranny."[11] Nevertheless, the Senate came within four votes of passing the measure over his veto. Republicans split 24–23 in favor of overriding the Republican President, in another confrontation of East against West. Democrats voted 33–12 in favor, split similarly on sec-tional lines.[12]

The Republican insurgents took their appeal to the 1928 Republican con-vention, but they lost both in the platform committee, 35–15, and on the convention floor, 807–277. Then Herbert Hoover—whom George N. Peek, president of the American Council on Agriculture, the McNary-Haugen

10. Saloutos and Hicks, *Agricultural Discontent*, p. 389. It is indicative of the temper of the farmers that the American Farm Bureau Federation replaced its national president with a McNary-Haugen advocate because the former had had the temerity to invite President Coolidge to address the federation's convention.

11. *Congressional Record*, 70 Cong. 1 sess. (May 23, 1928), pp. 9524–27.

12. Totals include those whose positions were announced as well as those voting. The actual vote was 50–31. Ibid. (May 25, 1928), pp. 9879–80.

lobbying organization, had called the "arch-enemy of a square deal for agriculture"—was nominated for President. The farm leaders headed for Houston to offer votes to the Democrats in exchange for a promise of farm relief. (This was their only recourse, since the third-party forces grouped around La Follette had disbanded after his death in 1925.) The agrarians were "welcomed with open arms" in Houston. Their farm plank was accepted practically verbatim.[13]

But in offering a candidate to the farm belt, the Democratic party made a choice less than ideal. Governor Alfred E. Smith of New York, rejected by the Democratic convention in 1924, had completed four more successful years as chief executive of the country's largest state and could not again be denied the Democratic nomination. But Smith had scarcely even visited the West or South and admittedly knew nothing about agriculture. Besides being a Catholic and a wet, he was a product of Tammany Hall and his manner of dress and speech could hardly have been more alien to rural and small-town America. He was not the man to lead millions of disgruntled Republican farmers into the Democratic party, but Peek and his colleagues were committed to the attempt. The Democratic National Committee put Peek in charge of a Chicago headquarters with the mission of corralling the farm vote of eleven states.

Try as they might, however, the Democratic strategists were unable to make McNary-Haugenism the paramount issue to the farmers. The farm issue, in fact, was blurred—Smith's statements on agricultural legislation were equivocal, while Hoover called agriculture "the most urgent problem in our nation today" and proposed a federal farm board with power to aid the farmers in marketing their products through cooperatives. So, most farmers, seeing little difference between the candidates on the farm question, could respond like other segments of the population to the two issues that *were* paramount in the 1928 campaign—Prohibition and Catholicism.

Nevertheless, when the ballots were counted, a substantial shift of voters to the Democratic party had taken place. Al Smith carried forty-five counties in Illinois, Iowa, Minnesota, and North Dakota—almost all of them rural—and while twenty of those counties were predominantly Catholic, the others, shown in Table 9-1, were not. Some of the counties showed spectacular pro-Democratic movement. Mercer County, North Dakota, for

13. This paragraph is based on Gilbert C. Fite, "The Agricultural Issue in the Presidential Campaign of 1928," *Mississippi Valley Historical Review*, Vol. 37 (March 1951). Fite gives the votes as 806–278. The 807–277 figures are from Richard C. Bain and Judith H. Parris, *Convention Decisions and Voting Records* (2d ed., Brookings Institution, 1973), App. C. Quotations from Fite, pp. 657, 659.

Table 9-1. *Democratic Gains in Twenty-five Predominantly Protestant Midwestern Counties, 1928*

State and county	Catholics as a percentage of all denomi- nations	Democratic percentage of presidential vote			Democratic gain in percentage points	
		1928	*1908*	*1916/20 (average)*	*1908 to 1928*	*1916/20 to 1928*
North Dakota						
Eddy	28	53	40	40	13	13
Foster	21	51	43	36	8	15
Logan[a]	37	56	16	19	40	37
McIntosh[a]	11	55	13	13	42	42
McLean	27	50	28	32	22	18
Mercer[a]	9	62	18	20	44	42
Sargent	35	53	35	32	18	21
Walsh	48	51	46	42	5	9
Illinois						
Effingham	43	52	59	49	−7	3
Franklin	28	53	46	40	7	13
Gallatin	39	54	55	52	−1	2
Macoupin	30	50	50	40	0	10
Monroe	46	52	46	32	6	20
Perry	24	52	48	39	4	13
Randolph	26	52	49	40	3	12
St. Clair	49	54	44	41	10	13
Union	4	55	59	58	−4	−3
Wabash	17	62	52	50	10	12
Minnesota						
Big Stone	33	56	34	31	22	25
Lincoln	29	51	41	39	10	12
Traverse	40	61	41	36	20	25
Iowa						
Audubon	9	50	38	35	12	15
Crawford	22	57	51	34	6	23
Plymouth	42	51	44	34	7	17
Shelby	45	51	48	40	3	11

Source: Col. 1, U.S. Bureau of the Census, *Religious Bodies: 1926;* cols. 2–6, Edgar Eugene Robinson, *The Presidential Vote, 1896–1932* (Octagon Books, 1970).
a. County had never voted for a Democratic presidential candidate before 1928.

instance, a county only 9 percent Catholic, which had given the Democratic presidential candidate 18 percent of the vote in 1908, 31 percent in 1916, and 9 percent in 1920, gave Smith 62 percent in 1928. Audubon County, Iowa, another solidly Protestant county, went from 38, 44, and 26 percent Democratic in the earlier years to 50 percent in 1928.[14] None of the forty-

14. Because percentages for 1912 and 1924 were distorted by third-party candidacies, 1908, 1916, and 1920 are used as base years for purposes of comparison. Percentages for 1916 and 1920 are averaged because the former was a year of abnormal Democratic strength and the latter a year of unusual Democratic weakness.

five counties had been carried by a Democrat since Wilson and some, including Mercer County, not even then.

To some extent, the shift to the Democrats represented a reaffirmation of the McKinley-Bryan alignment of 1896 and 1900 that had since been eroded by a steady drift to the Republicans, but some of it represented a wholly new accretion of strength above Bryan's levels—an influx of rural voters cut loose from their traditional Republican moorings by the La Follette candidacy of 1924 and McNary-Haugenism. When it is considered that this occurred despite Catholicism, the Prohibition issue, Tammany, Smith's fuzziness on the farm issue, and the refusal of almost every one of the major Republican leaders of the region to bolt his party, the shift takes on even greater significance.

The western agrarian protest movement in its sixth decade—frustrated once again by a standpat Republican conservatism, disenchanted with third-party experiments, supported now by most of the Democrats in the Congress and courted by the party's leadership—seemed about to find at last in the Democratic party the activist political instrument it had been seeking and thus bring about a party realignment in the corn and wheat belts. By the time of the next election, of course, the McNary-Haugen reformist movement was engulfed by the tide of protest that followed the onset of the Great Depression; the realignment that appeared on a minor scale in the Midwest in 1928 became part of the major realignment of the 1930s, and cannot be separately traced. But there is strong evidence to suggest that the realignment that occurred in the 1930s in the farm belt might well have happened anyway, on a smaller scale, without a general depression. The farm depression alone might have sufficed to realign the farming regions once the Democrats had nominated a candidate who would embrace the issue of farm relief wholeheartedly and who could appeal to the agrarian regions without Smith's handicaps. Franklin D. Roosevelt in 1932 presumably would have been such a candidate.

The "Al Smith Revolution" in the East

If Al Smith seemed to western rural and small-town Protestants like someone from an alien culture, he was to the members of that culture, to the masses of the East, one of their own—a folk hero, a poor boy risen from a Lower East Side tenement to the highest office in the nation's largest state.

He was urban in manner, in idiom, and in his approach to politics; versed in city problems, a Catholic, a friend of labor, a friend of the slum dweller, an enemy of Prohibition, and a leader who had made his mark in the enactment of factory laws and other pioneering social legislation. If he was the candidate least suited to channel the agrarian reformers of the West into the Democratic party, he was the one best suited to bring back to the party at least a large element of the urban working class whose switch to Republican ranks had marked the realignment of 1896.

The vitriol with which he was attacked by Protestant spokesmen and journals in the South and Southwest as "a subject of the Pope" was matched by the enthusiasm with which the Irish-dominated Democratic organizations of the Northeast rallied to his support. His appeal extended far beyond the Irish or even the Italians, Poles, and other Catholic groups; it extended also to the Jews and the Negroes who were congregated in the cities. He was "a popular idol with the masses" of Massachusetts; no presidential candidate in a generation matched Smith's "appeal to the reason and emotions" of that state's Democrats.[15] Negroes responded to the slogan "A vote for Al Smith is a vote against the Klan."[16] All the groups who felt like underdogs in an American society dominated by what today are called WASPs (white Anglo-Saxon Protestants) identified with the first candidate of either major party in the nation's history who was not a WASP.[17]

The issues of Catholicism and Prohibition made the 1928 election the most passionate since 1896. The intensity of feeling is shown by the voter turnout: 26.5 percent higher than in 1924.[18] In five states, the 1928 vote ac-

15. Michael E. Hennessy, *Four Decades of Massachusetts Politics, 1890–1935* (Norwood Press, 1935), p. 384.

16. Franklin D. Mitchell, *Embattled Democracy: Missouri Democratic Politics, 1919–1932* (University of Missouri Press, 1968), p. 115.

17. Protestant immigrant groups evidently identified with the WASPs rather than with Catholic immigrants. William F. Ogburn and Nell Snow Talbot concluded that "the influence of the foreign-born vote for Smith is . . . almost negligible when the influences of religion, prohibition, party, and residence are removed. . . . In other words, the foreign-born voted for Smith because they were wet and Catholic or for some other reason closely correlated with these, and not apparently for the sole reason that they were foreign-born." This would suggest that the Jews were not attracted to Smith as an ethnic group, but Ogburn and Talbot's sample of counties did not include New York City, where the evidence of a surge to Smith of Jewish voters along with other recent immigrant groups is unmistakable. Ogburn and Talbot, "A Measurement of the Factors in the Presidential Election of 1928," *Social Forces*, Vol. 8 (December 1929), pp. 175–83.

18. The increase between 1920 and 1924 was 8.7 percent; between 1928 and 1932, 8.0 percent. The 1928 increase was probably due mainly to the motivation of many women who, though enfranchised in 1920, had never voted to cast their ballots for the first time.

tually exceed that recorded four years later at the height of the national protest against the depression and Herbert Hoover—most conspicuously in Pennsylvania, where the total vote increased by 47 percent between 1924 and 1928, then fell off by almost 10 percent in 1932.

In a country polarized between Catholic and Protestant, wet and dry, the former were of course heavily outnumbered in 1928, and Smith was resoundingly defeated. The Democrats lost Virginia, North Carolina, Florida, and Texas for the first time since Reconstruction, barely carried Alabama, and received only 40 percent of the vote in Kentucky and 44 percent in Tennessee. In addition to the six states of the hitherto Solid South that remained loyal, Smith carried only Massachusetts and Rhode Island.

But the Democratic gains in many northern cities were impressive. Smith's enormous majority in Boston—more than 100,000, a two-to-one majority over Hoover—converted staunchly Republican Massachusetts into what it has since remained in presidential politics, normally a Democratic state. Rhode Island was similarly converted. So were New Haven, Albany, Scranton, Wilkes-Barre, and St. Louis. Other cities that were already Democratic turned out massive majorities. New York City gave Smith a plurality of 450,000, with 60 percent of the total vote; Hudson County (Jersey City) also gave him 60 percent. Some of the great Democratic strongholds of the present day thus trace their Democratic preponderance not to the New Deal but to the pre–New Deal election of 1928. "Before the Roosevelt Revolution," Lubell has written, "there was an Al Smith Revolution."[19]

Table 9-2 shows clearly the two-way flow of voters across party lines in major northern cities. While the Democratic share of the presidential vote in 1928 was almost double that of 1924 in Catholic Boston, it barely held its own in "Bible belt" centers like Kansas City and Wichita. But 1924 was a year when the anti-Republican vote was split. If the combined vote for the Democratic candidate Davis and the independent candidate La Follette is used as the basis for comparison with the Smith vote of 1928, Smith's weakness outside his northeastern stronghold becomes dramatically clear. He lost ground in most of the urban centers of the Midwest and Far West, by margins ranging up to 18 percentage points in Wichita.

The anti-Smith reaction was apparent in the smaller cities and rural areas of the East as well as those of the West and South. Despite Hudson County, Smith lost New Jersey. Despite New York City, he lost his own New York State while non-Catholic Franklin D. Roosevelt was elected governor on the

19. Samuel Lubell, *The Future of American Politics* (2d ed., Doubleday, 1956), p. 36.

Table 9-2. *Comparison of the 1928 Democratic Vote for President with the 1924 Democratic Vote and 1924 Democratic plus Progressive Vote, Selected Urban Areas*

Percent

Region and urban area[a]	Democratic, 1928 (1)	Democratic, 1924 (2)	Democratic plus Progressive, 1924 (3)	Increase of col. 1 over col. 2 (4)	Increase of col. 1 over col. 3 (5)
Northeast					
Boston	67	36	53	31	14
Providence	53	39	43	14	10
Hartford	46	28	38	18	8
New Haven	50	30	43	20	7
New York (city)	61	40	59	21	2
Buffalo	45	21	42	24	3
Albany	55	42	48	13	7
Rochester	41	21	43	20	−2
Philadelphia	40	12	22	28	18
Pittsburgh	42	9	41	33	1
Scranton	53	27	40	26	13
Newark	41	22	34	19	7
Jersey City	60	47	58	13	2
Baltimore (city)	48	37	57	11	−9
Midwest					
Cleveland	46	9	51	37	−5
Columbus	34	25	42	9	−8
Cincinnati	43	18	39	25	4
Detroit	37	7	20	30	17
Grand Rapids	24	14	23	10	1
Indianapolis	40	37	41	3	−1
Chicago	47	20	38	27	9
Springfield	40	28	48	12	−8
St. Louis (city)	52	36	47	16	5
Kansas City	43	43	48	0	−5
Minneapolis	39	6	41	33	−2
St. Paul	51	10	52	41	−1
Omaha	47	29	55	18	−8
Wichita	25	24	43	1	−18
West					
Denver	36	17	37	19	−1
Los Angeles	29	7	35	22	−6
San Francisco	49	6	52	43	−3
Portland	37	22	50	15	−13
Seattle	32	7	47	25	−15

Source: Robinson, *Presidential Vote.*

a. The figures are for the county that includes the designated city in each case except Baltimore and St. Louis, which are independent cities, and New York City, where the figure is for the five counties that constitute the city.

same Democratic ticket. For Smith, that was the cruelest of all the blows of the cruel election.

How much of all this crossing of party lines was deviation and how much can be considered realignment? In other words, if the Great Depression had not come on the heels of the 1928 election to transform politics, how much of the presidential voting pattern of 1928 would have been reflected in new and durable patterns of party identification expressed not only in presidential voting but in balloting for other offices and in voter registration? Surely the Democrats who bolted the party at the presidential level in 1928 would have proved to be mainly deviants. The South and the border states would have looked upon 1928 as an aberration, forgiven the Democratic party, and returned to it; so would most of the Democrats elsewhere who rejected the party that year only because they did not approve of the candidacy of Al Smith.

The pro-Smith movement in the northern cities, one may guess, would have had a more lasting impact on voting patterns. It is true, as Jerome M. Clubb and Howard W. Allen have pointed out, that the swing to Smith in northern cities was not reflected in corresponding shifts to the Democratic column in voting for lesser offices.[20] Nor was it accompanied by the kind of massive switching of voter registration that would occur in a major realignment (and that did occur in the 1930s).[21] And insofar as the Smith majorities were produced by the turnout of new voters, they measure only a shift in the party balance. On the other hand, Clubb and Allen do find some degree of carryover of the Smith vote to Democratic candidates for other offices. In analyzing Chicago's conversion from a Republican to a Democratic city, John Myers Allswang identifies 1928 as the critical election that brought into being a Democratic "ethnic vote."[22] It seems reasonable to believe that the varied minority groups that were caught up in the Smith candidacy in the northern cities would have been absorbed into the local Democratic organizations with appropriate recognition and rewards and would have retained an emotional identity with the party that could nominate a slum-bred Irishman for president. The immigrant–old-stock cleavage, already established, would have become even more pronounced.

20. "The Cities and the Election of 1928: Partisan Realignment," *American Historical Review*, Vol. 74 (April 1969), pp. 1205–20.
21. Voter registration trends for selected areas during both periods are shown in Figures 10-3 through 10-7, below.
22. "The Political Behavior of Chicago's Ethnic Groups, 1918–1932" (Ph.D. dissertation, University of Pittsburgh, 1967).

There remains the problem of interpreting the limited Al Smith revolution in relation to the Roosevelt revolution that followed. In some accounts of party realignment, they are treated as two stages of a single process; a single "realignment period" spanning the elections from 1928 to 1936 is identified. But the Smith and Roosevelt revolutions were stages of a single realignment only if they were impelled by the same political forces. And this was, in the main, not the case.

Aside from the western farm vote in some localities, discussed earlier, the 1928 vote for Al Smith did not represent the kind of protest against economic conditions that powered the later realignment. Except for the farmers, the country was prosperous. And Smith went to great pains *not* to be the voice of protest. His object was just the opposite: to reassure the business and financial communities that he was not another La Follette, "that he was safe, sound and as well liked by business as anyone could desire."[23] He selected as chairman of the Democratic National Committee the millionaire chairman of the General Motors finance committee, John J. Raskob. Raskob located the Democratic headquarters in the Manhattan building that housed GM's headquarters and assured the nation that Smith as President "would give the country a constructive business Administration." "Business, big or little, has nothing to fear from Governor Smith," he said.[24] Then Smith himself put to rest the notion being circulated by the Republicans that he contemplated a wholesale reduction of the tariff rates established by the Republican Congress in 1922 over Democratic opposition. The Democratic party, he said, was now committed to tariff schedules that would "to the very limit protect legitimate business enterprise, as well as American labor from ruinous competition." The American workingman would not lose a single "five-cent piece" from tariff reduction, and "nothing will be done that will embarrass or interfere in any way with the legitimate progress of business, big or small."[25]

The heavy movement across party lines in presidential voting in the cities

23. William V. Shannon, *The American Irish* (Macmillan, 1963), p. 179. Richard O'Connor says "those Democrats who hoped the campaign would be conducted along progressive lines were immediately disappointed" (*The First Hurrah: A Biography of Alfred E. Smith* [Putnam, 1970], p. 199).

24. Edmund A. Moore, *A Catholic Runs for President: The Campaign of 1928* (Peter Smith, 1956), pp. 119–25.

25. Campaign address at Louisville, Oct. 13, 1928, *Campaign Addresses of Governor Alfred E. Smith, Democratic Candidate for President, 1928* (Democratic National Committee, 1929), pp. 165–66. Repeated at Philadelphia, Oct. 27, 1928 (ibid., p. 229), and elsewhere.

in 1928 was obviously caused by the issues that dominated public (and to an even greater extent, private) discussion in that election—religion and Prohibition.[26] Those were not the dominant issues of 1932 and 1936. The minor realignment of 1928 in the cities can therefore be considered an episode in American politics distinct from the realignment of the 1930s.

The minor upheaval in the farm belt, as well as the realignment in Minnesota, on the other hand, sprang from the same kind of protest against economic hardship that became universal a few months later. That much of the rearrangement of political patterns in the 1920s can therefore be considered a precursor of—perhaps not improperly seen as an integral part of—the political revolution precipitated by Wall Street's "Black Thursday," October 24, 1929.

26. An analysis made after the election showed that in a cross-section of 173 northern counties the Smith vote exhibited a higher correlation with the "wet" vote (as shown in concurrent referenda on Prohibition issues) than with the percentage of Catholics, but that both were powerful factors in party switching. Ogburn and Talbot, "A Measurement of the Factors in the Presidential Election of 1928," pp. 175–83. Ruth C. Silva, using different statistical techniques, found no significant relation between the 1928 outcome and either religion or Prohibition; she found the Smith vote to be associated most closely with the proportion of "foreign white stock" in a state's population. *Rum, Religion, and Votes: 1928 Reexamined* (Pennsylvania State University Press, 1962). David Burner faults the methods used in both studies. After the findings of the Survey Research Center of the University of Michigan as to the importance of Catholicism as an issue in the 1960 election, he finds it difficult to accept Silva's conclusion that religion was not significant in the outcome thirty-two years earlier. *The Politics of Provincialism: The Democratic Party in Transition, 1918–1932* (Knopf, 1968), pp. 217–19.

CHAPTER TEN

The Realignment of the 1930s

UNLIKE the two great political upheavals of the nineteenth century, the realignment of the 1930s was precipitated suddenly. It was not the culmination of a protest movement that had been growing, steadily or intermittently, for decades. Protest there was, as evidenced in the minor realignments of the 1920s, but it was weak, and in the summer and early autumn of 1929 no polar force of significant national dimensions existed. The political revolution set in motion later in that year was the product of a single cataclysmic event—the Great Depression—which polarized the country. Inevitably, the two parties moved to the opposing poles.

The polarization was not an immediate or rapid process. When the stock market collapsed in October 1929, everyone was caught off guard, radicals and conservatives alike. Neither political party, nor anybody else, had a program to reverse the economic slide. President Herbert Hoover's instinctive response was to call a conference of the country's business and industrial giants and ask them to voluntarily maintain production and employment, a request to which they agreed. He called for a "prudent" expansion of public works and asked for a one-year federal tax reduction of $160 million, which the Congress promptly granted. Then he expressed a cautious optimism and waited for the upturn.

But it did not come, and the clamor grew for more vigorous governmental action. It was in the character of Hoover, a man philosophically committed to the concept of limited government, to resist such clamor. It was in the nature of the Republican party as the country's conservative political organization to oppose hasty and ill-considered change. Perhaps it is the tendency of any responsible incumbent administration, confronted by a crisis where every alternative course of action is fraught with risk, to temporize. In any case, as the demand for energetic governmental policies rose, the Republican party took with increasing firmness a position of resistance. It had a vocal group of dissenting insurgents, but the President spoke for the majority.

The Democratic party, out of power, had an obvious issue to exploit. But it could not do so at the beginning with clarity and force because the issue of governmental intervention in the economy cut across the party system, dividing Democrats as well as Republicans. Some of the Democratic spokesmen cried out for governmental action, but others shared the views of Herbert Hoover. Only after it elected a president in 1932 was the party able to make a full commitment on the side of activism and move as a unified body away from the center of the spectrum toward the pole.

The realignment of the 1930s was precipitated when Hoover placed the Republican party squarely on the side of conservatism as the country polarized. But the form and shape of the realignment were not determined until Franklin Roosevelt placed the Democratic party clearly on the other side. Then the parties confronted each other across a philosophical chasm. The millions of polarized voters on opposite sides of the chasm then conformed their political attachments with the new alignment—some immediately, some after a little time.

Herbert Hoover and Limited Intervention

President Hoover had not come to office as a representative of his party's doctrinaire conservative wing. He was a moderate progressive, in the Republican spectrum of the 1920s, and was presented by his party as a humanitarian and a practical man, an engineer in government. He had looked forward, in his acceptance speech, to "the day when poverty will be banished from this nation." He had acknowledged the existence of a farm problem, and while, like Coolidge, he had rejected McNary-Haugen, he had, unlike his predecessor, proposed his own activist alternative—his Federal Farm Board, created in 1929. In his memoirs, he dissociates himself from his party's extreme conservatives, from the Senate Republican leader, James E. Watson of Indiana, for example, whose "economic, social, and political faith differs from mine," and from Treasury Secretary Andrew W. Mellon, head of the "leave it alone liquidationist" faction within the administration.[1] In using the powers of government even to the extent he did, Hoover had to

1. *The Memoirs of Herbert Hoover*, Vol. 3, *The Great Depression, 1929–1941* (Macmillan, 1952), pp. 103, 30–31.

overrule the "leave it alone" conservatives and break the tradition of almost total nonintervention that, he said, had been steadfastly adhered to in earlier panics by previous presidents, including Van Buren, Grant, Cleveland, and Theodore Roosevelt.[2]

"ECONOMIC DEPRESSION CANNOT BE CURED BY LEGISLATIVE ACTION"

But if, compared to Mellon or Grant or Cleveland, Herbert Hoover was an interventionist, he was still a believer in keeping intervention as limited as possible. The principal responsibility of government, in his view, was a negative one: to do nothing that would destroy "confidence."[3] Specifically, that meant keeping expenditures under control and the budget in balance. And he was a man of principle. Like Grover Cleveland in an earlier crisis, he saw himself as the defender of the country's integrity, and his own, against the compromisers and the demagogues. Undoubtedly, again like Cleveland, he saw this course as politically advantageous too, for, along with everyone else, he fully expected the depression to be brief, and when the storm passed he would be respected and rewarded for having stood unflinching among the lightning bolts. So he extolled the principle of nonintervention in speech after speech and in his messages. On December 2, 1930, he told the Congress:

> Economic depression cannot be cured by legislative action or executive pronouncement. Economic wounds must be healed by the action of the cells of the economic body—the producers and consumers themselves. Recovery can be expedited and its effects mitigated by cooperative action. . . .
> The best contribution of government lies in encouragement of this voluntary cooperation in the community.[4]

Those who sought legislative and executive action concentrated initially on relief of hardship. The first test came in 1930 when drought compounded the miseries of the depression in the Mississippi Valley. The President recommended a loan fund for farming purposes, including feed for animals, but when Senator Joseph T. Robinson of Arkansas, the Democratic leader, persuaded the Senate to extend the loans to food for human victims of the

2. Ibid., p. 29.
3. In his opening statement announcing his conferences with business leaders, President Hoover twice used the word, proclaiming the "confidence" of his administration and insisting that "any lack of confidence" on anyone else's part was "foolish." Press statement, Nov. 15, 1929. William Starr Myers (ed.), *The State Papers and Other Public Writings of Herbert Hoover*, Vol. 1 (Doubleday, Doran, 1934), pp. 133–34.
4. Ibid., pp. 429–30. As examples of speeches on this theme, see his addresses to the Gridiron Club, Dec. 14, 1929, and April 26, 1930, in ibid., pp. 189, 268.

drought, the President objected. Relief for people, he said, was the function of the Red Cross. When the Senate then voted to give the Red Cross $25 million for drought relief, the latter organization refused to accept federal funds on the ground that to do so would discourage private giving. The appropriation thereupon died.[5]

This and other spending proposals before the Congress, asking as much as $4.5 billion and mostly for relief, the President denounced en bloc as "playing politics at the expense of human misery." "Prosperity cannot be restored by raids upon the public Treasury," he declared.[6]

The activists also seized the occasion to advance a series of reform measures dealing with unemployment that had been on the reformers' agenda for at least nine years, since the unemployment conference chaired by Herbert Hoover, then secretary of commerce, in 1921. One of them proposed creation of a national system of employment exchanges built on existing state and local public employment agencies (what is now the United States Employment Service) through a program of federal aid. The debate on that proposal in 1930 signaled, in both tone and content, the terms of the party struggle over the role of the federal government that was to dominate national politics for the rest of the depression decade and even afterward.

Senator Robert F. Wagner, New York Democrat, sponsor of the bill, talked of the "wan, half-starved children, pale and thin from undernourishment" and of the "waste of human life which is the price of demoralizing unemployment" and contended that "unemployment lies within the sphere of Federal action because many of the remedies to be applied can only be applied by national agencies."[7]

For the conservatives, Senator Hiram Bingham, Connecticut Republican, cited a brief by the National Association of Manufacturers that the bill was unconstitutional and warned his colleagues not to "do injustice to our Constitution and our fundamentals of government in order to go along with our sympathy for those who are in trouble." And he continued:

> If we take away from the localities concerned the need of providing for their own suffering, we do away with just that much incentive toward their taking part in local self-government. . . . It is an attack on the very self-respect of local com-

5. Harris Gaylord Warren, *Herbert Hoover and the Great Depression* (first published, 1959; Norton, 1967), pp. 177–83.
6. Press conference statement, Dec. 9, 1930; *Public Writings of Herbert Hoover*, Vol. 1, p. 460.
7. *Congressional Record*, 71 Cong. 2 sess. (April 28, 1930), pp. 7797–98.

munities, inferring that they should not be left to work out their own salvation in matters of this kind. . . . We may safely leave it to the citizens [in the states] to set up such agencies. . . . it is upon the development of sturdy, self-reliant citizenry that this Republic must in the long run depend for its long life. If we build up a body of citizens who are always depending on the central Government we will make weak citizens rather than strong citizens.[8]

The Democrats divided 22–4 in favor of federal action, the Republicans 23–11 against. The Republican division followed the old line of cleavage between East and West, between Old Guard and agrarian insurgents. When the measure finally passed, President Hoover denounced it as proposing "the most vicious tyranny ever set up in the United States,"[9] and killed it with a pocket veto.

Through the summer and fall of 1931 as the depression deepened, President Hoover resisted demands that he call an emergency session of the new Seventy-second Congress. But when it assembled for its regular session in December 1931, he had his antidepression program ready. It was basically a recovery program, embellished with a few reforms affecting financial institutions but with nothing at all in the way of relief. For months, the President had been preaching against federal appropriations for relief. They would, he said, impair "something infinitely valuable in the life of the American people" and strike "at the roots of self-government." Lincoln, he said (without documentation), would have been against them. Cleveland, he said (with documentation), believed "that though the people support the Government, the Government should not support the people." Unemployment insurance, he declared, would degenerate into a "dole" that would "endow the slacker." The sum of local community chest budgets "will meet the needs of the Nation as a whole," and "no governmental action . . . can replace that God-imposed responsibility of the individual man and woman to their neighbors." Death and sickness rates had actually declined. The objective should be "the least possible Government entry into the economic field, and that only in temporary and emergency form." "Shall we," asked the President, "regiment our people by an extension of the arm of bureaucracy into a multitude of affairs?"[10]

8. Ibid. (May 12, 1930), p. 8742.
9. Address to Indiana Republican Editorial Association, Indianapolis, June 15, 1931; *Public Writings of Herbert Hoover*, Vol. 1, p. 579.
10. The statements in this paragraph all appear in *Public Writings of Herbert Hoover:* Vol. 1, pp. 496, 500–04, 497, 579, 583; Vol. 2, pp. 14–15, 44–45. The items appeared between February and December 1931.

"HE HEARS OUR CRY UNMOVED"

The centerpiece of Hoover's legislative program was a proposal for a Reconstruction Finance Corporation (RFC) to lend to "established industries, railways, and financial institutions" to "protect the credit structure and stimulate employment" and, indirectly, to "strengthen confidence." The contrast between this proposal and his bleak pronouncement on relief—"I am opposed to any direct or indirect Government dole. . . . Our people are providing against distress from unemployment in true American fashion by a magnificent response to public appeal and by action of the local governments"[11]—was stark and obvious. Before passing the President's RFC bill, the Democrats could at least take a partisan stand on the issue of relief. Their opening speaker, when Congress convened, was George Huddleston of Birmingham, Alabama:

> With hundreds of millions the President would come to the rescue of the bondholders of the land banks, to the succor of the commercial banks, to the support of the railroads, and to the aid of industry of one kind and another. To these interests he would open the Treasury, but to starving men, women, and children he would not give a red cent. . . .
>
> The State is not in a situation to help. Uncle Sam can help, but the man at Uncle Sam's helm will not help. He hears our cry unmoved. Starving women and children appeal to him in vain. . . . we have a man in charge of the Government who is more interested in the pocketbooks of the rich than he is in the empty bellies of the poor.[12]

Responded Carroll L. Beedy of Maine, for the Republicans:

> Today I confess that I was amazed and somewhat disappointed to find that the majority party had given the floor in this first available hour . . . to a man who would commit his party to the principle that it is the legitimate function of government to go into the Public Treasury and take out money contributed to the support of Government by millions of our people and give it to a particular group which for the moment is in need. From that proposition, my friends, to which you gentlemen of the majority, judging by the enthusiasm of your applause, have acceded, we on this side of the House beg leave to dissent. . . . men . . . have here acquiesced in one of the underlying principles of the Marxian philosophy.[13]

A few days later, the director of President Hoover's Organization on Unemployment Relief, Walter S. Gifford, president of the American Telephone and Telegraph Company, testified that his organization "was not to do

11. State of the Union Message, Dec. 8, 1931, in ibid., Vol. 2, pp. 50–52. Industries were excluded from the bill introduced next day as S. 1 of the Seventy-second Congress. Aid was restricted to financial institutions and railroads.

12. *Congressional Record*, 72 Cong. 1 sess. (Dec. 9, 1931), pp. 240–42.

13. Ibid., pp. 242–43.

anything other than to encourage the States to do the work." He assured a Senate committee that each state would successfully "care for its own." He had no information on total relief needs and total expenditures, on standards of relief in the various states, or on tax and debt limits that might hamper community efforts, but he did "not think the data would be of any particular value" since "all we need concern ourselves about are the cases where matters can not be taken care of, and that is a very much simpler proposition to look into." In any case, federal aid should be opposed because it would lessen state and community responsibility and the "net result might well be that the unemployed who are in need would be worse instead of better off."[14]

And so, on the issue of whether the federal government should come to the aid of the unnumbered millions who had been plunged into destitution, the Republican party moved simply, logically, even righteously, to the conservative pole. The Hoover of 1928 may have been a moderate centrist, in the political spectrum of that time, but in four years of calamity the whole spectrum moved sharply to the left. By 1932 the center had slipped from under the President and had stranded him, his heels still dug in, at the extreme. And his party, save for its insurgent minority, was stranded with him.

Since the end of Reconstruction (except for the Theodore Roosevelt aberration, and after all, T.R. did leave the party) Republicans had stood on the principle that the federal government should not intervene in the affairs of business, states, local communities, or private charities. That principle had been well rewarded; Republicans had been the majority party during all that time, and never more decisively than in the decade that had just ingloriously ended. Depressions of the past had proved to be transitory and had been ridden out successfully without a sacrifice of principle. This one could be too. That was the confident consensus of the conservative majority of Republicans as they took the offensive in pinning the opprobrium of "dole" on the opposition. They entered the 1932 campaign with this platform: "The people themselves, by their own courage, their own patient and resolute effort in the readjustments of their own affairs, can and will work out the cure. . . . True to American traditions and principles of government, the administration has regarded the relief problem as one of State and local responsibility."[15]

14. *Unemployment Relief*, Hearings before a subcommittee of the Senate Committee on Manufactures, 72 Cong. 1 sess. (Jan. 8, 1932), pp. 310, 313–15.

15. *National Party Platforms: 1840–1968*, compiled by Kirk H. Porter and Donald Bruce Johnson (University of Illinois Press, 1970), pp. 339, 341.

Before 1932: The Democrats Move Slowly

The Democrats were slower in moving to the other, interventionist pole. When the depression struck, the minority party had no greater will or capacity than the Hoover administration to respond to the public demand for governmental activism. Its titular leadership was thoroughly identified with big business. Raskob retained control of the national party machinery and, along with Bernard M. Baruch and a few other Democratic financiers, paid the expenses of such headquarters as were maintained. Al Smith himself entered the world of big business as president of the Empire State Building, and moved in the social circle of the rich. The southern wing of the party, which provided its leadership in the Congress, had no intention of taking the offensive on economic issues either. The major preoccupation, on both sides, was the Eighteenth Amendment and the Volstead Act.

So it was that the editors of *The Nation*, in calling for a new liberal party in 1931, could say that the Republican party's "weaker twin, the hybrid Democratic organization, differs from the G.O.P. only in that its desire to become the party of privilege has never been satisfied. . . . Essentially there is no difference between these two major parties except that the bankers and businessmen have found the Republicans more dependable."[16] As the springboard for a new party, John Dewey, Paul H. Douglas, and other intellectuals had formed the League for Independent Political Action, and Douglas in a league publication had stated the rationale: "It is idle to hope that either the Republican or the Democratic parties as at present constituted can ever be forged into honest or progressive instruments." While the Democratic party has "its sprinkling of liberal spirits . . . it is basically controlled by conservative Southerners and the corrupt political machines of the North."[17]

The real political opposition to the Hoover administration, in its first three years, remained therefore where it had been during the Coolidge years —not in the official opposition party but in a bipartisan bloc of insurgents organized primarily in the Senate. In that coalition, Republicans were the senior partners both in numbers and in stature. Their leaders were westerners of the agrarian tradition like George Norris of Nebraska, William E. Borah of Idaho, Hiram Johnson of California, and Robert M. La Follette, Jr., of Wisconsin, who had succeeded to the office of his late father.

16. "A Party for the People," *The Nation* (Jan. 28, 1931), p. 88.
17. Paul H. Douglas, *Why a Political Realignment?* (League for Independent Political Action, 1930), pp. 5–6.

Insurgent Democrats in the Senate joined with Republican progressives in 1932 in support of a bill by La Follette for $375 million in federal grants to the states for relief of the unemployed, but they were repudiated by the party's Senate leadership. Democratic Leader Joseph T. Robinson of Arkansas would support nothing beyond emergency loans to states that could show their resources were exhausted. "If we recognize that the primary responsibility for emergency relief is . . . national," he argued, "the draft on the Federal Treasury will threaten to become immeasurable and unlimited."[18] And to defeat the bill he carried with him more than half the voting Democrats, twenty-one of forty.[19]

But the issue did not rest. "Complete breakdown is imminent," warned *Survey*, the journal of the private charity field, in April 1932, on the basis of reports from thirty-seven cities.[20] New York City's relief bureau closed its doors early in April, leaving the unemployed nowhere even to apply for aid. "Starvation is wide-spread," declared Republican Governor Gifford Pinchot of Pennsylvania, although other governors disagreed.[21] On a single day in April, one-fourth (in acreage) of the state of Mississippi—39,699 farms and 12 to 15 percent of all town property—was auctioned in sheriffs' sales.[22] Men talked of violence. "Unless something is done," seven railroad brotherhoods warned the President, "we cannot be responsible for the orderly operation of the railroads . . . disorder . . . is sure to arise if conditions continue. . . . The unemployed citizen whom we represent will not accept starvation."[23] A Methodist minister wrote Senator Royal S. Copeland of New York: "The entire north country is seething with communism. . . . Expect revolution."[24] Even the conservative Democratic leaders outside the Congress—Smith, Baruch, Owen D. Young—endorsed a bond issue for public works.

Finally, on May 11, after a visit by Young and Baruch, Democratic Leader Robinson took the Senate floor. "We have all hoped, and some of us have believed, that conditions would improve," he said, referring to the

18. *Congressional Record*, 72 Cong. 1 sess. (Feb. 3, 1932), p. 3314.
19. However, five Democrats were paired or announced in favor of the grant program. Including all senators who voted or whose positions were made known, Democrats split 24–21 for the grants, Republicans 30–19 against. Ibid. (Feb. 16, 1932), p. 4052.
20. "How the Cities Stand," *Survey* (April 15, 1932), p. 71.
21. *Literary Digest* (April 2, 1932), p. 12.
22. Ibid. (May 7, 1932), p. 10.
23. Statement of May 14, 1932, quoted in *Congressional Record*, 72 Cong. 1 sess. (May 16, 1932), p. 10253.
24. *Congressional Record*, 72 Cong. 1 sess. (May 11, 1932), p. 9971.

earlier debate; but "the information that reaches me is that . . . unemployment is increasing rather than diminishing." Some action should be taken before Congress adjourned for the presidential election campaign. He revived his proposal for emergency relief loans to the states and proposed, in addition, $2 billion in loans for self-liquidating state and local public works. At this, the President saw the political perils of standpattism and modified the stand he had maintained through three depression winters. He would accept the relief loan program if it were turned over to the RFC (thus keeping it out of the federal budget) and if it were coupled with a doubling of the RFC's general lending powers. Republican senators, reported *Time* magazine, were "aggrieved" at the President's "apparent desertion of them in their 'anti-Dole' fight."[25]

On the other side of the Capitol, Speaker John Nance Garner, a Democratic presidential candidate, had by this time developed an activist program of his own. On May 26 he called for a $900 million federal public works program to be financed by a bond issue, a billion-dollar RFC fund for loans to "any person," and $100 million of "mercy money" appropriated to the President for use at his discretion. On the public works program the President came down hard: "It is the most gigantic pork barrel ever proposed to the American Congress. It is an unexampled raid on the public Treasury." The "most urgent question today," he said, "is the prompt balancing of the Budget."[26]

Outside the Congress, those close to the urban scene saw even the boldest of the Democratic programs as in reality timid. "It is a crisis, imminent and terrifying," declared thirty-one mayors and other city executives in urging a $5 billion spending program.[27] An unterrified Senate defeated a program of that magnitude, 56–12, when La Follette offered it.

In the end, the issue was dramatized by a presidential veto of a bill embodying the Garner-Robinson proposals. The relief bill that was finally signed by the President had to be stripped of Garner's "pork barrel," his "mercy money," and his RFC loans to individuals. Finally, after more than two and a half years, the Democratic party had managed to pull itself together under its congressional leadership around a program that, however restrained and moderate by later standards, still offered an activist alterna-

25. *Time* (May 23, 1932), p. 10.

26. Press conference statement, May 22, 1932, in *Public Writings of Herbert Hoover*, Vol. 2, pp. 195–96.

27. *Congressional Record* (June 7, 1932), pp. 12147, 12182.

tive to the sluggish and reluctant course the GOP had chosen. The Democrats had at last set themselves up as the party of the Masses against the Classes, as *Time* magazine put it.[28] The party had moved some distance toward the activist pole. It remained for Franklin Roosevelt to take it the rest of the way.

After 1932 : The Democrats Commit Themselves

Barring a sudden, miraculous recovery from the depression, only one thing could possibly have saved Herbert Hoover in 1932—a division of the opposition between the Democratic party and a more radical third-party movement along the lines of 1924. But this time the potential organizers of a third party had no available leader of stature to make the try. Norris and Pinchot were too old, Bob La Follette, Jr., too young, other insurgent senators either too individualistic or too committed to party regularity. More important still, the Democratic party, again in contrast to 1924, appeared headed toward progressive leadership, for Governor Franklin D. Roosevelt of New York was its front runner for the presidential nomination.

A CAUTIOUS CAMPAIGN

Roosevelt did not enter the presidential race as a crusading progressive of the La Follette stamp. He had a head start for the nomination by virtue of his 1928 victory as governor of the largest state (while Smith was losing) and his reelection by a whopping 725,000 majority in 1930. He had had national exposure as the party's vice-presidential candidate in 1920 and as the man who nominated Smith in 1924 and again in 1928. He had maintained his political contacts across the country through incessant letter-writing, and his personal charm had registered. With all these advantages his strategy was to proceed cautiously and avoid mistakes. So his positions on some of the major issues of the day—the tariff, for instance, the World Court, and even Prohibition repeal—were disappointingly ambiguous to many would-be supporters.[29] He even agreed with Hoover that relief should be a state and local responsibility.

28. *Time* (July 18, 1932), p. 8; idem (July 25, 1932), p. 8.
29. James MacGregor Burns, *Roosevelt: The Lion and the Fox* (Harcourt, Brace, 1956), pp. 126, 133.

Roosevelt could afford to be cautious because his standing as a progressive was secure. He was an old Wilsonian. He had consistently maintained in his correspondence that the Democratic party should commit itself to progressive, though not radical, principles. As governor, he had supported public development of St. Lawrence River power, which endeared him to progressives everywhere, and he had made a positive record on conservation and on labor and welfare legislation. He was one of only three or four governors (others were Pinchot of Pennsylvania and Philip F. La Follette of Wisconsin, both Republicans) who had initiated significant programs of state aid for relief. He had endorsed the principle of unemployment insurance. Progressives were prominent in his state administration—Frances Perkins, Harry Hopkins, Leland Olds. As early as June 1930, Senator Burton K. Wheeler of Montana, the Democratic insurgent leader who had been La Follette's running mate in 1924, had come out for Roosevelt for President. "You more nearly typify the progressive thought of the Nation than anyone else," he told Roosevelt.[30]

As the campaign progressed, Roosevelt struck a progressive tone, even if he did not offer much in the way of a program. In April came his Forgotten Man speech—"These unhappy times call for . . . plans that . . . build from the bottom up and not from the top down, that put their faith once more in the forgotten man at the bottom of the economic pyramid." The following month, at Olgethorpe University in Georgia, he called for a "more equitable distribution of the national income" and expressed in purest form the activist temper: "Take a method and try it; if it fails, admit it frankly, and try another. But above all, try something." To some editors, this was "radicalism," and the idea that the country should "gamble its way out of the depression" was dangerous.[31]

Roosevelt's principal rival for the nomination, Al Smith, drew the ideological issue from the conservative side. Seizing on the Forgotten Man speech, he swore to "fight to the end any candidate who persists in any demagogic appeal to the masses of the working people of the country to destroy themselves by setting class against class and rich against poor."[32] But Roosevelt entered the convention with a majority of pledged votes and got

30. Arthur M. Schlesinger, Jr., *Crisis of the Old Order 1919–1933* (Houghton Mifflin, 1957), pp. 277–78, 389–93.
31. Quoted from newspaper comment on the Oglethorpe speech, by *Literary Digest* (June 4, 1932), pp. 3–4.
32. *Literary Digest* (April 23, 1932), p. 11.

the necessary two-thirds on the fourth ballot. The progressives once again had captured the Democratic party.

Paul Douglas, among others, continued to advocate a new party. Despite Roosevelt's "many progressive tendencies and a certain feeling for the underdog," he argued, the "Democratic party will remain the Democratic party under his administration."[33] But the response was negligible, and Douglas and many of his fellow members of the League for Independent Political Action finally voted for Socialist Norman Thomas. Others gave up their independence to throw in their lot with Roosevelt.

It probably did not matter what kind of campaign Roosevelt conducted, cautious or otherwise. When unemployment stands at 24 percent, as it did in 1932, an incumbent President is not reelected. The Democrats' share of the popular vote rose from 34 percent in 1920, 29 in 1924, and 41 in 1928 to 57 percent in the landslide of 1932. Almost one-third of the Republican strength of 1928 was lost to Roosevelt or to minor-party candidates.

But one landslide is not a party realignment. A realignment requires that the switching voters remain switched. In this case they would have to become more than just Hoover haters or Roosevelt supporters; they would have to come to think of themselves as Democrats.

The Democratic party was still an unknown quantity, however, in regard to the issues that had caused the massive crossing of the party line. It would have to prove, in office, that its philosophy and program were an improvement over those of Herbert Hoover. And it would have to find a way to absorb the newcomers into its institutional structure in order to retain them.

AN ACTIVIST ADMINISTRATION

As it was in the character of Herbert Hoover to lead the Republican party to the conservative pole on the issues of the depression, so it was in the personality and temperament of Franklin Roosevelt to cast his party in the role of activism. Yet while the distinctive quality of Rooseveltian leadership had much to do with the form and timing of the realignment that followed, he still seems to have been more instrument than author. At a time of suffering beyond all precedent, the policies of the government could not have remained forever frozen. An activist government would have been installed somehow;

33. Paul H. Douglas, *The Coming of a New Party* (Whittlesey House, 1932), pp. 168–69.

if not through Roosevelt, then through someone else; if not through the Democratic party, then through some other party; if not in 1932, then assuredly in 1936. And realignment would have come about in any case. The key variable in the 1930s was not leadership but the overwhelming intrinsic power of the Great Depression as a realigning issue.

If Roosevelt had not been on the scene as a declared activist, it still seems scarcely conceivable that the Democrats in 1932 would have joined the GOP and nominated another states' rights conservative. The candidacy of Governor Albert C. Ritchie of Maryland, who represented that point of view, never got off the ground. John Garner or Al Smith, one of whom might have been nominated if there had been no Roosevelt, would in all probability have campaigned for and accepted the nomination as a committed activist. Or someone else would have emerged. But if by any chance the Democratic party had halted the leftward movement that was so apparent in the Congress in 1932 and chosen instead to share the conservative side of the political spectrum with Hoover, then the insurgents of both parties would have had to unite behind someone—Wheeler or La Follette or Borah or someone less conspicuous—who would have caught the spirit of the times. The forces of protest were too powerful to be denied political expression in one of the major parties of the two-party system. If they had not captured one of the existing parties, as the forces of protest did in 1896, they would have formed their own, as in 1854. And in that case, if the new party did not at once appear as one of the two major parties, the strength of the issue would have carried it forward until it did attain that status. Realignment would have been different in form but not in essence.

As it happened, the forces demanding change captured the Democratic party. And even after Roosevelt's election, they, more than he, controlled the direction of the party and the government. If Roosevelt led his party and the people, he was also led by them. That the Congress during the Hundred Days passed major bills that had not even been printed suggests not only the depth of the crisis but Congress's reading of the depth of the President's support. And Congress was more than a "rubber stamp"; it too was responding to pressure from the country. Some major enactments of the New Deal were of congressional origin—including the National Labor Relations Act and public housing—and other measures credited to Roosevelt were spurred by pressure from the Hill. "In these early years," says Arthur M. Schlesinger, Jr., "Congress was as often to the left of Roosevelt as to the right."[34]

34. *The Coming of the New Deal* (Houghton Mifflin, 1958), pp. 554–55.

Mass organizations that were rising at the activist pole kept Roosevelt constantly reminded that, if the Democratic party flagged in its pursuit of reform, it could be superseded as the party of protest by a coalescence of formidable forces. The Reverend Charles E. Coughlin, a parish priest of Royal Oak, Michigan, had a radio audience of ten million people a week and was organizing a political movement called the National Union for Social Justice. Dr. Francis E. Townsend of Long Beach, California, author of a radical pension plan, was printing 200,000 copies of his weekly newspaper and forming "Townsend Clubs" across the country, which were potential components of a party organization. Senator Huey P. Long of Louisiana was planning a Share Our Wealth party for 1936 which, according to a poll commissioned by Democratic Chairman James A. Farley, would receive from three to six million votes. Milo Reno and his National Farmers' Holiday Association—a militant midwestern farm organization—were planning to support a third-party movement. The Democratic party in several states was far to the left of Roosevelt: in California, where Upton Sinclair ran for governor in 1934 on his End Poverty in California plan; in Washington State, where the Washington Commonwealth Federation captured control of the party. The Farmer-Labor governor of Minnesota, Floyd B. Olson, was a radical with a national following. The La Follettes in Wisconsin seceded from the GOP and formed a Progressive party that swept the state in 1934. The League for Independent Political Action became the Farmer-Labor Political Federation with a demand for "a new social order." While the programs of these organizations and leaders differed in scope and content, they tended in the same direction: a planned economy, public ownership of some or all basic industries, "production for use instead of for profit," redistribution of wealth and income. The radical threat had at least some effect on Roosevelt's decisions as he reinvigorated the New Deal, after a period of pause and uncertainty, in 1935. He cited Long's Share Our Wealth proposals and spoke of "stealing Long's thunder" when he proposed his own share-the-wealth tax plan: a federal inheritance tax, higher personal income taxes in the top brackets, a graduated corporation income tax.[35]

With these and other measures, Roosevelt maintained a pace of reform fast enough to keep the forces of the left from converging. Olson and the La

---

35. Arthur M. Schlesinger, Jr., *The Politics of Upheaval* (Houghton Mifflin, 1960), Chaps. 2, 3. T. Harry Williams, *Huey Long* (Knopf, 1969), pp. 843–47. John L. Shover, *Cornbelt Rebellion: The Farmers' Holiday Association* (University of Illinois Press, 1965), Chap. 12. Schlesinger, *Politics of Upheaval*, Chap. 7 and pp. 325–28.

Follettes remained loyal. Long's assassination in September 1935 removed the only other leader who might have seriously challenged Roosevelt. Coughlin, Townsend, and Gerald L. K. Smith finally formed a Union party in 1936 with Representative William Lemke, North Dakota Republican and Nonpartisan Leaguer, as its candidate. But Lemke polled fewer than 900,000 votes, a showing no better than that of Norman Thomas four years before.

Meanwhile the Republican party remained immobile at the conservative pole. As the government finally changed direction, under Roosevelt, Hoover continued to be the best-publicized spokesman both for the conservative ideologues and for the GOP. In his plea for vindication he denounced the New Deal and all its works in terms that grew harsher year by year: "a muddle of unco-ordinated reckless adventures in government," "the color of despotism . . . the color of Fascism . . . the color of Socialism," "flagrant flouting of the Constitution," "the era of the Great Fear," "dipped from cauldrons of European Fascism or Socialism," "the philosophy of collectivism and . . . greed for power," "repudiation of obligations . . . violation of trust," "the gospel of class hatred preached from the White House," "a revolutionary design to replace the American system with despotism," "the poisoning of Americanism."[36] Republican congressional minorities had gone along with some of the New Deal reforms, such as social security and the National Labor Relations Act, but they had gone down fighting against others—the farm bills, the reciprocal trade agreements act, the Tennessee Valley Authority, the public utilities holding company act. In 1936, Governor Alfred M. Landon as the Republican presidential candidate began his campaign attacking only New Deal extravagance and maladministration but ended sounding not much different from Hoover. The Republican National Committee talked of Stalin and Kerensky and Earl Browder and joined with organized business and the Hearst newspapers in a concerted effort to equate social security with European totalitarian ideas.

All this was a matter of compulsion as well as choice. If the country's activists were enraged by the fact of human suffering, its conservatives were no less incensed by the nature of the remedies proposed. To the conservatives, the New Deal genuinely threatened the very basis of the country's free economic system and political tradition. They too constituted a polar force that had to have political expression, and in the Republican party they found their instrument. A new generation of Republican moderates was to

36. Various addresses, November 1935 to June 1936; Herbert Hoover, *Addresses upon the American Road, 1933–38* (Scribner's, 1938), pp. 76, 88, 101, 105, 132, 175–78.

Figure 10-1. *The Realignment of the 1930s*[a]

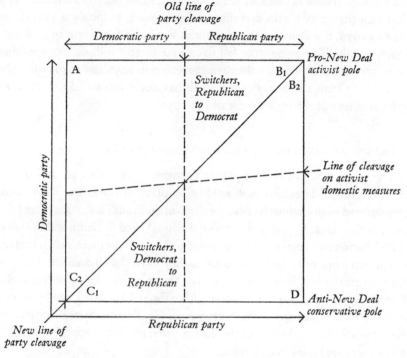

a. This figure is schematic rather than quantitatively precise. The size of the compartments does not measure the proportion of the electorate contained in each.

emerge later, but in the early New Deal years the militant conservatives had no difficulty retaining control of the national Republican party and stamping it with their philosophy.

By 1936, then, the polarization of the country was reflected in the polarization of the major parties. The election of that year, in which Roosevelt achieved his most stunning victory, therefore marked the climax of the realignment.

Substance of the Realignment

The realignment of the 1930s took the form shown in Figure 10-1. It followed the pattern of the second scenario in Chapter 2—realignment through the two existing major parties.

The millions of voters who switched from the Republican to the Democratic party, shown as block B_1 in the diagram, made the latter the country's clear majority party for the first time in eighty years. In the eight years from 1928 to 1936, the Democratic presidential vote rose from 15.0 to 27.8 million, while the Republican vote fell from 21.4 to 16.7 million. Some of that swing appears as a deviation that was corrected in 1938 and 1940, when the Republicans snapped back. But the GOP has never recovered the majority position it lost in the realignment of the 1930s.

URBAN, WORKING CLASS, AND ETHNIC SWITCHERS

The millions who switched parties between 1928 and 1936, and stayed switched, can be identified most readily by place of residence. They were concentrated in the industrial cities of the North. Franklin Roosevelt and the issues of the Great Depression completed what Alfred E. Smith and the issue of Prohibition had begun—the transformation of the northern urban centers into the network of Democratic bastions they have since remained. In cities that historically had been preponderantly Democratic, like New York, the Republican party ceased to be a competitive force. Cities that had been converted to Democracy in the Smith campaign, like Boston, were confirmed in their new allegiance. And cities that had resisted the Smith appeal responded to Roosevelt and were transformed.

Figure 10-2 shows the distinctly different voting behavior of three types of communities in the North. The top line shows the trend in the Democratic share of the presidential vote for a composite of the five northern counties of over 100,000 population with the highest proportion of Catholics and foreign born. These are the cities that were swept up in the "Al Smith revolution." With the combined La Follette-Davis vote of 1924 taken as the base, the Democrats showed an eleven-point gain in 1928. While that party enjoyed further gains in the next two presidential elections, most of its permanent increment in strength had come by 1928. The second line is a composite of the five urban counties of over 100,000 population at the other end of the scale of Catholic and foreign-born proportions. These communities the Al Smith revolution passed by, but they were caught up in the New Deal sweeps of 1932 and 1936. Although, as would be expected from their population composition, they are among the more Republican of urban counties, they still registered consistent Democratic majorities in the postrealignment period. Both groups of urban counties stabilized at a Democratic strength in 1948

Figure 10-2. *Democratic Percentage of the Presidential Vote in Selected Counties,
1920–48*[a]

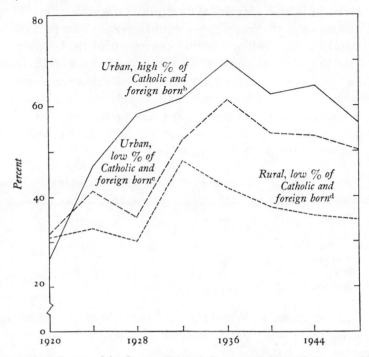

Sources: U.S. Bureau of the Census, *Fifteenth Census of the United States: 1930*, Vol. 3,
Pts. 1 and 2; *Religious Bodies: 1936*, Vol. 1, summary and detailed tables.

a. The percentages shown for 1924 are of the combined Democratic-Progressive vote.

b. Composite of the five counties of over 100,000 population in the North and West
with the highest proportion of Catholics and foreign born (as of 1930). They are Suffolk
(Boston); Wayne (Detroit); Passaic, N.J.; Bronx, N.Y.; New York, N.Y.

c. Composite of the five counties of over 100,000 population in the North and West
with the lowest proportion of Catholics and foreign born (as of 1930). They are Marion
(Indianapolis); Franklin (Columbus); Summit (Akron); King (Seattle); Hennepin
(Minneapolis).

d. Composite of thirty rural counties (ten contiguous counties each from New York,
Michigan, and Illinois) that lost population from 1900 to 1930 and had a low proportion
of Catholics and foreign born. In New York the counties are: Chenango, Columbia,
Delaware, Greene, Madison, Oswego, Otsego, Rensselaer, Schoharie, Ulster. In Michi-
gan: Barry, Branch, Clinton, Hillsdale, Huron, Mecosta, Montcalm, Sanilac, Tuscola,
Van Buren. In Illinois: Brown, Cass, Greene, Hancock, McDonough, Mason, Menard,
Morgan, Pike, Warren.

ten points above the La Follette-Davis 1924 base. The rural North, on the
other hand, experienced no such conversion. Thirty counties in three states
selected as representative of rural, old-stock, Protestant America (shown in

the bottom line) registered only a two-point Democratic gain over that time span. There the Democratic vote of 1932 turned out to be largely a deviation, and most of the Democratic gains of the depression years were lost by 1944. Within the cities, the Republicans-turned-Democrats were predominantly of the working class. Polling evidence confirms what the behavior of the parties and the politicians suggests: the party system that emerged from the revolution of the 1930s reflected a pronounced class cleavage. Businessmen and professional men were preponderantly Republican; the working class predominantly Democratic. Following is a breakdown of responses (by percent) given early in 1940 to the question, "In politics, do you consider yourself a Democrat, Independent, Socialist, or Republican?"[37]

	Republican	Democrat	Independent	Other
Total sample	38	42	19	1
Professional	44	29	25	2
Business	48	29	22	1
White-collar workers	36	40	22	2
Skilled workers	36	44	19	1
Semiskilled workers	33	47	18	2
Unskilled workers	27	55	16	2

And to another question, "Which party would you like to see win the Presidential election in 1940?" the breakdown of responses for each party (by percent) was:

	Democrat	Republican
Upper income	36	64
Middle income	51	49
Lower income	69	31
Labor union members	66	34

Since polling only began in the 1930s, comparative data are not available for the pre–New Deal period. The party system undoubtedly reflected some degree of class bias before the realignment, but there can be little doubt that it was accentuated by the event. It was in the New Deal era that tight bonds were formed between organized labor and the Democratic party, that ties equally close if less formal and overt were formed between business organizations and the GOP, and that partisan politics for the first time since 1896 sharply accented class issues. An activist-conservative line of cleavage and a

37. *Public Opinion Quarterly*, Vol. 4 (1940), pp. 340–41, summarizing American Institute of Public Opinion (Gallup) polls.

class-based rationale for the party system are two ways of describing the same structure, for it was the lower economic classes who wanted to use the powers of government for the relief of economic hardship and the reform of the economic system in their interests. The party conflict thus reflected at the same time a policy disagreement as to the role of government and a struggle between broad class and interest groups for the control of government.

Burnham and others have cited the *Literary Digest* polls to confirm not only that the realignment of the 1930s had a class basis but also that it took place after 1932 rather than before or during that year's election. The 1932 *Digest* poll accurately predicted the outcome of that year's election in spite of the pronounced bias of the sample in favor of upper-income groups. It missed Roosevelt's percentage of the popular vote by only three points, predicting 56 percent instead of the 59 percent he actually received. The 1932 Democratic majority must therefore have been relatively uniform among all groups in the population. But when the *Digest* used the same sampling technique in 1936, it miscalculated by eighteen points. It predicted 42 percent of the popular vote for Roosevelt; he received 60. This large discrepancy could only be accounted for by the underrepresentation of the lower-income groups in the sample, and their conversion to the Democrats in markedly disproportionate numbers must therefore have occurred after 1932.[38]

The polls have also consistently shown Democratic support to be far higher among Catholics, Jews, and blacks than among white Protestants, and while this disparity dates to 1928 in the case of the Catholics and perhaps the Jews, it was solidified by the realignment of the 1930s, as Figure 10-1 indicates. Perhaps the most careful study of the realignment of individual ethnic groups was done by John Myers Allswang, covering nine groups in Chicago during the period when the city was converted from a normally Republican one (it reelected its Republican mayor in 1927) to one so solidly Democratic that the Republican party could not offer a serious challenge.[39] Of Allswang's

38. Walter Dean Burnham, *Critical Elections and the Mainsprings of American Politics* (Norton, 1970), p. 56. For comments on the unrepresentativeness of the *Digest* sample, see George Gallup, *A Guide to Public Opinion Polls* (Princeton University Press, 1940), pp. 73–75, quoted in Julian L. Simon, *Basic Research Methods in Social Science: The Art of Empirical Investigation* (Random House, 1969), pp. 114–15. The sample was taken largely from telephone books and lists of automobile owners and so was heavily concentrated in the upper half of the income scale.

39. In 1928, the city was narrowly carried by Hoover. But in 1930 it helped elect a Democratic senator and defeated two of its five Republican congressmen; in 1931, it elected Anton J. Cermak as the first of a line of Democratic mayors; in 1932, it went for Roosevelt; in 1934, it replaced the rest of its Republican congressmen; in 1935, it voted overwhelmingly Democratic for mayor.

nine groups, only the Czechs and the Lithuanians gave a majority to the Democratic candidate for senator in 1924. In the 1928 presidential contest, five other groups swung over to Democratic majorities—the Poles (71 percent), Italians (63 percent), Jews (60 percent), Germans (58 percent), and Yugoslavs (54 percent). By that time, the Czech Democratic majority had risen to 73 percent and the Lithuanian to 77 percent. In 1932, a Protestant ethnic group, the Swedes, went Democratic by a bare majority of 51 percent. Finally in 1934, the ninth group, the blacks, left the party of Lincoln on their way to becoming the most solid of all the Democratic ethnic groups.[40] In that year they unseated Republican Congressman Oscar De Priest, the first black ever sent to the House of Representatives from a northern constituency and still the last black Republican to be sent there from any district.

EVIDENCE FROM PARTY REGISTRATION FIGURES

In addition to the data from public opinion polls, another source of quantitative data on party attachment is available in the twentieth century to supplement election returns, which are the only source of such data for the nineteenth. This new set of indicators consists of figures on voter registration (or enrollment) by parties, a requirement that was introduced in some states when direct primaries were instituted, beginning in the Progressive Era.

Registration is a positive act by a voter to identify with a party as such, as distinct from giving his support to the party's candidate in a particular election. For purposes of analyzing party alignment, therefore, registration data have the great advantage of ignoring the deviant voting behavior that so frequently confuses the interpretation of election returns: a deviant, by definition, does not change his party affiliation. On the other hand, registration data have their own weaknesses. Since registration is a public act, it is subject to coercive influences. In any local jurisdiction, the majority party will always be overregistered. Some voters who oppose that party in November in the secrecy of the voting booth may register with it because it holds the more significant primaries. Or they may find it prudent to affiliate publicly with the party that controls local patronage as well as the police, the courts, and property tax assessment.[41] And since registration requires a deliberate

40. John Myers Allswang, "The Political Behavior of Chicago's Ethnic Groups, 1918–1932" (Ph.D. dissertation, University of Pittsburgh, 1967), esp. table, pp. 39–40. The Irish, who were not among the ethnic groups whose political behavior was studied, were, as elsewhere, traditionally Democratic.

41. In one county in New York State, the local political folklore held that a change in enrollment meant an automatic $500 increase or decrease in the assessed value of a homeowner's real estate, depending on the direction of the change.

Figure 10-3. *Democratic Percentage of Two-Party Enrollment in New York, Selected Areas, 1915–70*[a]

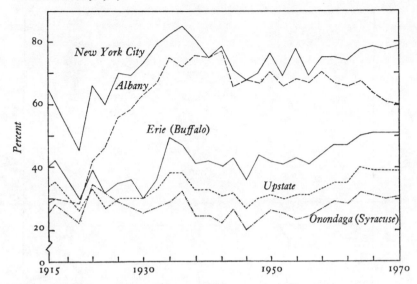

Source: *Manual for the Use of the Legislature of the State of New York*, various years.
a. Plotted biennially for even years, except 1915 is included and data for 1918 are not available.

overt act, registration shifts lag behind permanent shifts in voting behavior. Registrars are also slow in purging the voting lists of persons who have died or moved away.

Party registration data, moreover, are not universally available. In some states, voters are not required to register by party. In still other states, the figures are not centrally compiled and published. But for five states—New York, Pennsylvania, West Virginia, Oregon, and California—continuous series of party registration figures by counties have been published since the 1920s.

Registration trends in selected areas in the five states are presented in Figures 10-3, 10-4, 10-5, 10-6, and 10-7. They show how sharp and decisive was the break with the past in some areas and how limited it was in others. They also give evidence of the timing of the realignment where it appeared.[42]

Party enrollment trends in New York State (Figure 10-3) show a massive realignment in New York City and in Albany County, beginning from a

42. The trend lines begin at different dates in the several charts because the states began requiring registration, or began compiling and publishing the data, at different times.

Figure 10-4. *Democratic Percentage of Two-Party Registration in West Virginia, Selected Counties, 1928–70*[a]

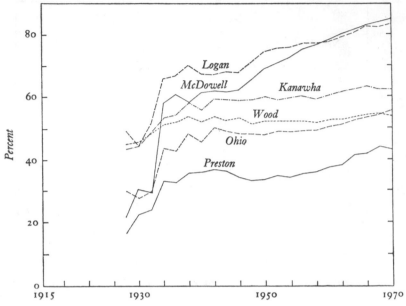

Source: *West Virginia Blue Books*, various years.
a. Plotted biennially.

Democratic low point in 1920 and reaching its climax in the 1930s, but no comparable trend in other places. Not only the rural areas but also some major industrial cities were bypassed in the New Deal realignment. In upstate New York as a whole the 1930s appear as a period not of realignment but of deviation. Political lines in Onondaga County (Syracuse), which Franklin Roosevelt could never carry, remained untouched by the New Deal era. Even Erie County (Buffalo) resembled the rural upstate more than it did New York City: Democratic strength stabilized at a level somewhat higher than in the 1920s, but the shift was limited. The new Democrats were primarily in the city of Buffalo, which elected a Democratic mayor in 1933. The rural areas of the county remained as Republican as the rest of upstate New York.[43]

43. The lines on the New York chart are less stable than those for other states because party enrollment has been annual rather than permanent. Since third-party registration or enrollment has been negligible in all states requiring registration by parties (rarely over 3 percent), it is disregarded wherever registration figures are cited in this book. The figures used are the Democratic and Republican percentages of the combined major party registrations or enrollment rather than of the total of all parties.

Figure 10-5. *Democratic Percentage of Two-Party Registration in Pennsylvania, Selected Counties, 1926–71*[a]

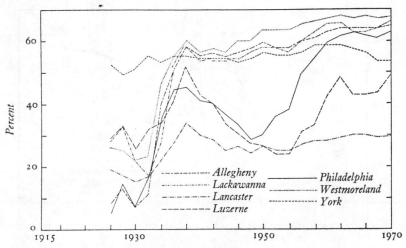

Source: *The Pennsylvania Manual*, various years.
a. Plotted biennially, except 1971 instead of 1970 data were used.

Figure 10-4, which presents the registration trends for six West Virginia counties, portrays again the sharp realignment of the 1930s—especially between 1932 and 1934—and a picture of relative stability since. The upheaval was greatest in the southern coalfields (Logan and McDowell counties) and in Ohio County (Wheeling, steel). In McDowell County, the Democratic percentage rose from 29.5 to 58 percent in a single two-year period following the election in 1932 of the first Democratic governor in a dozen years (along with Franklin Roosevelt). In the coal counties, the Republican party continued the struggle for a time after the Democrats had attained a clear preponderance, then gradually disappeared. The urban counties of Kanawha (Charleston) and Wood (Parkersburg) underwent a more limited realignment in the 1930s and have shown remarkable stability since. Preston County, which is agricultural, shows the typically lower Democratic strength of rural areas but reflects greater gains for the party than were recorded in the typical rural county of New York. Unlike the New York counties, the West Virginia localities in no case experienced a peaking of Democratic strength in the 1930s followed by a sustained decline. The shift of voters in the registration books was sudden, decisive, and permanent.

Registration figures for Pennsylvania (Figure 10-5) show some of the most revolutionary changes of all. In the metropolis of Allegheny County

Figure 10-6. *Democratic Percentage of Two-Party Registration in Oregon, Selected Counties, 1918–68*[a]

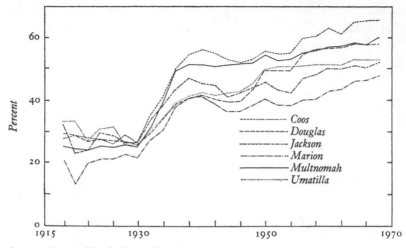

Source: *Oregon Blue Books*, various years.
a. Plotted biennially.

(Pittsburgh), the proportion of Democratic voters rose between 1930 and 1938 from 7 percent to 58 percent—a shift equivalent to more than half the county's voters. Rises nearly as steep were recorded in other coal and steel counties, including Westmoreland and Lackawanna. In these areas, the shifts took place mainly between 1932 and 1936, and they were sustained. By contrast, the Pennsylvania Dutch county of York, which was predominantly Democratic before the realignment, experienced no appreciable Democratic gain.

The political shifts in six of Oregon's major counties, shown in Figure 10-6, reveal a remarkable uniformity, unlike the divergent patterns of the East—a testament, probably, to the absence of disciplined party organizations in the West and also of sharp urban-rural and ethnic cleavages. In every county, Democratic registration declined slightly in the 1920s from the levels of the Wilson period, remained fairly stable until 1930, climbed steeply until 1938 or 1940, and stabilized at the new heights. A similar pattern is shown for California counties in Figure 10-7.

COUNTERMOVEMENT TO THE REPUBLICANS

In the cities, the early years of the realignment of the 1930s saw an almost entirely one-way movement. As the Democratic party gained its massive in-

Figure 10-7. *Democratic Percentage of Two-Party Registration in California, Selected Counties, 1928–70*[a]

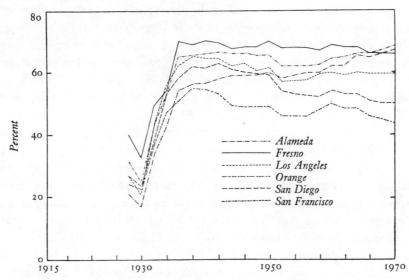

Sources: For 1928–62, Eugene C. Lee, *California Votes 1928–1960*, with 1962 supplement (University of California, Berkeley, Institute of Governmental Studies, 1961, 1963); for 1964 and later, *A Review and Analysis of Registration and Voting* (California legislature handbook).

a. Plotted biennially.

fusion of working-class Republicans who were ready for radicalism, it lost few of its own previous adherents who were not. In 1934, Al Smith, John W. Davis, and other eminent leaders of the pre–New Deal Democratic party organized the American Liberty League as a vehicle for anti–New Deal Democrats, but it never developed mass support and collapsed a few years later. Nevertheless, the net shift of voters to the Democratic side undoubtedly concealed some countermovement of conservatives. If leaders like Smith, who after all had been the archetypal urban Democrat, found the New Deal philosophically intolerable, he could not have been alone.

In traditional rural areas of native white Protestant Democratic strength, a measurable countermovement occurred. Particularly in Ohio, Indiana, and Illinois, Democratic losses among conservative rural voters were sufficient to substantially offset the party's gains in the cities. These were traditional Democrats, most of them living in communities founded by settlers from the South who had brought their Democratic politics with them. The communities had been steadfast through the Civil War, when many were Copperhead in sentiment, and through all the years thereafter until, having attained prosperity along with their neighbors of Yankee stock, they found they could not take "the spending, farm, and civil rights policies of the New Deal."[44] They were probably influenced too by the Democratic party's becoming, after 1928, even more markedly the party of the big cities, the Catholics, and the foreign born. Fenton finds a comparable pro-Republican reaction to the New Deal in the Bourbon rural areas of the border states, such as Maryland's traditionally Democratic Eastern Shore, and in areas of subsistence agriculture like south central Kentucky.[45]

That traditionally Democratic York County, Pennsylvania, showed no gain in its Democratic registration majority between 1932 and 1938 (Figure 10-5) could be accounted for in one of two ways: either all of its Republican industrial workers defied the national surge toward the Democrats or those who followed the trend were offset by an equal number of conservative Democrats—probably rural residents—who left their party when it was transformed. Since the former is hardly conceivable, the latter must be the case. A town-by-town examination of York County records would in all probability reveal what Fenton's county-by-county studies of the Midwest revealed—a two-way flow of voters across the party lines.

To be an integral part of the realignment of the 1930s, however, the countermovement did not have to take place immediately. In 1938, the Republicans began a comeback. That year they nearly doubled their strength in the House of Representatives, gained seven Senate seats, and recaptured the governorships of fourteen states, including the industrial strongholds of Massachusetts, Connecticut, Pennsylvania, Ohio, and Michigan. Most of the gains can undoubtedly be explained by the normal cycle of politics: the independent voters were by now rebelling against Democratic excesses and swinging to a Republican party that in many states had acquired new pro-

44. John H. Fenton, *Midwest Politics* (Holt, Rinehart and Winston, 1966), p. 145. Fenton identifies the areas of the three states where the defections took place and analyzes the reasons on pp. 145–46, 162–63, 182–83, 215–18.

45. John H. Fenton, *Politics in the Border States: A Study of the Patterns of Political Organization and Political Change Common to the Border States—Maryland, West Virginia, Kentucky and Missouri* (Hauser Press, 1957), pp. 75–78, 117–21, 162–63, 198–99. In addition, communities settled by Germans, particularly German Catholics, who had initially affiliated with the Democratic party because of the nativist tendency of the GOP made the transition to the Republican party. But it is not clear how many were alienated by the economics of the New Deal and how many realigned because of two "Democratic" wars against Germany. William H. Flanigan and Nancy H. Zingale observe that, in Minnesota, a significant proportion of traditionally Democratic rural voters, mainly in German communities, crossed to the Republican side in the 1930s. "Measurement of Electoral Stability and Change, 1832 to 1968" (paper delivered to the annual meeting of the American Political Science Association, September 1971; processed), p. 20.

gressive leadership, and deviant Republicans, having chastised their party sufficiently, were returning home.[46] But it may well be that a considerable part of the resurgence of the Republicans beginning in the late 1930s was due to a delayed flow of conservative Democrats into the GOP. In other words, the traditional Democrats who shared Al Smith's antipathy toward the New Deal did not leave in significant numbers when he did, but they began to do so not long thereafter.

DEMOCRATIC BOURBONISM DIES IN THE NORTH

When the Democratic party made its abrupt swing to the activist end of the political spectrum, during the first Roosevelt administration, it left stranded not only its national leadership of the 1920s—Smith, Davis, Raskob, and their associates—but a host of conservative Democrats in elected office. By James T. Patterson's calculations, eastern and midwestern Democrats in the Senate were actually more conservative during the 1933–39 period than their southern Democratic colleagues. The House also had a substantial conservative contingent of Democrats from the East and the Midwest.[47] At least two leading Democratic governors, Ritchie of Maryland and Joseph B. Ely of Massachusetts, were also vigorously opposed to FDR's New Deal.

The political base of the northern Bourbon Democrats was eroded not just by the leftward movement of the electorate as a whole and the conversion to the Democrats of action-minded Republicans, but also by the movement of a portion of the remaining conservative Democrats into Republican ranks. So the conservative strain in the Democratic party died quickly as the realignment of the 1930s took effect. (Where the realignment was delayed, of course, the conservative Democrats could hold their political support.)

A few of the anti–New Deal Democrats were unseated by pro–New Deal Democratic challengers; John J. O'Connor of New York City, the House

46. For a theory of party alternation that seems useful in explaining the 1938 Republican swing, see James L. Sundquist, *Politics and Policy: The Eisenhower, Johnson, and Kennedy Years* (Brookings Institution, 1968), pp. 499–503. While that discussion dealt only with elections resulting in shifts of party control, the reasoning is equally applicable to an election that produces a marked change in party support levels but stops short of a change in control.

47. James T. Patterson, *Congressional Conservatism and the New Deal: The Growth of the Conservative Coalition in Congress, 1933–39* (University of Kentucky Press, 1967), pp. 339–52. Defining as "conservative" Democrats the senators who opposed Roosevelt on at least 12 percent of key roll calls in the 1933–39 period and House members who opposed him on at least 25 percent, Patterson lists thirty-five senators and seventy-seven House members. These included half the eastern and midwestern Democratic senators and only 46 percent of the southern Democratic senators; 11 and 14 percent of eastern and midwestern House Democrats, respectively, and 32 percent of those from the South.

Rules Committee chairman, was the sole victim of Roosevelt's 1938 "purge,"
but in 1940 three of the most antiadministration Democratic senators—Rush
D. Holt of West Virginia, Edward R. Burke of Nebraska, and William H.
King of Utah—were deposed by the Democrats of their respective states.[48]
As other conservative Democrats retired, died, or were defeated by Republicans, they were not replaced by men of the same views. Men as conservative as Senators Peter G. Gerry of Rhode Island (who opposed Roosevelt on
68 percent of the roll calls selected by Patterson), Royal S. Copeland of New
York (50 percent), Francis T. Maloney of Connecticut (37 percent), or
David I. Walsh and Marcus A. Coolidge of Massachusetts (29 percent each)
no longer rose to leadership in the Democratic party of those states.[49] As the
generation of Democratic anti–New Dealers passed without replacement,
the Democratic party of the industrial North found itself with an extraordinarily high degree of philosophical and ideological unity—for an American
party.

The new Democratic party—the New Deal Democratic party—was issue-
oriented, working-class-based, even more urban-centered than before, activist, radical, and wholly devoted to Rooseveltian leadership. Within the
party, new groups—Italians, Jews, Poles, and all the other new ethnic groups
of European origin, blacks, and working-class Democrats of older Anglo-
Saxon and German stock—began to contest the entrenched Irish for a share
of party leadership and recognition. Organized labor, particularly the industrial unions that formed the Congress of Industrial Organizations (CIO) in
1936, became a virtual party adjunct, and labor wrote its legislative program
into Democratic platforms. Its leaders won a role—often a veto—in candidate selection and occasionally accepted nomination themselves.

Evolution of the New Deal Party System

In some communities, the movement of voters to Smith and Roosevelt at
the presidential level was translated at once into Democratic voting for other

48. Surprisingly, O'Connor's name does not appear in Patterson's list of the seventy-
seven most conservative House Democrats. But his anti–New Deal reputation was securely established by his actions as Rules Committee chairman in obstructing Roosevelt
administration measures.

49. After the war, Frank J. Lausche of Ohio, a conservative Democrat, was unique
in winning election as governor and senator of a northern industrial state, but even he was
finally unseated by a liberal, John J. Gilligan, in an ideological purge in the 1968 Democratic primary. Only in Indiana, among all the northern industrial states, is there still a
conservative Democratic strain strong enough to contest for party leadership.

offices, and the realignment was complete by 1936. Chicago and Pittsburgh are examples. But in other communities, the realignment set in motion in the critical presidential elections was completed only later—sometimes much later—at the state and local levels.

This introduced a new phenomenon into American politics. In the nineteenth century, a man who was a Whig, a Democrat, or a Republican in presidential politics belonged automatically to the same party in state and local politics, and vice versa. Tickets were split occasionally, especially in times of third-party turmoil, but not consistently, election after election, in the same direction.[50] In the four decades since 1932, however, a persistent pattern of divergence between voting behavior in presidential elections and behavior in state and local elections has appeared in many states.

In the South, tens of thousands of voters have regularly supported Republicans for president but Democrats for every other office. In the North, particularly during the early decades of the New Deal party system, the same phenomenon of divergence found its expression in the "Roosevelt Republicans" who supported FDR and the New Deal but maintained their Republican identification and voting habits (or, in Wisconsin and Minnesota, third-party identification and voting) in state and local elections.

Divergence between national and state-local political behavior is inherently unstable. A voter who identifies with one party nationally and another locally enters into such a contradiction with reluctance in the first place; once in it, he normally feels some degree of pressure to resolve it. This is evidenced by the steady if slow decline in the degree of divergence since the phenomenon first appeared in the 1930s. In other words, one of the striking trends of the decades since has been that of *convergence*—the conformity of state and local with national patterns.

A voter can resolve divergence by returning to his original party at the national level, but this is contingent on events that remove the reasons for his original disaffection. Or he can resolve it by changing parties locally, which may also be contingent on changes in the local party structure that will make his new party acceptable to him. The voter who resolves his conflict by returning to his original loyalty at the national level has simply deviated; the voter who resolves it by changing his party identification at state

50. One reason for the limited ticket-splitting in the nineteenth century was the use of party-printed, rather than government-printed, ballots. The party ballot listed only the party's nominees. The modern secret ballot, which lists the nominees of all parties and is a true "multiple-choice instrument," was introduced in most states in the 1890s. Jerrold G. Rusk, "The Effect of the Australian Ballot Reform on Split Ticket Voting: 1876–1908," *American Political Science Review*, Vol. 64 (1970), pp. 1220–21.

and local levels to accord with his new national loyalty has realigned. The realignment cannot be considered to have occurred until the reidentification is completed, for until that time the possibility exists that the conflict may be resolved the other way and the voter may turn out to have been only a deviant. As long as the conflict is unresolved—and that may last many years, even a lifetime—the realignment is only in process. It has not yet happened.

Unlike the major realignments of the nineteenth century, then, the realignment of the 1930s has been drawn out over an extraordinarily long period. Some voters were realigned in 1928, in the Smith campaign. Others were realigned in the early years of the Great Depression. But others shifted their party attachments at that time only at the national level, and the realignment has been completed gradually, as voters singly and in groups brought their state-local political attachments into line with those they had established at the national level. This evolution is taken up in Chapters 11 and 12.

The Retreat toward the Center

The Republican party, as might be expected, was first to move back toward the center of the political spectrum. The 1936 election made clear the people's verdict on the Republican position of that year; immediately the cry arose within the party for a new and different position, one that would accept the basic tenets of the obviously popular New Deal. But first those who took that position had to capture the party leadership from the GOP Old Guard, which stood on principle with its fallen leader, Hoover, and rejected compromise with New Deal activism, no matter what the tactical situation might call for. The GOP "cannot imitate the New Deal; cannot vacillate between two opinions, cannot stagger to the left," said Charles Hilles, the Old Guard leader of New York. The party would have to stand "for sound principles, whether they are temporarily popular or not," concurred Ogden Mills, Hoover's secretary of the treasury.[51]

But the debacle of the 1936 election gave rise to a new class of young Republican leaders. Even as Roosevelt was carrying Massachusetts in that year, along with forty-five other states, thirty-four-year-old Republican Henry Cabot Lodge, Jr., won a Senate seat by professing himself completely

---

51. Quoted by Judith Stein, "The Birth of Liberal Republicanism in New York State, 1932–38" (Ph.D. dissertation, Yale University, 1968), pp. 3, 80.

in sympathy with the New Deal's humanitarian goals and promising to bring an end to Roosevelt's neglect of New England.[52] By the time of the 1938 campaign, activist Republicans like Lodge emerged in state after state. "It is the duty of government to do everything within its power to solve the problems of poverty, unemployment, capital and labor," declared Leverett Saltonstall, then forty-six, in his successful campaign for governor of Massachusetts.[53] In New York a Republican party that had denounced unemployment compensation in 1933 as a "step toward sovietization" and social security in 1936 as "unsound financially and unworkable in practice" came under the leadership of Thomas E. Dewey, then thirty-six years old, who reversed its position on those issues in his campaign for governor, advocated public housing and public power, and directed his appeal to the urban vote. "It is not the function of a political party to die fighting for obsolete slogans," declared Dewey.[54] Republicans who had made peace with the New Deal were conspicuous among the dozen who that year displaced Democratic governors—like Payne Ratner of Kansas, who was attacked by the Democrats as a radical—as well as in the Republican congressional comeback.

"Younger Republican leaders seldom sniped at the President," wrote Milton Plesur in his review of the 1938 campaign; "more often they admonished the electorate to change leaders and put the New Deal, as it were, under new management. . . . On the whole, the Republican victors did not consider themselves Hoover reactionaries, but preferred to stress their descent from the progressivism of the Republican Roosevelt. Even Alf Landon conceded that the G.O.P. was committed to the social objectives of the New Deal. . . . He frankly advised his party to take over the New Deal, make it work, but to avoid recklessness."[55]

By 1940, the new leaders—now generally referred to as the party's "liberal" wing—were in complete control. A party program committee, headed by Glenn Frank, had issued its *A Program for a Dynamic America*, which "accepted most of the New Deal, with but slight camouflage."[56] The moderate ascendancy was established with the nomination of Wendell L.

52. Robert Keiser Massey, Jr., "The State Politics of Massachusetts Democrats, 1928–1938" (Ph.D. dissertation, Duke University, 1968), p. 214. The principal issue of the state campaign was Democratic corruption.

53. Ibid., p. 254.

54. Stein, "Birth of Liberal Republicanism," pp. 87, 206–07.

55. "The Republican Congressional Comeback of 1938," *Review of Politics*, Vol. 24 (1962), pp. 558–59.

56. Conrad Joyner, *The Republican Dilemma: Conservatism or Progressivism* (University of Arizona Press, 1963), p. 5.

Willkie for president in 1940, and confirmed in the national conventions of the next two decades, particularly those that nominated Dewey in 1944 and 1948 and Dwight Eisenhower in 1952. Until Barry Goldwater's campaign of 1964, the Republican party after 1936 did not engage in a frontal assault on the basic New Deal philosophy of governmental activism. While it always stood somewhere to the right of center on the activist-conservative spectrum, as it must, it was conciliatory, moderate, and on occasion genuinely activist. And some of the issues that were most bitterly contested in New Deal days, like social security, became part of the national consensus.

Correspondingly, the national leadership of the Democratic party remained after the realignment consistently on the activist side of the political spectrum. Strategically, there would have been no reason for the party's leadership to want to change directions; after all, it was Rooseveltian activism that had established the Democrats as the national majority, and it was the same philosophy that continued to give the party its unity, cohesion, and rationale. So every serious candidate for the Democratic presidential nomination since FDR has taken pains to identify himself as a worthy heir to the Rooseveltian legacy. (This is true even of southern candidates of conservative antecedents, like Senator Richard B. Russell of Georgia in 1952.) And Roosevelt's New Deal was followed by Truman's Fair Deal, Kennedy's New Frontier, and Johnson's Great Society—all consciously patterned on the model of the great reformist movement of the 1930s.

Nevertheless, while the party as a whole consistently embraced an activist philosophy, its *expression* of that philosophy became more moderate after the country recovered from the depression and the passions roused by the catastrophe subsided. Roosevelt himself abandoned New Deal reforms in order to unite the country during the war. After the war, the typical Democrat was no longer in or on the verge of poverty. He might be worried about unemployment, but he had a job, and he was enjoying an income far above what he had known before. He no longer cried for radical reform of the country's economic system. When the party's rank and file moved back from anger and extremism, its leaders were bound to follow.

Harry Truman appears, on the whole, as a leader unresponsive to the shift in the public mood. He was not by temperament a moderate; he echoed the rhetoric of Franklin Roosevelt, he advanced new reform measures in the spirit of FDR's New Deal, and he won election, in 1948, in a kind of "bloody shirt" revival of class antipathies of the previous decade. But all that changed when leadership passed to Adlai E. Stevenson in 1952. Stevenson purged the

Democratic party of some of the extremism of its program—like Truman's proposal for universal health insurance—and all of the extremism of its rhetoric. He proclaimed explicitly that the Democratic party was no longer against big business.[57] The party became conciliatory to the "economic royalists" once denounced so roundly by Democratic leaders. In return, enough royalists became party leaders—and campaign contributors—to dampen, if not squelch entirely, the prospect of a return to extremism in either rhetoric or program.[58]

So, as the polarization of the electorate that characterized the depression years dissolved into a wartime and postwar moderation, the conflict between the parties was somewhat muted. The parties remained anchored on either side of the activist-conservative line of cleavage, but the distance between them that had been so great in the early 1930s diminished. They retained their class bases, but the Republican party became more hospitable to working-class interests and the Democratic party less hostile to what businessmen saw as their interests. On issues like the Taft-Hartley Act, the coincidence between party and class conflict was sharply redefined, but gradually the Democratic party attracted a greater share of middle- and upper-class support, the Republican party overcame much of the hostility that working-class voters bore toward it in the 1930s, and the difference between the parties narrowed in class composition as well as in policy stance.[59]

57. See, for example, his article in *Fortune* of October 1955, reprinted in Adlai E. Stevenson, *What I Think* (Harper, 1956), pp. 3–17.

58. The authors of *The American Voter* show that what they call "status polarization"—the relation of class identity to partisan preference—rose sharply between the 1944 and 1948 elections, then declined just as sharply through 1956. Angus Campbell and others, *The American Voter* (Wiley, 1960), pp. 346–50.

59. Everett C. Ladd, Jr., Charles Hadley, and Lauriston King, in "A New Political Realignment?" *Public Interest* (Spring 1971), pp. 46–63, document the rise in Democratic middle-class support between 1937 and 1968.

CHAPTER ELEVEN

Aftershocks of the New Deal Earthquake—in the North

MOST OF WHAT HAS APPEARED as party realignment in the decades since the 1930s—including much of what is happening at the present time—has to be understood as simply a later phase of the realignment of the 1930s, a phase during which the new alignment settled into place. Various barriers prevented the electorate from conforming all at once, in every state and locality, to the new rationale of the party system that was established in the 1930s. As the barriers were removed, local realignments occurred. These appeared sometimes almost as independent changes in the party system, but since the essential result of each change was to bring a state or locality into conformity with the alignment established in the country as a whole in the 1930s, each must be considered an integral part—no less so merely because it was delayed—of that realignment episode. The deferred realignments are like aftershocks of the earthquake that changed the shape of the party system in the New Deal era.

The aftershocks occurred earlier in the North, later in the South, but they had the same character and origin in the two regions. In the North, delayed realignment made resistant areas of one-party Republican domination consistent with the two-party alignment. In the South, the process correspondingly converted one-party Democratic areas into areas of two-party competition. As the North became more Democratic, the South more Republican, the trends appear as mirror images. The process in the North is near completion, but it may be several decades before it has fully run its course in the South. What has happened in the North therefore provides one important set of guides for predicting the future of southern politics.

In the northern states where realignment was delayed, a typical two-stage pattern can be described. The first stage was, of course, the New Deal period, when a strong tidal movement to the Democrats was expressed at all levels

218

but most heavily in the vote for Roosevelt at the top of the ticket. Late in the decade the wave receded in elections for state offices and some or all local offices, restoring Republicans to a position of dominance approaching or even equaling the one they held before the New Deal era. The swing to the Democrats at the state and local level in the early 1930s thus appears on the charts as a deviation. At the presidential level, however, a larger portion of the Democratic gain was retained, with the result that a persistent divergence appeared between balloting for president and voting for state and local offices. Clearly, a substantial number of voters were behaving as Democrats nationally but as Republicans in state and local politics. To the extent that this was a matter of genuine party identification—as distinct from repeated deviational voting—it was bound to prove unstable. Those experiencing divided loyalties would feel some pressure, as noted earlier, to reconcile their conflict. This would be particularly true of aspiring politicians and their cadres of active supporters and followers. In that circle the pressure for party regularity is considerable, and those who depart from it must, at the least, explain and justify to the party regulars what appears to be disloyalty, and at the most, suffer penalties imposed by them.

Since the national parties were firmly fixed on opposite sides of the line of cleavage established in the 1930s, the conflict could be reconciled only by the reconstruction of the state and local party system in the national image. That is what happened in a second stage of the realignment process that took place after the barriers that caused the delay were removed.

The two-stage process can be clearly traced in several states where the second stage was sharp, violent, and distinct—where, in other words, identifiable blocs of voters changed party identification in response to particular chains of events. The experience of those states helps to clarify what happened in others where the process was less distinct, and a general pattern emerges that explains much of what has happened in a broad segment of the North in the postwar period.

North Dakota: The NPL Switches Parties

The two-stage process appears in its purest form in North Dakota, where one wing of the Republican party seceded and moved as a whole into the Democratic party.

After the Nonpartisan League (NPL) had collapsed in other northwestern states in the early 1920s, it remained in North Dakota as an organized faction within the GOP, a party within a party. To oppose the NPL, conservative Republicans established a continuing organization for their faction too—the Independent Voters Association (IVA). Where voters in other states identified as Republicans or Democrats, North Dakotans identified as NPLs or IVAs. The state had the equivalent of a two-party system, except that the arena of competition was the Republican primary rather than the general election. The Democrats, as a permanent minority, tried occasionally to maneuver in state politics as a balance-of-power group between the Republican factions but usually stood on the sidelines while the main political show took place wholly within the opposition party.

Accordingly, when North Dakota voted almost 70 percent for Franklin Roosevelt in 1932, it expressed its resentment against conservative Republicanism at the state level not by electing Democrats but by nominating in the Republican primary the entire NPL slate, and then electing it in the fall. The NPL gained control of both the state's executive branch and its legislature for the first time since 1919. The new NPL governor, William Langer, quickly established himself as one of the country's most radical state executives and also as North Dakota's most divisive political figure. He not only created in the conservative wing of the Republican party a legion of dedicated enemies, as might have been expected, but also managed to alienate by his political tactics a large segment of the NPL, including many of its established leaders.[1] To defeat Langer his enemies in 1934 bolted to elect the Democratic candidate for governor and in 1938 to elect another Democratic candidate, John Moses, who was reelected twice.[2]

But these were personal and coalition victories that added no permanent strength to the Democratic party. By the end of the war, the state was back to its traditional Republican voting habits, and the Republican party was

1. Striking out boldly on behalf of the distraught farmers, Langer proclaimed a moratorium on mortgage foreclosures—a policy not confirmed by legislation until four years later—and enforced it with the National Guard. He also used authority granted in new legislation to embargo wheat shipments in order to raise the price. Equally bold were his tactics of political organization. He had administered federal relief funds for only a few months before the Roosevelt administration felt constrained to remove them from his control, and shortly thereafter a federal grand jury indicted him for improperly collecting campaign contributions from federal employees. He was convicted in June 1934, and the state supreme court then removed him from office. He was subsequently cleared, enabling him to run for governor again in 1936 and win. Elwyn B. Robinson, *The History of North Dakota* (University of Nebraska Press, 1966), pp. 403–13. Langer was elected to the U.S. Senate in 1940 and served until his death in 1960.

2. The Democratic governor elected in 1934 was disqualified, and the office reverted to the Republicans until the 1938 election.

back in the hands of conservatives. In fact, according to one study, the Nonpartisan League itself had lost its crusading spirit and become "intrenched and conservative . . . a power structure without purpose other than to elect and re-elect to state office" and increasingly inclined to work in tandem with the conservative Republicans, especially on labor issues.[3]

So in the postwar years the shattered progressive forces had to fashion a new strategy and a new structure. Revival began when the triumphant conservatives overreached themselves in 1947 and launched a legislative attack on the insurance companies and other cooperatives of the Farmers' Union, the state's largest farm organization. This brought the Farmers' Union into politics. It created a political arm called the Progressive Alliance and launched a statewide membership drive for the new body. Next year, the Alliance joined with the NPL and organized labor in a Committee for Progressive Unity. Their chosen strategy was to revitalize the NPL with a mass infusion of new farm and labor members and then, as of old, use it to win Republican primary nominations. They almost succeeded in 1948: their candidates for state office ran strongly, and they won control of the lower house of the legislature.

Two groups within the Nonpartisan League, however, were critical of the new strategy: the conservatives who had controlled the league before the 1947–48 revitalization, and a group who wearied of the contradiction between voting Democratic for president and continuing as Republicans in state politics, which meant supporting for Congress men who would vote with the Republicans in organizing the national legislative bodies. This group, heavily sprinkled with young members, came to be known as the Insurgents of the NPL, their opponents as the Old Guard. The Insurgents' goal was to break the Nonpartisan League's long tradition by shifting its nominees from the Republican to the Democratic primary.

Over a span of nearly a decade, that was accomplished. The Insurgents captured the Young Nonpartisan League in 1950 and managed to rack the senior organization with controversy. But they did not capture clear control until North Dakota Democrats—seizing upon the example of Minnesota (pages 226–29, below)—formed a Democratic-Farm-Labor Association in 1954 with the mission of enrolling hundreds of Democrats in the Nonpartisan League. As this effort went forward, the Old Guard abandoned the field of battle and took its wing of the NPL into the Republican party un-

3. Lloyd B. Omdahl, *Insurgents* (Lloyd B. Omdahl, 1961), p. 204.

der the auspices of a Republican unity committee. Those who remained in
the NPL were then free to make, in 1956, the historic shift of the league's
candidacies to the Democratic party. Soon thereafter, aided by the unpopu-
larity of the Eisenhower farm policies, the Democratic-NPL candidates began to win. Quentin N. Burdick was elected congressman in 1958 and
senator in 1960, William L. Guy governor in 1960. When Governor Guy
was reelected in 1964 for the second time, the Democrats were able to extend
their victories beyond the governorship and one U.S. Senate seat; in that
year they captured control of the lower house of the state legislature. North
Dakota, for the first time in its history, had become a competitive two-party
state. It is symbolic of the realignment that when Quentin Burdick became
the first Democrat sent to the House of Representatives from the state, he
took the seat of his father, Usher L. Burdick, who had served twenty years
in the House as a Nonpartisan League Republican.

Wisconsin: La Follette Progressivism Changes Parties

In Wisconsin, a decade and a half elapsed between the first stage of the
realignment and the beginning of the second stage, and another decade before
the latter was complete.[4] In the first stage, in 1932, Wisconsin gave Roosevelt 63.5 percent of its vote and became for the first time since the Civil War
a genuine two-party state in national politics (Roosevelt carried Wisconsin
a .in in 1936 and 1940 and Truman in 1948). In 1932, the Democrats also
elected a governor for the first time in forty years, a U.S. senator, half the
state's congressmen (no Democratic senator or congressman had represented
Wisconsin since 1916), and a majority of the state assembly.

But this was accomplished with the support of the La Follette progressives—who had defected from Republican ranks after Governor Philip La
Follette had been defeated by a conservative in the Republican primary—and

4. Principal sources for this account of Wisconsin politics are Edward N. Doan, *The
La Follettes and the Wisconsin Idea* (Rinehart, 1947), Chap. 14; Leon D. Epstein, *Politics in
Wisconsin* (University of Wisconsin Press, 1958), Chap. 3; Roger T. Johnson, *Robert M.
La Follette, Jr., and the Decline of the Progressive Party in Wisconsin* (State Historical Society
of Wisconsin, 1964; Anchor, 1970); Charles H. Backstrom, "The Progressive Party of
Wisconsin, 1934–1946" (Ph.D. dissertation, University of Wisconsin, 1956); James R.
Donoghue, *How Wisconsin Voted, 1848–1954* (University of Wisconsin, University Ex-
tension Division, 1956); John H. Fenton, *Midwest Politics* (Holt, Rinehart and Winston,
1966), Chap. 3; and Frank J. Sorauf, "Extra-Legal Political Parties in Wisconsin,"
American Political Science Review, Vol. 48 (1954), p. 693.

the La Follettes and their fellow progressives never intended any such alliance to be permanent. They had looked on the Democratic party, which could muster only 17 percent of the vote for governor in 1926 and 30 percent in 1930, as "a political shell manned by job conscious people," in the words of one of them, and as no less conservative than the Republicans.[5] The Democratic politicians who made up the shell, suddenly thrust into power in 1932, did nothing to change that view. They enacted no program, displayed no impressive capacity for leadership, and steered what to the progressives appeared a conservative course. They alienated militant farm groups and their labor sympathizers by helping to break a milk strike. Moreover, to Wisconsin progressives in 1933 and 1934, even the national Democratic party seemed too cautious. Better to follow the example of their friends in neighboring Minnesota and entrust the progressive movement to a party of their own that would not be hamstrung by any traditional conservative elements. In three-way competition, with conservatives divided, the prospects for a new party would be bright.

At a convention in May 1934, the progressives voted overwhelmingly to launch a new party. They chose the name Progressive in preference to Farmer-Labor; they adopted a platform calling, among other things, for guaranteed employment for every able-bodied person, a government-owned central bank, a fair profit for the farmer, the right of labor to organize, and public ownership of the electric power, railroad, and munitions industries; and they nominated two sons of Old Bob La Follette—Philip for governor and Young Bob for reelection to the Senate. Carrying words of praise from Roosevelt that amounted to endorsement, Senator La Follette got more votes than his two opponents combined. Philip's margin over the Democratic incumbent was a narrow one, but in 1936 he was reelected handily.

At that point, however, things began to go wrong. When in May 1938 Governor La Follette announced formation of a national Progressive party, the enterprise drew no response from the country and was dead within a few days. That fall a committee of leading Democrats and Republicans worked out a coalition arrangement, the Democratic nominee for governor withdrew in favor of the Republican, and Governor La Follette's bid for another term was crushed. In 1940 the Progressives narrowly reelected Senator La

5. Former Representative Thomas R. Amlie, quoted by Johnson, *Robert M. La Follette, Jr.*, p. 28. The conservativism of the Wisconsin Democratic party in the 1930s is indicated by the fact that the state party chairmen from 1932 to 1940, the senatorial candidate in 1940, and all but five or six Democrats in the legislature after 1934 opposed the New Deal. Backstrom, "The Progressive Party of Wisconsin," pp. 293–94.

Follette, but two years later they suffered their final setback when the governor they had elected with slightly over 50 percent of the total vote died before taking office. The Republican lieutenant governor who became governor in his stead, Walter S. Goodland, proved both progressive and popular, and in 1944 the Progressives, with no La Follette on their ticket and running against both Goodland and the Democratic party in a presidential year, got only 6 percent of the total vote. There was nothing to do but reassemble in convention in 1946 and admit the experiment was over.

The question remained: through which major party should the Progressives seek to advance their principles? Tradition was powerful. Progressives remembered that the great triumphs of Robert La Follette, Sr., had been Republican triumphs. Both his sons had been elected as Republicans. Governor Goodland had defied the Republican conservatives in the La Follette manner and cordially invited the Progressives to return. The Republicans appeared in 1946 to be rising once again to their old dominance. To many outstaters, the Democratic party was too heavily dominated by Milwaukee and by labor. In a convention speech, Senator La Follette branded the national Democratic party of 1946 as "stalled in dead center" without "unity of purpose" and the Democratic party of Wisconsin as reactionary. In the vote, 284 ballots were cast for joining the Republicans, 51 for becoming Democrats, and 77 for remaining independent. But this decision did not save the Progressives. Senator La Follette, hurt in that postwar year by his record as an isolationist, was beaten in the Republican primary by Joseph R. McCarthy.

If the son and namesake of Old Bob La Follette could not win nomination in a Republican primary for a seat he had held with distinction for two decades, how could any other ambitious progressive hope to find a future in the GOP? It now became clear, at least to the younger progressives, that while they had been wandering with the La Follettes in the third-party wilderness the stalwarts who stayed home had made of the GOP an efficient, disciplined vehicle of conservatism. At the same time, it was equally clear that in most counties the minority Democratic party, kept by its old-line leadership in "a state of controlled dormancy,"[6] was ripe for takeover by new leadership. So a new generation of progressives united in their ideology but carrying various political labels—some of them liberal Democrats, some of them former Progressives, some German Socialists from Milwaukee,

---

6. Sorauf, "Extra-Legal Political Parties in Wisconsin," p. 693.

with substantial representation from organized labor—came together in 1948 and 1949 and formed the Democratic Organizing Committee to rejuvenate the moribund party as an effective statewide opposition to the Republicans.

The Democratic Organizing Committee (later renamed the Democratic party of Wisconsin), which was a mass organization that anyone could join, nominated candidates to contest the 1948 primaries and was immediately successful. From that time on, the party had a new generation of leaders and candidates and a new image as well. And then Democratic strength in presidential elections began to be translated into state and local party strength too. In 1948 the reorganized party broke through in Dane County (Madison), home of the La Follettes, and turned it into the Democratic stronghold it has since remained. From 1948 on, the Democrats made respectable showings every two years in campaigns for governor, and within ten years they had become a winning statewide party. William Proxmire was elected senator when McCarthy died in 1957, and the former Progressive Gaylord A. Nelson was elected governor in 1958—the first Democrats to win either office since the election of 1932. All but one of the Democratic state ticket were carried into office with Nelson. Wisconsin, after a century of Republicanism, was at last a two-party state.

Leon Epstein has tried to trace the flow of politically active members of the Progressive party into the major parties. In general, he has concluded, the older, more rural Progressives, particularly the officeholders, and those who had been "nurtured in La Follette isolationism" found the Republican party a more congenial refuge. Younger, more urban Progressives and those who agreed with Roosevelt and Truman internationalism turned Democratic.[7] But whatever happened to individual Progressive leaders, it is clear that the reborn Democratic party could not have grown as it did in the postwar years if the rank and file of Progressive voters had not shifted their allegiance predominantly to that party in defiance of the Progressives' 1946 decision. Between 1942, when the Progressive candidate for governor polled 50 percent of the vote to win a three-way race, and 1948, the Democratic share of the total vote rose from 12 to 45 percent, the Republican from 38 to 55; the Democratic gain as the Progressives disappeared was about twice the Republican gain. Ten years later, when the Democrats won the governorship with 54 percent, they were up forty-two points from the 1942 base, the Republicans only eight.

7. Epstein, *Politics in Wisconsin*, pp. 51–54.

By this time, moreover, the Democrats had lost to the Republicans much of their traditional strength in rural areas and small towns—conservative German Catholics, in particular, who were alienated both by the New Deal and by the war. In the 1948–54 period four of the fifteen counties that had been traditionally the strongest Democratic counties in the state were among the top fifteen Republican counties.[8] If the new Democratic party did not pick up all of the Progressive strength in rural areas, it surely absorbed almost the whole body of Progressives (and the new voters who were their philosophical descendants) in the metropolitan areas and was getting the votes, if not the allegiance, of former Republicans as well.

The nature of the party competition in Wisconsin confirms the lineal descent of postwar Democracy from the La Follette wing of the Republican party by way of the Progressive party. After 1948 the Wisconsin political cleavage was as cleanly on progressive-conservative lines as in all the decades before, but now this cleavage divided Republicans and Democrats rather than factions within the GOP or Republicans and third-party Progressives. The realignment is again embodied in the experience of a political family: when the politician carrying the name La Follette into this generation's political wars—Bronson Cutting La Follette, son of Young Bob and grandson of Old Bob—was elected state attorney general in 1964, it was as a Democrat.

Minnesota: The Farmer-Labor Movement Shifts Parties

As in Wisconsin, the movement of Minnesota progressives from Republican to Democratic ranks came by way of a third party—the Farmer-Labor party, which had provided progressives with their political vehicle throughout the 1920s. When the realignment of the 1930s began, Minnesota was already, in effect, halfway through the process. The Republican party had suffered the formal secession of its progressive wing, which would not happen in Wisconsin until 1934, in North Dakota until 1956. What re-

---

8. Ibid., pp. 53–54; also Fenton, *Midwest Politics*, pp. 48–49. Epstein points out that the county-by-county correlation of Progressive strength in gubernatorial and senatorial elections from 1934 to 1946 with Democratic strength in gubernatorial elections from 1948 to 1954 is only 0.50, "high enough to indicate some relation between the old Progressive and recent Democratic strength but not so close a relation as might have been expected on the assumption that today's Democrats occupy the leftward place in Wisconsin's political spectrum formerly filled by the Progressives." The low figure is explained by the stronger showing of the Democrats in the metropolitan areas and their relative weakness in rural and mixed rural-urban counties.

mained, then, was to absorb that wing into the Democratic party in a second stage.

When the depression brought disaster to the Republican party, the Farmer-Labor party as the principal opposition was the beneficiary. Floyd B. Olson, a self-proclaimed "radical," was elected governor by a landslide in 1930, and for eight years Minnesota was dominated by a party whose platform called for abolishing capitalism in favor of "a new sane and just society" in which "all the natural resources, machinery of production, transportation and communication shall be owned by the government."[9] At the national level, in the absence of a practical radical alternative, the Farmer-Laborites supported Roosevelt. In 1936, the Democrats returned the favor by staying out of the races for governor and senator.

But Olson died, and under Governor Elmer A. Benson, who was elected in 1936, the party disintegrated rapidly. Benson was discredited by charges of "fellow-traveling" with the Communists, the party split and entered into a bitter primary contest over the communist-infiltration issue, and the Democrats withdrew from the alliance that had been forged in 1936. Meanwhile, the Republicans had refurbished their image by nominating for governor a candidate who was young, energetic, and progressive—Harold E. Stassen. The result was inevitable. Stassen won in 1938 by a margin even greater than that of Olson eight years before.

While the effectiveness of the Farmer-Labor party was destroyed, it remained the only opposition to the Republicans of any consequence. The Democratic party had no standing in the state. Its candidate for governor could poll only 6 percent of the vote in 1938, 11 percent in 1940, 9.5 percent in 1942. The disgruntled anti-Benson Farmer-Laborites had obviously not become Democrats; they had returned at least temporarily, for want of a better haven, to the Republican party. One of them, Senator Shipstead, successfully ran for reelection as a Republican in 1940 (although he failed in the Republican primary six years later). The progressive forces that had made Minnesota a banner New Deal state in the first two Roosevelt elections were sundered.

The regrouping began, as in Wisconsin, with the rise of a new generation of leaders. A coterie of ambitious young New Dealers came together during the war in the Twin Cities, centered around Hubert H. Humphrey, a political science instructor at Macalester College. The impatient Humphrey

9. Party platform of 1934, quoted by Fenton, *Midwest Politics*, p. 85.

plunged into the nonpartisan race for mayor of Minneapolis in 1943 at the age of thirty-two, and in a near victory established himself as a dynamic campaigner and effective politician. The Humphrey group intended to make the Democratic party their vehicle, but it was clear that the prospect would be poor as long as many progressives remained loyal Farmer-Laborites. The obvious answer was to revive and carry through an idea that had been cast up from time to time for more than two decades—a merger of the Democratic and Farmer-Labor parties. The Farmer-Laborites had long looked on the Democratic party as too urban, too conservative, too Catholic,[10] and too Irish (the last four Democratic candidates for governor had been named Regan, Gallagher, Murphy, and Sullivan). But by 1944 they were ready to talk fusion; they were beaten and demoralized, and besides, this was a new Democratic party. As one of their leaders put it, they had to acknowledge the "wonderful fact that we now have in Minnesota a large group of liberal Democrats who practically subscribe to our progressive program."[11] Old-line Democrats, for their part, still distrusted the Farmer-Laborites as radicals associated with the Communists. But the new Humphrey Democrats provided a bridge, as did the national Democratic party, which wanted its Minnesota supporters united for the 1944 campaign and dispatched a representative to Minnesota to facilitate the merger. After negotiations that were said to require some 250 meetings,[12] the Democratic-Farmer-Labor party came into being.

That laid the basis. Humphrey established his right to leadership by a resounding victory in the Minneapolis mayoralty election in 1945. There remained only the problem of the party's radical taint. The Humphreyites solved that in 1948 when they defeated—first in precinct caucuses, then in the state convention, then in the courts, and finally in the primaries—the Benson group of former Farmer-Laborites that was trying to swing the party behind Henry A. Wallace's Progressive presidential candidacy.[13] That year Humphrey was elected to the Senate. But it was a while longer before the new party "succeeded in erasing the Catholic image of the Democratic party" and "in blurring the radical left-wing perception of the Farmer-Labor

10. Arthur Naftalin, "The Farmer-Labor Party in Minnesota" (Ph.D. dissertation, University of Minnesota, 1948), pp. 73–74.
11. Quoted by Leslie Gene Rude, "A Rhetorical Analysis of the Minnesota Farmer-Labor Movement" (Ph.D. dissertation, University of Illinois, 1962).
12. Michael Amrine, *This Is Humphrey: The Story of the Senator* (Doubleday, 1960), p. 90.
13. G. Theodore Mitau, "The Democratic-Farmer-Labor Party Schism of 1948," *Minnesota History* (Spring 1955), pp. 187–94.

party" sufficiently to bring back the moderate Protestant farmers who had left the Farmer-Labor party for the Republicans in 1938. The Eisenhower farm policies may have precipitated the switch.[14] In 1954, the farm areas finally joined with the cities to elect Orville L. Freeman, an early Humphrey associate, as the first governor since 1914 to win office under the Democratic label. All but one of the Democratic-Farmer-Labor state ticket were elected with Freeman. The realignment was complete.

Pennsylvania: Patronage Republicans Switch Parties

Pennsylvania is perhaps unique among states in the extent to which it illustrates a diversity of realignment patterns. Some counties completed a drastic realignment in a single stage in the early 1930s, others followed a two-stage process analogous to that of the upper midwestern states, and a third group showed no net shift at all in party strength.

The realignment patterns in Pennsylvania can be traced through party registration figures as well as through election returns. Figure 10-5 (page 207) shows the registration trends for seven Pennsylvania counties. Three of them—Allegheny, Lackawanna, and Westmoreland, all industrial and mining counties—experienced a sharp, one-stage realignment that was complete by 1938, and another, semirural Lancaster, showed a more limited one-stage realignment. In a fifth county, York, also semirural with a German (Pennsylvania Dutch) tradition, any pro-Democratic switchers were almost exactly offset by other voters shifting to the Republicans, with the result that no net realignment at all was recorded. But in two urban counties, Philadelphia and Luzerne (Wilkes-Barre), the registration figures show a sharp movement toward the Democrats in the 1930s, followed by a decade of decline after 1938, then by a second stage of switching to the Democrats that lasted through the 1950s and into the 1960s.

Local political control seems responsible for these differences. In Allegheny, Westmoreland, and Lackawanna, the reaction against Republicanism in the early 1930s carried through to the local level. Pittsburgh, in Allegheny County, elected a Democratic mayor in 1933 after twenty-seven years of Republican control of city hall. All three counties gave the Democrats control of the county government two years later in an abrupt transition from the unchallenged Republican domination of the preceding decades.

14. Fenton, *Midwest Politics*, p. 96.

At that point, the new Democrats had every reason to remain Democrats, and other Republicans had an incentive to join the new majority party. Local patronage cemented the Democratic majorities, and in each of those counties, as well as in the city of Pittsburgh, those majorities have remained invulnerable since.

In Philadelphia and Luzerne, on the other hand, the Republican organizations were entrenched deeply enough to withstand the upheaval of the 1930s. On the strength of national and state victories (Pennsylvania in 1934 elected George H. Earle as its first Democratic governor in forty years), Democratic registration climbed, but with the Republican recapture of the statehouse in 1938 and the concurrent decline in popularity of the New Deal the Republican organizations were able to reassert effective pressure on the voters' public political identification. Since the private political behavior of the voter on election day could not be so readily controlled, however, a situation of conflict—and of inherent instability—was created.

Figure 11-1 compares voting behavior and party registration since 1924 in Philadelphia. Unlike Chicago and Pittsburgh, Philadelphia did not become a Democratic city in state and local elections at the same time it became a Democratic city nationally. After voting heavily for Roosevelt in 1936, the city continued to give majorities to Democratic presidential candidates. But it was fourteen years before it delivered majority support to a Democratic candidate for governor, fifteen before it elected a Democratic mayor, and twenty-two before a majority of its voters were registered as Democrats. From 1936 through 1944, one voter of every five or six in Philadelphia (as measured by party registration) was a Roosevelt Republican, torn between his allegiance to the New Deal at the national level and his traditional loyalty to the dominant Republican organization in the city and state. By the early 1950s, one of three registered Republicans was regularly voting Democratic for governor and mayor as well as president.[15] Finally, these voters resolved their conflict by moving en masse into the Democratic party.

If the chart showed local off-year elections it would identify the initial breakthrough year as 1949, when Democrats elected Richardson Dilworth as city treasurer and Joseph S. Clark as city controller—the first local Democratic victories in decades. Dilworth and Clark, like their counterparts in the upper Midwest, were aggressive New Dealers, determined to

15. These calculations assume that registered Republican voters turned out at the polls in at least as high proportions as registered Democrats. This assumption could be faulty, but probably not to a degree sufficient to alter the calculations significantly.

Figure 11-1. *Democratic Percentage of Two-Party Vote Compared with Democratic Percentage of Two-Party Registration, Philadelphia, 1924–70*

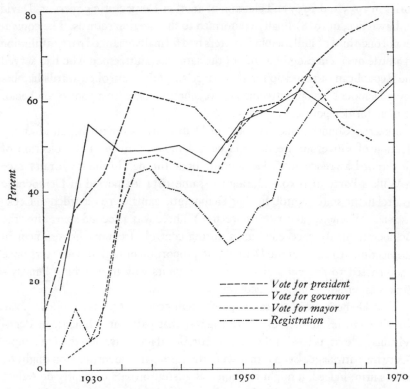

use a revived Democratic party as a vehicle for a liberal program, but they were also urban political reformers, campaigning against corruption and a patronage-oriented political system. Reform politics proved so attractive that Clark and Dilworth successively occupied the mayor's chair for twelve years, and other local offices regularly went Democratic as well.

During that period the lasting registration shift finally occurred. A modest gain in the Democratic percentage followed the 1949 off-year breakthrough, a sharper rise followed the election of Clark as mayor in 1951, and a still steeper rise occurred after George M. Leader was elected in 1954 as the first Democratic governor since the 1930s. The Republicans no longer had control of patronage; the Democrats had a new respectability and had demonstrated that they were finally a winning party. In short, the state and local victories broke the barriers that had prevented Philadelphians from identifying publicly with the party whose presidential candidate they had supported consistently since 1936; and the registration figures (after further local victories in 1955 and 1959 and election of another Democratic governor, David L. Lawrence, in 1958) finally conformed to the election returns. The equivalent of one-third of Philadelphia's voters had formally changed party affiliation in a little over a decade.[16] Many of the same committeemen who had served the Republican organization in that party's tightly controlled wards had become Democratic committeemen exercising the same firm control on behalf of their former political enemies.[17]

Luzerne County's second spurt in Democratic strength began after the election of Governor Leader and gained momentum with the election of Governor Lawrence and a Democratic breakthrough in the mayoralty race in Wilkes-Barre in 1959. (During the same 1954–62 period of Democratic control in the state capitol, further Democratic gains were recorded in Lackawanna, Allegheny, and Westmoreland.) There was a second spurt after the Democrats finally succeeded in capturing control of county government in the election of 1967 and the Democratic proportion of registered voters once again passed 50 percent and seemed to be on its way to matching Pennsylvania's other labor-industrial counties.

That Democratic registration gains seem generally to have followed the party's victories at the polls may suggest that party attachment, in Pennsylvania at least, is less a reflection of emotional identification than of simple desire for patronage. Even if that were the case, party identification might be no less firm; indeed, it might be firmer. Registration data evidently do reflect more than patronage hunger, however, for the lines have not moved in both directions as election fortunes alone would have dictated. The first two Roosevelt elections were signals of political revolution; the later Eisenhower landslides of roughly comparable proportions, in 1952 and 1956, were not. Instead, at the end of the Eisenhower period there was a higher proportion of Democratic voters in each of the seven counties than at the beginning. And while the election of a Democratic governor in 1954 was followed by an upturn in the party's registration, a Republican victory eight years later brought no downturn of similar magnitude. The conclusion is inevitable: new party identifications were formed by voters in the 1930s and were immediately re-

16. The one-third consisted in part of a substitution of immigrant Democrats for Republicans moving to the suburbs. This qualifies the general conclusion somewhat.

17. James Reichley, *The Art of Government: Reform and Organization Politics in Philadelphia* (Fund for the Republic, 1954), pp. 97–99.

flected in all aspects of political behavior, including registration, wherever the Democrats were able to win locally; where they did not, the expression (except in presidential voting) was delayed. Eventually, however, identification with the party at the presidential level proved controlling. Once the Democrats broke through at the local level the party's hidden strength was finally reflected in the registration figures and in sustained local Democratic victories.

Two-Stage Realignment in Other States

Across the whole belt of northern states, from Maine to California, were less dramatic counterparts of the two-stage realignment process so clearly expressed in the upper midwestern states and in parts of Pennsylvania. An examination of the charts of party strength compiled by Paul T. David show no fewer than sixteen states whose trend lines followed that pattern.[18]

Table 11-1 presents the experience of the sixteen states, and of the country as a whole. In each of the sixteen, the swing to the Democratic party in presidential voting during the Roosevelt (or Smith-Roosevelt) era was not matched by a comparable growth of basic Democratic party strength, as measured in David's "Composite B" index of the votes for governor, U.S. senator, and U.S. representative.[19] But in each case the divergence was overcome in the postwar period through a gain in basic party strength that far exceeded the gains recorded in the country as a whole. In all but two of the states, the second-stage spurt carried the index of party strength to a level as high as or higher than the one reached during the New Deal period, and the higher level appeared to be solidly established. In the second stage of the realignment, then, not only were the temporary gains of the early 1930s translated into a durable increment of basic Democratic party strength but additional strength was in most cases attained.

The gains and losses shown in the table are measured not from individual-year peaks and valleys but from sustained levels of party strength. For this purpose, the base in each case is the average of a period spanning four bien-

18. Paul T. David, *Party Strength in the United States 1872–1970* (University Press of Virginia, 1972).

19. Votes for the three offices are given equal weight in David's "Composite B" index, which is accepted here—since party registration data for most states is nonexistent or unavailable—as the best generally available measure of basic party strength. Chapter 3 (ibid.) presents David's argument that Composite B is "the best general measure of party strength."

Table 11-1. *The Two-Stage Realignment in Sixteen Northern States, Shown by Gains and Losses in Democratic Party Strength*[a]

In percentage points

| State | First-stage gain or loss | | Second-stage gain, between post-New Deal trough and second-stage peak[b] | Total gain from pre-New Deal trough to second-stage peak[c] | Period of principal second-stage gain |
	Between pre-New Deal trough and New Deal peak[b]	Between New Deal peak and post-New Deal trough[b]			
Minnesota	10	−7	41	44	1944–48
Wisconsin	16	−13	33	36	1942–58
California	16	−9	21	28	1954–58
North Dakota	16	−12	22	27	1954–64
Michigan	22	−5	9	26	1948–54
South Dakota	25	−13	11	22	1954–58
Pennsylvania	19	−3	5	21	1948–54
Iowa	21	−7	7	21	1954–58
Vermont	14	−11	18	20	1952–58
Connecticut	11	−2	10	19	1958
Oregon	9	−8	17	18	1952–56
Massachusetts	9	−5	11	16	1954–58
Maine	9	−14	18	14	1954–58
Nevada	13	−13	13	13	1954–62
New Jersey	8	−7	7	8	1954–64
Nebraska	6	−17	15	4	1954–58
United States	10	−4	3	9	1954–58

Source: Paul T. David, *Party Strength in the United States 1872–1970* (University Press of Virginia, 1972).

a. As measured by David's Composite B index; see note 19.

b. Base periods (average of four successive biennial elections) are as follows:

Pre-New Deal trough

1918–24: Massachusetts, South Dakota, Vermont
1920–26: Minnesota, Iowa, Connecticut, Nebraska, United States
1922–28: Wisconsin, North Dakota
1924–30: California, Michigan, Pennsylvania, Oregon, Maine, Nevada, New Jersey

New Deal peak

1928–34: Minnesota, Massachusetts, Nebraska
1930–36: Wisconsin, Connecticut
1932–38: South Dakota, Iowa, Vermont, Oregon, Maine, New Jersey, United States
1934–40: Michigan, Pennsylvania, Nevada
1936–42: California
1938–44: North Dakota

Post-New Deal trough

1936–42: Minnesota, Wisconsin
1940–46: Michigan, Iowa, Oregon, Massachusetts, Nebraska
1942–48: Maine
1944–50: Pennsylvania
1946–52: California, North Dakota, South Dakota, Vermont, Connecticut, Nevada, New Jersey, United States

nial elections. One period represents the bottom of the Democratic slump between the Wilson and Roosevelt victories. The second reflects the peak years of the New Deal era. The third represents the nadir of the Democratic decline in the war and immediate postwar years. The fourth measures the new and sustained level reached in the second-stage revival of the party's fortunes.

In the case of the three upper midwestern states whose realignments were examined earlier in this chapter—Minnesota, Wisconsin, and North Dakota —the decline in Democratic party strength after the New Deal boom came so close to wiping out the entire first-stage gain that the New Deal period, in terms of Composite B voting strength, appears as a deviation rather than a realignment. And the table confirms the suggestion of the earlier analysis that the second stage of the realignment would turn out to be the greater one. Both of these trends are found in other states as well. In Nebraska and Maine, the Democratic gains in the New Deal period were more than offset in the post–New Deal decline, leaving the party strength by the 1942–48 period at a lower level than in the 1920s. In Nevada, the entire Democratic gain of the 1930s disappeared in the party's postwar decline; and in Vermont, Oregon, and New Jersey almost the whole of the first-stage increment was lost. The second-stage aftershock was more severe than the original earthquake not only in three midwestern states but in California, Vermont, Oregon, Massachusetts, Maine, and Nebraska, and it was of equal power in Nevada.

All this is qualified by the fact that while the David index that is the basis of Table 11-1 may be the best available measure of party strength, it is not fully satisfactory as a measure of party *identification*, the concept on which an analysis of alignment and realignment must be based. The offices of governor and U.S. senator, which make up two-thirds of the index, are undoubtedly, as David argues, less subject to deviational voting than is the office of president; hence, election returns for those offices provide a better measure of basic party attachment than do the returns in presidential balloting. Never-

---

Second-stage peak
1954–60: Pennsylvania, United States
1956–62: California, South Dakota, Oregon
1958–64: Minnesota, Michigan, Iowa, Vermont, Connecticut, Massachusetts, Maine, Nevada, New Jersey, Nebraska
1960–66: North Dakota
1964–70: Wisconsin
  c. Rows may not add to totals because of rounding.

theless, gubernatorial and senatorial candidates are still conspicuous public figures who cause voters to stray across the party line temporarily. The more faceless the office, the less the deviation, perhaps; on that basis the vote for state treasurer or clerk of court might be a better measure of true party strength than votes for either president, senator, or governor. But not much better, for even in such cases deviations occur; voters who deviate at the top of the ticket may do so for lower offices as well, particularly in states where the form of the ballot encourages straight-ticket voting, or they may cross the line at the lower levels to support competent incumbents whose names are well known. The basic weakness of election returns as a measure of party attachment simply cannot be eliminated no matter which returns are used for the purpose; when elections show a shift in party strength, there is no way to determine exactly—even long after the event—how much of the shift is deviation and how much is truly realignment.

Among the two-stage realignment states listed in Table 11-1 are three of the states whose party registration figures are available, and the two sets of data (voting behavior and registration) can be compared to provide clues to the interpretation of both. This is done in Figure 11-2. The data for Pennsylvania are mutually supportive in their description of a two-stage realignment. In the first stage, the rise in the registration trend line is probably the more accurate indicator of the timing of the realignment, for its upturn came entirely *after* 1932, which accords with the evidence assembled in the preceding chapter that the realignment took place during the New Deal years rather than in the initial Roosevelt election. The second-stage Democratic gain is shown clearly in both the Composite B and registration lines, with a lag of eight years between them. Democratic strength was sustained in voting for Composite B offices after 1954 and was reflected in the party registration figures. By 1960 all three trend lines had come together, and (if the 1964 deviation in the presidential vote is disregarded) they remained together throughout the 1960s in a pattern suggesting that the period of adjustment had ended and stability had been attained.

The three trend lines for Oregon show striking divergence in the initial stage of the realignment. All show sharp Democratic gains in the early 1930s, with the registration shift lagging, as in Pennsylvania. But the registration gain proved durable, while the voting gains, particularly those for Composite B offices, did not. Since party identification is presumably a stable attribute of the electorate, it seems likely that the relatively level trend of registration percentages is a fairly accurate indicator of basic party identification. If so,

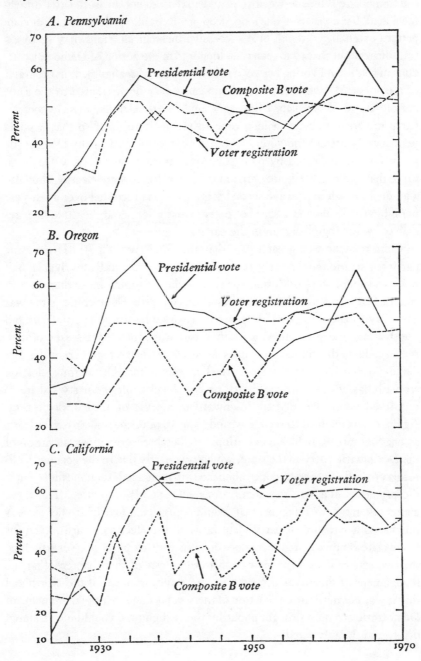

Figure 11-2. *Democratic Percentage of Two-Party Vote Compared with Democratic Percentage of Two-Party Registration, Pennsylvania, Oregon, and California, 1924–70*

the Composite B line between 1936 and 1956 does not measure party attachment at all but consists of one long, deep pro-Republican deviation. A deviant pattern extending through nine successive biennial elections may seem extraordinary, but that time span is no longer than the period of Democratic decline in state-level voting between the two stages of realignment in the states of the upper Midwest. And the slump can surely be attributed to the same reason. As in Wisconsin, Minnesota, and North Dakota, the Democratic party in Oregon needed a long time to reconstitute itself so that it could permanently attract the voters who had been converted to the Democratic party (and so indicated by their party registration) in the New Deal era. Once that had occurred, not only did the party win in state elections but also a gradual though impressive second-stage gain was recorded over a ten-year period in the Democratic share of party registration. And the three lines remained closer together than in the earlier decades.

California shows a greater gain than the other two states in Democratic party registration in the early 1930s. In sharp contrast to Pennsylvania, half the gain came before or during 1932. But while claiming more than 60 percent of California's registered voters after 1936, the Democratic party was able only in the two landslide years of 1958 and 1964 to translate its full registration strength into votes either for president or for lesser offices. Nevertheless, the three trend lines have come closer together in the last decade; since its second-stage revival in the 1950s, Democratic election strength has hovered around the 50 percent level while the party's share of registered voters has drifted downward to a level of around 58 percent. Again, one is inclined to see the period from 1934 to the mid-1950s, at least, as one long pro-Republican deviation, attributable to the disorganization of the Democratic party in the state, which was partly due to the peculiar California cross-filing system (since abolished) that enabled Republicans to enter the primaries and win the nominations of both major parties. The three charts taken together suggest that, while registration figures are not always reliable as a measure of party identification, the election returns, even for Composite B offices, are much more dubious for that purpose. Nevertheless, the two sets of data do at least confirm the thesis of this chapter—that the realignment of the 1930s occurred in two stages in much of the North and that it was not until the completion of the second stage that the increments of Democratic strength brought about by the realignment could be considered firmly and durably fixed.

The Rise of the Programmatic Liberal Democrats

What accounts for the delay of twenty years or more between the first and second stages of the realignment? If a massive shift of voter allegiance to the Democratic party occurred at the presidential level, why was it not translated at once into Democratic strength at other levels in all the northern states, as it was in some? If the voter put one foot across the party line, why did he not go all the way across? Again, the experience in the four states analyzed earlier in this chapter suggests the answer. The barrier that got in the voter's way was the unattractive character of the state and local Democratic parties.

The Democrats who rode into positions of power on the crest of the Roosevelt tide lacked the appeal, the public respect, the motivation, and the competence that would have enabled them to quickly consolidate the support the party had temporarily gained in the early 1930s. The leadership was too old or too conservative to appeal to Roosevelt supporters, or more deeply committed to the party's patronage than to its program, or all of these. By the 1930s it had probably lived down some of the disabilities that had kept the aroused farmers of the nineteenth century from moving into its ranks; it was no longer significantly damaged, presumably, by its identification with rum and rebellion. But the third of the old obstacles—Romanism—remained. The Democratic party in many states was still too Catholic to appeal to the Protestant majority, and it was too urban to appeal to the rural and small-town population. The second stage of the realignment could not take place until a new group of Democrats rose to the top of the party structure, as leaders and as candidates, to give the party a new image and vitality.

In the postwar years, a generation of new leaders did arise throughout the belt of northern states where the process of realignment had not been completed in the 1930s—in other words, in most of the states that appear in Table 11-1. The characteristics of the new generation have already been indicated in the discussion of the upper midwestern states. The new leaders were as different from the old as the Conscience Whigs in their time were from the Cotton Whigs, say, or the La Follette Republicans of Wisconsin from the stalwarts. They were invariably young. They were as issue oriented as the old leaders were patronage oriented. They had been attracted into politics by the excitement of the New Deal and, in many cases, by war experience that had fired in them an interest in world politics; and while they were ambitious, it was not for the pecuniary rewards of politics.[20] They were intellectual and argumentative, devoted followers of the Roosevelt New Deal, as liberal as their elders were conservative. They were activist and reformist, mid-century inheritors of the progressive tradition. Among them were issue-oriented representatives of organized labor and liberal farm groups. And they were zealous to build the party and win elections. To use a term that has attained currency among politicians and political scientists, they were "programmatic liberals."

As soon as a nucleus of programmatic liberals determined to remold the Democratic party in their own image came together in a particular state and began to make their voices heard, a spiraling reaction took place. The new coloration they gave the party made it attractive to Roosevelt Republicans and independents, especially among the younger voters and those attaining voting age. They began to gather recruits. As their bloc grew in number and influence, the party became attractive to still more recruits. Ultimately, a whole new generation of liberals had cast its lot with the Democratic party, along with those of the older generation who were able to break from Republican tradition.

As the main body of liberals consolidated itself in the Democratic party, the old progressive wing of the GOP dwindled, and that party became more solidly conservative. This too had a spiraling reaction; the more conservative it became, the more it forced progressives of all ages into the Democratic party. The distinction between the parties sharpened.

Eventually the programmatic liberals were sufficient to outnumber the professionals in the Democratic party and capture for their own leaders the party's nominations for high office. With that, the party's old image was erased, and the new programmatic party with its young, reformist leadership

---

20. John H. Fenton emphasizes the distinction between the old and the new in his comparative study of politics in six midwestern states, three of which (Michigan, Wisconsin, and Minnesota) he calls "issue-oriented states" and three (Ohio, Indiana, and Illinois) "job-oriented states." He writes: "The important distinction between the two types of parties is that the people in the traditional parties are active in politics because they want a job, and issues are perceived as tools by which to secure the job, whereas the people in the programmatic parties are in politics not for the jobs as such, but because the job is seen as the means of securing the policy goals they regard as desirable" (*Midwest Politics*, p. 4).

A penetrating study of the new programmatic Democratic party and its leaders in one state is Robert Lee Sawyer, Jr., *The Democratic State Central Committee in Michigan, 1949–1959: The Rise of the New Politics and the New Political Leadership* (University of Michigan, Institute of Public Administration, 1960).

proved its appeal to independent voters and its ability to win elections. Once the new leaders gained statewide office, particularly the governorship, they could consolidate their position and complete the transformation of their party and the realignment of the party system. As they built and consolidated their own power, they also brought about a sharp and lasting accretion of Democratic strength in state and local elections, which is shown in Table 11-1.

Thus the long progressive stream of American political history changed course; the part of the stream that had been flowing in Republican channels —in much of the North, this had been the major part—shifted to the Democratic. Where the progressives were organized, the diversion might occur through a single conscious decision, as in North Dakota and Minnesota. There the stream was suddenly dammed and diverted to a new channel. But in many places the transition was neither so abrupt nor so distinct. Usually the progressive current in the Republican party dwindled imperceptibly, almost disappeared for a time, and reemerged in a reborn Democratic party —like a lost river that goes underground, flows hidden for a time, then bursts forth suddenly as a spring.

The realignment was most dramatic and complete in the states of the agrarian tradition where Republican insurgency had always centered. By the beginning of the 1960s, the "Sons of the Wild Jackass" who had plagued Presidents Coolidge and Hoover had no survivors in the Republican party in the Senate. Some were defeated by Republican conservatives, as George Norris by Kenneth S. Wherry in Nebraska and Robert La Follette, Jr., by Joseph McCarthy; when others retired or died in office, no new Republican of the same stamp, with two exceptions, came to join their ranks. One exception was Wayne L. Morse of Oregon, but he found the Republican party uncongenial and declared himself an independent in 1953 and a Democrat in 1955. The other was William Langer of North Dakota. He remained a nominal Republican to the end—while voting faithfully with the Democrats on almost every issue—but when he died in 1960 the Republican agrarian tradition died with him. The farm-belt Republican of the early 1970s is the most stalwart of all his party's conservatives, and the insurgent Republican senators of the earlier generations have found their spiritual heirs in Democrats: La Follette of Wisconsin in William Proxmire and Gaylord Nelson; Langer in Quentin Burdick; Peter Norbeck of South Dakota in George McGovern and James G. Abourezk; Smith Brookhart of Iowa in Harold E. Hughes and Richard Clark; William Edgar Borah of Idaho in Frank Church.

Like the Republican progressive strain, the Democratic conservative strain generally disappeared, although enclaves have survived in Kansas and Nebraska, the southwestern ranching areas, and Nevada.

The last column of Table 11-1 dates the rejuvenation of the Democratic party in the sixteen states. In most cases, the period of the party's revival included one or both of the years 1954 and 1958, when the country veered in the Democratic direction primarily in response to economic recessions that occurred during the Eisenhower administration. But the timing of the gains is also associated with the rise to power in those states of the programmatic liberals. While this is clearest in the states of the upper Midwest discussed earlier, it seems demonstrable in other states as well.

In traditionally Republican Maine, for instance, the programmatic liberal Democrats burst through in 1954 in electing Edmund S. Muskie governor and continued their progress during his term; it was "a new sort of politics—a politics of youth, of amateurs, substantially without patronage or corruption" that "revived the Democratic party and revitalized politics," according to John C. Donovan, who became Maine's Democratic state chairman in 1956.[21]

In Oregon the revival of Democratic fortunes began when "a new generation of young liberal Democrats," spawned by the New Deal and centered in the growing Portland metropolitan area, joined with farm and labor groups to form a Commonwealth Federation. This coalition challenged the established conservative leadership of the Democratic party and captured control in 1948. At that point, the state grange and the CIO unions, particularly the lumber workers, cast their lot with the Democratic party. Capitalizing on discontent with the economic policies of the Eisenhower administration, the Democrats succeeded in electing Richard L. Neuberger to the Senate in 1954 and elected a governor in 1956 for the first time in twenty years; at that time also, Senator Morse switched to the Democratic party and was reelected as its candidate.[22]

In South Dakota, the party gains date from 1953, when George McGovern resigned his Dakota Wesleyan professorship to become executive secretary

---

21. *Congressional Campaign: Maine Elects a Democrat*, Eagleton Foundation Case Studies in Practical Politics (Holt, 1958), p. 13.

22. Lester G. Seligman, "A Prefatory Study of Leadership Selection in Oregon," *Western Political Quarterly*, Vol. 12 (1959), p. 57; idem, "Political Change: Legislative Elites and Parties in Oregon," *Western Political Quarterly*, Vol. 17 (1964), pp. 184–86; and John M. Swarthout, "The 1958 Election in Oregon," *Western Political Quarterly*, Vol. 12 (1959), p. 330.

of a state Democratic party with no treasury and very little life; by 1958, the party was able to elect a governor for the first time since 1934. In Michigan, the period of sharp Democratic growth coincided with the rise to power of new programmatic liberal leadership in the persons of Governor G. Mennen Williams, state chairman and party organizer Neil Staebler, and their associates. Robert Lee Sawyer, Jr., who has traced the rise of Michigan's postwar Democratic party, notes that by 1946 the state appeared to have lapsed back to "the Republican 'normalcy' of the predepression era" but that under the Williams-Staebler leadership "the Democratic revival was both swift and vigorous."[23] In California, the mobilization of thousands of programmatic liberals in the state's Democratic club movement[24] and the new-style leadership of Governor Edmund G. (Pat) Brown were factors. And to the list can be added Pennsylvania, where the Democratic gain (smaller than in the other fifteen states but still enough to bring the party to its highest sustained level since the time of President Buchanan) followed the rise to the top of the Philadelphia Democratic party of reformers Joseph Clark and Richardson Dilworth and the subsequent election as governor of young George Leader, another program-oriented liberal.

Whether the Democratic gains in some of the other states can be attributed in whole or in part to the rise of new leadership is not so apparent, but in some of those states programmatic liberals did play conspicuous roles in the party's revival. Senator John F. Kennedy of Massachusetts and Governors Abraham A. Ribicoff of Connecticut and Robert B. Meyner of New Jersey all provided leadership during the second-stage Democratic revivals, and all were liberals of the new stamp not associated with old-line Democratic organizations.

In states that showed a less pronounced second-stage Democratic spurt— or none at all—programmatic liberals also appeared in the postwar years. Governor Adlai E. Stevenson and Senator Paul H. Douglas of Illinois (both elected in 1948), Senator Stuart Symington of Missouri (1952), Mayor Raymond R. Tucker of St. Louis (1953), and Governors Averell Harriman of New York (1954) and Michael V. DiSalle of Ohio (1958) all fit the clas-

23. *Democratic State Central Committee*, p. 3; tables showing the shift from Republican dominance of lesser offices in the 1932–53 period to Democratic dominance in the 1954–59 period are on pp. 3–4. Fenton (*Midwest Politics*, pp. 28–29) observes that before 1948 organized labor had not been attracted in full force to the Democratic party because of the conservatism of the party's gubernatorial candidates but that under Williams a "liberal-labor alliance" was consummated.

24. Francis Carney, *The Rise of the Democratic Clubs in California*, Eagleton Foundation Case Studies in Practical Politics (Holt, 1958).

sification. So did Democratic National Chairman Paul M. Butler (1955–60) of Indiana. But just as there were smaller Democratic gains in those states than in Michigan or Minnesota, so there was less reconstruction of the party organization. When Stevenson and Harriman left their respective state-houses, the professional politicians were still in control of the party. In fact, there had been no confrontation, for the professionals had participated in the original nominations and there had been collaboration all along. It would be an overstatement to suggest that destruction of the old-line Democratic orga-nizations is in all cases a prerequisite for a second-stage surge in party strength, for in some of the sixteen two-stage states the professional poli-ticians still flourish. All that can be said is that in the states where the pro-fessionals were plainly and decisively superseded—where a genuinely new party was created, controlled by a new social group with a liberal program orientation and an image of zeal and amateurism—a significant and lasting accretion of party strength did follow. Despite their one-party Republican tradition, many of these states were to take their places among the strongest Democratic states in the union.

The appeal that the programmatic liberals gave the Democratic party, as well as the popularity of the program they wrote for it, contributed to the party's national resurgence expressed in its election victories of 1954, 1958, 1960, and 1964. Those years marked the culmination of the pro-Democratic component of the realignment of the 1930s, when the Democratic party reached a peak of strength, whether measured by election returns, party registration figures, or attitudes reported in public opinion surveys. The culmination of the pro-Republican component of the realignment, taking place mainly in the South, is yet to come.

CHAPTER TWELVE

Aftershocks of the New Deal
Earthquake—in the South

POLITICAL REALIGNMENT in the one-party Democratic South has followed essentially the same course as realignment in the one-party Republican states of the North. As the country polarized around the issues of the New Deal, many southern Democrats found themselves at the anti–New Deal pole just as many northern progressive Republicans found themselves to be New Dealers. And the southern conservatives were as acutely uncomfortable in a party led by Franklin D. Roosevelt as the northern progressives had been in a party led by Herbert Hoover. Like the Roosevelt Republicans, they could resolve their conflict very simply by changing parties. But the barriers to such a course were even greater in the Solid South than in the one-party strongholds of the North. So the process of realignment set in motion in the 1930s, which took as long as three decades to work its way to completion in the one-party states of the North, is taking even longer in the South.

The bitterly intransigent anti–New Deal southern Democrats of the 1930s—senators like Carter Glass and Harry F. Byrd of Virginia and Josiah W. Bailey of North Carolina, congressmen like Howard W. Smith of Virginia and Edward E. Cox of Georgia—were the counterparts of the La Follettes in Wisconsin or the Nonpartisan League (NPL) Republicans of North Dakota. They were just as reluctant to transfer their allegiance to the major party that reflected their views and for the same reason. Even more securely than their counterparts, they and their conservative allies controlled the majority party of their states and districts. They could at least determine *its* policy and philosophy. They could take on a qualifying adjective, become *Southern* Democrats or *Virginia* Democrats (like *NPL* Republicans), and what matter the road taken by the national party? By remaining Democrats, in fact, they could to some degree influence and restrain the national party; under their influence, the national party might even recover its

senses. Their votes in Congress, meanwhile, counted equally for the conservative position no matter which side of the aisle they came from. Even
more important, the conservative Democrats retained their seniority in the
Congress and with it their domination of major committees and, much of the
time, of the congressional Democratic party as a whole. So they continued to
enjoy great personal and regional power as Democrats, while they saw the
minority Republican party in their states (as the minority Democrats had
formerly been seen in the one-party North) as a hopeless, discredited band of
stragglers, disreputably led, without tradition of victory or prospect of it,
and bearing the taint of regional disloyalty and (in the South) the opprobrium
of having once been responsible for Negro and carpetbagger rule.

So the obstacles to realignment were enormous. Carter Glass could brand
the New Deal, as early as 1933, "an utterly dangerous effort of the federal
government to transplant Hitlerism to every corner of the nation"[1] yet declare, "I'm a Democrat, not a half-way Democrat" two years later when the
radicalism of the New Deal was even more abhorrent to him.[2] Southern conservative Democrats would develop a working coalition with Republicans in
Congress, but any kind of electoral coalition—which would threaten the
unity and supremacy of the Democratic party in their own southern states—
was anathema. Proposals for a national Republican–conservative–Democratic alliance to oppose Roosevelt in 1936 had no takers in the South.[3]

The tension grew as Roosevelt led the Democratic party toward the left,
even to the point of attempting a "purge" of leading southern conservatives
in the 1938 primaries. Nevertheless, throughout the Roosevelt years, the
lines held. The Republican vote for president in the South,[4] which had stood
at 19 percent of the total in 1932 and again in 1936, rose to only 22 percent
in 1940 and 25 percent in 1944 (though the GOP gain in 1944 well exceeded
the national increase of 1.1 percentage points). The war, which suspended
New Deal reforms, may have been a factor in deferring political disruption
in the South. For almost as soon as the war ended, the Democratic party
accelerated its march toward the inevitable rupture.

1. Carter Glass, letter to Walter Lippmann, Aug. 10, 1933, quoted by James T.
Patterson, *Congressional Conservatism and the New Deal: The Growth of the Conservative
Coalition in Congress, 1933–39* (University of Kentucky Press, 1967), p. 13.
2. *Washington Post*, June 1, 1935, quoted in ibid., p. 254.
3. Patterson, *Congressional Conservatism*, pp. 251–57.
4. Unless otherwise indicated, "the South" refers to the eleven states of the Confederacy.

The Dixiecrat Revolt

Harry Truman had even less chance than did Franklin Roosevelt to bridge the chasm between the Democratic North and the conservatives of the Democratic South. The liberalism of the new Democratic party, if less yeasty than in the prewar years, was being defined and institutionalized within the party by the new generation of programmatic politicians. President Truman had to choose between his party's wings, as did his predecessor, and he made the same choice, for the same reasons.

Like Roosevelt, Truman was by sympathy and outlook with the left. Like Roosevelt, he relished controversy. Politically, he faced the same compulsions. To his left, where Huey Long had stood in Roosevelt's first term, Henry Wallace now stood, threatening a party schism. The Negro, who in the 1930s was just entering the Democratic party, was now on the inside, settled, numerically important, and demanding.

"I believe in the brotherhood of man," Harry Truman had said in his 1940 campaign for the Senate, "not merely the brotherhood of white men but the brotherhood of all men before law."[5] After the war, Truman's dedication was put to the test. A series of anti-Negro incidents aroused the country. Truman anticipated a southern defection, he says, but "I wanted to get the facts . . . and to see that the law was strengthened, if necessary."[6] He appointed the President's Committee on Civil Rights, made up entirely of northerners and southern liberals. In October 1947 the committee announced its unavoidable conclusion: the Negro and other minorities in America were the victims of segregation and gross discrimination, and the government should act to right those wrongs.[7]

The professional politicians in the Truman circle instinctively recoiled.

---

5. Quoted by Jonathan Daniels, *The Man of Independence* (Lippincott, 1950), pp. 339–40. But Truman was not an advocate of "social equality" for blacks, he told a Negro audience during the same campaign. Barton J. Bernstein, "The Ambiguous Legacy: Civil Rights," in Bernstein (ed.), *Politics and Policies of the Truman Administration* (Quadrangle, 1970), p. 272. Truman "shared the views of many decent men of his generation and thought that equality before the law could be achieved within the framework of 'separate but equal,'" Bernstein concludes. "His vision was parochial. . . . Like many Americans, he found racial matters peripheral to his interests and considered the problem only when it was thrust upon him." Ibid.

6. *Memoirs by Harry S. Truman*, Vol. 2, *Years of Trial and Hope* (Doubleday, 1956), p. 180.

7. President's Committee on Civil Rights, *To Secure These Rights* (1947).

The cabinet was split.[8] But Truman's principal planner of political strategy for the 1948 campaign was Clark M. Clifford, his special counsel, and Clifford had just written a brief for boldness. Negroes might hold the balance of power in several large northern states, wrote Clifford. "The Negro voter has become a cynical, hard-boiled trader," and the Republicans were bidding high. Besides, Clifford argued, "as always, the South can be considered safely Democratic. And in formulating national policy, it can be safely ignored."[9]

Truman decided to ignore the South. He proclaimed in his State of the Union Message in January 1948 that the nation's "first goal" was "to secure fully the essential human rights of our citizens." A month later he sent to the Congress a message which, while omitting the most far-reaching proposals of the Committee on Civil Rights (such as federal sanctions to end segregation), proposed a fair employment practices law, an antilynching law, protection of voting rights, and a series of other measures that foreshadowed the legislation enacted in the 1950s and 1960s.[10]

The reaction in the South was immediate and vehement. The Southern Governors' Conference, then in session, issued a hurried statement declaring, "The President must cease attacks on white supremacy or face full-fledged revolt in the South." Four hundred Democrats walked out of a party dinner in Little Rock when Truman's voice came over the loudspeaker. After meeting with the Democratic national chairman, a committee of southern governors issued a statement warning that the southern vote was not "in the bag" for the Democratic party. In May, Governor Fielding L. Wright of Mississippi played host to a southern political conference, which agreed to reconvene after the Democratic national convention.[11]

To keep the party from disrupting, the administration and its congressional leaders found reasons to delay the introduction of bills and the issuance of executive orders. The draft of the 1948 Democratic platform written at the White House proposed only to repeat the comparatively mild stance of the 1944 convention on civil rights. But on both sides of the Mason-Dixon line there were politicians opposed to compromise, men with convictions and

8. Alfred Steinberg, *The Man from Missouri: The Life and Times of Harry S. Truman* (Putnam's, 1962), p. 303. John M. Redding, *Inside the Democratic Party* (Bobbs-Merrill, 1958), pp. 129–30.

9. Memorandum to the President, Nov. 19, 1947, quoted by Irwin Ross, *The Loneliest Campaign: The Truman Victory of 1948* (New American Library, 1968), pp. 22–23, 27.

10. *Public Papers of the Presidents: Harry S. Truman, 1948* (1964), pp. 3, 121–26.

11. Redding, *Inside the Democratic Party*, pp. 133–34. Ross, *Loneliest Campaign*, pp. 63, 64. Steinberg (*Man from Missouri*, p. 304) says 750 walked out of the Little Rock meeting.

men who had a political interest in disruption. So at the national convention both sides denounced the platform plank sent from the White House. Southerners cried that it promised too much, northerners that it promised too little. Hubert Humphrey and his programmatic liberals provided the rhetoric and the passion for the northern revolt, but the northern professionals— worried now about Negro defections to Henry A. Wallace—provided the practical support. A civil rights fight, said Boss Ed Flynn of the Bronx, was "what we need to stir up this convention and win the election." The Illinois, New Jersey, and Pennsylvania professionals agreed. So the convention beat down the southern amendments and adopted the northern amendment, $651\frac{1}{2}$ to $582\frac{1}{2}$, with those who spoke for Truman voting against it. Then the entire Mississippi delegation and half the Alabama delegates walked out.[12]

But in their farewell, the Alabama delegates made clear that they were still Democrats and would have no truck with the Republicans. When the southern political conference reconvened at Birmingham in July, it declared that "principle is above any party" and endorsed Governor J. Strom Thurmond of South Carolina for president and Governor Wright of Mississippi for vice-president. The object was not to create a third party; it was to maneuver Thurmond-Wright electors onto the ballot under the Democratic symbol. This stratagem succeeded in four states—South Carolina, Alabama, Mississippi, and Louisiana[13]—where the candidates and their backers retained their status as Democrats. But elsewhere in the South, the Thurmond-Wright ticket was forced to run as a States' Rights (popularly known as Dixiecrat) third party.

The intraparty struggles between Dixiecrats and loyalists for the Democratic label on the ballot tended to follow the same liberal-conservative factional lines that had developed over economic issues in state politics through the years and in national politics in the 1930s. Economic conservatives saw and seized the opportunity to exploit the race issue as a means of strengthening their position in state politics in general. Thus the Arkansas Free Enterprise Association, a planter-industrialist organization that had sponsored a "right-to-work" amendment to the state constitution, became prominent in Dixiecrat maneuvers there. "It is no accident," wrote the *Arkansas Gazette*, "that those who are loudest now in denouncing Mr. Truman [on civil rights]

12. Ross, *Loneliest Campaign*, pp. 64–65, 120–21, 125.
13. V. O. Key, Jr., *Southern Politics in State and Nation* (Knopf, 1949), pp. 335–44; Alexander Heard, *A Two-Party South?* (University of North Carolina Press, 1952), pp. 20–23. In Alabama, the national Democratic party could not even get a slate of Truman electors on the ballot.

are the same Southern Democrats who have also taken issue with him and with his predecessor on many other matters—labor legislation, price controls, public power, federal spending, etc." The Associated Industries of Florida took the lead in condemning Truman's civil rights program as "iniquitous, insidious and malicious." In Louisiana the Dixiecrats were the anti-Long conservative Democratic faction; in Georgia, the Talmadge conservative faction flirted with a Thurmond-Wright endorsement. Throughout the South, the more liberal of the established factions "usually went down the line for the national Administration." In their campaign, the Dixiecrats crusaded for states' rights not only on the civil rights issue but also, as Thurmond put it, on "many other like questions."[14]

Thurmond easily carried the four states in which he was the official Democratic nominee. He won every county in Mississippi, all but one (traditionally Republican Winston) in Alabama, and all but two in South Carolina. In the other states, where Thurmond had to run as a third-party candidate, few Democrats of standing, no matter how sympathetic, risked their political careers by openly supporting him. Senators and congressmen had their seniority to worry about, and state and local politicians their Democratic credentials to protect. Even so, the Thurmond ticket carried twelve counties in Georgia, including Richmond (Augusta); three in northern Florida; three in the Arkansas delta; two in Tennessee, including Shelby (Memphis); and one in southern Virginia. The Dixiecrats also scored impressively, though short of a plurality, in a large belt of eastern Texas and in southern North Carolina. President Truman responded that he was "proud" to have won "without the solid South"—a remark for which he was not forgiven there.[15]

The areas of Thurmond strength define a political Deep South, which corresponds closely to the region's "black belt,"[16] its area of rich black soil, of antebellum plantations and postbellum sharecropping, and of highest proportion of blacks in the population. This has been consistently the area most sensitive to the civil rights issue and most responsive to racist politics. A comparison of maps A and B in Figure 12-1 shows the close relationship be-

14. Key, *Southern Politics*, pp. 338, 339, 342. *Arkansas Gazette* (Little Rock), Feb. 21, 1948, as quoted by Key. Heard, *Two-Party South?* p. 27.

15. Press conference, Dec. 2, 1948 (*Public Papers of the Presidents, 1948*), p. 952. Key felt that Thurmond would not have carried Alabama and Louisiana if he had not been the "Democratic nominee" (*Southern Politics*, p. 342).

16. Donald S. Strong defines each state's "black belt" as the top quartile of counties ranked according to the percentage of Negro population in 1950. "The Presidential Election in the South, 1952," *Journal of Politics*, Vol. 17 (1955), p. 345. The term will be used similarly here.

Figure 12-1. *Five Maps Showing "Black Belt" and Voting Behavior in the South, 1948–68*

A. *Areas of highest proportion of blacks, 1950*

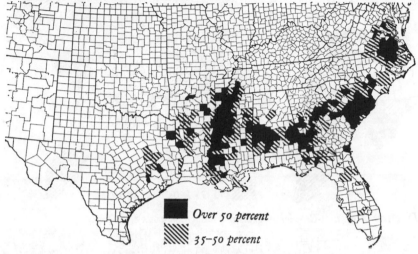

■ *Over 50 percent*

▨ *35–50 percent*

B. *Areas of greatest Thurmond strength, 1948*

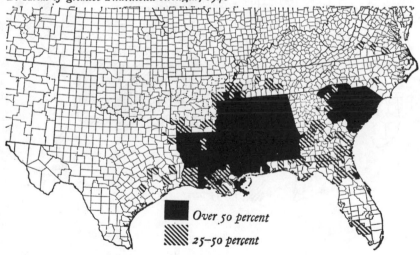

■ *Over 50 percent*

▨ *25–50 percent*

C. Areas of greatest Republican gains in presidential voting, 1948–52

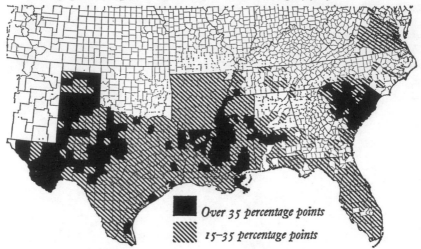

Over 35 percentage points

15–35 percentage points

D. Areas of greatest Republican gains in presidential voting, 1960–64

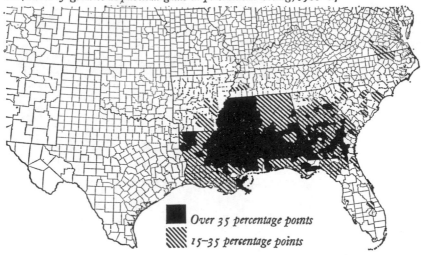

Over 35 percentage points

15–35 percentage points

E. Areas of greatest Wallace strength, 1968

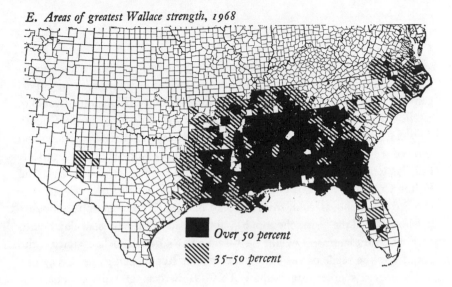

■ *Over 50 percent*

▨ *35–50 percent*

tween the ethnic "black belt" and the Thurmond movement. For the South as a whole, the percentage of the vote for Thurmond correlates at the high level of 0.682 with the percentage of blacks in the population. And despite the participation of economic conservatives in the Thurmond movement, economic class seems to have had no relation to the Dixiecrat vote. A precinct-by-precinct study of the 1948 election returns in Jacksonville, Florida, showed that the proportion of the Thurmond vote in high- and low-income neighborhoods was approximately the same.[17]

Outside the Deep South lies another political zone—often called the "rim South" but extending into the border states—nearly as solid in its Democratic allegiance but more moderate in its racial attitude. In this zone Thurmond had little appeal, and anti-Truman feeling expressed itself in a significant shift to the Republicans. In 1948 Republican candidate Thomas E. Dewey's share of the total national vote fell from the 1944 level by one percentage point, from 46 to 45, but it rose seven points in Texas, four in Florida, and four in Virginia.

17. Charles D. Farris, "Effects of Negro Voting on the Politics of a Southern City" (Ph.D. dissertation, University of Chicago, 1952), cited by Strong, "Presidential Election in the South," pp. 354–55. The Thurmond vote in precincts classified by rental levels was as follows: upper, 28.3 percent; middle, 27.9; lower, 27.0.

Metropolitan Republicanism in the South

In the rim South, the striking Republican gains in 1948 were in the metropolitan centers. In Texas, the Republican proportion rose from 22 to 32 percent in Dallas County, from 11 to 35 in Harris County (Houston), from 8 to
28 in Tarrant County (Fort Worth), from 10 to 28 in Smith County
(Tyler), and from 10 to 26 in Galveston County. In Virginia, Richmond
showed a Republican gain, from 28 to 41 percent, Norfolk, from 29 to 41.
Pinellas County (St. Petersburg), Florida, rose from 42 to 56 percent. And
Fulton County (Atlanta), Georgia—rim South in its political moderation—
showed a Republican gain, from 17 to 29 percent. Thus first appeared what
has been called the "metropolitan Republicanism" of the present-day South.

Four years later, in Dwight D. Eisenhower's first landslide victory, the
South was the scene of even more spectacular Republican gains. Every one
of the eleven southern states showed a GOP percentage point gain exceeding the national average of 10 points (from 45 to 55 percent of the total
vote). The southern gains ranged from 13 points in Tennessee to an incredi-
ble 29 in Texas, 37 in Mississippi, and 46 in South Carolina. Four of the rim
states—Virginia, Florida, Tennessee, and Texas—gave their electoral votes
to Eisenhower.

This massive flow of votes to Eisenhower represented the convergence of
two streams—first, the metropolitan Republicanism that had made its appearance in 1948; second, a part of the Dixiecrat protest movement of that
earlier election. As can be seen from map C (Figure 12-1), the Republicans
registered gains of 35 percentage points or more in most of South Carolina,
in part of the Alabama black belt, in the Mississippi delta, and in some of the
counties in Louisiana (and one in Tennessee) that Thurmond had carried.
The one state of the Deep South that had resisted Thurmond—Georgia—
was also most resistant to Eisenhower.

In subsequent elections, the metropolitan Republicanism was to prove
durable. Figure 12-2 compares the transformation of presidential voting behavior in four large metropolitan centers of the rim South with the national
trend. In the first two postwar elections, the voting patterns of these centers
came into conformity with that of the nation as a whole. And essentially
they remained in conformity, staying with Eisenhower in 1956, giving
Nixon somewhat less support in 1960, and rejecting Barry Goldwater in
1964. Their Republican vote also held up remarkably well against George

Figure 12-2. *Trend in Republican Percentage of Total Presidential Vote, Selected Metropolitan Centers of the Rim South, 1936–68*

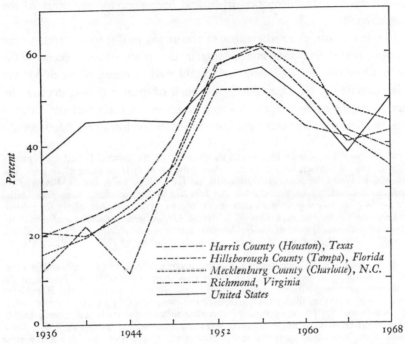

Source: Richard M. Scammon, *America at the Polls* (University of Pittsburgh Press, 1965).

Wallace's southern campaign of 1968; one of the four actually showed a gain.

Within each metropolitan area, moreover, the new party alignment at the presidential level conformed with that of the nation as a whole. Donald S. Strong analyzed the 1952 vote by precincts in fifteen metropolitan counties in states of both the Deep South and the rim South and found that in every instance the party division was on class lines (just the opposite of the 1948 Dixiecrat-Democratic division, which was unrelated to class). The 1952 election separated more affluent Republicans from less opulent Democrats, Democratic black and white slums and working-class districts from white Republican suburbs, exactly as in the North. "They're acting like Yankees!" concluded Strong. "The prosperous folk of Richmond, Charleston, and Dallas voted just like their economic counterparts in Syracuse, Indianapolis, and Cleveland."[18] Sixteen years later they were still doing so. Strong's analysis of the 1968 election showed that southern presidential Republicanism remained based on the urban and higher-income segments of the population.[19]

In other words, the realignment of the 1930s finally took effect, in the 1948–52 period, in presidential voting in the metropolitan centers of the South. Once the new alignment was established, it remained fixed. Metropolitan centers in the Deep South realigned to greater or less degree, depending on their size and the "metropolitanism" of their outlook. In each area, smaller cities lag behind the large cities in developing reliable Republi-

18. Strong, "Presidential Election in the South," p. 382. Samuel Lubell's analysis of the 1952 vote in thirteen southern cities shows the same division along class lines. For Houston, he traces the political stratification as far back as 1936. Lubell, *Revolt of the Moderates* (Harper, 1956), pp. 182–86. An analysis by Strong of the 1956 presidential vote produced comparable findings, except that blacks were much less solidly for Stevenson than they had been in 1952. Donald S. Strong, *Urban Republicanism in the South* (University of Alabama, Bureau of Public Administration, 1960), Chap. 2.

19. "Further Reflections on Southern Politics," *Journal of Politics*, Vol. 33 (1971), pp. 245–49.

A survey of political attitudes of voters in eleven southern states, conducted in 1961, provides further corroboration for the thesis that the growth of Republicanism in the South represents primarily the movement of economic conservatives to the Republican party. Asked what they liked or disliked about the two parties, 63.3 percent of the Democrats who voted for Nixon in 1960 gave replies indicating dissatisfaction with Democratic liberalism on domestic economic policies and social welfare programs. The positive appeal of the Republican party lay in the same area; 58.3 percent specified a liking for the GOP's conservatism in domestic policy. These figures were far higher than those for the next categories (which related to party leadership and style of operation). Civil rights were clearly not a direct factor; more voters were alienated by the Republicans' position on civil rights than by the Democrats' (a difference probably accounted for by black respondents' preference for the Democratic civil rights position). Once more the class structure of the emerging two-party system was confirmed: middle class voters were 54 percent for Nixon, working class voters 70 percent for Kennedy. Blacks were 75 percent for Kennedy, whites only 55 percent. "Most of the deviation from party identification in the 1960 election can be shown to be class related," concluded George Robert Boynton, Jr., who analyzed the data. "Class polarization in voting is increasing in the South, while in the nation as a whole it is decreasing." Boynton, "Southern Republican Voting in the 1960 Election" (Ph.D. dissertation, University of North Carolina, 1963), pp. 193–94.

A three-city analysis of Dallas, Texas, and Charleston and Columbia, South Carolina, also showed that in 1960 Nixon received his strongest support from upper-income white precincts. Bernard Cosman, "Presidential Republicanism in the South," *Journal of Politics*, Vol. 24 (1962), p. 320. A study of 1956 presidential voting in a single precinct in Tallahassee, Florida, also showed that Eisenhower Democrats had a higher income, on the average, than Stevenson Democrats. Civil rights was not found to be a significant factor in the movement of 40 percent of the Democratic voters to Eisenhower. James W. Prothro, Ernest Q. Campbell, and Charles M. Griggs, "Two-Party Voting in the South: Class vs. Party Identification," *American Political Science Review*, Vol. 52 (1958), pp. 131–39.

can strength, and the rural areas lag still farther.[20] In communities of each size class, the Deep South lags behind the rim.

In some rural areas at the edge of the rim South—far from black belt political influence, close to the North, and weak in Civil War tradition—the presidential voting pattern looks much like that of the metropolitan centers. The heavy Republican gains in western Texas in 1952 (shown on map C in Figure 12-1) have resulted in a permanent accretion of GOP strength in subsequent presidential voting. The retirement counties of central and southern Florida and the upland regions of Virginia and Arkansas show similar patterns. To these realigned areas of the rim South can be added others of the border states themselves, like New Mexico's "little Texas" and the more urbanized counties of southern Oklahoma.

In communities that have completed the conformance of their presidential voting to national patterns, like those charted in Figure 12-2, one of every three or four habitual Democratic voters (or new voters of Democratic families) has become a reasonably reliable Republican supporter. Such a large bloc of switchers is obviously not made up of Democrats who were New Dealers in the 1930s. Just as obviously, it is not made up of racist voters; Figure 12-2 shows that Goldwater's subtle exploitation of the racial issue and Wallace's blatant utilization of it left the metropolitan Republicans equally unmoved. The switchers must therefore consist of a large part of the anti–New Deal wing of the Democratic party—of voters who were left behind, philosophically, when Roosevelt transformed the traditional Democracy as they had known it. In short, they were *latent* Republicans who had been kept within the Democratic party by some kind of pressure. When the pressure was suddenly released after the war, the latent Republicans began to express themselves as Republicans, free at last to behave in presidential elections as they would have behaved all along had they lived somewhere else (though not necessarily ready yet to identify themselves as Republicans in state and local politics).

20. Strong found that the Republican percentage of the vote in 1956 in metropolitan areas exceeded the percentage in nonmetropolitan areas in every southern state, and that the larger of the nonmetropolitan areas were more Republican than the smaller. If Republican *gains* rather than absolute percentages are used, the metropolitan areas exceeded the nonmetropolitan areas in each of the eleven states except Florida, where immigration of northern Republicans into nonmetropolitan retirement and resort communities distorted the pattern. "Durable Republicanism in the South," in Allen P. Sindler (ed.), *Change in the Contemporary South* (Duke University Press, 1963), pp. 179–81. See also Strong, *Urban Republicanism in the South*, Chap. 1.

What was the pressure, and what released it? Donald Strong has offered an explanation. "The historic Solid South was an artificial device to assure white supremacy," he wrote. "When the Democratic party ceased to be the champion of white supremacy Southern whites began to act like other Americans and vote in harmony with what they perceived to be their economic interest."[21] In other words, the same Democratic platform and Truman policies that triggered the Dixiecrat revolt also produced the move of economic conservatives to Dewey and to Eisenhower.

Certain it is that the aggressive civil rights stance of the national Democratic party was the one big *new* event, from the southern viewpoint, of the 1944–52 period. Its traumatic effect can hardly be overestimated. The South, after all, had managed, without leaving the national Democratic party, to accept the Wagner Act, minimum wages, public housing, public power, federal welfare programs, the Farm Security Administration, deficits and debt and devaluation of the dollar, Roosevelt's "purge," and his attack on the Supreme Court. But in the single year of 1948 the issue of civil rights drove out of the national Democratic party almost nine-tenths of its supporters in Mississippi, almost three-fourths in South Carolina, and more than half in Louisiana, and all of its support (by providing the pretext for keeping it off the ballot) in Alabama. In an atmosphere of regionwide hostility to the Democratic party, it was natural that the opprobrium hitherto attached to voting Republican would lose its force and, in the more cosmopolitan localities, disappear entirely.

But perhaps it does not detract from the validity of Strong's thesis to suggest that there were other, reinforcing factors in the postwar situation. The war and early postwar years were a period of extraordinarily rapid urbanization in the South. Thousands of young men had been uprooted from the rural South during the war years and thrust into the company of men from other regions, and had then returned not to their farms or small towns but to the urban centers. This was a mobile, traveled generation, which had shed much of the old parochialism and yankeephobia. The new industrialization infused the southern cities with northern executives and technicians, many of them Republican. Southern businessmen were developing ever closer ties with northern businessmen, bankers with bankers, brokers and insurance men and lawyers with their northern counterparts. In the postwar years, a forward-looking, national-minded leadership was coming to the top in southern cities.

21. "Durable Republicanism in the South," pp. 174–75.

The emergence of a new postwar social, economic, and intellectual climate came at a time of transition in national Democratic leadership. As long as Roosevelt lived, his personal hold on the mass of southern voters might alone have been enough to forestall any organized revolt, and he was a wartime president besides. But at the war's end, in Roosevelt's chair sat Harry Truman—politically lonely, weak, and vulnerable. He caught the country's fancy for a time, but by 1952 he and his party were out of favor everywhere, South and North alike.

At this juncture came the candidacy of Dwight Eisenhower. Alexander Heard, in a prophetic passage written in 1951, speculated that only the nomination of General Eisenhower by the Republicans would be likely to upset the conventional Democratic pattern of the South "because he would be viewed by many voters as essentially nonpolitical."[22] When Eisenhower ran, a southern Democrat could in a sense vote against Truman (or Adlai Stevenson, as his political heir) without voting Republican. Eisenhower was everybody's hero—the South's as well as the North's, the Democrats' as well as the Republicans'. He stood for national unity, national strength, a confident military and foreign policy, above the partisan struggle. He gave the southern Democratic conservatives a kind of absolution to vote Republican, and they voted for him not once but twice. A psychological threshold had been crossed; a Republican vote for president every four years became natural, normal, acceptable, even fashionable, among the middle and upper economic classes in the cities.

Even without the civil rights issue, then, it seems likely that the South would have realigned on the national pattern in the postwar years, and most rapidly in the cities. The fact that the Republican party gained strength in nine of the eleven southern states at a rate higher than the national average between 1940 and 1944—before the civil rights issue emerged—suggests this conclusion.

From Thurmond to Wallace: The Protest Vote

While the metropolitan Republicanism that appeared so decisively in 1952 has proved to be solid and reliable, the other element of the GOP surge that year has turned out to be just the opposite. The support given the Re-

22. Heard, *Two-Party South?* p. 167.

Figure 12-3. Trend in Republican Percentage of Total Presidential Vote, Three Rural Dixiecrat Counties, 1936–68

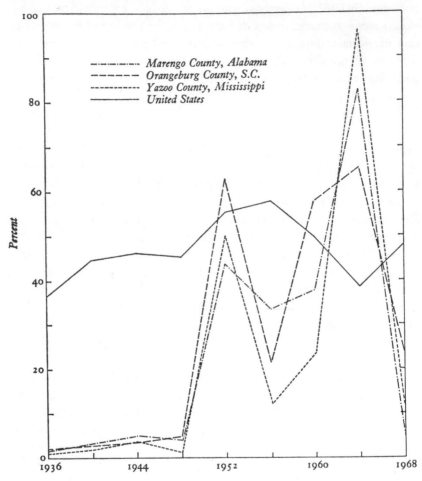

Source: Scammon, *America at the Polls.*

publican party in the Dixiecrat black-belt counties has fluctuated wildly since 1948, as shown by the voting record of some typical counties in Figure 12-3.[23] With regularity since 1952, the trend lines in these counties have moved in the opposite direction from those of the rim metropolitan centers (Figure 12-2) and of the nation. These counties were disillusioned with Eisenhower

23. The chart shows the trend in the rural black-belt county, in each of three states, that showed the strongest Republican surge in 1952.

in 1956 (voting for a States' Rights ticket when one was on the ballot, otherwise swinging to Stevenson). They rejected Kennedy in 1960, plumped enthusiastically for Goldwater in 1964, but dumped Nixon in 1968 in favor of
Wallace (the white voters, that is; the blacks, who had not voted in significant numbers in most of the rural black belt in previous presidential elections, turned to Humphrey).

Plainly, the white voters in the Dixiecrat black-belt counties lost their
moorings in national politics in the postwar period. They cut loose from the
national Democratic party in 1948, and did not return to it in six presidential elections afterward—except in 1956, when the only choice was between
Eisenhower and Stevenson. But neither did they settle anywhere else. They
gave their vote in each election to the candidate who promised—or appeared
to promise—the strongest position against integration. That candidate
proved to be Republican in 1952, 1960, and 1964, but the national Republican party as such did not command their permanent allegiance. Whenever a
third-party candidate (or a slate of independent electors) ran on a platform
tailored for the white voters in the black belt—1948, 1956, and 1968—they
deserted the Republicans as readily as they had rejected the Democrats in
1948. The black-belt protest vote could be described as anti-Democratic at
the national level, but it was not yet Republican. In the absence of a continuing third party, it had become a floating, unattached vote. It might be in
the process of realigning. It was clearly available for realignment. But by
1968 it had not yet realigned.

The solid 1972 vote for Nixon among white voters of the black belt can
probably be explained on the same basis. The President took the stronger
stand against busing, and came much closer to the black-belt view on racial
issues generally than did Democratic candidate George McGovern. But
whether Nixon won any more permanent converts to the GOP than did
Goldwater in his earlier Republican sweep of that area is yet to be determined; if George Wallace, or someone of like views and stature, is in the
presidential contest in November 1976, the Republican presidential strength
of 1972 may melt away as quickly as did the strength of 1964.

A comparison of the maps in Figure 12-1 makes clear the continuity of
the anti-Democratic protest movement. George Wallace's popular vote in
1968 (map E) was more than eight times that of Thurmond twenty years
earlier, but it was still centered in the same Dixiecrat belt of the Deep South.
In spreading beyond that belt, it found its greatest response in the black-
belt counties of the other southern states (map A)—the North Carolina-

Virginia tobacco region, the delta counties of Arkansas, the Florida pan-
handle, western Tennessee, eastern Texas.

The figures below show the generally high positive correlation in the rim
South of the 1968 Wallace vote (map E) with the proportion of blacks in the
population (map A) and with the original Dixiecrat movement (map B):[24]

	Percentage of blacks, 1950	*Thurmond percentage of 1948 vote*
Arkansas	0.433	0.411
North Carolina	0.738	0.098
Tennessee	0.472	0.534
Texas	0.476	0.571
Virginia	0.528	0.628

The Second Stage of Southern Realignment

As in the one-party states of the North two decades earlier, the transformation of voting behavior at the presidential level in the South (in the counties, particularly the metropolitan centers, where it proved lasting) was no
more than the first stage of the party realignment process—the realignment
of the 1930s, that is, even its first stage twenty years delayed. Full identification of GOP presidential voters with the Republican party as an institution
would have to await a second stage of the realignment process corresponding
to the one in the North.

A survey in December 1956 of 225 white registered Democratic voters
in one precinct in Tallahassee, Florida, showed that 109, or nearly half,
voted for Eisenhower but only 6 of them would admit to being Republicans.
Of the remaining 103, 15 called themselves independents, 2 identified with
"other" parties, and 12 refused to answer the question, leaving 74 insisting
they were still Democrats. Of these, however, only a quarter considered
themselves "strong Democrats."[25] The 1961 regionwide survey analyzed by
Boynton confirmed that Democrats who voted for Nixon (most of whom,
presumably, had also voted twice for Eisenhower) still generally considered

24. Computations by Gary Greenhalgh.
25. Prothro, Campbell, and Griggs, "Two-Party Voting in the South," pp. 137–39.
That some, at least, of the Eisenhower Democrats were in transition to becoming normally Republican in presidential voting (beyond the 6 admitted Republicans) is indicated
by a finding that 80 percent of the Eisenhower voters were undecided about their 1960
voting intention, while 69 percent of the voters who had stayed with the Democratic
party in 1956 intended to stay with it again in 1960.

themselves Democrats. Of the total sample, only 13.5 percent identified themselves as Republicans, whereas Nixon had received 48 percent of the popular vote. (Another 19.5 percent were independents, 8.5 percent were apolitical, and the remaining 58.5 percent were still Democrats.) Presidential voting habits had changed drastically by 1961, but the change had not extended to party identification; indeed, Boynton observes, a smaller proportion of voters had switched in the South than in the nation as a whole.[26]

The Eisenhower Democrats resembled the Roosevelt Republicans of twenty years before. Truman played the role of Hoover, a president who alienated large blocs of voters in the areas where his party was dominant. Eisenhower played the role of Roosevelt, an enormously popular leader who at last made his party respectable, as a national institution, in the region where it had been discredited. The Eisenhower party in the South in 1952 would still have the same distance to go as the Roosevelt party in the North had had in 1936 to convert its presidential voters, even the habitual ones, into genuine *party* strength. Yet the experience of the North did show that the conversion could ultimately be made—indeed, that it seemed inevitable. Eventually, the barriers would have to tumble, and the realignment of the 1930s would be nationwide.

The barriers also were the same. Local Democratic organizations had powers of coercion. "You want to get your road built? Then you'd better not be seen at a Republican meeting."[27] The minority Republican party in the southern states in 1952 was, if anything, even less attractive and suitable as a political vehicle than the minority Democratic party of the one-party northern states had been in 1932. "Southern Republican leaders—save those

---

26. Boynton, "Southern Republican Voting," p. 117. A further analysis showed that Democratic families were holding to their political traditions more solidly than Republican families: of voters whose parents were Democrats, 82 percent considered themselves Democrats; the corresponding figure for voters of Republican parentage was only 54 percent (a Republican loss undoubtedly accounted for largely by black switchers).

In analyzing the southern segment of the 1956 and 1960 samples of the University of Michigan's Survey Research Center, Philip E. Converse reached conclusions consistent with those of Boynton. Partisan conversions among southern whites between 1956 and 1960 amounted to 4 percent, the converts divided equally between the parties. The younger southern white generation was as Democratic as the older generation. The most significant factor in the growth of southern Republicanism was in-migration, concentrated in the cities and along the littoral. Civil rights was not a clear party-splitting issue in 1960 since some southerners blamed the Republicans for desegregation pressure and others blamed the Democrats. Converse, "A Major Political Realignment?" in Sindler (ed.), *Change in the Contemporary South*, pp. 206–16. Revised as Chap. 12 in Angus Campbell and others, *Elections and the Political Order* (Wiley, 1966).

27. This was the comment of a Texas Republican official in 1970 in explaining the slow growth of the GOP in rural areas. Interview, September 1970.

who get themselves elected to local office—are not politicians in the usual sense of the word," wrote V. O. Key, Jr., in the pre-Eisenhower years. "They might be called palace or bureaucratic politicians, since their chief preoccupation is not with voters but with maneuvers to gain and keep control of the state party machinery. . . . These party officials often have only the foggiest notion where the Republican voters in the state live and who they are. Most of them are overwhelmed by the futility of it all, but they keep the faith in a quiet spirit of dedication not unlike that of the Britisher who, although living in the jungle surrounded by heathen, dresses for dinner."[28] "The most signal characteristic of the party's southern 'leadership,' " wrote Alexander Heard in the same pre-Eisenhower period, "has been a lack of interest in winning elections. There are exceptions . . . but Republican officials in the South by and large have not wanted to build a party worthy of the name. They have been big fish in little ponds and they have liked it. . . . Republican officials have not sought to disrupt their closed corporation by electing local candidates. . . . They have been 'patronage referees' or 'palace politicians' but not candidates or campaign managers."[29] In 1952, Key observed, several Republican organizations "seemed bewildered by the prospect of the accession of a mass-following and even resented the intrusion of converts."[30] All reminiscent of what had been said of North Dakota and Wisconsin Democrats.

The first requisite for a change in Republican party fortunes, then, was a change in the attitude of the party leadership, and that usually required a change in the leadership itself. The palace politicians who suddenly found themselves at the head of a mass movement and were incompetent to lead it had to be deposed. But that took time. No substitute corps of Republican leaders—dynamic, dedicated, devoted to party-building rather than to party control and patronage—had been standing in the wings, waiting for just such an opportunity to come on stage. Such an alternate leadership corps would certainly have long since taken over, for the "closed corporations" that ruled the party had little depth of support and could not have offered stout resistance. After 1952, with what seemed like a new Republican era emerging, was a time to encourage fresh challenges. But first those who would emerge as challengers had to discover themselves and one another, form their alliances, establish their power bases, and develop their support.

28. *Southern Politics in State and Nation*, pp. 292–93.
29. Heard, *Two-Party South?* p. 97.
30. Key, "The Erosion of Sectionalism," *Virginia Quarterly Review*, Vol. 31 (1955), p. 167.

The Programmatic Republican Conservatives

There is no evidence that the Eisenhower administration gave any appreciable support to party-building. In at least some southern states, it accepted the traditional practices of minority politics; it acquiesced in understandings with conservative Democrats that in return for the latter's continued support at the national level the Republicans would not seek to undermine them locally[31] (reminiscent of Roosevelt's 1934 endorsement of La Follette in Wisconsin). Texas Republicans in particular were bitter that the only two southerners appointed to the Eisenhower cabinet—Oveta Culp Hobby and Robert Anderson, both of Texas—had been lifelong Democrats. The patronage awarded to local Republicans could hurt as well as help; some of the most energetic and promising young party leaders were taken out of politics with appointments to the bench.

Figure 12-4 presents several indicators of the rise of southern Republicanism. The first measures party effort, the number of seats in the U.S. House of Representatives for which the party ran candidates. The others measure party success. All tell the same story: party gains were meager in the 1950s; not until the 1960s did they gain momentum.

Southern Republican strength in the House of Representatives, for instance, rose from two in 1950 (both in eastern Tennessee) to seven in 1954, but not another seat was won until 1962.[32] In the state legislatures, the Republicans held 2.9 percent of the seats in the year before Eisenhower was first elected; this had risen to only 3.5 percent ten years later, the year of his retirement.[33] In 1958, six years after the first Eisenhower landslide, southern Republicans were still so dispirited that they contested only 33 of the 106 southern congressional district elections, just 4 more than they had entered in the pre-Eisenhower election of 1950. In 1957, only 22 of Louisiana's 101

31. See, for instance, O. Douglas Weeks's account of the understanding in Texas in 1954. "Republicanism and Conservatism in the South," *Southwestern Social Science Quarterly*, Vol. 36 (December 1955), p. 252.

32. The five new seats, as might be expected, were in metropolitan areas of the rim states. They were the districts that centered on Charlotte and Roanoke, where a heavy strain of traditional mountain Republicanism exists; Tampa–St. Petersburg and the Virginia suburbs of Washington, where northern in-migrants had swelled the GOP vote; and Dallas, where Republican Bruce Alger may have been given his crucial margin by liberal Democrats seeking to punish his conservative Democratic opponent. See below, pp. 270–71.

33. It should be noted, of course, that malapportionment by Democratic legislatures held down Republican strength in both the legislatures and the House of Representatives, and the one-man, one-vote decisions of the 1960s account for part of the rise in Republican membership in that decade.

Figure 12-4. *Rise of Southern Republicanism in Contests below the Presidential Level, 1950–73*

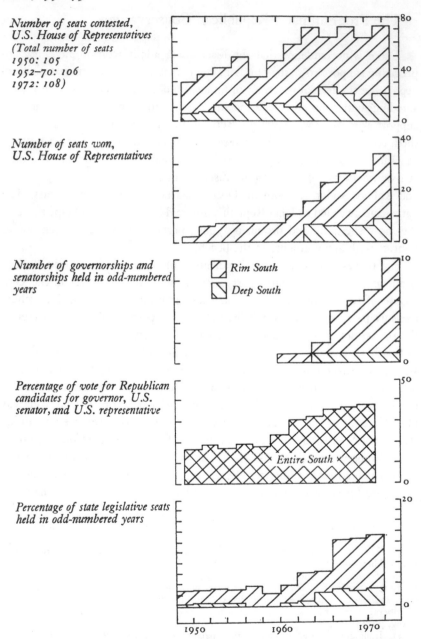

Number of seats contested, U.S. House of Representatives
(*Total number of seats
1950: 105
1952–70: 106
1972: 108*)

Number of seats won, U.S. House of Representatives

Number of governorships and senatorships held in odd-numbered years

Rim South
Deep South

Percentage of vote for Republican candidates for governor, U.S. senator, and U.S. representative

Entire South

Percentage of state legislative seats held in odd-numbered years

1950   1960   1970

Sources: *Congressional Directory*, various Congresses; Paul T. David, *Party Strength in the United States 1872–1970* (University Press of Virginia, 1972), Composite B index; *Book of the States*, various years.

parishes had Republican committees, and only one city, Shreveport, had a truly active Republican organization.[34]

Nevertheless, during this period the new generation of political leaders who were to lay the foundation of competitive Republicanism was maturing. The new southern Republicans were the counterparts of the North's programmatic Democratic liberals who in the war and early postwar years were impelled to enter politics by their enthusiasm for the New Deal philosophy. The new generation of Republicans in the South felt equally strongly about that philosophy—but against it. As ambitious and dedicated as the Humphreys and Williamses of the North, they were determined to have done with defeatist minority politics and to build an effective political instrument for conservative ideas. Like their counterparts, they were young, energetic, concerned with program rather than patronage, disinclined to compromise on party principle. Just as the programmatic northern liberals were more liberal than the Democratic party as a whole, so the programmatic southern Republicans stood to the right of the center of their national party—many of them near the extreme right of the whole liberal-conservative spectrum.

Their task was more difficult, however, than the one the northern liberals had faced. Not only was the one-party tradition more deeply entrenched, but the minority party had no hero around whom to rally. Franklin Roosevelt had dominated an era, revolutionized a government, defined and personalized a philosophy; and the programmatic liberals could use his name and his program as a rallying point long after he was gone. Here the analogy blurs: Dwight Eisenhower was not himself a programmatic conservative; he searched for what he called "the middle of the road" and laid down no standard for conservatives to follow. To many of the rising Republican leaders of the South, the man who sent the army into Little Rock and advocated his own versions of Medicare and federal aid to education was hardly a bona fide conservative at all.

Not having a hero around whom to rally, the programmatic conservatives found—or created—one, Barry Goldwater. It was the South that gave Goldwater his preconvention heartland; of the South's 278 votes, 271 went to the Arizona senator on the first ballot.[35] And in the topsy-turvy general election of 1964, while the Republican North and the metropolitan centers of the rim

34. Robert J. Steamer, "Southern Disaffection with the National Democratic Party," in Sindler (ed.), *Change in the Contemporary South*, p. 168. For the story of Shreveport Republicanism in the 1950s, see Kenneth N. Vines, *Two Parties for Shreveport*, Eagleton Foundation Case Studies in Practical Politics (Holt, 1959).

35. Bernard Cosman, *Five States for Goldwater: Continuity, Change in Southern Presidential Voting Patterns* (University of Alabama Press, 1966), p. 40.

South rejected Goldwater, he crashed through to stunning victories in the Deep South—87 percent of the vote in Mississippi, 69.5 percent in Alabama, 59 percent in South Carolina, 54 percent in Georgia, all states that Eisenhower had never carried.

The secret, of course, was that Goldwater combined in an unprecedented way the two streams of southern discontent—the rebellion against New Deal–Fair Deal–New Frontier–Great Society liberalism on economic and social welfare measures and the revolt against the Democratic commitment to civil rights. His record on both scores was impeccable; he had voted not only against virtually all of the Kennedy-Johnson economic and social welfare programs but against the 1964 Civil Rights Act as well. He adopted an overt "southern strategy," announced he would "go hunting where the ducks are"—that is, in the South, where the conservative latent Republicans were most numerous—and caught fire there as the first candidate of either major party since Herbert Hoover who genuinely acknowledged and embraced the southern concept of states' rights.

Most of the latent Republicans whom Goldwater flushed out of hiding turned out to be merely anti-Democrats, and four years later they were off in a new direction, following the banner of George Wallace. But he did leave the South a legacy of revived Republican organization. The programmatic conservatives now had control of most of the state and local committees. They were prepared to contest elections from top to bottom. They had learned how to do precinct work, to proselyte recruits, to outorganize and outmaneuver the flaccid Democrats in locality after locality. Norman L. Parks has trenchantly described the "New Guard" Goldwater Republicans of Tennessee as "politically inexperienced, but deeply ideological and impatient with the supineness of the Old Guard"; as "prepared to exploit the older norms of white supremacy, laissez faire, anti-unionism, and businessman Bourbonism"; and as proposing "to bring to politics the hard sell, the grass roots drive, and the systematic organization which generated success in the business world."[36]

The results are apparent in each of the panels of Figure 12-4. In 1964 the party cracked the Deep South for the first time in congressional races, electing five congressmen from Alabama, and one each from Georgia and Mississippi. In 1966 the Republicans won the governorships of Arkansas and Florida, elected senators in Tennessee and South Carolina, won a plurality in the race for governor of Georgia (though losing the office when write-in

36. "Tennessee Politics Since Kefauver and Reece: A 'Generalist' View," *Journal of Politics*, Vol. 28 (1966), p. 151.

votes for an independent candidate threw the choice into the legislature), and in spite of losing some of the Deep South congressional seats won in 1964, made a net gain of seven congressmen. The most striking gains, however, were in the state legislatures, where the number of Republicans in 1967 was nearly twice that in 1965 (223 as against 113) and exceeded 10 percent of the total for the first time since the Solid South became solid. Since then, the party has continued its steady progress; by 1973, every state of the erstwhile Solid South had elected a Republican as governor, senator, or congressman, and Virginia and Tennessee had the distinction of being the first southern states since Reconstruction with GOP majorities in their delegations to the U.S. House of Representatives.[37] No fewer than seven of the twenty-two senators from the former Confederate states were Republicans, and three of the eleven governors.

Variations in the Second Stage

In the translation of presidential Republican voting strength into election victories below the presidential level, three distinct processes can be identified. The first is conversion: popular leading Democrats, usually officeholders, announce their conversion, run for office as Republicans, and carry their followers with them across the party line. The other two are opposite forms of Democratic mass defection. In the first case, liberal Democrats defect to the Republicans to defeat a conservative Democratic nominee; in the second, conservatives defect to defeat a liberal Democratic nominee.

Outright conversions of leading Democratic conservatives, for reasons already discussed, have been as rare as were conversions of progressive Republican leaders of the 1930s. Conservative southern Democrats have been able to uphold their principles to their satisfaction within the Democratic party; they may find it distasteful and, on occasion, inconvenient to be identified with the liberal national party, but to shift parties would be to abandon the standing and (in the case of members of the Congress) the seniority already achieved for the sake of tidiness in political nomenclature. Yet there have been two conspicuous examples: Senator Strom Thurmond of South

37. Party registration figures are not available in a continuous, published series to facilitate the analysis of realignment in any of the eleven southern states. But they are available for a southwestern state, Arizona, which until the 1950s had a record of Democratic predominance as solid as some of the southern states. The percentage of Republican registrations has risen steadily for every county in Arizona throughout the postwar period, with the sharpest increases in the 1950–54 period and another spurt between 1966 and 1968. For the state as a whole, the Republican percentage rose from 18 in 1950 to 44 in 1970. *Bill Turnbow's Arizona Political Almanac*, various issues.

Carolina, who courageously switched parties in 1964 to campaign for Senator Goldwater; and Representative Albert W. Watson, also of South Carolina, who switched the following year when the House Democratic caucus stripped him of his seniority for having supported Goldwater and who in 1970 was the GOP gubernatorial candidate in his state.[38]

The second type of process—election of Republicans through defection of liberal Democrats—is best illustrated by events in Texas. The story begins in 1954. Wallace Savage, who as Democratic state chairman had deserted to Eisenhower two years earlier, won the party's nomination for Congress from Dallas County. Incensed at Savage's 1952 "betrayal," some national Democrats of Dallas determined to repay him in kind by organizing a campaign in the union and black areas to hold down the Savage vote in favor of his conservative Republican opponent, Bruce Alger.[39] Savage aided their cause by saying at one point that he did not want "the Negro vote." Alger was elected. The Dallas *Morning News* said Alger had won "overwhelmingly" in black precincts.[40]

The next occasion for organized liberal defection came in a nonpartisan special election in 1961 to choose a successor to Senator Lyndon B. Johnson, who had become vice-president. The candidates in the runoff, after a seventy-one-candidate initial election, were two conservatives—Democrat William Blakeley, incumbent by interim appointment, and Republican John G. Tower. To a workingman, said the president of the Texas AFL-CIO, that looked like a choice "between arsenic and blowing his brains out." A small group of liberals, financed with Republican money, organized a statewide drive to persuade their fellow national Democrats either to vote for Tower or, if they could not bring themselves to vote Republican, to "go fishing." Their long-term objective was to enable liberals and moderates to win control of the Democratic party, and that required a short-run strategy of assisting the Republicans to develop a party strong and successful enough to begin inducing a substantial number of conservative Democrats to switch parties.

---

38. The importance of congressional seniority in holding conservative Democrats within the party is illustrated in the remark attributed to Leon Bramlett, chairman of the state executive committee of the Mississippi "regular" Democratic party: "If it weren't for the Democratic congressional delegation from Mississippi, I'd rather be a Republican." *New Republic* (Feb. 5, 1972), p. 10.

39. Hawkins Hanley Menefee, Jr., "The Two-Party Democrats: The Study of a Political Faction" (Master's thesis, University of Texas at Austin, 1970), p. 26; James Reichley, *States in Crisis: Politics in Ten American States 1950–1962* (University of North Carolina Press, 1964), p. 116. Except as otherwise indicated, this account of Texas politics follows Menefee, esp. pp. 34–40.

40. Quoted by Paul D. Casdorph, *A History of the Republican Party in Texas 1865–1965* (Pemberton Press, 1966), p. 204.

The campaign was highly successful. Democratic liberals of Harris County (Houston) formally resolved through their factional organization not to endorse either candidate. The weekly *Texas Observer*, organ of the liberals, told its readers that they and the Republicans shared "some decisive political objectives." Labor withheld any endorsement. When the vote was counted, only 53 percent of those who had voted for liberal candidates in the first primary had supported Blakeley in the second, by the *Observer*'s computation. Of the others, half had switched to Tower, half had "gone fishing." In Houston, the total vote had fallen to 25 percent in "typical labor boxes," to 10 percent in some Negro areas, reported the Houston *Chronicle*. Liberal and moderate Democrats had "defected . . . in droves," said the *Observer*. Tower won by a narrow margin. The liberals jubilantly forecast that his victory would lead to the realignment that would permanently break the conservative hold on the Democratic party.

Since then, those who joined the Tower forces to defeat Blakeley have organized similar campaigns (under the label of "Texans for a Two-Party Texas" or "Democratic Rebuilding Committee") whenever a conservative has won the Democratic nomination for a statewide office. Only once, in the reelection of Tower in 1966, has the Republican-liberal coalition repeated its initial triumph, but since 1961 Texas has remained a two-party state in state-level politics. And gradually the realignment is extending to the local level: the GOP has firmly established its control of three seats in the House of Representatives, has mounted strong challenges in other districts, and has made modest gains in the state legislature.

In Arkansas in 1966, enough liberals and moderate Democrats defected from their party's segregationist candidate to elect Winthrop Rockefeller as the state's first Republican governor since Reconstruction. Liberal Democratic votes have occasionally contributed in other southern races to a strong Republican showing, short of election.[41] But the more common pattern by

<hr />

41. Such a race was the Virginia gubernatorial election of 1953, when the Republican candidate received strong support from the Democratic liberal-moderate faction. Robbin L. Gates, *The Making of Massive Resistance: Virginia's Politics of Public School Desegregation, 1954–1956* (University of North Carolina Press, 1964), p. 22; J. Harvie Wilkinson III, *Harry Byrd and the Changing Face of Virginia Politics 1945–1966* (University Press of Virginia, 1968), pp. 104–05. When the Republicans finally captured the governorship in 1969 with the election of Linwood K. Holton, it was also with considerable support from normally Democratic liberals, including a large segment of the black population. This does not fit the pattern of Texas and Arkansas, however, for the Democratic candidate, William C. Battle, was from the moderate rather than the conservative wing of the Democratic party. The shift of liberal voters was attributed primarily to Holton's positive appeal rather than to rejection of Battle.

which Republicans have been elected, as might be logically expected, is through the defection of Democratic conservatives.

An early prototype of this type of realigning election was the 1962 congressional race in the eastern Tennessee district centered on Chattanooga. This district contained several traditionally Republican counties, but the party had not elected a congressman since 1920 and had become so accustomed to playing minority politics that in 1960 it had not even run a candidate against Democratic incumbent J. B. Frazier, Jr. But Frazier, reflecting the basic conservatism of his district, was one of the southern Democrats who had cast the deciding votes against President Kennedy's Medicare proposal in the House Ways and Means Committee. Liberal Democrats in the district saw an issue with which to beat Frazier and, with encouragement from national organizations backing Medicare, entered Wilkes T. Thrasher, Jr., as a candidate in the primary. Thrasher narrowly beat Frazier. At that point a larger group of young Republicans who had been preaching the need for vigorous two-party politics seized *their* opportunity. William E. Brock III, thirty-one-year-old businessman and a leader of the Young Republicans, challenged Thrasher in the general election.

Thrasher sought and received Kennedy's endorsement and continued his campaign for Medicare, federal aid to education, and other measures in the national Democratic program. The issues were cast in rhetoric hardly changed from that of the 1930s—"socialism" and "increased federal intervention in our daily lives," as Brock defined them, or "federal-state partnership" in the solution of national problems, as Thrasher saw them.[42] "Many of Frazier's supporters joined with the Republicans" in the campaign, noted the Chattanooga *Times*, but neither they nor the official Republican leadership were in the vanguard. Most of the burden of electioneering was borne by Brock's contemporaries in the Young Republicans—men and women in their twenties and early thirties.[43] Their energetic and systematic precinct activity was unprecedented. In November, Brock won a narrow victory, centered in the traditional Republican counties and in new metropolitan Republicanism in Hamilton County (Chattanooga). He carried some of the upper-income suburban precincts by more than 75 percent.

Here again are aspects reminiscent of the northern postwar realignments

42. Chattanooga *Times*, Nov. 1, 1962. But Brock shied away from the word "Republican," calling himself a "conservative" instead, and attacked Thrasher not as a Democrat but as a "liberal."
43. Ibid., Nov. 4, 7.

—young, crusading, issue-oriented politicians, who displace the older leaders and their minority politics; vigorous and efficient precinct work; a clearly stated ideological appeal to like-minded voters to put principle above party. Here again is the generational nature of the realignment symbolized in the history of individual political families—Republican William E. Brock III, who went on to become senator in 1970, is the grandson of William E. Brock, Jr., once a Democratic senator from Tennessee.

The pattern of the Brock race was repeated over and over in the years to follow, particularly in the metropolitan centers of the rim South. There, thousands of traditionally Democratic conservatives had become accustomed to rejecting their party at the national level. It was a natural next step for them to also reject the state and local Democratic candidates who were clearly identified with the leaders and principles of the national party.

Thus, at the opposite end of Tennessee, Republican Daniel R. Kuykendall was elected to Congress from the Memphis district in 1966, when the freshman Democratic incumbent openly supported the national party and in particular its position on civil rights. Republican Claude R. Kirk was elected governor of Florida in 1966, when the Democrats, after a divisive primary campaign, nominated an outspoken liberal and associate of the Kennedys. Republican William L. Scott, in the same year, was elected to Congress from Virginia's newly reapportioned eighth district after a liberal Democrat had ousted the conservative Howard W. Smith, chairman of the House Rules Committee, in the primary. In Virginia's second district in 1968 and seventh district in 1970, Republican victories came when Democratic nominations went to liberals seeking to succeed conservative incumbents who were retiring. Both of the Georgia districts won by the Republicans in 1966 were in the Atlanta metropolitan area, where the Democratic party had come under the control of liberals and moderates, had become heavily black in composition, and had nominated candidates for Congress identified with the national party.

In every case where a congressional seat was captured by the Republicans against liberal Democratic competition, it has remained solidly in GOP hands or has been the object of strong two-party competition, which indicates that realignment in these areas has now been completed at the congressional as well as at the presidential level. And enough Republican state legislators, mayors, and county officials are being elected to suggest that realignment is progressing at the local level too. The process, like the earlier process in the North, appears to be one of spiraling interaction: as some conservatives, particularly the younger ones, move into the Republican party, the liberal Democrats have an increasing chance to displace the remaining conservatives who control their party locally. At some point, liberals begin to win nominations. This drives out still more conservatives, which places party control even more firmly in the hands of the liberals. The increase in Negro voting has expedited the process, and in some instances reapportionment has accelerated it as well. The Democratic party will no doubt harbor a conservative strain in the South for a long time, but as the spiral gains momentum the strain will steadily dwindle. Liberals will control an increasing number of state and local party organizations (Virginia's once solidly conservative state party organization was captured by the liberals in 1972); they will exercise an expanding influence on party policy and win a rising share of nominations for public office. As they do, the Republican party will continue to gain strength from the accession of conservatives who no longer find the Democratic party acceptable at any level. Through a series of aftershocks the realignment of the 1930s—pitting an activist, liberal Democratic party against a conservative Republican party—will settle into place throughout the region.

CHAPTER THIRTEEN

The Realignment Process:
An Amplified Statement

THE ACCOUNTS in the preceding nine chapters of some of the major and minor events of American party history can be used as the basis for a more careful statement of the realignment process, to amplify what was said in a preliminary fashion in Chapter 3. The statement will be in the form of a series of generalizations that derive from analysis of the three major realignments studied in this book and of such of the minor realignments as were examined. They are intended to describe not the cases as such but realignment as a phenomenon—in other words, to apply to *any* major realignment of the American party system, whether past, current, or prospective.

While three major cases is not a large number on which to base a comparative analysis, this is all that can be found without going even further back into history than one hundred and thirty years. But given these limitations, the generalizations are offered as hypotheses that will bear more testing against earlier major realignments and other minor realignments in this country, and against the experience of other democratic countries.[1]

The discussion is written in terms of major realignments, but the generalizations, with appropriate modification of the wording where it indicates scale, seem applicable to minor realignments as well.

1. *A realignment is precipitated by the rise of a new political issue (or cluster of related issues).*

Political parties have great stability, resilience, and adaptability. An upheaval in the party system occurs only when new political forces generated by circumstances and events within the society—in other words, by a new

---

1. The generalizations appear to be consistent with the characteristics ascribed to "critical realignments" by Walter Dean Burnham in the opening chapter, "Toward a Definition of Critical Realignment," of his *Critical Elections and the Mainsprings of American Politics* (Norton, 1970).

issue or a cluster of related issues—become strong enough to shatter the system's characteristic inertia.

The issues that brought about the three major realignments discussed in the preceding chapters are easy to identify. In the first, what should the government do about slavery? In the second, what should the government do about the hardships of the farmers and about inequality in the distribution of wealth and income among regions and classes? In the third, what should the government do about the Great Depression?

Everett C. Ladd, Jr., has written a history of the successive party systems in the United States that relates each, with impressive documentation, to significant alterations in the social, economic, and demographic composition of the society—the Industrial Revolution, the urban revolution, and so forth.[2] Yet such changes do not in themselves produce realignments. They must first give rise to genuine *political* issues. It is entirely possible that a profound change in the structure of society, particularly one that occurred gradually, might never produce a political issue of realigning force; on the other hand, a major political issue might arise in the absence of fundamental structural change.

The realignment of the 1890s seems to support the Ladd thesis best; the dislocations arising from the Industrial Revolution were surely at the bottom of the farm and labor discontent. Nevertheless, had political and governmental leadership been wise enough, the dislocations conceivably could have been ameliorated and the discontent contained. The realignment of the 1930s indicates even more clearly that structural change in the society does not by itself produce a new party system. For three decades after the 1890s, American society evolved with unprecedented speed in every social, economic, and demographic aspect. Yet in the summer of 1929, there was little evidence of strain in the party system that had been established more than thirty years before. Within the space of a few years, the existing system was shattered and replaced by another. But the cause was not any gradual change in the economy or the structure of society; it was a sudden event that precipitated momentous new issues with which the party system immediately had to cope.

2. *To bring about a realignment, the new issue must be one that cuts across the existing line of party cleavage.*

In each of the realignments, the new issue was clearly of that type. The

2. *American Political Parties: Social Change and Political Response* (Norton, 1970).

slavery issue did not follow the existing line of party division between Whigs and Democrats but split each party, separating northern Whigs from southern Whigs and northern Democrats from southern Democrats. The monetary question that became the focus of the struggle of the 1890s divided the two postwar parties along a still different line, separating East from West, gold Democrats from silver Democrats and gold Republicans from silver Republicans. The issues of the depression split the parties not on regional but on class and ideological lines, separating New Deal Democrats from conservative Democrats and progressive Republicans from conservative Republicans.

A powerful new issue does not have to be crosscutting, of course. It may closely follow the existing line of party cleavage. In such a case (discussed later as point 16) the existing line of cleavage is reinforced rather than altered.

3. *To bring about a major realignment, the new issue must also be one powerful enough to dominate political debate and polarize the community.*

The two relative terms contained in this proposition—"powerful enough" and "dominate"—correspond to the two relative terms—"major" and "minor"—used earlier to describe the magnitude of individual realignments. For the more powerful and dominating the issue, the greater the number of people affected by it and hence the greater the magnitude of the realignment.

Power has two dimensions, breadth and depth. The former relates to the number of persons on which it has impact; the latter to the strength of the impact. And strength depends on the degree to which an issue not only persuades intellectually but stirs emotionally. A major realignment cannot occur unless the realigning issue becomes dominant to the electorate as a whole and a substantial segment of that electorate is passionately aroused. It is thus characteristic of realignment periods that political interest and participation, and voter turnout, are high.

In some instances it takes time for an issue to acquire power, in one or both of its dimensions. In the first realignment, time was needed for the slavery issue to acquire breadth. At the outset only a few people—the abolitionists—were deeply stirred, but they were driven to stir other men, and within a couple of decades the issue became clearly dominant.

The second realignment had a slow buildup, both in breadth and depth, and the buildup was cyclical; the power of the issue, among the farmers, varied with the depth of the rainfall, the bounty of the harvest, and the fluctuation of prices in the Chicago pit. Yet it would be difficult to interpret the cyclical political uprisings as unrelated episodes without cumulative effect.

The Grange, the Farmers' Alliance, and the Knights of Labor played the role of agitators, and the agrarian issue and related labor issues grew spasmodically in breadth and depth for a generation until they dominated the political debate.

The third realignment grew from an issue so powerful that it became dominant almost instantaneously. Even so, it grew in breadth and depth with each successive bank failure and factory shutdown and each successive winter of distress.

The depth of an issue's power can be discerned by examining the tenor of political debate. In each of the three realignment periods, political discourse took place in language charged with a passion that in the intervening periods of stability would have been unconvincing and unacceptable. The community was rent. To each party, the other party was not the opposition but the enemy. It was denounced not just as weak or misguided or guilty of errors of judgment—the normal language of politics—but as guilty of *moral* dereliction. Political policies were invested with moral absolutism. Thus antislavery politicians like Seward appealed to a "higher law" than the Constitution, while their opponents identified slavery with the will of God; Cleveland rallied the churches to equate defense of the gold standard with the defense of Christianity itself, while Bryan invoked the image of the Crucifixion in opposing it; Hoover, like Cleveland but with less success, sought to identify conservative fiscal policy with fundamental Christian ethics, self-reliance, and the "God-imposed responsibility" of neighborliness, and he branded the New Deal with terms like "Fascism," "despotism," and "the poisoning of Americanism." When political positions become moral absolutes, compromise becomes impossible, for who can tolerate a pact with evil? Normal conciliatory processes of politics are discarded. Men talk of violence as the alternative to victory; in the first realignment, both sides accepted civil war in preference to compromise. If the country has been close to internal violence on that scale since, it was in the 1890s and the 1930s. When a community polarizes in hatred and distrust, the moderates are ostracized by both sides. The center becomes uninhabitable political territory. The centrists move to the poles, or they are crushed.

4. *The realigning issue must be one on which major political groups take distinct and opposing policy positions that are easily dramatized and understood.*

Issues on which all major groups profess essentially the same position may arouse deep electoral passion, but they result mainly in deviations from normal voting behavior. Similarly, voters may cross party lines for reasons that have nothing to do with a party's policy positions, but these also turn out to be mainly deviations.

The issues that brought about the major realignments of the past involved profound questions of public policy, on which major political groups took distinct and opposing policy positions.

The extension of the institution of slavery in the nineteenth century was a clear policy question, and one that was simply and easily dramatized. By its very nature, it compelled distinct and opposing positions. Slavery had to be either legal or illegal in a given territory; a middle position could not be found. The same was true of the issue of secession, and the post–Civil War question of the full rights of citizenship for Negroes.

The economic questions that underlay the two later major realignments were more complex, and party positions could be more readily blurred and compromised. That they were not was due in large part to the character and temperament of the presidents who happened to be in office at the critical times—Grover Cleveland and Herbert Hoover. Consequently, sharp and easily understood opposing positions were allowed to develop.

The policy confrontation may be over a primary question as to the government's objective, or in cases where the objective is not in dispute, it may be over the subsidiary question of the means for achieving the goal that is agreed upon. Primary questions about the appropriate objectives of the government are more likely to appear to the voter as endowed with moral significance and more closely related to the composition and intrinsic nature of a *party*, and therefore more likely to provide both the emotional impulse and the rational basis for his identifying with a party. It is probably no accident, then, that all three major realigning issues (or complexes of related issues) centered on the appropriate objectives of the government—whether it should prevent the extension of slavery, whether it should help relieve the farmers' plight by inflating (or ending the deflation of) the currency, whether it should assume responsibility for alleviating widespread distress caused by a great depression and undertake fundamental reform of the economic system.

On subsidiary questions of means to agreed-upon ends, the voter is likely to assume that each major party has its share of skillful leaders and bunglers, and he may see little to choose between them on that score. So his normal recourse, if he thinks his party's leadership has been unwise, is not to change parties—his party identification rests on something more fundamental than that—but to use his vote, and if he is politically active his participation, to change his party's leadership. If he fails he will normally, at most, deviate.

Nevertheless, in the realignment of the 1930s, some subsidiary questions were so crucial and so hotly contested that they took their place with the primary question in the complex of realigning issues. Both parties wanted to end the depression and bring about recovery, but were the economic recovery and reform measures embodied in the New Deal the appropriate means to the agreed-upon objective? That was a phase of the issue on which the voters realigned.[3]

Differences between the parties on subsidiary questions are likely in most cases, however, to be narrow and technical rather than distinct and easily dramatized, as specific measures are advanced, defended, and attacked. Consequently, campaign strategy will attempt to transmute subsidiary issues into primary ones; each party will attempt to portray itself in simple terms as more deeply devoted to the *objective*—more strongly in favor of peace, more strongly against depression or unemployment or inflation or crime. To the extent that a party can succeed in convincing voters that its superiority is of a primary order, relating to the objective, rather than of a secondary order, relating to the choice of means or to administrative skill and wisdom, it can bring about some realignment in its favor.

Elections may turn also on issues unrelated to policy positions.[4] Parties have often been expelled from office by the voters, for example, because of scandal and corruption. Where corruption is particularly associated with one party for a prolonged period, as in the case of the Democratic big-city machines, it may enter into the party image and result in minor realignment. But in the main, the voters see each party as having its share of crooks and reformers, and the usual effect of scandal is deviation rather than realignment.

Another electoral factor that may be of crucial importance quite apart from policy positions is personality, and for the same reason, it leads to deviation rather than to realignment. The Smith-Hoover contest of 1928, for

3. It is important here to reemphasize that the realignment of the 1930s is traceable, in the main, to the sharp party conflict over the New Deal as a body of measures to cope with the depression rather than simply to the fact of the depression and its association with the Republicans. See Chapter 10 above, particularly p. 203.

4. Donald E. Stokes, "Spatial Models of Party Competition," in Angus Campbell and others, *Elections and the Political Order* (Wiley, 1966), pp. 170–71, calls these "valence issues" as opposed to "position issues." He defines the former as "those that merely involve the linking of the parties with some condition that is positively or negatively valued by the electorate" and the latter as those "that involve advocacy of government actions from a set of alternatives over which a distribution of voter preferences is defined." See also David Butler and Donald E. Stokes, *Political Change in Britain: Forces Shaping Electoral Choice* (St. Martin's, 1969), p. 189.

example, aroused more intense involvement and brought out a higher proportion of the voters than most elections before or since, but while policy issues (notably Prohibition) were involved, the main issue was the personality of Smith. Similarly, the personality of Dwight Eisenhower brought massive crossing of party lines. But the crossover voters in both cases were preponderantly deviants. Leadership is seen as a transitory and accidental thing, subject to change at the next election, and is no reason for permanently shifting party attachment.

5. *Whether a new issue becomes dominant depends not only on its intrinsic power but also on the extent to which the older issues underlying the party system have faded with the passage of time.*

Since domination means the displacement of old issues by newer ones, it depends not only on the power of the new issue but also on the weakness of the old. When a community goes through a realignment period, as observed earlier, it is in the grip of an issue of transcendent power. The voters who have polarized on the issue have experienced deep emotions—fear and hatred of the opposing polar forces; kinship and solidarity with compatriots at their own pole; contempt for people in the middle. When the party system realigns to reflect the polar forces, these emotions are transferred to the parties. The individual voter loves and identifies with his party just as he loves and identifies with his family, his community, his country, or his church; and he hates, fears, and distrusts the opposing party as a real or potential enemy. In time his passion abates, but the basic attitudes and feelings remain and can be aroused during campaigns when party politicians adroitly employ the language and manipulate the symbols of the past. For many people the emotional attachment to one party and the hostility toward the other formed at a time of crisis remain an essential part of their personal identities for the rest of their lives. To abandon one's party would be as unthinkable as to abandon one's country or convert to another church. For a powerful issue to fade, then, is in part a generational process, as new voters too young to have identified emotionally with either side at the time of polarization displace their elders. Even the passing of a generation may not be enough, however, for attitudes and feelings are transmitted from parents to children, crises are experienced vicariously, and children through social encounters are drawn into the politics of their neighborhoods and communities.

So the Civil War remained the dominant force in the alignment of American politics long after the issues of the war were settled. Orators in the North waved the "bloody shirt," their counterparts in the South called up memories of the glōrious war and the indignities of Reconstruction, and audiences in both regions forgot the current issue—hard times or monopoly or the maldistribution of wealth or income—that might be crying for attention. "Vote as you shot," they were instructed, and they did. By the end of the 1870s, economic issues had become the truly pertinent political questions of the time, and logically the political system should have been organized around them. The Democratic party in much of the North, particularly in the Northwest, was ready to exploit those issues and could have been used by the agrarians and other protest forces for the purpose, but Republicans of the generation that had fought a war against Democrats could not conceive of joining that party whatever its economic policies. By 1896 the wartime generation was no longer a majority of the electorate; nevertheless the barrier remained. The realignment of the party system on economic lines was severely limited by the old attachments. Party switching occurred when it was in a direction consistent with the Civil War alignment, but was obstructed by the old loyalties when it ran counter to them. Thus gold Democrats did not become Republicans in the South, and in the North the Democratic party absorbed only a small portion of the powerful agrarian protest movement. The regional configuration imposed on the party system in the 1850s could not be redrawn; it could only be reinforced.

As the country entered an era of prosperity, the monetary issue of the 1890s faded more quickly, and by the 1930s the attachments formed forty years before were no great barrier to realignment on the issues of the depression, although the attachments formed even earlier, during the Civil War, still proved insurmountable in some places, particularly in the South.

The issues of the depression cut deeper than those of the 1890s and lingered long. Democratic orators in the 1950s were still regularly denouncing Herbert Hoover and refighting the old battles of the New Deal, and even in 1970 a traveling political observer—particularly if he ventured into rural America, where audiences are older—would occasionally hear a Democratic candidate still waving the modern version of the bloody shirt. Perhaps in this case, too, a generation would have to pass before any other issue or set of issues, no matter how strong, could supplant those created by the Great Depression.

Kevin Phillips's emphasis on the periodicity of realignment at thirty-two- to thirty-six-year intervals[5] therefore has a measure of justification; it sometimes, though by no means always, may take that long for the issues

5. Kevin P. Phillips, *The Emerging Republican Majority* (Arlington House, 1969), pp. 36–37.

underlying an existing alignment to fade to the point where they can be supplanted. Nevertheless, even then, a realignment does not automatically occur. A new issue, or set of issues, powerful enough to cause realignment must arise.

6. *A new issue is likely to have greater inherent appeal to the voters of one of the major parties and thus potentially a more disruptive effect on that party than on the other.*

It would be an improbable coincidence if the new issue were to cut across the existing line of party cleavage exactly at right angles. Because the two parties are differently composed, the new issue is likely to encounter substantially different measures of support and opposition from the respective major parties.

Thus in the pre–Civil War North, because of the geographical and religious makeup of the Whig party, the abolitionists found a readier audience among the Whigs than among the Democrats. In the later realignments, the Democratic party was more responsive to the farm and labor protest classes than was the business-dominated, establishment-oriented Republican party.

7. *The normal response of both major parties at the outset is to straddle the new issue.*

The established leadership of a party consists of politicians who are, by definition, the beneficiaries of the party system as it is. Moreover, the leadership includes a heavy mixture of professionals who are not crusaders on any issue, whose main interest may be in patronage or in organization, and who are flexible and pragmatic in their approach to public problems. Even among politicians who are issue oriented, those who are part of the party leadership are the ones who are oriented toward the old issues that are the party's rationale, the issues of the last realignment, which brought the existing party system into being and are still the basis for the party's unity, cohesion, and strength. The leaders of each party have an abiding interest in keeping these issues alive as a constant source of reinforcement, but by the same token they have a powerful incentive to suppress or avoid the crosscutting issues that threaten the party's unity. Both attitudes are especially characteristic of the majority party, which has benefited most from the ascendancy of the old issues and therefore has the most at stake in maintaining their ascendancy.

The crosscutting issue erodes the natural cohesion of both parties and spawns new leaders to challenge the old. The normal reaction of the established leaders to the new issue is therefore defensive. They try to straddle it, to change the subject, to find policy compromises that will conciliate the polar forces developing within the party, and to nominate candidates who are uncommitted and able to make gestures in both directions, all the while hoping that the issue will somehow solve itself or disappear. If it does not, they hope at least to gain time to take soundings and determine which side of the issue offers the greatest political advantage.

In each of the realignment crises of the past, then, a well-delineated group of straddlers (or, if one prefers, conciliators) appeared within each of the major parties. They seemed to appear especially in the Congress, whose members live in a world of daily compromise and whose leaders tend to be those most skilled in the arts of straddle and conciliation. The most celebrated group of conciliators were of course the Democratic "doughfaces" and their Whig allies who sought to avert the breakup of their parties—and the Union—through a long series of conciliatory measures that culminated in the Compromise of 1850. In the next prerealignment period, the preeminent compromisers were John Sherman, the Republican who steered his party's financial course between the gold and silver poles, and President Harrison; the Democrats were represented by the congressional leaders who broke with the inflexible Cleveland. In the 1930s the straddlers were exemplified by the southern congressional Democratic leadership centered in such men as Vice-President John Nance Garner and Senate Majority Leader Joseph T. Robinson, who tried to moderate the course of the New Deal, and by the younger Republicans who led their party toward accepting the principle of governmental activism that underlay the New Deal program.

Straddling is easier for the out-party, which can officially hedge and at the same time speak with many voices, including some from near the poles. So it can stand ambiguously on the sidelines, demanding action and decision but not necessarily united on a program of its own, like the Democratic party between 1929 and 1932. It stands to profit whenever the in-party is forced by events to take a stand and in so doing to alienate one or the other of its contending wings; alternatively, it can expect to gain from the public reaction against the in-party's timidity if it puts off the hour of decision. So some, at least, of the leaders of the out-party may find ways of inflaming the new issue to maintain the pressure on the in-party's leaders and keep public attention focused on the in-party's handling of an issue on which it can only lose politically. These out-party leaders may make common cause, somewhat cynically, with the polarizing elements of both parties. Yet other leaders of the out-party will sense that in the long run they and the leaders of the in-party have a common interest in suppressing the crosscutting issue. Putting principle and long-run interest ahead of the party's short-term benefit, they may enter into a joint effort at conciliation. The bipartisan Compromise of 1850 is again the best example.

8. *Within each of the parties, however, there form at each pole political groups that are more concerned with victory for their position on the new issue than with their party's electoral success.*

As the new issue arises, politicians inevitably emerge to exploit it. At first they may appear to most of the public as nothing more than agitators bent on stirring up trouble for the established political and governmental order, and that, of course, may be what many of them are. In any case, they will include not only political independents but persons who have at least some standing within the major political parties and who will see the party as an available and useful vehicle for advancing their cause.

At the point where the party leaders sense the danger of the new issue and adopt, implicitly or explicitly, a policy of straddling, those exploiting the issue within the institutional machinery of the party must make a choice. Those who are devoted to their party and who have innocently embraced the issue in ignorance of its disruptive potential may submit to the demands of party loyalty and dissociate themselves from it. But others will choose to continue espousing the issue. The latter fall into three overlapping classes:

First, the *zealots*, who are exploiting the issue through dedication to the cause it represents and who may be totally selfless in doing so.

Second, the *opportunists*—out-of-power politicians who may care nothing for the issue but see in it a means to political advancement.

Third, *established political leaders in local areas* where the issue has its greatest appeal, who are forced by constituency pressure to embrace it.

These groups will appear on both sides of the issue. Zealots will produce counterzealots. Wherever the zealots appear, so too do the opportunists. Local constituencies press in both directions.

Whichever their category and whichever their side of the issue, those who have chosen to continue agitating, in defiance of the party leadership and at the expense of disrupting the party, have at that point an overriding personal and political concern that their position on the issue be successful. If it fails, their hope of early political advancement, perhaps even their political careers, will be at an end. If on the other hand, it succeeds, they may ride to power with it. They must defeat, then, not only their opponents on the issue, but also the straddlers and the policy of straddling. Indeed, they and their opponents have a mutual interest in a further polarization of the community that will discredit the straddlers and remove the basis of their support. Those who occupy the polar position on either side of the issue and who positively seek further polarization in order to advance the issue and themselves, I have referred to as a political polar force.

The first two of the categories that make up the leadership of the polar force—the zealots and the opportunists—are not easy to distinguish. Most politicians, if not all, blend the motives of the two in varying and indeterminable proportions: whether Daniel Webster, William Jennings Bryan, or Franklin Roosevelt was basically opportunistic or basically "sincere" is still debated. Even the most selfless of the zealots can readily come to the conclusion that the best way to advance his issue is to advance himself by seizing political opportunity as it comes along, and he may be entirely correct. By the same token, the opportunist, if he is to succeed in politics, usually develops a facility for becoming genuinely converted to an issue, if only *after* he has embraced it. Many years ago E. E. Schattschneider said, "It is futile to try to determine whether men are stimulated politically by interests or by ideas, for people have ideas about interests."[6]

Shortly after the zealots and opportunists appear at the poles of the party spectrum, they will be joined by the established politicians in the geographical areas where the issue has its greatest appeal. This group is distinguishable from the other two groups in a highly important respect: its members have a stake in the existing party system, while the first two classes have a stake in its disruption. Nevertheless, if his followers are on the move, an established leader must move with them or lose his leadership. So to save his stake in the *local* party system, a local leader may find himself compelled to advocate the disruption of the *national* system, although he will be slower than the zealots and the out-of-power opportunists to come to that position.

As the new issue comes to public attention, the zealots are likely to predominate at the outset among the three groups of its supporters, for it is among the issue oriented, necessarily, that the issue arises. But the two groups of politicians—the opportunists and the established leaders—are not slow to join. The zealots and the politicians recognize and distrust one another. The "true believers" sense that the politicians—particularly the in-power politicians who may join their cause—may take over their issue and ultimately compromise it. The "practical" men fear that the zealots will overreach themselves and bring discredit on the joint endeavor. And the two

6. *Party Government* (Farrar and Rinehart, 1942), p. 37.

groups of practical men are at odds, for one consists of leaders who may be part of the party's "establishment," while the other is made up of politicians intent on displacing that establishment.

In a party already divided on other matters of patronage or policy, one entire party faction may turn opportunistic and use the issue as a weapon in the intraparty battling. Thus the bolt of the New York Barnburners to the Free-Soil party in 1848 was motivated not just by antislavery sentiment but also by the desire to exploit that sentiment to wrest control of the Democratic party from the Hunkers. The challenging faction that rides the new issue is apt to be led by younger persons on the rise who hope to displace an older generation of political leaders and officeholders (the Conscience Whigs, for example, challenging the Cotton Whigs of Massachusetts). Their supporters may also consist disproportionately of the younger elements of the population, who usually have more impatient zeal and less tolerance of compromise than their elders.

Whatever the motivation, however, the groups making up the polar force in a party are defined as such by a common commitment that if they are forced to choose between their party and the issue they will go where the issue leads them. In a distinction that Samuel Lubell has made, they are less interested in *belonging* to a party than in *using* it. And they will so announce, as Richard P. Bland did to his Democratic party in 1893.

If the crosscutting issue loses it momentum before the realignment crisis is reached (point 11, below), the realignment is averted. It is not necessary for the issue to disappear completely, but only to cease winning new support. For a polar force grows not on the appeal of the issue alone, but on expectations as to the outcome too. An issue that "looks like a winner" develops bandwagon support, but if the bandwagon appears to be slowing it attracts few new riders, and once the issue looks like a loser the bandwagon can quickly go into reverse as those already aboard jump off as nimbly as they got on. The remainder of this discussion presupposes that the issue maintains momentum, as did those that produced the realignments of the past.

9. *The polar forces coalesce most rapidly if the party out of power is the one with the greater predisposition toward the new issue.*

The polar forces supporting the new issue—that is, those demanding governmental action in response to what they perceive as a grievance—have difficulty organizing and coalescing within the party in power. Policy making there is centered in the chief executive and he normally reflects the party's interest in straddling the new issue. Moreover, he can use the party's patronage to suppress the development of polar forces. The Democratic "doughface" presidents are the preeminent example of leaders who used their patronage to force a straddle position on a restive party rank and file.

The out-party, however, is in a wholly different position. It is usually the arena of a divisive struggle for leadership and control, and in that struggle some of the prospective leaders embrace the polarizing issue as the means of developing and consolidating a following, hoping to attract the potential adherents of a third party organized around the issue, or the actual adherents if one has formed. In the process, they publicize and incite the issue, increase its credibility and respectability, and bring to it at least a portion of their own following. They are free to pursue their course with a measure of irresponsibility. They are subject to no one's discipline. Indeed, since the party's interest is in finding issues on which to challenge the incumbents, the party's official leadership and principal spokesmen may give open or tacit encouragement to the polar forces to make whatever they can of the new issue. This is particularly true if a third party is draining, or threatening to drain, substantial elements away from the out-party.

If the out-party is the one less predisposed toward the new issue, it may develop slowly. But if the out-party has the stronger predisposition, circumstances are right for its rapid development. And the minority party in any period has somewhat the same outlook as an out-party, even during its occasional intervals of power.

In the pre–Civil War realignment, the party with the greater predisposition toward the new issue, the Whigs, happened also to be the minority party out of power most of the time. The northern Whigs were surely impelled to solidify their antislavery position by the opportunity the issue gave them to challenge and discredit the national Democratic administrations with northern voters.

The realignment of the 1890s may appear to contradict the proposition, since it was within the incumbent Democratic party that the polar forces supporting change coalesced in the period between 1893 and 1896. Yet in defense of the proposition it can be argued that leadership of the polar forces that grew within the Democratic party was concentrated in western agrarian states where the Democrats from the beginning of the protest movement had been in the minority, looking for issues. Others came from southern states where no truly effective minority party existed, and both sides of any argument had to be represented within the majority party. Nationally, the Democrats had been out of power most of the time before the 1890s. Cleveland ceased to be an effective party leader early in his second term and so could not impose upon his fellow Democrats the kind of restraints normally employed by an incumbent president; even so, he probably retarded the development of the polar forces more than would have been the case if the Republicans had been in power.

At the beginning of the Great Depression, the Democrats—who were the party that by the nature of its composition would be more responsive to the victims of the catastrophe—were also the out-party looking for issues with which to batter the entrenched Republicans. So when the economy collapsed, it was easy and natural for the polar forces demanding governmental action to develop within, and ultimately win control of, the Democratic party.

The polar forces on the opposition side of the issue—those who oppose the changes in governmental policy advocated by those who advanced the issue in the first place—have greater opportunity to coalesce in the incumbent party. For as out-party leaders begin to demand change, the in-party is inclined by virtue of its responsibility to be cautious and defensive. This gives the advantage in intraparty debate to those of the in-party who are opposed to a shift of governmental policy and who offer a rationale for resisting it.

10. *If both major parties persist in their straddle or come under the control of the polar forces opposing change, supporters of the new issue at some point form a third party.*

The tendency of the existing parties to straddle strengthens the argument of those among the polar forces who advocate independent political action through organization of a new party to compete directly with the major parties. The true believers, skeptical of all politicians, are quick to give up on the major parties. They argue that one major party is as bad as the other and both are hopeless as instruments of action. The established politicians continue to urge working through one or both existing parties. But if neither party embraces the issue and it continues to grow in power, sooner or later a third party is formed.

In each of the first two realignments, those with slowly developing issues, more than two decades elapsed while both major parties were either straddling or under the control of the opposition. Third parties were therefore the crux of the realignment story—the Liberty, Free-Soil, and Republican parties, in the first case, and the Greenback, Union Labor, and People's parties, in the second. In each case, the rise of the new issue as a polarizing force was reflected in a slow and intermittent but inexorable rise in the voting power of the third-party movements.

In the third realignment, the issue struck so suddenly that everyone was caught unprepared, extremists and moderates alike. As the polar forces formed, those at the activist pole within the Democratic party were strong enough at the outset to promise control of that party, and the impetus for a third party therefore did not develop. After 1933, President Roosevelt pursued policies of governmental intervention in economic and social welfare matters with sufficient vigor to contain the bulk of the forces that had formed at the interventionist pole. The threat of third-party activity, however, was a factor in keeping the New Deal on its activist course.

Even if a third party forms, it does not initially contain more than a fraction of the polar forces supporting the new issue. Those supporters have strong reasons for not joining a third party: the major parties, in a two-party system, are where the action is; better to vote for the major party candidate who is the lesser of two evils than "throw away the vote." Third parties have trouble getting on the ballot in many places. They have little hope of victory or prospect of patronage. By staying within the major parties, the polar forces can hope to win one or both over to their point of view.

11. *A realignment crisis is precipitated when the moderate centrists lose control of one or both of the major parties—that is, of party policy and nominations—to one or the other of the polar forces.*

As the issue grows in heat and the community polarizes, the polar forces gather strength and gain in influence at the expense of the moderate forces in the center who are dedicated to holding the party together. Each party is subjected to severe internal strain, as the two polar blocs contend for intraparty supremacy against each other and against the centrist straddlers. Anyone who has seen the circus act in which a rider stands with one foot on the back of each of a pair of galloping horses has the picture. The rider is the centrist, hoping that the two galloping elements of his party team will stay close enough together to enable him to remain astride. But in the intraparty contest, ambitious men try to drive these elements apart, sometimes with the express purpose of bringing the centrist tumbling to the ground.

The three-way split was plainly visible in both major parties at the time of each realignment. The crisis was precipitated and realignment became inevitable when the centrists lost control of one or both parties.

In the first realignment, the Whig straddlers—Clay, Webster, and Fillmore—lost control of their party in the fight over the Compromise of 1850, which led to the nomination two years later of a candidate for president identified with the antislavery polar forces led by Seward. This split the Whigs irrevocably, setting the northern wing of the party free to coalesce with the Free-Soil party and dissident Democrats and, in so doing, realign the party system.

In the second realignment, the party that was in power during most of the prerealignment period—this time the Republicans—again maintained a successful straddle well into the period of polarization. In the Democratic party, however, the centrist leadership in the Congress was overshadowed by the personality of Grover Cleveland, who did not fit the normal pattern of the party politician, whose whole career had, in fact, been built on opposition to the professionals. Cleveland himself became the leader of the polar forces on the gold side of the monetary issue, and when economic depression thrust the monetary issue to the fore, the lack of a controlling centrist bloc in the Democratic party made a split inevitable. With the leader of one polar force in the White House, the other polar group had no choice but to organize for a showdown. When it came, at the Chicago convention of 1896, the realignment followed.

When the third realignment issue—government response to the Great Depression—arose, in the White House was a president who, like Cleveland, was essentially a nonprofessional politician with neither the temperament nor the skill for centrist leadership. Accordingly, like Cleveland, he took his stand as leader of the polar forces at the conservative end of the party spectrum, suppressing the centrist elements among the party's insurgents in the Congress. When he did so, the realignment crisis was precipitated.

It is theoretically possible that a realignment could occur without the capture of either major party by a polar force and a consequent realignment crisis of the kind described here. Conceivably, for example, in the 1850s the Democratic and Whig parties could have remained under the control of moderate centrists while the Free-Soil party (or a new Republican party) rose to major-party status. Or in the 1890s, if the Democratic party had been in the hands of centrists, the Populists might have grown into a major party through defections from the existing major parties without benefit of a crisis that split either of them. No major realignment in American national politics followed such a pattern during the period covered by this book, and there is strong reason why this type of realignment would be unlikely: any issue powerful enough to carry a new party to major-party status would surely be powerful enough to force at least one of the existing major parties to end its straddle and take a stand. However, some realignments in state political systems may fall into this category: the rise of the Populists to major-party status in several states, or the Farmer-Labor realignment in Minnesota. Some realignments in other democratic countries appear also to have been of this type.

12. *If the polar forces supporting the new issue gain control of one major party and so precipitate a realignment crisis, realignment may still be averted if they also succeed in capturing the other major party simultaneously or shortly thereafter.*

The Progressive Era was a period in American history when realignment was avoided despite powerful crosscutting issues that came to dominate the political scene. True, in retrospect these issues do not appear to have stirred the electorate as deeply as those of the Civil War period or the 1890s or to have polarized it as sharply, but the reason is by no means clear. They may have had less intrinsic power. Yet had either party been adamant in opposing progressivism, it seems clear that the issues would have grown steadily more powerful. What stunted their growth and averted polarization was the early capitulation of both major parties to progressive leadership. When that happened, progressives in neither party felt compelled to change allegiance, nor did antiprogressives. This, rather than any lack of intrinsic power in the progressive movement, was probably the safety valve that prevented an explosive impact on the party system.

It follows that if the country had responded promptly and in a bipartisan manner to the demands of the abolitionists in the 1850s, the farmers in the 1890s, and the unemployed in the 1930s, the wave of reform in each case would simply have washed over the party system without upsetting it. The reason for realignment would have disappeared.[7]

If both parties yield to the forces supporting the new issue, die-hard elements of the opposing polar force may organize a third party to seek reversal of the major parties' decision. Then their success in bringing about a realignment would depend, as in the case of a new issue, on whether the question of reversal could be made to gather momentum, become dominant, and polarize the community. Such a movement seems unlikely to gain the necessary force, but the theoretical possibility exists.

13. *In any other circumstance, however, the crisis eventuates in a realignment.*

---

7. Perhaps it should be repeated that the discussion here, as elsewhere in this chapter, refers to major realignments. Some degree of minor realignment is likely to occur under the circumstances described in this proposition.

The form of the realignment is determined by the degree of difficulty encountered by the polar forces supporting the new issue in gaining control of one of the major parties.

a. *If they gain control at an early stage of the new issue's development, a realignment may occur without the appearance of a third party.*

This was the case in the 1930s. As Hoover placed the Republican party at or near the conservative pole, the Democrats moved gradually to the other. After the election of Roosevelt, the party's straddlers—chiefly its southern congressional leaders and Garner as vice-president—were pushed aside and the activists gained full control before a third party had had time to form. The polarized voters were able to reidentify politically according to the new alignment within three or four years after the issue arose.

b. *If they gain control at a later stage, after the formation of a third party, realignment may occur through absorption of the new party by one of the old ones.*

This was the case in the 1890s. Neither party could be captured at the outset by the polar political forces that had organized around the demand for new economic policies. That left the reformers no course but to devise a political instrument of their own, and a series of third parties were formed, which finally gathered strength. In the climactic Democratic convention of 1896, however, polar forces supporting change captured control of a major party with the nomination of Bryan. The third-party protest movement, represented at the time by the Populists, also nominated Bryan, and the Populist party was in effect absorbed.

If there is institutional continuity, and continuity in name, between an old party and a new (as in either this or the preceding variant), there is also continuity in attachment of the voters who did not, even at the time of crisis, come to view the new issue as paramount. Even in a major realignment, such a bloc of voters will be considerable. They will carry with them the policy positions of the party on the old issues, and when those issues come to the fore again after the new issue is resolved, the image and posture of both parties may appear much the same as under the previous party system.

c. *If they gain control at a late stage, realignment may occur through replacement of one of the existing parties by a third party.*

This was the case in the 1850s. The realignment crisis was precipitated when the antislavery polar forces gained control of the Whig party at the 1852 convention, provoking a party split. After their defeat that year, antislavery Whigs joined in organizing a third party, the Republicans, which was much stronger than the earlier third parties that had formed around the slavery issue. In doing so, they acquiesced to the replacement of the Whig party as one of the major parties and ultimately forced the rest of the northern Whigs to do the same.

Presumably, the same party split would have occurred if the southern Whigs and their northern allies had been triumphant at the 1852 convention, and the outcome would have been the same.

Under some circumstances, particularly if the Whig centrists had been able to maintain control of the party a little longer and defections of the antislavery polar bloc had been more gradual, the defectors might have been absorbed into the existing third party, the Free-Soil organization, thus elevating that party to major-party status when the Whigs finally collapsed. The outcome would have been essentially the same; the new major party would simply have carried a different name.

d. *As a variant of the preceding outcome, realignment can occur through replacement of both of the existing parties by new ones.*

In individual states during various periods of crisis, the two major parties have combined against a third party. Whigs and Democrats joined forces against the Free-Soilers in the Western Reserve of Ohio in 1848; Democrats and Republicans united in some states against the Populists. These formal coalitions were sometimes parties in everything but name, and were kept from taking on a party identity only because they were made up of constituents of national organizations that maintained separate identities.

However, this type of realignment of the national party system has not occurred and is the most remote possibility for the future. The major parties of the United States are so deeply entrenched that a realignment in which even one of them were replaced by a new party, as in the 1850s, is an unlikely outcome of a realignment crisis. Our present parties have survived every realignment for twelve decades, and their relative openness now to participation by new groups with fresh views and interests makes them more adaptable and increases their chances to survive.

14. *The realignment reaches its climax in one or more critical elections that center on the realigning issue and resolve it, but the realigning process may extend over a considerable period before and after the critical election.*

The effect of the realignment is to end the straddling of the major parties and place them squarely on opposing sides of the realigning issue. Originally a crosscutting issue that divided both parties, it is now an issue that unites each party and separates one from the other. It is no longer avoided and suppressed. It becomes the focus of each election until it is resolved. This may come in a single critical election, as in 1896, or it may require two presidential elections (and an intervening congressional election) before the decision of the people is clear, as in 1856–60 and 1932–36. If public sentiment on the polarizing issue is closely balanced, more than two presidential elections might be required. (Elections are only one way of resolving polarizing issues, of course. In 1860, the people made a decision, but the losers chose secession rather than accept it, and the issue was resolved by war.)

But if realignment is defined as the reallocation of voters on either side of the new line of cleavage (rather than as merely the establishment of the line), realignment does not occur in a single critical election, or even in a series of them. It is the sum of a myriad of individual decisions that may be made at any time. Many of them may be made before the first critical election, and others have still to be made after the last. To understand a realignment, one must look at the whole course of the realigning issue, from its rise to its final disposition.

In the states or localities where the realigning issue has its greatest initial appeal, realignment may come early. Thus in the turmoil of the 1850s, the party systems were substantially realigned in Michigan and Wisconsin and the realignment process well under way elsewhere in the Northwest in 1854, two years before the first election in which the two major parties collided on the slavery issue. The critical election of 1896 was preceded by a period of six years in which lifelong Republicans on the agrarian frontier broke from their political moorings and became Populists en route to becoming, for a season at least, Democrats.

The realignment period of the 1930s was even more drawn out. This reflected, in part, a feature peculiar to the twentieth-century political scene—a lag between realignment of voter affiliations at the national level and realignment of the party system at state and local levels. In much of the nation, the realignment was completed before or during the critical presidential election of 1936. But in the South, the realignment of national political affiliations did not appear on any significant scale until 1948, and in both the North and the South it required (or will require) a decade or two, or even longer, after that for the realignment process to work its way through the state and local party systems.

15. *After the critical election or elections in which the voters make a clear choice*

on the issue that has polarized the country, polarization gives way to conciliation. As it does, the parties move from the poles toward the center and the distance between them narrows.

After the critical elections of 1896, polarization gave way to conciliation almost at once. After 1936, the Republicans conceded defeat and moved quickly back toward the center; by 1940, moderates were in control of the GOP again. The 1860 election has to be treated as a special case in which normal conciliatory processes were rejected; yet with the end of the Civil War, the spirit of conciliation gradually prevailed.

The victorious party, of course, has an incentive to keep the issue that produced the realignment alive and to exploit it, for it is to the issue that it owes its original cohesion and its success. The Republicans appealed to wartime patriotism for a full generation after the Civil War, and Democratic orators attacked Herbert Hoover and his administration with vigor and venom long after the end of the New Deal era. National leaders of the losing party, especially in Congress, have reason to keep old issues alive, too, for in their own states and districts they came to power because the losing cause nationally was the winning side locally. So the post–Civil War Democrats in the South, victorious in their region, cemented their position by continuing to appeal to the Confederate principles of states' rights and white supremacy.

But as time passes, the leaders who exploit old issues seem increasingly anachronistic. Once the critical issue has been resolved, people weary of conflict and yearn for political peace. New issues demand attention. A new generation that has not lived through the realignment period does not respond to the old slogans and symbols. Yesterday's courageous battlers are now seen as shrill and raucous troublemakers, seeking to capitalize on turmoil. The old enmities seem divisive and distracting, and the new generation demands, and produces, political leaders who will put an end to them.

As the parties move back from the poles, a cycle is completed. An issue arose, polarized the community, realigned the party system, was resolved, and spent its force. Now the parties lose the sense of moral purpose that energized them in the crisis. They become cautious. Participation in party affairs slackens, the amateurs drift away and the professionals move to the center, and the ratio of issues to patronage in the party cements shifts in favor of the latter. People are again heard to say, "The parties don't stand for anything" and "There's no difference between the parties."

Yet over the years, the political loyalties of those who passed through the realignment crisis harden. Though they no longer need the party for its original purpose, they still belong. Ties of habit and sentiment become stronger. A new generation comes to political maturity with attachments less firm than those of the one preceding, but the basic pattern established during the realignment remains until a new crosscutting issue, capable of again arousing powerful emotions and of polarizing the community, appears. Indeed, it is always possible that a new realigning issue has been in the process of germinating even before the old one was laid to rest.

16. *However, if new issues arise that coincide with the existing line of party cleavage, they strengthen party cohesion, increase the distance between the parties, and reinforce the existing alignment.*

A powerful new issue (or cluster of related issues) need not be crosscutting. The new issue may run along, rather than across, the existing line of party cleavage. In that event, its effect is to increase each party's internal cohesion, again widen the distance between them, and reinforce the existing alignment.

As the new issue, which may be called a "coincident issue," comes to dominate public discussion, it will polarize blocs of voters just as the cross cutting issue did. But since the major parties are already established on either side of the line of cleavage on the new issue, they will reflect the growing polarization rather than straddle. The polarized voters therefore will not have to realign the party system to find or create a political vehicle through which to express their will.

The effect on the individual polarized voter is the same as in any other case of polarization. He forms a lasting emotional attachment with the party that adopts his cause. In this case, it will be for most of the electorate a matter of *reidentification*, and so the existing bonds that unite the people who make up a party are strengthened and the existing system of party competition is reinvigorated.

The events of the Civil War and Reconstruction presented the electorate of that time with new and powerful issues that coincided, in the main, with the line of party cleavage that had been drawn in the 1850s. The effect was to powerfully reinforce the alignment then established and intensify party attachment.

In the post–New Deal period, many specific issues operated similarly to revitalize and reinforce the alignment established during the New Deal. Each of the new issues turned on one or both of the two related questions that defined the New Deal alignment—the question of governmental activism in regulating, reforming, or ameliorating the consequences of the private economy, and the question of whose class interests the government was to represent. The Taft-Hartley Act, public housing, federal aid to education, antirecession measures, health care programs, the war on poverty, all dominated public discussion for long periods, if not individually, then as a cluster, and aroused as much excitement in some segments of the population as did the original issues of the 1930s. On some occasions, the party division was as sharp as it was in the New Deal period. The result has been an intermittent reinforcing of the New Deal alignment that has offset to some extent the tendency, described under preceding points, for party attachments to weaken through generational change in the electorate and for parties to draw closer together after a realignment.

CHAPTER FOURTEEN

Some Further Notes on Party Dynamics

FROM THE GENERALIZATIONS about party behavior set out in the preceding chapter, two even more general statements can be drawn. First, the party system is dynamic, not static. Second, it is multidimensional, not unidimensional. These conclusions merit some further explication, because they challenge conceptions of the party system that have been widely accepted in both academic and popular discussion and that have been incorporated into the models of the party system presented in standard textbooks.

The generalizations also have a bearing on normative concepts of the party system—about how American political parties *should* behave and what constitutes a healthy party system.

The Static, One-Dimensional Model

Writing in 1959, V. O. Key, Jr., suggested that analysis of the political party system must take account of what he called "the time dimension." Characteristically, said Key, analysts of the party system have used static models, and these "may exclude from attention fundamental aspects of party behavior."[1] A few years later, Donald E. Stokes called attention to a number of defects in the prevailing model of the party system used by both journalists and academicians; among the defects he listed were not only that the model was static, which Key had criticized, but also that it was unidimensional. In the model, voters and parties are thought of as arrayed along a single spectrum from left to right, from liberal to conservative, when in fact political competition is multidimensional. Stokes pointed out, for example,

1. "Secular Realignment and the Party System," *Journal of Politics*, Vol. 21 (1959), p. 198.

that the evidence from public opinion polls indicates *no* relation between a voter's attitude on social welfare policies and his view on American involvement in foreign affairs. If he takes a "liberal" or "conservative" stand on one set of policies, he is no more likely than any other voter selected at random to take a "liberal" or "conservative" stand on the other set.[2]

If the propositions offered in the preceding chapter are valid, they emphasize the importance of both those criticisms of the prevailing party model. They suggest that political party behavior follows one course in a prerealignment period, another during the realignment crisis, another in the immediate postrealignment period, and still another a generation after the realignment. And the response of parties to particular issues varies not only with the time but with the axis of conflict that an issue represents; if the issue cleaves the electorate along the same line as the issue that brought about the most recent realignment, the parties respond in one manner, while if it cuts across the electorate along a different line they respond in quite another. Other variables might be introduced as well: the incumbent party behaves differently than the out-party, the majority party differently than the minority party, and so on.

Any generalization about political party behavior that does not take these variables into account is to that extent invalid. The treatise on politics that has had perhaps the greatest influence on American politicians of the early 1970s, for example, advances as its major thesis "that the center is the only position of political power." The thesis is restated by the authors, Richard M. Scammon and Ben J. Wattenberg, in various forms throughout their book: "It can safely be said that the only extreme that is attractive to the large majority of American voters is the extreme center." "Presidents get elected by occupying the center territory." "It can be noted again that centrists win elections." "A man or a party who forgets the center forgets the name of the game."[3] The same advice appears in academic works. One textbook in current use, after presenting a diagram arraying voter attitudes on a one-dimensional curve that approaches a normal distribution, bulging at the center and sloping downward toward the two extremes, goes on to conclude: "Obviously, if a party wishes to win, it needs to appeal to the large center."

2. Donald E. Stokes, "Spatial Models of Party Competition," in Angus Campbell and others, *Elections and the Political Order* (Wiley, 1966), pp. 165–68.

3. Richard M. Scammon and Ben J. Wattenberg, *The Real Majority* (Coward-McCann, 1970), pp. 200, 21, 117, 131, 160. Similar comments are found on pp. 78, 137, 179.

Both parties "must stay close to where the majority of the constituents are located—the great middle."[4]

But that ignores the time dimension. What is true today was not true yesterday and may not be true tomorrow. It all depends. If the country polarizes, the normal distribution becomes bimodal, and centrists are crushed. Then presidents are defeated because they occupy the center territoty—Millard Fillmore, for example, and Benjamin Harrison. When Franklin Roosevelt moved away from his relatively centrist position of 1932 to his more extreme position of 1936, he gained voter support. The victory-to-the-center thesis may be true *most* of the time, and in *most* places, but if it were true *all* the time, in *all* places, as a categorical proposition, then Sumner and Seward, Chase and Calhoun, Bryan and Cleveland, and Lincoln and Franklin Roosevelt would occupy a much lesser place in history, or none at all.

Related to the centrist theme in the literature on party behavior is another prevailing concept: because the parties try to move toward each other and toward the center where the voters are massed, they avoid taking distinctive ideological and policy stands. Their interest is in patronage rather than program, they adopt platforms that are deliberately vague and straddle the issues, they try to be all things to all voters. Occasionally, this description is qualified with "usually" or "normally," but the exceptions are not set forth.

"Both parties try more or less successfully to spread over the whole political rainbow from one extreme to the other," said Schattschneider in his standard work of a generation ago,[5] and his words have been echoed ever since. "The American major party is . . . lacking in party principles," declares a later textbook.[6] A characteristic of the American party system, according to another authoritative work, is a "striking . . . lack of ideological or programmatic commitment in both the front and the rear ranks of the two major parties. . . . The parties . . . are interested in the votes of men, not in their principles."[7] According to still another, party ideologies "tend to converge," and "party leaders will talk in generalities and be intentionally vague and ambiguous in their programs."[8] In Anthony Downs's model of

4. Hugh A. Bone, *American Politics and the Party System* (3d ed., McGraw-Hill, 1965), pp. 119–21.
5. E. E. Schattschneider, *Party Government* (Farrar and Rinehart, 1942), p. 88.
6. Ivan Hinderaker, *Party Politics* (Holt, 1956), p. 27.
7. Clinton Rossiter, *Parties and Politics in America* (Cornell University Press, 1960), p. 11.
8. Bone, *American Politics*, p. 121.

the party system, which occasioned the Stokes critique, "politicians . . . never seek office as a means of carrying out particular policies; their only goal is to reap the rewards of holding office *per se*," and the parties deliberately make their platforms "vague and ambiguous."[9] Herbert Agar, reacting to the 1964 Goldwater campaign, generalized that "a successful American political party must be a non-ideological affair, accommodating many points of view."[10]

Once more, it all depends. The party system may have been nonideological in the 1880s or the 1920s, when the parties were between realignments. But no one would contend that the Republican party of the 1860s, the Democratic party of 1896, or either party in 1936 lacked ideological or programmatic commitment, and some of those parties were notably successful. And their commitment was not a transitory phenomenon. The sharp programmatic differences between the Republican and Democratic parties on matters pertaining to slavery and civil rights lasted through more than two decades, from the middle 1850s to the 1870s. The different views of the two major parties on the role of government, dramatized in the 1930s, was still significant in the 1960s. Hinderaker cites the major parties' stand on four issues to demonstrate what he describes as their normal tendency to straddle the fence on policy questions: women's suffrage, direct election of U.S. senators, the income tax, and regulation of business.[11] These examples are all taken from the Progressive Era, when the line of cleavage between the parties was singularly blurred, for reasons discussed earlier. But a textbook writer could, if he chose, select as many examples from the issues that arose at a time when the line of cleavage in the party system was sharp and distinct and that ran along, rather than across, the line of cleavage—issues on which the parties therefore took clear and differing stands. The Social Security Act and the Agricultural Adjustment Act in the 1930s could be cited, say, or the Taft-Hartley Act, federal aid to education, or Medicare in the postwar period. Since political conflict is not unidimensional, whether a party straddles an issue depends on the direction of conflict the issue represents, as well as on the time dimension. On the latter point, one can return to Key. "If the parties are viewed in [a] temporal framework," he wrote in his own textbook, "one may better appraise the old saw that the parties offer the electorate only a choice between tweedledum and tweedledee. In fact, the dif-

9. *An Economic Theory of Democracy* (Harper and Row, 1957), pp. 28, 115.
10. *The Price of Union* (2d ed., Houghton Mifflin, 1966), p. ix.
11. *Party Politics*, p. 34.

ferences between the parties vary from stage to stage in the conversion of controversy into new consensus."[12]

An Open or a Closed Party System?

The most eloquent, even passionate, plea for Tweedledum and Tweedle-dee as the ideal party system is perhaps that voiced by Herbert Agar. "The price of union," he wrote in concluding the volume that bears that title, is a political system in which the major parties lack principles and straddle the major issues. In doing so, he argued, the parties can reconcile conflicting points of view in the society before they become disruptive. He saw it as "a sign of health" in the party system, not a "sign of failure and decay," that the Republican party lost its principles between 1856 and 1886—the former year "had been the exception and the danger, 1886 the reassuring norm." The "purpose" of an American party, Agar went on, should be patronage:

> The party is intended to be an organization for "getting or keeping the patronage of government." Instead of seeking "principles," or "distinctive tenets," which can only divide a federal union, the party is intended to seek bargains between the regions, the classes, the other interest groups. It is intended to bring men and women of all beliefs, occupations, sections, racial backgrounds, into a combination for the pursuit of power. The combination is too various to possess firm convictions. The members may have nothing in common except a desire for office. . . . They tend to ignore any issue that rouses deep passion. And by doing so they strengthen the Union.
>
> The decisive American experience—the warning against politics based on principles—took place between 1850 and 1860. . . .
>
> A federal nation is safe so long as the parties are undogmatic and contain members with many contradictory views. But when the people begin to divide according to reason, with all the voters in one party who believe one way, the federal structure is strained.[13]

This view, somewhat modified perhaps, has also found its way into what may be called the textbook model of the American party system. Political scientists always acknowledge and usually admire the achievements of the major parties in moderating political conflict. It is "healthy," says one textbook, that both major American parties are broad coalitions; the fact that neither party "can 'fly' off toward either political extremity of conservatism or progressivism without disintegrating" has a "stabilizing" effect on the

---

12. *Politics, Parties, and Pressure Groups* (5th ed., Crowell, 1964), p. 225.
13. Agar, *The Price of Union*, pp. 689–90. In this passage, Agar was refuting Lord Bryce, whose language he quotes.

political system.[14] It is a "basic function" of American parties, says another, "to soften sectional, group, economic, and other tensions. . . . Accommodation is made in the interests of the larger objective of control of government. Because parties are flexible, paralyzing deadlocks are avoided and compromises worked out."[15] "Without the important contribution of American political parties in compromising important issues, there might now be no United States of America," says a third.[16]

If Agar is to be taken literally, one may well ask who defined the "purpose" of American parties, and by whom it was "intended" that they be parties of patronage instead of principle. Not the founding fathers, assuredly; they hoped to avoid a party system altogether. Not the founders of the Republican party, who gave that party the principles Agar deplores. Their explicit intention was to create a party of principle that would put an end to what they viewed as the unseemly straddling of the country's moral issue. And they defeated the centrist Democrats because they reflected, at the time, the political will of the majority of the people of the North.

To talk about how the party system *should* behave or how it was *intended* to behave is largely futile. American parties do not and cannot arrive at policy positions as rationally as the textbook models suggest they do. To say that parties "try" to design their own composition, their strategies, or their ideologies on the basis of something like political market research has limited validity. Such interpretations impute to parties a rationality that bodies of such size and such remarkable looseness of organization and absence of discipline do not often have. The in-party, during periods when the president is exercising firm control, may at times approach the textbook model of rationality, but only at times. The out-party approaches that model for only a few months out of four years, between the time the presidential candidate is chosen and the election, when the candidate is setting policy. The rest of the time, an American party should be thought of not as a rational organism with some kind of collective brain making coherent strategic judgments, but as a terrain to be fought over, conquered, and controlled first by one element, then by another.

American parties are unusually decentralized, in our federal system, and extraordinarily open to participation by any group that seeks to use a party

14. Hinderaker, *Party Politics*, p. 42.
15. Bone, *American Politics*, p. 662.
16. Dayton David McKean, *Party and Pressure Politics* (Houghton Mifflin, 1949), p. 24.

for its purposes. An American party has multiple centers of power and multiple points of entry. Each center of power is, indeed, a kind of fortress commanding a part of the terrain being contested. The wider the participation in party affairs, the more vigorous the struggle for power. In the out-party in particular, the federal, decentralized party structure positively encourages rival leaders to vie for power by espousing rival strategies, and these rivals (except sometimes for the front runners) are impelled not to "talk in generalities" but to be clear, bold, and specific in order to attract attention and gain support. Americans see, and participate in, a struggle for control of at least one of the two major parties every four years and sometimes oftener, and struggles are frequently bitter, as witness the internal Republican contest of 1964, the Democratic conflict (even though the Democrats were the in-party) in 1968, and the 1972 feud within the Democratic party that was still going on in 1973. The struggles really never end; they are only suspended at times. The terrain known as the Republican party is sure to be a battlefield again when President Nixon ends his term of office.

So parties are not beings with calculating minds; they are instruments. They serve whatever purpose their leaders, subject to the ultimate control of their rank and file, define for them at any given time. Some leaders will define the purpose as one of patronage, others as one of principle and program. In periods when principles and programs are hotly contested, the latter group increases in number and prevails. Accordingly, when a society polarizes, so do the parties. If the mood of the country is extreme, the parties cannot "fly" off toward moderation either. To admonish the parties against polarization, or to suggest that it is the *party system* that has become "unhealthy" if polarization occurs, is to put the blame in the wrong place.

True, the leaders of a political party do more than just reflect the will of the party members; they also lead. Political leaders, particularly presidents, have a major role in influencing public opinion, and it may be the part of statesmanship at some times to use that influence to forestall polarization (as the pre–Civil War presidents tried to do, although with the present day's perspective some might question the statesmanship of compromise on the issue with which they dealt). But many other institutions also influence the public attitude toward controversial issues—all the media, all the organizations to which people belong, all the country's leaders outside of politics. If those influences are creating a polarized society, then political leaders who try to bridge the schism through compromise may only isolate themselves and lose their influence. Even if, in a time of polarization, all the established political leaders of both parties were to stand together in the center with the president (one recalls the Compromise of 1850), new leaders would arise to reflect the points of view not represented and, if necessary, throw out of office the entire compromising crowd. In a democratic society, extremists as well as centrists find their instrument of political expression. If they cannot capture the existing parties, they create new ones.

Insofar as it is now futile to prescribe how political parties should behave, it may be destructive. For the logic of arguing that parties *should* behave in a certain way leads to designing the system so that they *will* behave that way. And if the judgment is made that the ideal behavior is the avoidance of polar positions, it follows that the parties should be organized so that they will fail to reflect the sentiment of a community when and as it polarizes. To that end, responsiveness and participation must be limited. That, of course, can be done. Barriers to participation are easy to devise. The American South demonstrated that for decades, and the polarization of politics that the white South feared was certainly avoided.

If the object is to enhance the power of the centrists in the major parties, to protect them from the extremists, to keep them in power even though they are no longer responsive to the party membership, devices to accomplish this purpose can be designed as well. Nominations can be made by conventions rather than through primary elections. The unit rule in conventions can be permitted. Convention delegates can be selected by party committees rather than through primaries or mass meetings. Election laws can be written to make it difficult for third parties to get on the ballot. And so on. There are many means of closing an open party system.

But the trend throughout the last three-quarters of a century has been in the opposite direction. The reformers of the Progressive Era found that, if a closed political system was rigged in favor of moderation, it was also rigged in favor of inertia and of an intolerable amount of boodling. The cure they advanced for the weaknesses of democracy was, in that day's phrase, more democracy; in the current phrase, power to the people. The direct primary was introduced. The secrecy and honesty of elections were safeguarded. The initiative, referendum, and recall were adopted. Women's suffrage was approved. And the reforms continued through the years. The Democratic national convention abandoned its two-thirds rule. The Congress finally acted to enforce the enfranchisement of southern blacks. The poll tax was outlawed. The voting age was lowered to eighteen. Many more states adopted the direct primary for selection of party convention delegates. The

Democratic party, for its 1972 convention, adopted radically revised rules to ensure a greater measure of democracy in the delegate-selection process.

If moderation, centrism, and compromise are the signs of party health, then virtually everything the country has been doing in the way of institutional reform in the past seventy-five years has worked against this end. The reforms of the twentieth century have gone a long way toward ensuring that whenever the country polarizes on an issue the polarization will be quickly and faithfully reflected by the parties. If the polar groups can gain enough public support, few institutional barriers remain to prevent their gaining control of party policies and nominations. This prospect will encourage more politicians to take their chances with extremism, giving it even greater potential.

That is the hazard of an open party system. But, on balance, the reformers have surely been right in sensing that a closed system is ultimately more dangerous, as well as impossible to justify in terms of the democratic ethic. For if zealots devoted to the pursuit of a particular principle, policy, or measure find that the political system is closed to them, their only recourse is to challenge the legitimacy of the system itself. Throughout our history, and the history of other countries, those who have been denied a full right of participation in the party system have taken their case to the streets. Even so suppressed and intimidated a group as the southern blacks, after a century of waiting, finally did that. The young people who tried to settle the 1968 Democratic presidential nomination in the streets of Chicago were not willing to wait at all. After the chaos of that convention subsided, the dissident young were advised from all sides to "work within the system." But if zealots and extremists are to work within the party system, they must be granted the right to take control of a major party if and when there are enough of them. When they do, the party will inevitably cease to be Herbert Agar's "ideal" party of patronage and compromise, if it had been that; the polarization of the political system that he dreaded will reappear. But whether people who believe deeply in either making or forestalling what seem radical changes in government policy *can* make a party over and attain effective expression of their views is the true test of the health of a political system in a democracy.

CHAPTER FIFTEEN

Crosscutting Issues since
the New Deal

To RETURN to the questions of the first chapter: Has the American party system entered a period of major realignment? If so, why and how? If not, what *is* happening to it?

In the four decades since the New Deal party system came into being, the most distinct changes in the party balance have been the pro-Democratic trend in the former predominantly Republican areas of the North and the pro-Republican trend in the formerly solid Democratic South, which were discussed in Chapters 11 and 12. These two trends were interpreted there as the product of aftershocks of the political earthquake of the 1930s, as the new alignment created in that stormy decade settled into place, locality by locality, state by state, and generation by generation. In other words, they constituted a secular realignment set in motion by the critical realignment of the 1930s and still continuing.

Yet the aftershock interpretation may not account for all that has happened during the past forty years. New issues have arisen, some of them with realigning potential. They have cut across—or at first appeared to cut across—the existing party structure. They have been powerful enough to dominate political debate. They have aroused deep emotions and polarized large segments of the voting population. Political groups of significant size have formed at the respective poles. What has been the influence of these crosscutting issues? Have they set forces in motion that may be now at work within the political system, pointing toward a major realignment?

Four such issues can be identified. The first, in the late 1940s and early 1950s, was communism. The second, which developed in the 1950s, was race. The third, in the 1960s, was Vietnam. The fourth, equally recent, was "law and order," which came to be combined with aspects of race and Vietnam into what has been called "the social issue" by Richard M. Scammon and Ben J. Wattenberg.[1] Only the first of these—communism—has so far run its course.

The Republican party, as the minority party throughout the period, has had a stake in the exploitation of crosscutting issues. To the extent that segments of the electorate can be polarized on those issues, and Republicans can identify with the popular side and drive the Democrats to identify with the unpopular side, voters will be realigned in favor of the GOP. The quick and obvious means by which the Republicans can become the majority party once again is an intense polarization of the country that will lead to realignment on a major scale.

But an American party, to repeat, is rarely able to function as an entity with a rational collective mind. In between campaigns, especially when out of power, it is no more than an arena for the struggle of contending forces; so the Republican party of the postwar period has been no better able than any other party in any other extended period to adopt a consistent strategy. Crosscutting issues, by definition, divide both major parties, and the Republican party has been split no less severely than the Democratic. In the 1940s and again in the 1960s, the GOP in typical out-party fashion spoke with many voices as various candidates and factions jockeyed for supremacy. When in power as both the minority party and the incumbent party, it has been torn between the former's temptation to exploit divisive issues and the latter's tendency to straddle them.

The interest of the Democratic party has been just the opposite. As the majority party, it has had nothing to gain and everything to lose by realignment. Accordingly, most of its leaders have sought to suppress the divisive questions and emphasize the kinds of issues—the "bread-and-butter," class-related issues—that carried the party into majority status in the 1930s and have provided the basis of its strength and unity ever since. Yet even when in power, it too has had no means of forestalling the rise within its ranks of leaders and factions determined to exploit crosscutting issues, divide the party, and use those issues as the means of achieving party leadership and national power.

So both parties have been and still are battlegrounds of competing groups who respond to the crosscutting issues in diverse ways. By their nature, some of these issues do not permit early resolution, and it is in the interest of the polar political groups to keep them agitated. So the prospect is that the political scene will remain tumultuous.

1. *The Real Majority* (Coward-McCann, 1970).

The four postwar issues are examined below in the light of the characteristics of the realignment process detailed in Chapter 13.

Communism as a Realigning Issue

Communism as a political issue was born when Franklin Roosevelt recognized the Soviet Union in 1933, but it did not flourish immediately. The act of recognition affected few Americans directly; it lent an element of plausibility to the cries of economic conservatives that the New Deal was "communistic," but that was all. The more visible menace in those days was fascism. Then came the war, and the Soviet Union was an ally.

After the war, however, all at once world communism became a peril. The iron curtain fell across Europe, and millions of Eastern Europeans (with millions of relatives in America) found communism imposed upon them, all seemingly with the acquiescence of Roosevelt at Yalta. The American and Russian military colossi confronted each other, and all over the globe the Russians probed for weaknesses in the Western lines. They blockaded Berlin. They menaced Turkey. They supported powerful internal communist threats to the governments of Italy, Greece, France, and any other country that had not yet achieved postwar stability. The question, How had communism become so strong? could be answered, Because of Democratic policies—policies from Roosevelt's recognition of the Soviet Union to wartime lend-lease to Yalta. This answer gained credence when the name of Alger Hiss was emblazoned in the headlines, followed by those of Harry Dexter White and scores of lesser figures in an alleged conspiracy.

True to predictable party behavior, the leaders of the Republican party straddled. Many of them had supported Roosevelt's wartime policies in a spirit of bipartisanship, believed in them, and shared a measure of responsibility. Perhaps they were afraid to attack the record of the era's most popular political figure. At any rate, most of the established Republican leaders showed a marked reluctance to take so divisive a course as to suggest that their opponents had connived with, or been duped by, communism. Yet if established leaders would not step forward, the situation was made to order for new leaders to advance themselves by doing so. An obscure freshman Republican senator from Wisconsin, Joseph R. McCarthy, moved to the center of the political stage. Beginning with a dramatic speech in Wheeling, West Virginia, in February 1950 ("I have here in my hand . . ."), McCarthy in a couple of years built communism-in-government into an emotionally compelling national issue. He mobilized and led a powerful and growing polar force.

The established Republican leaders continued to straddle. They found McCarthy too crude and ambitious to be admitted to the leadership circle, but still they sought to make use of him and his following. So Robert A. Taft, "Mr. Republican" of the Senate, encouraged McCarthy both publicly and privately while not associating himself with the latter's style and methods.[2] The party selected McCarthy as a convention speaker in 1952, but not on prime time. General Eisenhower in the 1952 campaign was careful neither to embrace McCarthy nor to join personally in impugning the loyalty of leading Democrats. But Eisenhower was equally careful not to repudiate McCarthy, and he chose as his running mate the most acceptable of the new politicians who had come to national attention on the anticommunism issue —Senator Richard M. Nixon of California, who as a congressman had been largely responsible for exposing Alger Hiss. On the anticommunism issue, Eisenhower and most of his closest associates could be classed as "moderate centrists."

The national Democratic party leaders, of course, could hardly take refuge in straddling. Since their own loyalty and competence were being challenged, they had to respond by condemning McCarthy and all his works. But as it happened, the Wisconsin senator's greatest appeal was to one of the traditional pillars of the Democratic party, its Catholics. American Catholics had participated in their church's struggle against international communism with as much intensity as their fellow religionists anywhere. So when one of their own—Irish, Catholic, and tough—launched a crusade to purge their own American government of communism, thousands of them, especially the Irish and those from the "captive nations," rallied behind him. Diocesan papers like the Brooklyn *Tablet* glorified him. The hierarchy in some cities openly supported him. He received a "tumultuous reception," wrote Daniel Patrick Moynihan, at the annual communion breakfast of the Police Department Holy Name Society of the New York Diocese.[3] And these were Democrats.

2. Taft was quoted by newsmen in 1950 as saying that McCarthy should "keep talking and if one case doesn't work out he should proceed with another." William S. White, *The Taft Story: Biography of Robert A. Taft* (Harper and Row, 1954), pp. 85–88.

3. Nathan Glazer and Daniel Patrick Moynihan, *Beyond the Melting Pot: The Negroes, Puerto Ricans, Jews, Italians and Irish of New York City* (M.I.T. Press and Harvard University Press, 1963), p. 270.

But other Democrats recoiled. Among them were the Jews, who sensed in McCarthy's style antilibertarianism at best and fascism at worst. Also among them were both Catholic and non-Catholic intellectuals, who saw the attack on communism as a facade for an assault on all things liberal. And the men under attack had friends. "I do not intend to turn my back" on Alger Hiss, said Secretary of State Dean Acheson, to the applause of one wing of the party and the dismay of the other. The party was indeed divided.

The communist issue contributed some imponderable proportion to the Eisenhower landslide of 1952. By that time it had been linked through a web of association to almost everything else that troubled Americans. The Democratic liberals, soft on communism and under the influence of traitors in government, had "lost" China and given away Eastern Europe to the Communists, went the chain of argument. Then aggressive communism, encouraged by blunders of the Truman administration, had attacked Korea and dragged the United States into war. The war in its turn had brought inflation, which brought price and wage controls. The affinity of Democratic liberalism with communism was at the bottom of it all. It was, the people decided, "time for a change."

But a polar leader, if he is to retain leadership, must oppose the centrist leaders of whatever party is in power, even his own. So in 1953 and 1954, McCarthy continued his attack on communism-in-government with the same flair and recklessness as before, striking each time closer to President Eisenhower. Finally the Republican straddlers saw the danger, came down off their fence, isolated and repudiated McCarthy, and joined in censuring him. McCarthyism then expired.

The 1952 Republican landslide turned out to be a deviation; no major realignment resulted from the communism issue. Why? The answer appears to lie in the fourth proposition of Chapter 13: the realigning issue was not one on which major political groups took distinct and opposing policy positions. There was no disagreement as to the government's objective; only a minuscule fragment of the electorate favored communism as such. When the attempt to label their enemies procommunist proved less than credible, McCarthy and his allies tried to label them "anti-anticommunist," and then tried to equate that with procommunism. But that approach was ineffective too.

So the issue had to be shifted to the question of means to achieve the universally agreed-upon end of stemming communist advance. What the polarizers required was some anticommunism measure that could be easily dramatized and understood, that could be made to appear of great significance, that would have majority support in the country, but that would so offend substantial elements of the electorate—especially within the Democratic segment—that they would be driven to the same pole as the Communists. Then the issue would be clearly defined.

Unfortunately for the anticommunists, they were unable to come up with such a measure. McCarthy himself had only a posture, not a program; he was identified with no major legislative proposals. Other anticommunists had measures, but on none of them did political polarization take place. The two major pieces of legislation that were enacted—the Internal Security Act of 1950 and the Communist Control Act of 1954—both had overwhelming bipartisan support. True, Harry Truman vetoed the first of them, but no one could seriously argue that he sympathized with communism as such. It was he who established the government loyalty program; he who checked communism in Europe with the Truman doctrine and in Asia with the Korean war. Besides, he did not even speak for his party with his veto; more than three-fourths of the Democrats in the House and more than two-thirds of those in the Senate voted to override. In 1954, it was the liberal Hubert Humphrey who sponsored the amendment (supported by Senate Democrats 37–1) that would have made it a crime to belong to the Communist party— an amendment too extreme even for the House.

These events made it clear that the two parties did not differ on the basic policy objective, and this reduced the debate to the secondary level. The parties could quarrel only over the selection and administration of means to the agreed-upon end. The Democrats could be accused only of short-sightedness and blundering. Truman could be attacked for not moving soon enough to eliminate communism from government, for calling the charges against Hiss a "red herring," for (as Attorney General Herbert Brownell claimed in the White case) "knowingly" promoting a communist spy, for speaking kindly of Stalin ("I like old Joe! He is a decent fellow"). But this is the kind of issue that produces mainly deviation, not realignment. An anticommunist Democrat did not have to change parties to oppose communism; he had only to support for leadership in his own party men who had demonstrated their clear-headedness on the subject. Moreover, McCarthy had attacked the Eisenhower administration for the same kind of errors he had earlier accused the Democrats of making.

In 1960, with the Democratic nomination of an Irish Catholic for president, the party was purged of any association with communism that may have lingered from the McCarthy era. If some voters had strayed from Democratic ranks in the 1940s and 1950s because of the communism issue, they would thereafter have to stay outside for other reasons.

It is these other reasons, I believe, that explain for the most part the residue of minor realignment left from the agitation over communism. The steady drift of Catholic voters, particularly Irish Catholics, to the Republicans in the urban centers has been well documented.[4] But the explanation for this trend too, I suggest, lies in the aftershock interpretation. The rise of Irish Republicanism in the North is analogous to the rise of metropolitan Republicanism in the South. The Irish Catholics, like the southerners, were Democratic by habit and tradition. In any solid bloc of traditional Democrats would naturally be found voters both liberal and conservative on questions of domestic economic policy. In the South, in Donald Strong's argument, the Democratic stance on civil rights discredited the party as a reliable vehicle of white supremacy and so set economic conservatives free to vote as their views on economic issues dictated.[5] In the North, the anticommunism issue in the early 1950s served a similar purpose by making it respectable, within the Catholic community, to vote Republican. (It should not be overlooked that anticommunism had its impact in the South as well, helping to pry economic conservatives from their traditional Democratic attachment. In both regions, the hero image of General Eisenhower was a facilitating factor.)

In this interpretation, then, anticommunism was not a realigning issue in itself. But by agitating the political structure it shook individual voters loose from old attachments and set them free to conform to the alignment established in the 1930s. In short, like the race issue in the South, it broke some of the barriers that had delayed conformance to the New Deal party system of party alignments at the local level.

Race as a Realigning Issue

Proposition 11 in Chapter 13 stated that a realignment crisis is precipitated when the moderate centrists lose control of one or both parties on a

4. See, for instance, Kevin P. Phillips, *The Emerging Republican Majority* (Arlington House, 1969), pp. 151–75, esp. pp. 165–75.
5. See p. 258.

powerful crosscutting issue. Race has been such an issue; for generations it has been the most powerful of all issues in one large region of the country, the South. A realignment process should thus have been set in motion when the Democratic party, immediately after the war, made its commitment to support the black demand for civil rights. Events have shown that this is exactly what happened. A realignment process affecting a significant segment of the electorate, mainly in the South, began. It has lasted an unusually long time and is still not finished.

The principal events surrounding the civil rights controversy of the postwar years were narrated earlier, but they can be reviewed here in terms of realignment theory. The party system was plunged into its realignment crisis on the day in 1948 that President Truman sent Congress his civil rights proposals, reversing the moderate policy of his predecessor, Franklin Roosevelt. The Democratic party was polarized at once. Then began the struggle for control among three contending party elements that is characteristic of a prerealignment period. At one end of the party spectrum was the civil rights polar force—black activists and their white liberal allies from the programmatic wing of the Democratic party, who were determined to press their cause even at the risk of disrupting the unity of the national party. At the other end was the polar force of southern white resistance, sworn to bolt the party when and if the northern zealots attained clear control. In the middle were the moderate centrists who sought to find the areas of compromise that would maintain the party's unity.

The centrists dominated the party in Congress, the Truman administration itself drew back to a less activist position, and none of the Truman civil rights measures were enacted. When the Democratic convention of 1948 assembled, the centrists, tacitly supported by Truman, also controlled the platform committee, on which senior members of Congress traditionally served. But they did not control the majority of delegates. The northern programmatic liberals, led by former Congressman Andrew J. Biemiller of Milwaukee and Mayor Hubert Humphrey of Minneapolis, won the convention for their amendment to strengthen the civil rights plank of the platform; then some of the southern delegates made good their pledge to leave the party, and the Dixiecrat third-party movement got under way.

The loss of thirty-nine electoral votes to the Dixiecrats in the 1948 election so shook the Democratic party that at the next convention the centrists were firmly in control. They lost the opening skirmish, when the convention by voice vote adopted a requirement for a "loyalty oath" from each delegate before he could be seated,[6] but thereafter they held what amounted to a veto over any action that might provoke another southern walkout. The convention seated the delegations from Virginia, Louisiana, and South Carolina in spite of a ruling from the convention chairman that those delegates had not complied with the loyalty oath requirement. The centrists successfully backed Governor Adlai E. Stevenson of Illinois, "a man . . . whose record was good, but who was not publicly committed deeply to the divisive issue that threatened to split the party,"[7] over the liberals' candidates, led by Senator Estes Kefauver of Tennessee. And the convention carried the symbolism of party unity further by nominating for vice-president a man from the Deep South, Senator John J. Sparkman of Alabama. In the campaign Stevenson did not crusade on the civil rights issue, as a Truman or a Kefauver might have, and in the November election the four Dixiecrat states all returned to the Democratic fold.

If centrist politicians had succeeded in healing (or, perhaps more accurately, papering over) the party rupture, the Supreme Court in 1954 reopened it. With the decree that year outlawing dual school systems, the polar forces in the Democratic party regrouped. The northern zealots demanded that the Supreme Court decision be carried out forthwith, with full support of the executive and legislative branches. The southern polar forces solidified under the banner of "massive resistance." And the centrists, led by Senate Majority Leader Lyndon B. Johnson, worked out legislative compromises in the classic fashion when the issue forced its way to the Senate floor, in 1957 and 1960.[8] But the continuing turmoil over school integration in the South increased polarization throughout the country. The lunch counter "sit-ins" heightened it. When the 1960 Democratic convention met, the polar forces demanding an unqualified commitment to civil rights regardless of the consequences to the party were in clear control. They wrote a platform that was, for its time, a clarion call to action, and they steamrollered the southern protest when it was made in the platform committee and on the convention floor.[9]

---

6. While called a "loyalty oath," it only required each delegate to "exert every honorable means available to him" to see that the Democratic nominees appeared on the ballot of his state under the Democratic label. Richard C. Bain and Judith H. Parris, *Convention Decisions and Voting Records* (2d ed., Brookings Institution, 1973), p. 288.

7. Ibid., p. 287.

8. Rowland Evans and Robert Novak, *Lyndon B. Johnson: The Exercise of Power* (New American Library, 1966), pp. 119–40; James L. Sundquist, *Politics and Policy: The Eisenhower, Kennedy, and Johnson Years* (Brookings Institution, 1968), pp. 233–50.

9. Sundquist, *Politics and Policy*, pp. 250–53.

President Kennedy tried to steer a centrist course, despite the convention mandate, to conciliate the southerners who still held the dominant power in the Congress. Even after the freedom riders, the riot over integration at the University of Mississippi, the fire hoses in Birmingham, and Governor George C. Wallace's "stand in the schoolhouse door," the President still tried to prevent an aroused Congress from going too far. He presented a relatively cautious program and strenuously resisted efforts by some members of the House Judiciary Committee to strengthen it.[10] But he was out of step with the preponderance of northern Democrats; the House Judiciary Committee did indeed strengthen his bill. And Lyndon Johnson, the first president from a southern state in a century, chose to take his place as the head of the civil rights activists he had opposed as Senate leader. On national television he intoned the refrain of civil rights marchers everywhere, "We Shall Overcome." Unlike the northerners Roosevelt and Kennedy, he chose to align his party directly and openly with its northern polar forces. The result was a repetition of the crisis of the Truman era. The opposing force again bolted to a third party, led this time by Governor Wallace of Alabama. But this crisis was far more severe. The Democrats who might try to moderate the civil rights issue could make no comeback. They were destroyed.

By this time, moreover, the civil rights movement had moved north. Voices had begun to demand that, in the course of righting ancient southern wrongs, the more recent northern sins be atoned as well. Civil rights activists marched not just in Birmingham and Selma but in Chicago and Milwaukee and elsewhere in the North. And President Johnson's commitment, characteristically, was total. He cast his lot with the northern marchers, too, and offered the first legislative proposal that would arouse fiercer opposition in the North than in the South—open housing. That and the riots of the mid-1960s in Watts, Hough, Detroit, Newark, and scores of other black ghettos broke the unity of the northern Democratic party.

Now the Democrats were no longer split simply along regional lines; resistance from whites developed in the North. Wherever the civil rights issues became heated, this resistance took on the character of a polar force, more concerned with resisting black demands—for housing integration, for equal employment opportunities, for police review boards, for the end of de facto school segregation, or whatever—than with the unity of the Demo-

10. Ibid., pp. 254–65; Theodore C. Sorensen, *Kennedy* (Harper and Row, 1965), pp. 473–506; Arthur M. Schlesinger, Jr., *A Thousand Days: John F. Kennedy in the White House* (Houghton Mifflin, 1965), pp. 928–77.

cratic party. The realignment crisis once confined to the South became a crisis everywhere.

The strength of the resistance from northern whites became apparent as early as 1964 when the leader of the polar anti-integration forces within the southern wing of the Democratic party, Governor Wallace, entered the Democratic presidential primaries in Wisconsin, Indiana, and Maryland as a segregationist, anti–civil-rights, states' rights candidate and shocked the party by capturing from 25 to 43 percent of the primary vote, including majorities in some whole counties. In September 1966 the public opinion polls showed for the first time that a majority of northerners thought the national administration was "pushing racial integration too fast."[11]

That same month, George P. Mahoney was able to win the Democratic nomination for governor of Maryland with a single-issue appeal to the state's white voters to reject integration of white neighborhoods: "Your home is your castle—protect it!" The depth of the party split was revealed two months later when the party's integrationist wing defected as a bloc to elect Mahoney's Republican opponent, Spiro T. Agnew.

The effect of the race issue on the Republican party was less disruptive. The zealots at both ends of the civil rights spectrum happened to be from groups predominantly Democratic—blacks and liberal intellectuals, on the one hand, and southern traditionalists, on the other. The Republican party, too, had its committed pro-integration wing—senators like Thomas H. Kuchel of California and Jacob K. Javits of New York were co-leaders with the northern Democrats in the legislative struggles—and zealous anti-integrationists like Senator Strom Thurmond, the erstwhile Dixiecrat, but its moderate centrist bloc was able to maintain control of party policy (if the few months of Goldwater control are disregarded). Whatever his private views, as chief executive President Eisenhower was a centrist on the civil rights issue, a straddler. He disapproved the civil rights enforcement proposals advanced by Attorney General Brownell in 1956,[12] and while he sent federal troops to Little Rock, he conspicuously declined to endorse at any time the decision of the Supreme Court that called them there. In the 1960s, the key Republican figure on civil rights legislation was Senator Everett McKinley Dirksen of Illinois, the minority leader, whose flexibility on this and all other matters was legendary. And after Richard Nixon became party

11. Sundquist, *Politics and Policy*, pp. 498–99.

12. J. W. Anderson, *Eisenhower, Brownell, and the Congress* (University of Alabama Press for the Inter-University Case Program, 1964); Sundquist, *Politics and Policy*, pp. 223–30.

leader in 1968, he steered a course on racial questions somewhere near the center of his party, not fully satisfactory to either of the party's polar groups.

As of 1968, then, the realignment crisis precipitated by the race issue was well advanced. By that time, it had become intertwined with a complex of related issues that came to be known collectively as "law and order," or "the social issue." Moreover, the controversy over Vietnam had risen to its height. These two other potentially realigning forces at work in the current political scene need to be examined before the impact of the race issue can be finally appraised.

Vietnam as a Realigning Issue

It is significant that none of the major realignments of the American party system in the past have been produced by a crisis in foreign policy. True, there have been minor shifts of party affiliation induced by international events—the Democrats suffered some loss as a result of World Wars I and II (particularly of persons of German descent) and other defections as consequences of the Yalta agreements relating to Eastern Europe, the "loss of China," and the subsequent entanglement in Korea. The Democrats also gained Jewish support because of Roosevelt's stand against Nazism and Truman's support of the creation of Israel. But cleavage on foreign policy has at no time been the basic rationale for the country's two-party system. On the contrary, foreign policy has been traditionally bipartisan; politics, in the old phrase, has "stopped at the water's edge."

The reason is probably inherent in the nature of foreign policy. The degree of polarization necessary to bring about a major realignment can hardly develop on an issue of foreign policy. A president is usually unwilling—and when he is not unwilling, he is usually unable—to pursue a course in international affairs that bitterly divides the country. A not insignificant reason is the requirement of a two-thirds vote of the Senate for ratification of treaties. After Woodrow Wilson lost his fight for U.S. entry into the League of Nations, even though a majority of the Senate supported it, presidents have been assiduous in courting broad public support and obtaining bipartisan collaboration in foreign policy ventures. Franklin Roosevelt took great pains in the pre–World War II period not to bring the country closer to intervention than the preponderance of public opinion and the political opposition would support. He and Harry Truman were careful to ensure full bipartisan participation in the founding of the United Nations. Politicians have halted politics at the water's edge because they have understood implicitly that they had to. Any foreign policy venture undertaken with less than preponderant public support, expressed directly and through both parties, would be futile.

The Vietnam episode is a striking case in point. American intervention in Vietnam could be escalated as long as it had the backing of the public, reflected in strong bipartisan support within the political system. But when the campus revolt against the war broke out, President Johnson's Vietnam policy quickly became untenable. However a majority of the country's voters might feel about the policy on its merits, they were bound to weary of the internal dissension it created. If the war stirred up that much trouble, if it produced such alienation in the young, even to the point of sending many into exile, clearly the objective was not worth the cost. Any prospective gains from the Vietnam policy were deferred, intangible, and speculative. The costs in national, even family, disunion were immediate and real. So the majority lost whatever will it may have had to keep the war in progress. A vocal minority centered in young people, it turned out, had an effective veto, compelling the retirement of a president and a redirection of the country's policy on Vietnam.

Until the end of 1967, the polar forces that had been mobilizing against the Vietnam war for more than two years were operating almost wholly outside the existing political establishment. A growing number of senators were identifying themselves with the peace movement, but they were senators on the fringes of the party leadership structures. President Johnson, who every Democrat assumed would be his party's nominee for reelection, had the majority party securely in his grip. Republican leaders, both in and out of the Congress, made the Vietnam policy bipartisan. But since polar forces create their own leaders in the absence of available established leadership, one was bound to appear as the 1968 presidential campaign approached; he came forward in the person of another back-bench U.S. senator, Eugene J. McCarthy of Minnesota, who challenged Johnson for his party's nomination.

In the early months of 1968, the Democratic party appeared to be split into irreconcilable polar forces: one, led by the President, escalating the Vietnam war; the other, led by McCarthy, who was subsequently joined by Robert F. Kennedy, demanding that the policy be reversed. Centrist leadership on the Vietnam issue seemed to have vanished.

Yet suddenly it reappeared. Once the depth of the party division became apparent—in McCarthy's astonishingly strong showing against Johnson in the New Hampshire primary—Johnson himself took the essential steps to heal it. He moved abruptly back from the pole toward the center. He called a halt to the bombing of most of North Vietnam and later all of it, and entered into peace negotiations. Most important of all, he announced his retirement from office.

There was still a bitter confrontation over the platform and the presidential nomination at the party's 1968 convention, and "peace" forces who had followed McCarthy and Kennedy, not only defeated but manhandled and tear-gassed by police, left Chicago with more than the normal anger and frustration of a losing faction. Yet the issue was damped down sufficiently to avert a realignment crisis. Hubert Humphrey, the Democratic nominee, struck a conciliatory note in his campaign, promising to do his best to negotiate a settlement. While unmeasured numbers of peace Democrats either deviated to other candidates or did not vote at all—the numbers were certainly sufficient to account for Humphrey's defeat—they did not organize any concerted course of action. For the time being, the polar force on the Vietnam issue was politically homeless. It had neither captured a major party nor formed a party of its own.

Before many months, however, it was given every reason to return, for the Democratic party, once it was out from under Johnson's leadership, moved quickly toward the peace position. Most of its leading spokesmen, including Humphrey, began to advocate the policies of withdrawal the party had rejected in 1968. In 1970, northern Democrats solidified behind a demand that a date be fixed to end the war; on September 1 northern Democrats in the Senate voted 29-6 for an amendment by Senators George S. McGovern (D., South Dakota) and Mark O. Hatfield (R., Oregon) to withdraw all troops by the end of 1971. (Republicans voted 34-7 and southern Democrats 15-3 against it.) As the 1972 convention approached, Democrats could choose between McGovern and half a dozen other candidates committed to a unilateral ending of the Vietnam war.

So the 1968 crisis on the Vietnam issue was surmounted without a major realignment. There is no reason to think that many of the peace Democrats who defected from their party in 1968 made new party attachments. Richard Nixon as the Republican nominee had no positive appeal to them, although some voted for him to punish their own party for its behavior at Chicago. The average voter perceived Nixon in the campaign as slightly more "hawkish" than Humphrey.[13] Like Humphrey, he was for negotiation toward a peaceful settlement; he was for "Vietnamization" of the war, and he was just as adamant as Humphrey against unilateral withdrawal. George Wallace, of course, campaigned unequivocally as a hawk.

There is also little reason to think that very many peace Republicans were won over to the Democrats in the years after 1968. Nixon as president invigorated the policy of de-escalation that Johnson had begun in 1968. He proceeded with "Vietnamization," and by 1972 had withdrawn all ground combat troops. Meanwhile, he pursued a policy of negotiation. The parties were then agreed on the objective, and when George McGovern tried to win votes in 1972 by stressing his differences with Nixon on the means toward the agreed end, he clearly failed. If anything, the polls and the election returns indicate that his Vietnam position cost him votes. But that was of little significance in terms of party realignment, because any such loss of support evidently did not extend to the Democratic party as a whole—which actually gained U.S. Senate seats, governorships, and control of several state legislative houses despite the Nixon landslide. In sum, realignment of the party system on the Vietnam issue was averted because the two major parties both yielded at about the same time to the basic demand of the peace advocates that American policy be reversed.

Law and Order and the "Social Issue"

In the mid-1960s, at the very time the race and Vietnam issues were the focus of public and political attention, still another powerful crosscutting issue arose, labeled "law and order."

Law and order might or might not be a separate and independent issue. Crime in the streets—the alarming rise in yokings, muggings, robberies, and rapes—had made half the women in America, and 19 percent of the men, afraid to walk alone in their neighborhoods at night.[14] To some, the rise in crime had nothing to do with race: criminals were simply criminals, whether black or white. Yet a disproportionately high share of the criminals were black, and it was in black neighborhoods that people were particularly afraid

13. Benjamin I. Page and Richard A. Brody, "Policy Voting and the Electoral Process: The Vietnam War Issue" (paper prepared for delivery at the annual meeting of the American Political Science Association, September 1971; processed).

14. American Institute of Public Opinion (Gallup) poll, February 1968; cited by Scammon and Wattenberg, *The Real Majority*, p. 95.

to walk. Moreover, the most terrifying breakdown in law and order had everything to do with race; between 1964 and 1968 the black ghettos in almost every major city in America and in scores of smaller cities were convulsed with riot. So when some whites talked of "law and order," they did mean something beyond law and order in a literal sense. They meant keeping black crime and disorder out of white neighborhoods, which in turn meant continued confinement of blacks to their ghettos, continued segregation of the black population by the white. In short, "law and order" might be "a code word for racism," as the saying went, or it might not, depending on the perception and intent of the user. Law and order was a *separable* issue from race, but it was not always a *separated* issue.

Law and order was not completely separated from Vietnam either, for disrespect for law also took the form of direct action against the war by its opponents, mainly the young—burning of the flag and of draft cards, ransacking of draft offices, interference with military and industrial recruitment on campuses, harassment of defense research and ROTC organizations, burning of their buildings, and demonstrations that had a way of getting out of control.

So the issues of crime, race, and Vietnam were intertwined. And there were still other issues related to them that contributed to the national anxiety of the late 1960s. The young were not only alienated by the war but disaffected generally, experimenting not just in new styles of hair and music and language but in the more dangerous world of drugs. The campuses exploded over both Vietnam and a range of other grievances. Police and national guard units were summoned, and at Kent State, Jackson State, and elsewhere students were shot down. Old standards of conduct and morality seemed everywhere to be disintegrating, expressed in many ways besides black and student riots and rising crime. In the spread of pornography, for instance. In the direct-action tactics of many groups, from "sit-ins" by welfare mothers to the "poor people's march" on Washington to the seizure of land for a "people's park" in Berkeley. In the breakdown of family responsibility and of the work ethic that caused (or was assumed to have caused) expenditures for aid to families with dependent children to increase year by year at an accelerating rate—10 percent in 1965, 13 percent the next year, then 22 percent, then 26 percent in 1968 and again in 1969. While increasing millions were supported by welfare, rising state and local taxes made the citizen more and more aware of who paid the bill. And while he armed himself for protection against thieves or militants, the liberals were trying to pass legislation to take away his guns. And their Supreme Court would not even allow his children to say prayers in school.

In the public perception, all these things merged. Ghetto riots, campus riots, street crime, anti-Vietnam marches, poor people's marches, drugs, pornography, welfarism, rising taxes, all had a common thread: the breakdown of family and social discipline, of order, of concepts of duty, of respect for law, of public and private morality. In 1968, 81 percent of the public agreed that "law and order has broken down in this country"; only 14 percent disagreed.[15] Whatever terms he used, the average American was disturbed, anxious, fearful, alarmed. And so, as in the case of any other widespread anxiety or fear, a political issue was born. Richard Scammon and Ben Wattenberg gave to the composite issue the name that appears likely to prevail, "the social issue."

They suggest a date for the full emergence of the social issue: May 9, 1965, the date that "crime" appeared for the first time on the list of what the Gallup poll respondents designated as "the most important problem" facing the nation. This was some time after racial problems first appeared on the list but three months before Vietnam appeared. By 1968 crime and lawlessness were bracketed with Vietnam and race relations as the three top problems of concern to the American people, and they remained that throughout the 1968 campaign and into 1969.[16]

The social issue, especially when reinforced, as it was bound to be, by the long-standing and related political schism over race, was powerful enough to be a realigning issue. It was personal and immediate in its impact, dramatic on the television screen, easily understood, evocative of strong emotion. At any time, in any place, it could quickly become the dominant, overriding issue.

Yet it was an issue too diffuse for the formation of polar political groups. Not all of the elements of the issue cut across the electorate on the same axis. One could be a hawk on street crime but a dove on young people's antiwar demonstrations, for instance. White and black "hard hats" might react with equal antipathy to student demonstrations, but differ in their views on Negro protest. No single simple solution, no legislative panacea, offered a rallying point for anxious voters. Putting the disorderly in jail was no answer; there were too few jails. Changing the Supreme Court might help, but that

15. Louis Harris poll; cited in ibid., pp. 95–96.
16. Ibid., pp. 38–39.

was a remote kind of solution. Rhetoric about national and individual disci-
cipline could be uttered and endorsed, but that did not constitute a program.

If the polar forces could not coalesce around a program, however, they
could come together around an attitude and an approach. Their common cry
was for those in authority to "get tough" with whatever group disturbed the
peace of that night's television screen. They opposed "coddling" criminals
or welfare mothers. They denounced "permissiveness." They favored discipline. They defended the police. They demanded that government, at every
level, stop making excuses for the rise in crime and take the issue of law and
order seriously. "Security from domestic violence, no less than from foreign aggression, is the most elementary and fundamental purpose of any government," Barry Goldwater told the Republican convention that nominated
him in 1964, even before the issue of domestic violence had fully flowered.[17]

RISE OF THE SOCIAL ISSUE, 1966–69

Goldwater's attempt to capitalize on domestic violence came a couple of
years too soon. The political power of the social issue did not become fully
clear until 1966. Then Ronald Reagan, picking up where Goldwater left off,
skillfully and aggressively exploited the social issue in all its aspects—welfare, crime, ghetto riots, and student disorder—in the state of Watts and
Berkeley, and won the governorship by an overwhelming margin. Across the
nation in the congressional elections, the disenchanted voters turned out
forty-seven Democratic congressmen and three Democratic senators in favor
of Republicans. While the election did not turn on crime and disorder alone
(Vietnam and inflation were also major issues), the Republicans had made
lawlessness a central campaign theme. High officials of the Johnson administration, charged the Republican Coordinating Committee in October of that
year, "have condoned and encouraged disregard for law and order."[18]

By 1967 the Republicans were pulling out all the stops. Declared Republican House Leader Gerald R. Ford, for example:

The War at home—the war against crime—is being lost. The Administration
appears to be in full retreat. The homes and the streets of America are no longer
safe for our people. This is a frightful situation. . . .

The Republicans in Congress *demand* that this Administration take the action
required to protect our people in their homes, on the streets, at their jobs. . . .
There can be no further Administration excuse for indecision, delay or evasion.

17. Ibid., p. 37.
18. Statement entitled "Crime and Law Enforcement," issued Oct. 3, 1966.

When a Rap Brown and a Stokely Carmichael are allowed to run loose, to threaten law-abiding Americans with injury and death, it's time to slam the door on them and any like them—and slam it hard![19]

Next year, the issue was propelled by so many events that it hardly needed partisan exploitation. There were riots in the spring in many cities, including the nation's capital, after the assassination of Martin Luther King, Jr. And in the summer the serious purpose of the Chicago Democratic convention was all but drowned in a sea of turbulence.

To turn the social issue into an effective polarizing issue that would realign voters in their favor, the Republican spokesmen would have to maneuver the Democrats into a position where their party would be perceived as procrime and proviolence. The Democrats were inadvertently helpful to the GOP at first. For years, as part of their appeal for governmental intervention to solve social problems, they had been predicting dire consequences if the government did not act. When the dire consequences did occur, their reaction was inevitably, "I told you so." When the flames went up from Hough in 1966, the response of Ohio's Democratic Senator Stephen M. Young was to demand "federal action on a large scale. . . . The housing program is too small. The poverty program is too small. The program for slum schools is too small. . . . It is clear that the elimination of slum misery will require new programs and much money."[20] "I could lead a mighty good revolt myself," said Vice-President Humphrey, if he and his family were "stuck on a fourth floor of a tenement with rats nibbling on the kids' toes—and they do—with garbage uncollected—and it is—with the streets filthy, with no swimming pools, with little or no recreation."[21] Humphrey was careful to disavow violence, but the Democratic tendency to blame black disorder not on the blacks but on society at large gave the Republicans the basis for charging their opponents with "condoning" and "encouraging" violence. Then the Johnson-appointed Kerner Commission made it official. Whites, not blacks, were at fault: "White racism is essentially responsible for the explosive mixture which has been accumulating in our cities."[22] When the 1968 Democratic convention met, television watchers could not help noting that a large

19. Press conference statement, Aug. 29, 1967, in "A Record of Press Conference Statements made by Senator Everett McKinley Dirksen and Representative Gerald R. Ford for the Republican Leadership of the Congress," S. Doc. 61, 90 Cong. 1 sess. (1967), p. 10. Brown and Carmichael were black leaders of the Student National Coordinating Committee (SNCC).

20. *Congressional Record*, Vol. 112 (July 26, 1966), p. 16246.

21. *New York Times*, July 19, 1966.

22. *Report of the National Advisory Commission on Civil Disorders* (New York Times Co./Bantam Books, 1968), p. 10. The commission was chaired by Democratic Governor Otto Kerner of Illinois.

segment of the 1968 Democratic convention had at least some sympathy with the unruly, unkempt youths who stench-bombed the party's headquarters hotel and taunted and provoked police. The Democrats had indeed responded to the sudden new crosscutting issue in the accustomed way of politicians—with a straddle. Sure, violence was bad, but there was good reason for it, too. The Democratic party by 1968 had been branded "soft" on the law and order issue, much as it had been branded "soft" on communism two decades earlier. Hubert Humphrey took a stern line in the campaign. "Rioting, burning, sniping, mugging, traffic in narcotics and disregard for the law are the advance guard of anarchy. They must—and they will—be stopped."[23] But the image of Chicago could not be erased.

For many of the TV viewers, the Republican party was too tame an alternative for a pusillanimous incumbent party. True, Nixon took the appropriate strong posture on crime and lawlessness and he achieved the appropriate symbolism in his choice of running mate: Spiro Agnew had first come to national attention through his forceful dressing down of Baltimore's black leadership after the riots there a short time before the convention. Yet Nixon was not Goldwater or Reagan, and the Republican party as a whole did not come through clearly on the social issue; Republican Mayor John Lindsay of New York City as a symbol was the direct opposite of Agnew— mayor of a city rife with disorder who identified himself with black demands even to the point of advocating a police review board. Yet he was the man who had nominated Agnew. So the "get-tough" advocates turned to the original polar leader of the race issue, now combined into the racial-social issue. By the end of September, the polls showed George Wallace with 21 percent of the total vote, 12 points higher than in April. On election day, his support had fallen to 13.5 percent, but this did not mean that public support of his strong stand on the social issue had fallen too; Nixon and Humphrey and their supporters hammered away with the "he can't win" argument, and Wallace as an individual lacked credibility as a potential president.[24] That Wallace's early strength grew out of the social issue is indicated by polling data. A Gallup poll in September showed that more than one in four voters thought Wallace was the candidate who "could do the best job in handling law and order," a vote of confidence higher than that accorded Humphrey.[25]

23. Speech to the American Legion National Convention, New Orleans, Sept. 11, 1968.
24. See Scammon and Wattenberg, *The Real Majority*, pp. 191–92, for an analysis of the Wallace falloff.
25. The responses were Nixon 36 percent, Wallace 26 percent, Humphrey 23 percent, not sure 15 percent. Ibid., p. 167.

In 1969, the social issue dominated a whole series of municipal elections
—Cleveland, where the city polarized between blacks and whites in re-
electing Mayor Carl Stokes (as it had done in Stokes's first election two
years earlier); Minneapolis, where Charles Stenvig, a policeman, was
elected mayor on a platform of "taking the handcuffs off the police"; in Los
Angeles, where Mayor Sam Yorty was reelected over a black opponent
whom Yorty accused of being "antipolice" and the candidate of "black militants and left-wing extremists"; in New York City, where Mayor Lindsay,
with his problack and pro–Puerto Rican image, lost the Republican nomination in the primary and got only 42 percent of the vote in a three-way final
election; in Buffalo, where Mrs. Alfred Slominski, the Republican nominee,
ran strongly as a law-and-order candidate; in Boston, where Mrs. Louise
Day Hicks ran a similar campaign; and in many other cities.[26]

CLIMAX OF THE SOCIAL ISSUE, 1970

The Republican leadership needed no more encouragement. Even before
the 1969 elections, President Nixon made the calculated decision to try to
polarize the country on the social issue, taking care, however, to separate
the social issue from the race issue and avoid any overt appeal to the "white
backlash." Agnew, designated the principal party spokesman in the 1970
national campaign, even used the word: what he sought, he said at the outset, was a "positive polarization" of the electorate.[27] At one pole would be
"the silent majority," to whom Nixon had appealed directly for support of
his Vietnam policy;[28] at the other, their enemies. In a series of major
speeches to party gatherings, Agnew defined the enemy. He called on his
majority to "mobilize" against youthful demonstrators, "misfits," indulgent
parents, "tomentose exhibitionists," campus "hellraisers" and their college
administrators, "permissivists," rioters, "thieves and traitors and perverts,"
"avowed anarchists and communists," "sunshine patriots" and "apologists

26. These interpretations of the 1969 municipal elections, as well as the quotations,
are taken largely from ibid., Chaps. 16–18.
27. Speech in Harrisburg, Pa., Oct. 30, 1969. In an October 1971 speech in El Paso,
Texas, Agnew observed that "dividing the American people has been my main contribution to the national political scene since assuming the office of vice president." He said,
"I not only plead guilty to this charge [as made by his enemies] but I am somewhat flat-
tered by it." Reuter dispatch from El Paso, printed in the *Washington Post*, Oct. 6, 1971.
28. Television address, Nov. 3, 1969. Nixon had signaled his approval of the Agnew
course on Oct. 30 when he said the vice-president was "doing a great job for the Administration." John Osborne, "Spiro Agnew's Mission," *New Republic* (Nov. 15, 1969), pp.
17–20.

for Hanoi," "professional pessimists," the "garbage" of society—whatever discordant element happened to be in the news on a particular day, along with the "elitists" in the television networks and selected newspapers, universities, and elsewhere who encouraged and glorified these elements. And above all, against the "radical liberals" running for office on the Democratic ticket who created the "permissive" climate that led to the breakdown of law and order.[29] Others picked up the Agnew theme. Democrats were just "posturing" on law and order, charged GOP National Chairman Rogers C. B. Morton, but "people won't be fooled. They know that Democrat permissiveness has contributed to crime, violence and campus unrest."[30] In the end, President Nixon personally entered the campaign to associate himself with Agnew's polarizing effort.

The effort failed. Far more of Agnew's "radical liberals" won than lost; indeed, few Democrats were clear casualties of the social issue. Senator Ralph Yarborough in Texas, certainly, but he was beaten in the Democratic primary and the winning Democrat, Lloyd Bentsen, went on to defeat Republican George Bush in November. Senator Albert Gore in Tennessee, probably, but Tennessee like Texas is in the South, where oratory on the social issue was most often heard, even if not expressed, as an echo of time-worn racial themes. In the North, Joseph Duffey, the Senate candidate in Connecticut, perhaps, but his was a complicated three-way race against Republican Lowell P. Weicker, Jr., and incumbent Democrat Thomas J. Dodd running as an independent. And that was all. The Democrats, despite the social issue, made a net gain of eleven governorships and twelve seats in the House while losing two in the Senate (in a year when most of the contested Senate seats were held by Democrats).

What is the explanation? It can only be that the social issue, like communism twenty years before, did not find major political groups taking distinct and opposing policy positions. As in the case of communism and Vietnam, all were on the same side. All were against crime. All were against disorder. And they vied with one another in advancing proposals to do something about these social evils.

Since 1968, the Democrats as a party had set themselves right on the social issue. Liberal Democrats (and Republicans) might still believe that

29. Quotations are from the Harrisburg speech and later Agnew speeches in Washington, May 4; Cleveland, June 20; San Diego, Sept. 12; Milwaukee, Sept. 25; and Belleville, Illinois, Oct. 30; as reported in various newspapers.

30. Washington, D.C., speech, Sept. 21, 1970, as reported in the Memphis *Press-Scimitar* and other newspapers.

Negro unrest as well as street crime could only be controlled through an attack on basic social ills, but they talked less and less about it. And while they praised housing and education and antipoverty programs, they were increasingly careful to praise crime suppression and riot control programs also. In 1968 the Democrats in the Congress manifested their good faith by hastily devising an Omnibus Crime Control and Safe Streets Act (analogous to the manner in which they showed their good faith by legislating anticommunist measures in an earlier era). The 1968 platform contained a long section on, if not "law and order," then "justice and law." The disorders at the 1968 convention set them back, but the Democrats were gradually making clear that there was no essential difference between the parties on crime and disorder. Fortunately for them, the wave of ghetto riots came to an end in 1968, and the campuses suddenly became calm as well. Republicans could still assert that they had had sharper vision on the issue from the beginning and hence could be trusted to combat crime with greater determination and efficiency, but they could not credibly claim to have a monopoly on commitment to the objective itself. Moreover, the polls suggest that the voters are ambivalent; at the same time that a majority wants toughness in putting down disorder, a majority also acknowledges the need to get at the social ills that plague the slums. The Democrats, once they corrected their image of "softness," may have struck closer to the general public view with their continuing advocacy of social measures than did the Republicans with their almost exclusive stress on law enforcement.

As the 1970 campaign began, Democratic candidates could avail themselves of a book-length lecture on the crucial importance of the social issue, concluding with some pointed advice to Democrats. Separate the race issue from the other aspects of the social issue, said Scammon and Wattenberg in *The Real Majority*. Continue to be problack but remember that blacks are injured more by crime, drugs, and violence than anybody else; so be as much against mugging and disruption and drugs as any Republican. Talk about "law and justice" but in no instance talk about justice or civil liberties or racism *without* talking about law.[31]

Whether the Democratic candidates of 1970 took their lesson from the book or from their own sensitive political antennae, the lesson was clearly learned. Democratic candidates in 1970 wore flags in their buttonholes, had their pictures taken inspecting police stations and shaking hands with the men in uniform, denounced the legalization of pornography, and advocated

31. See esp. pp. 274–76 and 284–89.

various legislative measures to aid the fight on crime. By October, according to a Louis Harris poll, the voters had just about as much confidence in the Democratic party as in the Republican party as an instrument for combating crime.[32] When Senator Edmund S. Muskie rasped his indignant *"How dare they?"* in his election eve telecast, the defense was credible.

After that, the social issue went into decline. True, some of the positions that George McGovern took in his preconvention campaign and some of the activities of his followers at the 1972 convention revived the issue sufficiently to give the Republicans their "three A's" slogan—"acid, amnesty, and abortion"—and contribute to Nixon's victory. But since the Democratic party retained or even increased its strength in the voting for other offices, it is clear that the social issue inflicted little damage on the party as a whole.

In short, a clear distinction between the parties on the social issue never did develop, despite the efforts of the GOP's "positive polarizers." They could place their own party squarely at one pole, but they could never find a way to drive their opposition to the other. In effect, the Democrats as a party beat a hurried retreat, only a step or two behind the Republicans, to the same pole. The major parties had yielded in something like unison to the forces demanding toughness on the law-and-order issue, and they remained together. The Democrats no doubt lost some adherents by their early show of sympathy for lawbreakers and by their association with the bearded young, and the Republicans lost some by their show of lack of sympathy for civil liberties, but the basis for a major realignment of the party system did not exist.

32. In answer to the question, "As far as the elections are concerned, who do you feel would do a better job on [cutting crime]—the Republicans or the Democrats?" the responses were: Republicans, 28 percent; Democrats, 25; neither, 22; not sure, 25. *Philadelphia Inquirer*, Oct. 15, 1970. An earlier Gallup poll showed comparable results. In response to the question, "Which party . . . do you think can do a better job of dealing with crime and lawlessness?" the responses were: Republicans, 24 percent; Democrats, 21; no difference, 44; no opinion, 11. American Institute of Public Opinion release, Feb. 4, 1970.

CHAPTER SIXTEEN

Current Trends in Party Strength

IF THE CROSSCUTTING ISSUES since the New Deal have not provided the impetus for any major realignment of the party system established in the 1930s, how much minor realignment has taken place? It was the Democratic party that was most disrupted by all four issues, and sometimes the opposing political forces at both poles were made up primarily of Democrats. Has there been any significant loss of Democratic strength as the result of all the turmoil? Is there an emerging Republican majority?

If one looks at comparative Democratic-Republican strength, the answer is, until 1972 at least, no. In registering to vote and in casting ballots for party candidates, the voter has shown no significant and sustained shift in favor of either party, as measured in aggregate national figures. The Democratic majority established in the 1930s appears to have survived communism, race, Vietnam, and the social issue virtually intact.

But if one looks at another set of statistics—public opinion polls, where a voter has the opportunity to describe himself as an independent instead of as a Democrat or Republican—quite a different picture appears. Between the mid-1960s, when the Vietnam, race, and social issues rose to their dominant position, and 1972, the Democratic party lost a substantial segment of its former strength to the independents, about five million voters. But so did the Republican party, about the same number. The loosening of party attachments all across the electorate and the movement of masses of voters from party identification to independence has been the most striking development within the party system in the past decade.

The Convergence of Party Strength

The distribution in the population of basic attitudes toward the aligning principle of the New Deal party system—activism versus conservatism in domestic policy, to state it in somewhat oversimplified terms—presumably does not differ greatly from region to region and from state to state. Some states and some metropolitan areas may have more conservatives, and some more activists, but an activist-conservative cleavage provides no basis for a one-party political system in any community whose population is distributed in near-normal proportions on the socioeconomic scale. And if the activist-conservative cleavage is somewhere near 50-50, any 70-30 or even 65-35 distribution in a particular community can only represent the persistence of old patterns protected by some artificial barrier against conformity with the national party system. As the barriers weaken, through the processes described in Chapters 11 and 12, each community can be expected to come to rest somewhere near the national average of party strength. In other words, communities that have been at the extremes will converge on the center. Trends having the character of what Key called "secular realignment" will appear in favor of the minority party wherever the distribution of party strength has been unbalanced.

Earlier chapters presented considerable data documenting the convergence toward the center of former Republican and Democratic one-party strongholds. But they can be summarized in a single chart, adapted from those in a book by Paul T. David, who grouped the states into three categories: those that were predominantly Republican during the 1896–1930 period, those that were predominantly Democratic, and those that were competitive. The trend for each of these three groups, employing his "Composite B" index,[1] is shown in Figure 16-1. The twelve Democratic states (the eleven Confederate states plus Arizona) showed a loss in Democratic strength from a high of over 90 percent in 1942 to 57.9 percent in 1970. The eighteen predominantly Republican states (northern and western, from Maine to California) showed a Democratic gain from a low of 39.9 in 1946 to an actual majority, 54.1 in 1958, followed by a decline to 47.1 in 1966 and a rise to 52.3 in 1970.[2] The eighteen competitive states (northern, western,

1. *Party Strength in the United States 1872–1970* (University Press of Virginia, 1972). The "Composite B" index gives equal weight to the vote for governor, U.S. senator, and U.S. representative. These votes are a better measure of basic party strength than the vote for president, which is more subject to deviational influences. See Chapter 11, pp. 233–35, above.

2. This group corresponds closely to the group of states identified in Chapter 11 as having realigned in two stages. Fourteen of the eighteen states in David's group are among the sixteen states listed in Table 11-1. The eighteen include New Hampshire, Illinois, Kansas, and Idaho, which are not in the table, and the table includes New Jersey and Nebraska, which David lists among the competitive states. The two-stage realignment discussed in Chapter 11 is clearly shown in Figure 16-1 in the line for the formerly Republican states.

Figure 16-1. *Convergence of Party Strength, as Shown in Democratic Proportion of Vote for Governor, U.S. Senator, and U.S. Representative, 1926–70*

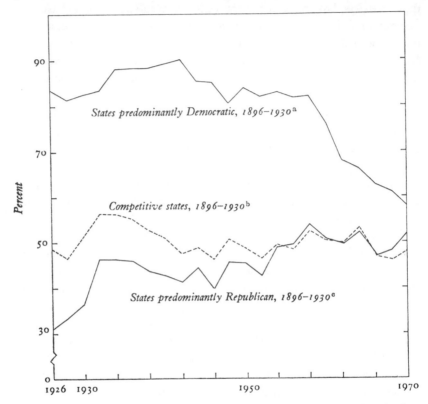

Source: Paul T. David, *Party Strength in the United States 1872–1970* (University Press of Virginia, 1972). Composite B index.

a. Alabama, Arizona, Arkansas, Florida, Georgia, Louisiana, Mississippi, North Carolina, South Carolina, Tennessee, Texas, Virginia.

b. California, Connecticut, Idaho, Illinois, Iowa, Kansas, Maine, Massachusetts, Michigan, Minnesota, New Hampshire, North Dakota, Oregon, Pennsylvania, South Dakota, Vermont, Washington, Wisconsin.

c. Colorado, Delaware, Indiana, Kentucky, Maryland, Missouri, Montana, Nebraska, Nevada, New Jersey, New Mexico, New York, Ohio, Oklahoma, Rhode Island, Utah, West Virginia, Wyoming.

and border) showed a postwar Democratic gain less sharply defined, from a low of 46.3 in 1946 to a high of 53.3, this time in 1964, followed by a drop to 46.3 in 1968 and a slight rebound, to 48.4, in 1970.

The sharpest movements, then, have been in the states with the deepest one-party tradition. The closer a party's strength is to zero in a state, as a general proposition, the stronger is its rebound toward the 50 percent level.

Logically, convergence should appear and be measurable within individual states as well as between groups of states. Some of the registration data referred to earlier suggest that this is the case. In New York (Figure 10-3), for instance, the postwar Democratic trend has been much more striking in Republican upstate New York than in Democratic New York City, and among the upstate counties the banner Democratic county, Albany, has become more Republican since 1946, countering the general upstate trend. In Pennsylvania (Figure 10-5) the one traditionally Democratic county charted, York, is the one that does not show great Democratic gains measured either from the 1920s or from the Democratic party's postwar low point. In West Virginia (Figure 10-4) the most Republican of the selected counties, Preston, has one of the strongest Democratic gains. A more detailed analysis of the county-by-county registration trends in these states would shed further light on the convergence phenomenon.

Convergence of two disparate sections of New Mexico has been analyzed by Jack E. Holmes.[3] While the traditionally Democratic "little Texas" area of that state has been moving toward the Republicans, the historically Republican Spanish-speaking counties have been shifting toward the Democrats. The steady drift of two Democratic rural counties of Indiana, Auglaise and Dubois, toward the Republican side, as measured by presidential balloting, has been charted by Key to illustrate his concept of secular realignment.[4]

A steady, secular shift in party strength like that reflected in the convergence phenomenon has to be compounded of three factors: (1) net conversion of voters from the majority to the minority party; (2) net effect of in-migration and out-migration; and (3) net effect of replacement of one generation of voters by another. Of these, the first may be the least important, since it is unlikely that a party attachment so firm that it cannot be upset during the critical phase of a realignment will be disturbed by the weaker influences that prevail later. Generational change is probably the most important.[5]

3. *Politics in New Mexico* (University of New Mexico Press, 1967).
4. V. O. Key, Jr., "Secular Realignment and the Party System," *Journal of Politics*, Vol. 21 (1959), pp. 205–06; and Key, *Politics, Parties and Pressure Groups* (4th ed., Crowell, 1958), p. 585.
5. Data from the University of Michigan's Survey Research Center show that voters who came of age during the Great Depression became, and remained, Democrats in far higher proportions than did their elders. While 57 percent of the voters who came of age

Insofar as convergence of Republican and Democratic states and counties is attributable, as most of it is, either to conversion or to generational change, it measures the weakening of the influence that geographical community and family have had on the political identification of voters. One might speculate that some of the other bases of traditional voting have been eroding at the same time, ʾand that similar charts tracing the political behavior of religious and ethnic groups, for example, might also show convergence toward the center. In these days of ecumenicity, religious differences have lost their sharpness, and the readiness of voters to follow the political lead of clergymen and lay church leaders has probably slackened too.[6] With upward so-

---

between 1921 and 1926 and who identified with a party in the 1950s called themselves Democrats, that party claimed 65 percent of those who reached voting age from 1931 to 1944 and 62 percent of those who came of age between 1945 and 1951. The generational change was bound to produce a large secular shift in the direction of the Democrats in the nation as a whole, as a generation 57 percent or less Democratic was giving way to one with a much higher proportion of Democrats. Angus Campbell and others, *The American Voter* (Wiley, 1960), pp. 153–56. The analysis covered 10,000 cases, combined from seven surveys made from 1952 to 1958. The authors conclude that a larger component of the long-term Democratic increase came from new voters (including not only young voters but older people who had previously failed to vote) than from party switchers. They also suggest (pp. 163–65) that the Republicans may enjoy the advantage of a secular drift as people age and move upward in the economic and social scale and that this drift might have been offsetting, in the 1950s, the advantage that the Democrats were then getting by continuing to attract a disproportionate share of new young voters.

Samuel Lubell's interviewing in the 1960s documents both the extent and the nature of party realignment through generational change. He found that one of every seven college students from Republican families was identifying with the Democrats (or with a party or political movement further to the left), while one of every eleven from Democratic families was turning to the Republicans. He found that "the most important" influence on those breaking from family tradition was their choice of careers; specifically, whether they identified with the public or private sector of the economy. The new Democrats were students from middle-class Republican families who planned careers as professors, researchers, or government workers, or in other jobs that involved "working with people." Often they were bitterly antibusiness. The new Republicans were students who had no quarrel with the competitive economic system and were planning business or professional careers. They were disproportionately from southern Democratic families. Thirty years after the New Deal, then, the new generation was aligning on the basis of attitudes regarding governmental intervention in the economy, just as when the New Deal party system was established. Lubell, *The Hidden Crisis in American Politics* (Norton, 1970), pp. 191–93, 211–13. The politically undecided also tended to be the vocationally undecided.

David Butler and Donald E. Stokes have traced a similar process by which generational change is working to extend the class alignment of British politics that was established during the realignment in which the Labour party replaced the Liberals as a major party. The extension occurs as children of working-class parents who have retained traditional ties with the Conservative party identify with Labour. *Political Change in Britain: Forces Shaping Electoral Choice* (St. Martin's, 1969), pp. 110–11.

6. Of Lubell's college student inverviewees, one-half termed themselves "not religious" but only one-fifth described their parents that way. *Hidden Crisis*, pp. 209–10.

cial and economic mobility, intermarriage, and the movement from ethnic neighborhoods to heterogeneous suburbs, some Irishmen may feel less Irish, Jews less Jewish, Poles less Polish, and so on. The candidacy of Dwight Eisenhower made the Republican party respectable for voters of staunchly Democratic ethnic groups, just as it did for southerners. The importance of patronage distributed to minorities on the basis of their political loyalties has also waned. So political attitudes are less apt to be based on ethnic and religious identity. (However, in at least one major ethnic group, the blacks, group identity has intensified in recent years, and so they have been, predictably, the one ethnic group that has shown a strengthening of identity with party, in their case the Democrats.) With the upward mobility of immigrant groups, white Anglo-Saxon Protestants too may feel their WASPishness— or nativism—less. Perhaps the clincher for them was the election of the first non-Protestant president, John Kennedy, who made voting for a Catholic (and, by extension, a Jew or a black) acceptable. To the extent that the American melting pot has served the purpose of blending populations of diverse origins, then, it has served also to erode some of the bonds that have traditionally tied people to parties.

A Competitive Party Balance

Figure 16-1 offers no persuasive evidence that the major crosscutting issues of the postwar period, particularly those of the last half of the 1960s, had much effect on basic party strength.

While the South shows a continuing decline in the Democratic vote in the late 1960s, the decline was slower than in the earlier period, particularly 1958–62, before the new issues had developed. The index line for that region in the last half-dozen years appears simply as a continuation of the general convergence trend of the post–New Deal period.

One group of northern states—the eighteen that were predominantly Republican before 1930—showed greater Democratic strength in 1970 than at any previous time except in the party's peak years, 1958 and 1964. The second-stage realignment during the 1950s in these states has clearly been sustained, with no subsequent realignment evident in the opposite direction.

The other group of northern states—the eighteen that were competitive before 1930—does show a Democratic falloff between 1964 and 1966 that was not recouped by 1970. How much of this decline is due to the new issues and how much to temporary and cyclical factors is a matter for conjecture. If the 1964–70 decline represents a minor realignment, it balances a minor pro-Democratic realignment in the 1950s and in 1964 and returns the party balance to what it was before.[7] On the other hand, the Democratic strength between 1958 and 1964 may have been essentially a deviation based on the two unusually favorable Democratic years that began and ended that period. In any case, the Democratic strength remained stable during the 1966–70 period when the crosscutting issues were being exploited most vigorously.

What stands out in Figure 16-1 is not change but continuity. By far the most significant factor affecting the shifts in party strength throughout the postwar period has been convergence. This is further borne out by another glance at the charts of party registration figures in Chapter 10. In the five northern states for which figures are available (New York, Pennsylvania, West Virginia, California, and Oregon), the long-term postwar Democratic trend may have slowed or even stalled in some places during the late 1960s, but there is no sign of reversal.

In Oregon (Figure 10-6) the Democratic lines in all of the counties charted still tilt upward through 1970. In West Virginia (Figure 10-4) the Democratic trend continued into 1970 in some counties but lost force in others. In California (Figure 10-7) the mid-1960s do not appear as a turning point; the trend lines run in the same direction as in the previous period, some favoring the Republicans, some the Democrats. In upstate New York (Figure 10-3) the impressive shift to the Democrats of the 1958–64 period (a 9-point rise, from 31 to 40 percent) leveled off, but it leveled off near the peak Democratic percentage of the 1964 Goldwater year. In the Pennsylvania counties shown in Figure 10-5, the Democratic trend came to a halt in

7. Evidence suggesting that the 1960s saw significant realignment in both directions, much of which would be concealed in the aggregate figures, is offered in a recent article by Gerald Pomper, "From Confusion to Clarity: Issues and American Voters, 1956–1968," *American Political Science Review*, Vol. 66 (1972), pp. 415–28. During the 1960s, and particularly in 1964, Survey Research Center data show that the voters "did align their partisan loyalties far closer to their policy preferences" on a series of domestic issues involving the role of government. Voters favoring the activist, or "liberal," position on aid to education, medical care, job guarantees, fair employment, and school integration identified more consistently with the Democratic party (and conservatives with the Republican party) in 1964 and 1968 than they did in 1956 or 1960. During the same period the proportion of the electorate who perceived differences between the parties on these issues increased. Pomper suggests that the readjustment of party loyalties in 1964 was sufficiently sharp to warrant classifying that year's election as a "critical election" (p. 425). In any event, the effect of 1964 was to accelerate the convergence trend by stimulating the conformance of individual party identification to the national party rationale established by the critical elections of the 1930s—not to upset the trend. And it was to reinforce the existing alignment of the party system rather than to alter it.

1962, but that was the year the governorship passed from Democratic to Republican hands; as noted in Chapter 11, Pennsylvania registration figures respond to party political fortunes, especially at the state level where large patronage rewards are controlled. In the case of two of the counties charted, Philadelphia and Westmoreland, the Democratic trend resumed after 1968.[8] As in the other four northern states, there is little evidence in the Pennsylvania figures to indicate that the issues of the middle and late 1960s have caused any significant shift in strength from the Democrats to the Republicans.

Moreover, if the Democratic trend had approached or exceeded the 50 percent level when it slowed or stalled (as is the case in most of the counties where a slowdown appears to have occurred), the leveling off does not in itself indicate a reaction against the Democratic party. An end to the Democratic trend by the late 1960s or even earlier would be the entirely natural consequence of convergence. For the secular realignment set in motion by the upheaval of the 1930s could hardly go on forever. At some point, the crossing of party lines would be finished, the Republican party would be reduced to those who belonged there by virtue of their attitudes and principles, and the realignment would have run its course.

Figure 16-1 suggests that this ultimate outcome of the long-term convergence trend may be close at hand. In both groups of northern states (the formerly Republican and formerly competitive), the party balance reached 50-50 by 1954 and has hovered within a few percentage points of that line ever since. In formerly Democratic states (the South plus Arizona) it is below 60 percent and will undoubtedly continue downward.[9] When it

8. Philadelphia political observers attribute the rise in Democratic registration there to the switching of Italian-Americans who wished to support Frank L. Rizzo, elected mayor in 1971, in the bitterly contested Democratic primary of that year.

9. When the index for 1972 is compiled, it will almost surely show a continuance of the decline of Democratic strength in the states classified as formerly predominantly Democratic, for the party's losses were concentrated there. The party lost to the Republicans one governorship (North Carolina), two Senate seats (North Carolina and Virginia), and a net of five House seats. Of the GOP's net gain of thirteen House seats in the nation, eight were in the states formerly predominantly Democratic. (The difference between the Republican gain and the Democratic loss is accounted for by the net Republican gain of three seats through reapportionment.)

The 1972 trend in the other two groups of states is not so readily apparent, but it seems probable that the Democrats suffered no heavy loss of strength despite the Nixon landslide. They had a net gain of two governorships (winning in Delaware, Illinois, and Vermont while losing in Missouri) and four Senate seats (winning in Colorado, Delaware, Iowa, Kentucky, Maine, and South Dakota while losing in New Mexico and Oklahoma); and a net loss of eight House seats (five to the Republicans, three to reapportionment).

reaches the 50 percent mark, a leveling off can perhaps be expected. At that point, the whole nation will be in a system of competitive politics in a roughly uniform pattern with an approximately equal balance between the parties. The regional distortions embedded in the party system in the 1850s, solidified by the Civil War, and exaggerated by the realignment of the 1890s will have finally been eliminated. The party system will have been nationalized and aligned on the basis of issues of the twentieth rather than the nineteenth century.

Alienation and Independence

But the relationship between a political party and the electorate has another dimension—depth. The Democratic party may get as high a proportion of the total vote in the 1970s as it did in the 1940s yet still be significantly weaker, *if the voters who ultimately support it are less firmly attached to the party.* And it is in this dimension that the Democratic and Republican parties have both lost ground in recent years, particularly in the 1960s. Voters have been deserting the major parties by the millions in favor of independent political attitudes and behavior. A far greater number call themselves independents than ever before in the thirty-five years of polling. On election day, they split their tickets with far greater abandon than at any time in the country's history.

The magnitude and sharpness of the trend toward political independence has led politicians and students to ponder whether the party system is undergoing a different kind of transformation—not just a realignment of its constituent elements, like those of the past, but a decay of the system itself. So the journalist David S. Broder entitles a 1972 book *The Party's Over*,[10] and the political scientist Walter Dean Burnham subtitles a chapter of a 1970 book "The Onward March of Party Decomposition."[11] Any analysis of where the American party system is heading must include the possibility that it is heading into oblivion.

The evidence of the growth of independent politics is readily available from two sources: electoral behavior and public opinion polls. Interpretation of the evidence is not so simple.

10. Harper and Row. Broder explains (p. xvi) that the title is not a prophecy or a wish but an expression of alarm at the erosion of party loyalties that has already occurred.
11. *Critical Elections and the Mainsprings of American Politics* (Norton, 1970).

THE RISE OF TICKET-SPLITTING

The electoral expression of independent politics is ticket-splitting. This is well illustrated by the behavior of Arkansas in 1968, when the state's voters elected a Republican governor (Winthrop Rockefeller) and a Democratic senator (J. William Fulbright), while giving their electoral votes to a third-party candidate for president (George C. Wallace). Or by the results in 1970, when every one of the half dozen largest northern states that elected a governor and a senator chose men of different parties for the two offices. California, Michigan, and Massachusetts elected Republican governors and Democratic senators; Pennsylvania and Ohio, Democratic governors and Republican senators; New York, a Republican governor and a senator running on the Conservative ticket. For the first time since 1934 two senators who were not the candidates of either major party were elected— James L. Buckley, the New York Conservative, and Harry F. Byrd, Jr., elected as an independent in Virginia.[12] The latter state—until only a few years ago noted for the monolithic discipline of its dominant Democratic party—repeated its eccentric behavior the following year by electing another independent, Henry Howell, as lieutenant governor. In 1972 only one (North Carolina) of the twelve states that voted for governor, senator, and president favored the candidate of the same party for all three offices—a degree of consistency only one-third of what would be expected if the voters made their choices entirely on a random basis. In only six of the twelve did the voters select governors and senators of the same party—exactly what would be the normal expectation in a situation of random behavior.

Burnham has assembled a mass of statistical evidence from election returns to illustrate his thesis of "party decomposition."[13] In 1964, for example, one of every three congressional districts in the nation gave majority support to presidential and congressional candidates of different parties, far higher than the 1.6 percent in 1904, 3.2 percent in 1920, and 14.1 percent in 1932 and 1936—other years of landslide victories. As Burnham points out, in the nineteenth and early twentieth centuries a presidential candidate who lost by a wide margin would drag his party down to disaster in the House of Representatives, but in 1964 the voters seemed to go out of their way to pre-

12. In the Senate, Buckley calls himself a conservative Republican and has full standing in the Republican caucus. Byrd calls himself an independent but has retained the seniority as a member of the majority Democratic party that he earned in his first term as a Democrat.

13. *Critical Elections*, pp. 106–19.

serve anti-Goldwater Republican congressmen. Split decisions amounted to
31.7 percent in 1968, a year of three-party competition; but in the year of
the strongest third-party movement of the century, 1912, split decisions
were 25 percent, and in another third-party year, 1924, only 12 percent.
When comparable data are compiled for the 1972 election, they will undoubtedly show a proportion of split decisions even higher than 1964.

A comparable analysis of split outcomes in gubernatorial and senatorial
elections between 1914 and 1970, made by Howard Reiter, shows the same
trend. In each of the five most recent elections in his series, from 1962
through 1970, more than 44 percent of the states electing both a governor
and a senator split their choices between the parties (and 1972, with 50 percent, becomes the sixth in his series). Only once in the twenty-four election
years from 1914 to 1960 had the proportion exceeded 28 percent.[14]

Looking at election return series for five states, Burnham found the tradition of straight-ticket voting preserved only in Indiana, where the job-
oriented political culture of the nineteenth century is also uniquely preserved. In his other four states—Massachusetts, Rhode Island, Michigan,
and Wisconsin—he found a startling rise in ticket-splitting, as measured by
the variance in percentage of votes cast for candidates of the same party for
different offices, with most of the increase again occurring (except in Wisconsin) in the 1960s. In Massachusetts in 1966, as an extreme case, the
Democratic percentage of the two-party vote ranged from 37.1 percent for
the gubernatorial candidate to 70.7 percent for the candidate for secretary
of the commonwealth. In such an election, Burnham noted, "Party identification in the electorate obviously counts for very little in general-election
results."[15] In that year, the University of Michigan's Survey Research Center reported that only 50 percent of its respondents identified themselves as
straight-ticket voters in state and local elections, although 73 percent had so
identified as late as 1960.

THE GROWTH IN INDEPENDENT ATTITUDES

If ticket-splitting represents a rise in independent attitudes, one would
expect to find those attitudes reflected in voters' self-identification when re-

14. In Walter De Vries and Lance Tarrance, Jr., *The Ticket-Splitter: A New Force in
American Politics* (Eerdmans, 1972), p. 31. The one year exceeding 28 percent was 1940,
when the figure was 42.3 percent.
15. *Critical Elections*, pp. 117–18, n. 26.

sponding to survey questions about party preference. The polls can give the voter more choices than he is usually given on the ballot. When asked his preference between the major parties, a respondent can call down a plague on both their houses. And increasingly, this is what he has been doing.

The upper panel of Figure 16-2 summarizes the responses to the question asked regularly since 1952 by the Survey Research Center (SRC) of the University of Michigan: "Generally speaking, do you usually think of yourself as a Republican, a Democrat, an Independent, or what?" The lower panel presents the responses obtained in the same period by the American Institute of Public Opinion (Gallup) to a corresponding question: "In politics, as of today, do you consider yourself a Republican, Democrat, or Independent?" Both polls show an impressive rise in the 1960s in the proportion of voters describing themselves as independent. They differ slightly in the timing of the independent movement: the SRC's 11-point rise in the proportion of independents begins from a low point in 1958 and was still continuing in 1970, while the Gallup rise takes off from a 1960 low and climbs by more than 9 points to a peak in 1968. These minor differences are within the margin of sampling error, but the upward trend that the two sets of polls mutually corroborate is large enough to be significant and has been sustained long enough to be judged more than an aberration. The increase in the percentage of eligible voters calling themselves independents is equivalent to something like ten million actual voters.[16]

The two polling organizations also agree on the general trend lines of the two major parties and hence on the magnitude and timing of their respective losses to the independents. During the first half of the period (through 1964), when independent voting was on the rise, the independent gains were wholly at the expense of the Republicans, and the Democrats apparently also profited from the Republican decline. But the Democrats' peak came in 1964, and then they had their turn on the toboggan, with an even steeper downhill slide. After 1964, the independent gains were predominantly or wholly from the Democrats, and by 1970 the party's strength was, in both polls, 6 percentage points below the peak.[17] The Democratic losses after 1964 were

16. The newer Louis Harris poll, which asks its question in a somewhat different form, comes up with a much smaller, but also rising, proportion of independents: 17 percent in 1968, 19 in 1970, and 23 in May 1971. Everett C. Ladd, Jr. (*American Political Parties: Social Change and Political Response* [Norton, 1970], p. 232) charts the Gallup results since 1937.

17. As suggested in note 7, referring to Pomper's findings, the Democratic gains and losses were probably made up of different persons for the most part, reflecting some minor realignment centering on 1964.

Figure 16-2. *Party Identification of the Electorate, According to Two Public Opinion Surveys, 1952–70*[a]

A. *Survey Research Center data*[b]

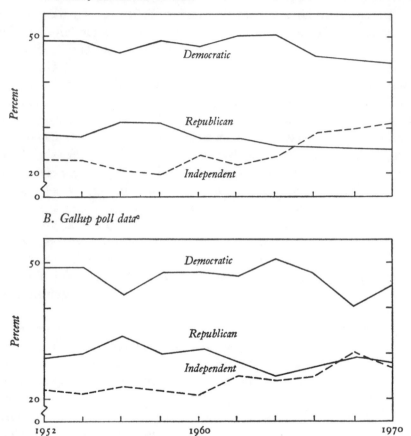

B. *Gallup poll data*[c]

Sources: Top panel, University of Michigan, Survey Research Center, Ann Arbor, Mich. Bottom panel, American Institute of Public Opinion, Princeton, N.J.

a. Plotted biennially. All figures exclude those who failed to respond to the question or who gave an answer classified as "apolitical," "don't know," or "other party."

b. Each entry based on election survey taken in October or November, except 1956, which averages two surveys in April and October; 1962, which averages two in May and November; and 1964, which averages three in January, May, and October.

c. Each entry based on the average of three surveys taken during calendar year, except 1970 figures, which average polls taken in October 1970 and April and October 1971.

about equal to the Republican losses before 1964 in both polls, and the aggregate gain of the independents over the whole period was therefore about evenly divided between the major parties. Since the Republicans started their slide from a lower base, however, they lost a higher proportion of their support than did the Democrats.

It will be noted that the trend lines of party strength as measured by the polls, particularly the more volatile Gallup poll,[18] correspond to the trend lines of party strength as reflected in the election returns. From this it can probably be inferred that the factors that brought about election losses for the Republicans in the 1958–64 period and for the Democrats in 1966 and 1968 were the same factors that drove people out of the major parties into the independent ranks. In other words, the loss of confidence in Republican economic policies in the recession-plagued late 1950s and the nomination of the unpopular Barry Goldwater caused about five million Republican voters not just to deviate, as they might have done in other years, but to leave the Republican party for good. After 1964, the debacle of Lyndon Johnson's later years in office—riots, Vietnam, inflation—caused a similar exodus of Democrats. By 1970, according to the SRC data, neither party had begun to recoup its losses; according to the Gallup poll, each had made a partial comeback. But the outstanding features of the 1972 political season—the heavy deviation at the presidential level and the extraordinarily high degree of ticket-splitting—lead one to expect that when party identification data for that period become available they will show, if anything, a further increase in the proportion of independents.

WHO ARE THE NEW INDEPENDENTS?

An analysis of who made up that ten-million-eligible-voter exodus from the major parties in the 1960s may give some clues not only to their motiva-

---

18. Perhaps the greater volatility of the Gallup poll trend lines is attributable, at least in part, to the slight difference in the wording of the question. The Gallup pollsters ask the respondents their party preference "as of today," while the SRC asks for a preference "generally speaking." A deviant voter would be encouraged by the former wording to express his *current* attitude and by the latter to report his *general* outlook over a longer period. A southern Wallace voter, for example, asked in 1968 his position "as of today," might call himself an independent (Gallup reported that more than half the southern Wallace voters that year so classified themselves), but asked his *general* party identification might term himself a Democrat. Whether or not this is the explanation, the Gallup poll reflects much more strongly than does the SRC the deviant voting for Eisenhower in 1956 and for Johnson in 1964, and the independent (presumably Wallace) preference of 1968.

tion but also to whether the major parties will be able to win them back. A comparison of the party identifications of various population groups at the beginning and end of the decade, as reported in two Survey Research Center polls, provides some indication of who the ten million defectors were. The principal findings are given in Table 16-1.

The first thing that stands out in an analysis of the makeup of the two blocks of independent voters is that the increase was entirely attributable to whites (section 2 of the table). Indeed, the white exodus from the major parties was greater than the net movement of both races, for the decade saw a pronounced solidification of party attachment on the part of black voters. Even though the samples of black voters are small, the swing shown is of sufficient magnitude to confirm the evidence from the election returns and from political observers that the Democratic party solidified its hold on the black segment of the electorate during the Kennedy and Johnson years. The remainder of this analysis will therefore disregard the blacks and attempt to further identify the white voters who are the new independents.

A comparison of the two surveys shows the Democrats-turned-independents as being mainly in the alienated South (section 3 of the table). Whatever loss the Democrats suffered among some voting groups in the North and West is offset by a corresponding gain in others, leaving their hold on 39 percent of white voters outside the South unchanged. The growth in independent political attitudes in the South is entirely among those opposed to government action to enforce school integration, or without an opinion (section 4 of the table). Southern integrationists show no increase in independent voting.

Another group can be identified among the Democrats-turned-independents. The proportion of independents among Catholic voters rose in the decade from 18 to 30 percent, all at the expense of the Democrats (section 5). Since relatively few Catholics live in the South, the defection of that religious group appears to account for a large share of total Democratic losses in the North and West.

People over forty were virtually undisturbed in their party allegiance by the turmoil of the 1960s. But many younger voters were detached or reluctant to form any allegiance at all. Since polling began, younger voters have invariably shown looser party ties than their elders,[19] and this is still the

19. See, for example, the tabulations of various Gallup and SRC polls in Everett C. Ladd, Jr., Charles Hadley, Lauriston King, "A New Political Realignment?" *The Public Interest*, No. 23 (Spring 1971), pp. 60–61.

case in our 1960 and 1970 samples. But the significant fact is that, apparently for the first time, individual voters as they have gotten older have actually shown a weakening of party attachment rather than the usual solidification. Thus 26 percent of the voters who were in their twenties in the 1960s, as shown in section 6 of the table, were independents then, but the proportion had risen to 40 percent ten years later, when they were in their thirties. The proportion of independents in the group that was between thirty and forty in 1960 increased from 24 to 34 percent. Only those over forty maintained the same proportion of party identification. Each age group shows a greater proportion of independent voters than the corresponding age group a decade earlier, and the disparity in the younger age brackets is especially high. And among college students the proportion of independents is even higher. Two Gallup polls in 1969 and 1970 each put the figure at 52 percent.

While the Republican losses are distributed among all regions (see section 3 of the table), they are most heavily concentrated in the Northeast, which has also been the region of the GOP's most conspicuous electoral decline, especially in 1964, the Goldwater year. (Seven northeastern states are among the fifteen where the Republican proportion of the total major party vote for president declined by more than 15 points between 1960 and 1964.) The Republican loss of party identifiers in the South contradicts the sharp GOP gains in state and local elections (if the total sample, rather than the white component, is used, the Republican loss is even greater, 5 percentage points instead of 3). The contradiction confirms the evidence of other polls, summarized in Chapter 12, that most of the new GOP voters in the South still have not crossed the realignment threshold. As noted, in their own eyes they are only "independents," not yet "Republicans."

The Republicans-turned-independents are less easily identified than the former Democrats. But an examination of the many categories of voters into which the SRC respondents can be divided reveals three groups where independent gains of more than ten points have been made preponderantly or wholly at the expense of the GOP. These groups are identified by place of residence, education, and social class (sections 7, 8, and 9).

The figures show heavy Republican losses in the suburbs of the country's largest cities, among the college educated, and among voters who consider themselves middle class. If these data are combined with those from the other sections, the prototypical Republican-turned-independent can be described. He or she is a young, middle-class, college-educated, Protestant suburbanite in a large metropolitan area of the Northeast who left the party

Table 16-1. Changes in Political Affiliation of Various Population Groups, 1960 and 1970

Identification of group	1960[a]				1970[a]				Change[a]		
	N	D	R	I	N	D	R	I	D	R	I
1. Gross shift in party identification											
All voters	1,864	46	30	23	1,490	44	25	31	−2	−5	8
2. All voters, by race											
Whites	1,700	46	31	23	1,324	40	27	33	−6	−4	10
Blacks	147	50	19	31	144	78	4	18	28	−15	−13
3. Whites, by region											
South	542	61	21	18	430	44	18	38	−17	−3	20
Rest of country	1,158	39	36	25	894	39	31	30	0	−5	5
Northeast	(431)	(37)	(39)	(24)	(299)	(35)	(31)	(34)	(−2)	(−8)	(10)
Midwest	(476)	(36)	(38)	(26)	(390)	(38)	(33)	(29)	(2)	(−5)	(3)
West	(251)	(47)	(28)	(25)	(205)	(46)	(26)	(28)	(−1)	(−2)	(3)
4. Southern whites, by attitude on school integration issue[b]											
For integration	118	53	20	27	114	47	26	26	−6	6	−1
Against government action to enforce integration	332	65	22	13	204	46	19	35	−19	−3	22
Not sure, no opinion	92	58	19	23	80	38	13	50	−20	−6	26
5. Whites, by religious affiliation											
Protestants	1,170	39	38	23	912	37	32	31	−2	−6	8
Catholics	335	64	18	18	270	52	18	30	−12	0	12
Jews	57	61	9	30	42	55	5	40	−6	−4	10
6. Whites, by age group											
20–29	228	45	29	26	277	36	19	45	−9	−10	19
30–39	384	49	27	24	239	33	27	40	−16	0	16
40–49	384	46	29	25	241	42	24	34	−4	−5	9
50 and over	704	45	36	19	567	45	32	23	0	−4	4

7. *Whites, by place of residence*

	N				N						
Central cities in 12 largest metropolitan areas	*186*	54	22	24	*106*	52	25	23	−2	3	−1
Suburbs of 12 largest metropolitan areas	*212*	32	44	24	*218*	39	26	35	7	−18	11
Other cities (over 2,500)	*628*	48	31	21	*558*	38	28	34	−10	−3	13
Rural	*554*	49	28	23	*442*	41	27	32	−8	−1	9

8. *Whites, by education*

	N				N						
Some college	*392*	33	46	21	*352*	32	34	34	−1	−12	13
No college	*1,307*	50	27	23	*968*	43	24	33	−7	−3	10

9. *Whites, by social class[c]*

	N				N						
Working class	*1,047*	51	26	23	*655*	44	22	34	−7	−4	11
Middle class	*595*	37	42	21	*627*	37	31	32	0	−11	11

Source: University of Michigan, Survey Research Center, 1960 and 1970 polls. Percentages may not add to 100 because of rounding.

a. N = number of respondents. The apolitical, "don't know," "no answer," and other-party respondents are excluded. They amounted to 4.6 percent of the 1960 sample and 1.1 percent of the 1970 sample. The number of respondents in the different sections of the table are further reduced by eliminating those who did not respond to particular questions or whose responses were not recorded, as well as by those (as in sections 2 and 5) who would be classed as "other."

D = Democrat; R = Republican; I = independent. The numbers under each of these designations are percentages of the number of respondents in the same line.

b. The 1960 survey asked whether the respondent agreed or disagreed with the proposition: "The government in Washington should stay out of the question of whether white and colored children go to the same school." A "disagree" answer is classified as pro-integration. The 1970 question was: "Do you think the government in Washington should: see to it that white and Negro children are allowed to go to the same schools or stay out of this area as it is not its business?"

c. As self-identified.

sometime between 1960 and 1964. Along with southern segregationists and northern Catholic former Democrats, northern suburbanite Protestant former Republicans take their place as a third identifiable, substantial element among the ten million new independent voters who appeared in the 1960s.

The movement of all three groups again illustrates the principle of convergence discussed earlier. Over the years each of these three groups has been an anchor of one of the major parties, tied to it by bonds of regional patriotism, of family-community tradition, of class consciousness, of religious or ethnic group identity. With the fraying of some or all of those bonds at an accelerating pace in the postwar years, younger voters in particular have been set free from the party allegiances of the past. Many of these younger voters, who belong to a mobile, better-traveled, better-educated generation, have simply not formed the traditional allegiances at all.

So a growing body of millions of voters remains independent, detached, atomistic, floating. Even among those who do identify with party, the ties have weakened.[20] Party members as well as independents split their tickets with increasing freedom. "I vote for the man, not the party" has become the political norm. David Broder and Haynes Johnson of the *Washington Post* in interviewing voters in twenty precincts around the country in 1970 "found it rare to encounter a voter—anywhere—who thinks of politics in terms of political parties."[21]

LONG-TERM AND SHORT-TERM INFLUENCES

Burnham suggests that what has happened since the 1950s, and especially since the mid-1960s, is merely the latest phase in "a secular trend toward the gradual disappearance of the political party in the United States,"[22] which he dates from about the turn of the century. Certainly, at the time of the progressive movement, the political party was in disrepute. The muckrakers condemned it. Political reformers rose up against the party bosses. Many of

---

20. This conclusion is supported not only by the data on ticket-splitting but by a more refined analysis of the Survey Research Center data. The SRC asks each person who identifies himself as a party member, "Would you call yourself a strong (R) (D) or a not very strong (R) (D)?" From 1952 to 1962 the proportion of strong party members in the electorate remained stable, at about 36 percent; by 1968 it had dropped to 30 percent and by 1970 to 29. Those who identify themselves as independents are asked, "Do you think of yourself as closer to the Republican or Democratic party?" In 1952, only 5 percent denied any leaning toward either party; by 1966, that figure had risen to 12 percent and by 1970 to 13.

21. *Washington Post*, Oct. 9, 1970.

22. *Critical Elections*, p. 133.

the reforms they espoused were deliberately designed to weaken the "political machines" of the times; others, if not so intended, had that effect. Ballot reform not only substituted government-printed for party-printed ballots, but often arranged the new ballots in such a way as to discourage straight-ticket voting. The reformers undermined the party machines by instituting nonpartisan elections or through creating local independent parties. They steadily replaced patronage with civil service, which served the dual purpose of improving administration and weakening the party organizations. Civic groups like the League of Women Voters spread the gospel that it is the "independent" voter who is the watchdog of the political system; it is he or she who holds the balance of power between two more-or-less corrupt party organizations and who should wield it to put into office whichever party may be the lesser of the evils. This doctrine found its way into high school civics courses. At the same time, the party newspapers characteristic of the nineteenth century gave way to the independent press that prevails today. Rare, nowadays, is the metropolitan newspaper that endorses a party slate without deviation; a self-respecting editor feels obliged to advise his readers to split their tickets. The same is true of "good government" groups, ethnic political associations, farm organizations, and even many labor unions. All these influences toward independent politics have had their greatest influence on the more highly educated and economically secure, and the proportion of these citizens has been rising constantly.[23]

With the realignment of the 1930s the parties became more salient, but not to the degree of the nineteenth century. The "march of party decomposition" resumed in the 1950s. By this time, public assistance programs had largely superseded the parties' welfare activities, and rising pay levels and greater job security in the private economy had lowered the value of their remaining patronage jobs. Then came a revolution in political campaign techniques that helped to rob the party of one of its basic functions—the organization and management of campaigns. Television became, almost overnight, the principal channel of communication between the candidate and the voter. While a party structure might have been needed to stage rallies and torchlight parades and to distribute literature from door to door, for television one needed not political organizers but film makers and advertising specialists. Candidate-marketing firms sprang up and began to crowd the tradi-

---

23. The proportion of ticket-splitters is always higher among better-educated, higher-income, and higher-occupational-status groups. See De Vries and Tarrance, *Ticket-Splitter*, esp. Chap. 3.

tional party organizations out of campaign management. And professional fund raisers appeared also, to challenge the role of the party as an organization for campaign financing. They discovered that contributors would rather give to a candidate than to a party anyway.

The party organization lost control not just of campaigning but of the candidate selection process. As the voter lost touch with the party organizations, aspirants for office came to ignore it. Money, media, and marketing could build a political following for an ambitious unknown in the same way and about as quickly as they could build sales for a new deodorant. Rich men, or men with access to money, could defy the established political organizations and win the party nominations. In 1970, Democrat Milton J. Shapp, through a media campaign, defeated one of the most deeply entrenched political organizations in the country to become governor of Pennsylvania. In 1972, the most powerful old-style machine of all, Mayor Richard J. Daley's Chicago Democratic organization, failed for the first time to control the Illinois party nominations. Some state and local party organizations ceased to even try to influence the party nominating process.

The long-term trends are surely irreversible: the old-fashioned closed political system is not going to be reestablished, old-style bosses restored to power, media campaigning outlawed, or the levels of affluence and education that make for independent politics reduced. Nevertheless, it is easy to overestimate the degree of change. Insurgents found ways to beat party organizations long before television was invented. The whole progressive movement grew by toppling one entrenched machine after another. Robert La Follette, Sr., and Ben Tillman and Hiram Johnson were able to create powerful personal political organizations even before the days of radio. And George McGovern's success in winning the Democratic presidential nomination in 1972, which was attributed more to superb organization than to superior use of the media, shows that even in the age of television meticulous old-style organization in the precincts is still important, although it may have to be done by new-style people.

If the indicators show a phenomenal growth in ticket-splitting and rejection of the major parties in the 1960s, so do they show a remarkable stability until about a dozen years ago. If there was a long-term trend toward party decomposition before the middle or late 1950s, it was so slow as to be at times imperceptible. The party identification data from the polls show nothing like a gradual, steady increase in the proportion of independents; rather they show an essentially level line until the upheaval of the 1960s. Even

Burnham's analysis covering ninety years of ticket-splitting in five states shows no increase in one state, Indiana; less ticket-splitting in Michigan in the 1950s than in any decade in this century; and less in Wisconsin in the 1950s than in any decade since 1910. Rhode Island showed very little ticket-splitting before 1956. Only Massachusetts, among the five states, displayed a clear secular trend. Even if one concedes the existence of long-term influences, the sharp, abrupt departures from party regularity that marked the 1960s have to be explained by short-term factors.

The nature of these factors has been suggested. The rise in independent attitudes in the 1960s coincided with the rise to a dominant position of the three powerful and related issues detailed in Chapter 15—race, Vietnam, and the social issue. By cutting across the existing line of party cleavage, these issues blurred the distinction between the major parties and created polar forces that found no satisfactory expression through those parties. Identifying the population groups most affected by the new crosscutting issues also indentifies a large proportion of the added millions of voters shown in Table 16-1 who are rejecting the major parties and calling themselves independents. One group of new independents is the young, the group most alienated by Vietnam. Another consists of southern segregationists, the group most stirred by the race issue.[24] Another is made up of traditional Democrats, southerners and Catholics, the blocs most aroused by the social issue. A fourth consists of northern middle-class, well-educated suburbanites of Republican antecedents, the Republicans probably most offended by their party's exploitation of the race issue, particularly during the Goldwater campaign, and its subsequent position on law and order. One cannot say with certainty just why any particular group of voters left their party to take an independent stand, but the coincidence of those who *did* leave their party and those who would be *expected* to leave because of the new issues is strong circumstantial evidence that those issues were in fact the cause.

The party system is always thrown into turmoil when powerful, crosscutting issues are at work. Fluidity, independence, and party switching are characteristic of the prerealignment and realignment periods that such issues generate. The present time, when millions of voters have been jarred loose from past allegiances and are floating unattached in political space, has all the characteristics of a prerealignment period.

24. More than half the southerners who voted for Wallace in 1968, reported Gallup, called themselves "independents" in 1969. American Institute of Public Opinion release, July 19, 1969.

Such periods in the past led to realignment when polarization around the realigning issue reached a crisis stage and the major parties gravitated to the poles. Alternatively, as postulated in Chapter 13 (point 16), party systems weakened by the passage of time can be reinforced if powerful new issues arise that run along, rather than across, the existing line of party cleavage. In either event, parties become relevant again and new and durable party attachments are formed. Whether either is likely to occur to arrest the onward march of party decomposition remains to be examined.

CHAPTER SEVENTEEN

Whither the American Party System?

OF THE FOUR crosscutting issues that have disturbed the New Deal party system in the four decades since its establishment, three remain alive. They are race, Vietnam, and the social issue. Of these the last two can probably be dismissed as having finally lost their force.

As was observed in Chapter 15, polarization on the Vietnam issue, which reached its peak in 1968, has declined steadily since that time as the Nixon administration has carried out its policy of de-escalation, negotiation, and withdrawal, and the social issue also lost its potency as a realigning agent once the parties were seen to take essentially the same position on crime, disorder, and the related social questions troubling the electorate. While these two issues may still result in some further minor realignment, they are not likely to be revived to the point where they could cause a major upheaval that would establish a new (post–New Deal) rationale for the party system.

That leaves race, and this is an issue that has maintained its polarizing power. There have been strong and determined political forces at both poles for a quarter of a century now, and while their strength has waxed and waned over the years according to the course of events affecting racial questions, the long-term trend has probably been upward. The blacks and their allies at one end of the spectrum are better organized and more assertive politically than ever before; their opponents, due largely to the busing controversy, are also organized to militantly resist black demands in more communities throughout the country than has been the case in other years. The long-term potential of this explosive issue for realignment of the party system needs therefore to be explored.

A Black-White Political Alignment?

As noted (Chapter 13, proposition 10), if a strong polar force encounters resistance or straddling by the major parties, a third party is likely at some point to be created. When the realignment occurs (proposition 13) the third party is absorbed by one of the major parties (variation b) or it replaces one of the existing major parties (variation c or d). Until such a realignment occurs, the political system can only continue in a state of instability as long as the issue retains its polarizing power.

THE WALLACE THIRD-PARTY MOVEMENT

In the case of the race issue, the polar force supporting civil rights was able to gain clear control in 1948 and again in the 1960s of a major party, the Democratic; and in the intervening years the prospect of its regaining domination of the Democrats was good enough to discourage any impulse to create a third party. But the polar force at the other end, which can be called the white resistance to black demands, was rejected, always by one major party and usually by both. So a third-party movement did arise. The movement has been continuous since; whether it took the form of a third party in any particular presidential year depended on the attitude of the major parties that year. When the Democrats first rejected its claims outright in 1948, the movement flowed into the States' Rights party. It took a third-party course again in 1968. In between, it gave its support sometimes to Democrats and sometimes (notably in 1964) to Republicans. In 1972, it followed George Wallace into the Democratic primaries and found the Republican candidate acceptable in the general election.

During the quarter century, the power of the movement grew, spurred by the Supreme Court's school integration decision, the agitation and demonstrations and violence, and the civil rights legislative battles. In 1968 Wallace ran in all fifty states and won 9.9 million votes, more than eight times as many as Thurmond had received as a regional candidate twenty years before. Wallace's 13.5 percent of the popular vote was the highest proportion given a third-party or independent presidential candidate since 1924. He carried five states, all in the Deep South, the strongest showing of a third party in the electoral college since 1912. He outpolled the Democrats in eight states, forming a solid belt from North Carolina to Louisiana. He did well in the border states: 20 percent of the popular vote in Oklahoma, 18 percent in Kentucky, 14.5 percent in Maryland. In the North, he received 12 percent of the vote in Ohio, 11 percent in Indiana, and 10 percent in Michigan. Nearly five million of the Wallace ballots came from outside the eleven southern states.

Yet even that impressive vote undermeasured the degree of polarization in 1968 on the racial issue. In gauging the basic support of the third-party movement, a more significant figure is probably the 21 percent of the voters who favored Wallace in the public opinion polls in late September; his share of the actual vote in November was reduced to 13.5 percent only by dint of the concentrated "he can't win" campaign of his opponents. "The vote Wallace drew in the North," Lubell has written, "was not the measure of the racial anger that prevailed; it was a measure of the anger that could not be repressed or restrained by Medicare, Social Security, high employment, and other appeals of the Democratic party."[1] Not all the Wallace support was racially motivated, of course—some undoubtedly came to him for other reasons—but Wallace was clearly perceived as the country's leading die-hard segregationist; he was originally a one-issue man, who rose to national prominence when he "stood in the schoolhouse door" to prevent integration. It is unlikely that many who did not share his views on racial questions gave him their vote; he got almost none, for example, in black precincts. That as many as one-third of the voters in many northern working class precincts were ready in September to dump their traditional Democratic affiliation to follow a third-party candidate with essentially a one-issue platform demonstrates the depth of their feeling and the extent of their alienation from the Democratic party on that issue.[2]

In 1972, Wallace chose to take his following back to the Democratic party—that is, until convention time. Hammering away at the 1972 version of the race issue, busing, as well as at various aspects of the social issue, and broadening his appeal with a "populist" economic program, he showed that the movement he led in 1968 had lost none of its appeal. He finished well ahead of his rivals in all the southern and border states that held preference primaries. Most spectacular of all, he received 51 percent of the party's vote in the northern industrial state of Michigan, which happened to be the state most inflamed by court orders on school busing and before that by the issue

1. Samuel Lubell, *The Hidden Crisis in American Politics* (Norton, 1970), p. 87.
2. Richard M. Scammon and Ben J. Wattenberg (*The Real Majority* [Coward-McCann, 1970] Chap. 13) detail the rise and decline of the Wallace strength in 1968, the nature of his support, and the voter perception of his candidacy. In the end, much of the race-motivated vote went to Nixon. This was surely true in some parts of the South, notably South Carolina, a Deep South state carried by Nixon where Senator Strom Thurmond, the original Dixiecrat, vouched for Nixon's sympathy with southern racial views. Lubell's data for white areas of northern cities where racial antagonism was high (South Philadelphia, Chicago's west side, Gary, East Baltimore) show Nixon inroads into the traditional Democratic vote that can be accounted for in no other way. *Hidden Crisis*, pp. 95–96.

of housing integration in the suburbs. He also finished second in Indiana, West Virginia, New Mexico, Wisconsin, Pennsylvania, and Oregon, with from 20 to 42 percent of the Democratic vote.

As newspaperman Jim Clark has pointed out, Wallace's popular strength within the Democratic party was about equivalent to George McGovern's. In ten primary states where Wallace made a serious effort, he received one out of every three votes, by Clark's figures, for a total of 3.4 million. In fourteen states where McGovern campaigned, he also received one out of every three votes, for a total of 3.8 million. Wallace won fewer than half as many delegates in the primary states because he concentrated on the presidential preference side of the primaries and failed to file a complete slate, or sometimes any slate at all, in the delegate selection contests. Had he mounted a campaign for delegates as well organized as McGovern's in the states with primaries and those without, Clark argues, he could have gone to the convention with a first-ballot strength comparable to McGovern's.[3]

When Wallace declined to run as a third-party candidate after the 1972 Democratic convention, most of his supporters undoubtedly voted Republican in the presidential election. But there is no reason to think that they have yet identified themselves as Republicans, presaging a realignment of the party system on the race issue. For that to be the outcome, one of three things would have to happen: the polar force represented in the Wallace movement[4] would have to capture the Democratic party, gain control of the Republican party, or attain major-party status independently and supplant one of the existing major parties.

THE RACE ISSUE AND THE MAJOR PARTIES

The prospect that the polar force represented in the Wallace movement might capture the Democratic party appears least likely. If the white resistance elements are predominantly within the Democratic party, so are

3. "Could Wallace Have Won?" *Washington Post*, July 9, 1972. Clark is writing a book on the Wallace campaign.

4. This does not imply that all of Wallace's support is racist, in the pejorative sense of the term. Even if his appeal in northern states such as Michigan did rest heavily on his position as the most emphatic opponent of busing (as seems to have been the case), that was not necessarily a racist appeal, for busing is opposed on other than racist grounds. Race as an issue, as used in this section, and racism as an attitude are two different things. Busing is treated as a manifestation of the race issue, in political terms, because it polarizes people along racial lines; at one pole are those who support the demands of the blacks and their rights as interpreted by the courts; at the other are those who resist these demands, on whatever grounds.

the blacks and their liberal allies. Since 1948, whenever the party has had to choose between the two polar blocs, it has consistently taken its stand with the blacks. It reaffirmed that choice emphatically in 1972, when it rejected the Wallace substitute for its affirmative platform plank on busing and then nominated as its candidate the one among the major aspirants who had probably made the fewest concessions to the antibusing clamor in his primary campaign.

Given its record of commitment and the numerical weight of the blacks and their liberal allies within the party—blacks cast one-quarter of the Democratic vote for president in 1968 and must have equaled that proportion in 1972—only one contingency could bring about a reversal of the party's position and its realignment with the other polar bloc. That would be a divisive, well-organized, all-out campaign by George Wallace or an equally effective leader that would fully mobilize the latent antibusing, white-resistance sentiment within the party and win the party's nomination. This would polarize the party internally and split it as surely as the same racial issue split the Whigs in 1852. But since the attempt on Wallace's life in May 1972, his future as a vigorous campaigner has been in doubt, and no one of his stature with similar views has appeared on the political horizon. Moreover, his latent support would dwindle quickly if the busing issue faded; and the issue may well fade, as the courts respond to pressure from the President, the Congress, and the public and draw back from the issuance of new orders that involve extensive busing.

The vulnerability of the Republican party to capture by the white resistance forces was demonstrated temporarily in 1964, when the segregationists in the South rallied behind Barry Goldwater as a states' rights advocate, although Goldwater did not express the personal segregationist views of a Wallace or cast his appeal in overt racist tones. Since then, the party leaders have followed the accustomed course of party leaders in coping with crosscutting issues—they have straddled.

President Nixon in his first term took such conspicuous steps to conciliate the white resistance that liberals accused him of straying well to the other side of the center. Particularly conspicuous were his nomination of "strict constructionists" to the Supreme Court, his demand for legislation to stop any further court-ordered busing, and his denunciation of quotas as a means of assuring blacks of their rights. But there were still outspoken integrationists among the administration's top officials, notably the secretary of housing and urban development, George Romney, who continued to press for housing

integration in the suburbs. The President had managed to stay close enough
to the center to retain the support of the black members of his subcabinet
and of the only black Republican member of Congress, Senator Edward W.
Brooke of Massachusetts. This is ultimately the definition of a successful
straddle: one that gives enough satisfaction to both sides of an issue to prevent any significant loss of party strength. In 1972, the Republican party
was still managing to bridge the chasm between Senators Brooke and Jacob
Javits at one extreme and Strom Thurmond at the other, and between rank-
and-file Republicans of both persuasions as well.

RACIAL POLITICS AT THE LOCAL LEVEL IN THE NORTH

More significant, perhaps, as an indicator of the prospect of a black-white
political alignment is what has happened at the local level. In northern communities that have been polarized on racial issues, the opportunity has existed
for the Republican party to become the party of the "white backlash." Yet
this has happened only occasionally. On the one hand, the white resistance
movement has not sought to make the Republican party its political instrument. On the other, local Republican leaders have not usually been willing
to exploit the racial issue.

Those at the white resistance pole have not sought to take over the Republican party because they have not had to. Being for the most part Democrats, they have found it more convenient and more effective to use their
own party for their ends. Where established local Democratic leaders stood
in their way, they have been able to contest for party leadership, often successfully. Thus the symbol of the white resistance in Philadelphia has been
Mayor Frank L. Rizzo, the "tough cop" police chief nominated by the Democratic organization. In Boston, it has been Louise Day Hicks, school board
member and later congresswoman, a Democrat. In Cleveland, it has been
James V. Stanton, city council president and later congressman, a Democrat.
In the New York City mayoralty election of 1969 it was Mario Procaccino,
Democratic candidate running against Mayor John V. Lindsay. In Gary, In-
diana, it was the Democratic county organization. In Los Angeles, it was
Mayor Sam Yorty, nominally a Democrat. And so on.

Even in such a citadel of Democratic liberalism as Michigan, Democratic
politicians proved no less responsive than Republicans to the white suburbanites who mobilized to resist a federal court order for busing school-
children across district lines between Detroit and its suburbs. Every white

Democratic member of the House of Representatives from Michigan, along with most Republicans, voted for the series of legislative measures that came before the House in 1971 and 1972 seeking to curtail the issuance, or delay the effectiveness, of school busing orders. "Shocking," said black Representative John Conyers, Jr., describing the way the "knee-jerk liberals . . . deserted the Constitution once it got to the suburbs."[5]

Sometimes the local symbol of sympathy with black demands has been a Democrat, like Mayor Carl B. Stokes of Cleveland, Mayor Kevin White of Boston (called "Mayor Black" by his enemies), or Mayor Joseph H. Mc-Dowell of Kansas City (called "Old Black Joe"), but perhaps as often it has been a Republican. In Philadelphia in 1971, it was W. Thacher Longstreth, Rizzo's opponent, and in New York it has been Mayor Lindsay, a Republican during his first six years in office. In Michigan, said a Democratic leader in 1970, "the suburbs are on fire on the open housing question—but against George Romney. It was Romney the pictures showed them spitting on when he visited Warren."[6]

Even when the Democrats at the white resistance pole had occasion to vote Republican with unanimity, as in Cleveland's three mayoralty elections between 1967 and 1971, they showed no sign of changing their basic party affiliation. The Cleveland municipal election was simply treated locally as though it were nonpartisan. White Democrats who voted for Mayor Ralph J. Perk, Republican, were not looking at the party label but voting for Perk, white, against Stokes or Arnold Pinkney, black. The Republican party of Cleveland steadfastly resisted the temptation to exploit racial issues in order to bring the mass of racially motivated deviating Democrats into the Republican party. "I would fire any ward leader who tried it," said Robert E. Hughes, chairman of the county GOP committee. And the same attitudes are found in Republican leadership throughout the North. Political necessity, as well as idealism, is involved. "The Republican party will never go racist

5. *Detroit Free Press*, Nov. 5, 1971. Four antibusing amendments came to roll call votes in the House on Nov. 4, 1971. On one of the amendments, Conyers cast the only negative Michigan vote. The other amendments received three, two, and one additional negative votes, all from Republicans. On a motion on March 8, 1972, to instruct the House conferees to uphold its antibusing amendments against a milder Senate version, only one Republican and two Democrats, both blacks, voted in the negative. Again, on Aug. 17, 1972, the two black Democrats and two white Republicans cast the only Michigan votes against a strong antibusing bill.

6. Warren is a Detroit suburb, which was the center of conflict over housing integration. Quoted remarks in this chapter, if not otherwise identified, are from interviews conducted in the course of visits to twelve states during the off-year election campaign in the fall of 1970. The interviews were generally on a "not for attribution" basis.

because the liberals won't let it," a liberal Republican explained. "They can't afford to lose us. We include the big contributors and the press, and they can't win without us." That was perhaps demonstrated in 1964, when Barry Goldwater's open appeal to the southern segregationist vote was one of the factors that cost him millions of votes in the North, which he needed for victory.

For all these reasons, a black-white political alignment has so far been averted in the North.

RACIAL POLITICS AT THE LOCAL LEVEL IN THE SOUTH

The picture is somewhat different in the South. There, a black-white political alignment has been established in some localities and gives some indication of stability. It can be dated from 1964, when Goldwater successfully merged the Dixiecrat-racist stream of southern white voting with the metropolitan Republicanism that developed in the Eisenhower years. In the metropolitan counties where this occurred, the Democratic party was reduced to little more than its hard core of liberal-integrationist and black supporters and was easily branded by its opponents as "the black man's party." When this became its local image (and the Republican party began to be identified as "the white man's party") the black-white party alignment was in place, marked by a movement of some Democratic officeholders and established politicians into the Republican ranks.

As late as 1970, at least, the black-white alignment was largely confined to the communities where the two streams Goldwater brought together were strongest—in other words, communities that were both metropolitan in character and located in the black belt. In the rim South and in the smaller cities and rural areas of the Deep South, the Democratic party had been able to maintain its position as the majority party of the whites in state and local politics (outside traditionally Republican areas). Even in the metropolitan centers of the Deep South where the new black-white alignment is in place, the GOP has had trouble consolidating its position.

The two streams that have come together there within the Republican party have entered into a marriage of convenience, but they are in many ways quite incompatible. The metropolitan Republicans have their base in the upper-income, more highly educated strata—the "country club set"— and it is in these strata, which are the most insulated from the blacks in housing and job competition, that the most liberal attitudes on race are found.

Racial demagoguery is not the style of its leaders, and social distance prevents an easy amalgamation of metropolitan suburban Republicans and racists. "The country club set and the Wallace rednecks have nothing in common; they can't even talk to each other," said one political observer.

The difference in racial attitudes carries over into a profound difference in strategy and tactics. In Shelby County (Memphis), Tennessee, one of the southern centers where the black-white political alignment is most pronounced,[7] the Republican county chairman, Alexander W. Dann, Jr., said in 1970, "We will not have a black-white political system in this county if I can help it," and he recited the party's policies and programs designed to attract black voters to the GOP. But a young Republican campaigner in Tennessee expressed another view: "We should leave them [the blacks] strictly alone and let the Democrats have them all. There are more whites."

This argument has rent the Republican party throughout the South, but those who advocate renouncing racism and seeking black support have on the whole prevailed. The success of GOP candidates who wooed and won a large proportion of the black vote has helped to set the pattern; for instance, Governors Winthrop Rockefeller in Arkansas and Linwood K. Holton in Virginia. In his two election victories, Rockefeller reportedly received 85 percent of the black vote.

If a clincher were needed, perhaps it was in South Carolina in 1970. There the Republican strategists reasoned that a Wallace-type campaign along racial lines would enable the party to put together the Nixon vote of 1968 (38 percent) and the Wallace vote (32 percent) for an unbeatable majority. Congressman Albert W. Watson, the gubernatorial candidate, made "discipline in the schools" his central issue and featured television spots of the Watts and Washington, D.C., black riots; "wallowed in the filth of racial hatred" was the description of his campaign by the liberal Republican journal *Ripon Forum*.[8] But the intended Republican coalition came unstuck: the 70 percent combined vote for Nixon and Wallace in 1968 fell to 46 percent for Watson. On the one side, according to a newspaper report, "dozens . . . of South Carolina conservatives from the established world of business and the suburbs were outraged by the pungently racist Republican campaign."[9]

7. In one poll in Memphis in 1968, 94 percent of black respondents supported Humphrey for president, but only 12 percent of white respondents. Yung Wie and H. R. Mahood, "Racial Attitudes and the Wallace Vote: A Study of the 1968 Election in Memphis," *Polity*, Vol. 3 (Summer 1971), pp. 536–37.

8. December 1970, p. 15.

9. Rowland Evans and Robert Novak, *Washington Post*, Jan. 14, 1971.

Table 17-1. *Democratic Gains in Five Southern States, 1968–70*

State	Percentage of presidential vote, 1968			Percentage of gubernatorial vote, 1970		Gain	
	D	R	AIP	D	R	D	R
Arkansas	30.4	30.8	38.9	62.3	31.7	31.9	0.9
Tennessee	28.1	37.8	34.0	45.9	51.9	17.8	14.1
Georgia	26.7	30.4	42.8	59.0	41.0	32.3	9.6
Florida	30.9	40.5	28.5	56.8	43.2	26.9	2.7
South Carolina	29.6	38.1	32.3	51.7	45.6	22.1	7.5

D = Democrats; R = Republicans; AIP = American Independent party.

On the other, the bulk of the Wallace vote reverted to the Democrats. The so-called southern strategy advocated by Kevin Phillips for the national GOP, to "undercut" the Wallace movement and absorb its strength by paying "sufficient attention" to its viewpoint,[10] had not worked even in the Wallace heartland.

"State government in South Carolina must be color-blind," said the new Democratic governor, John C. West, in his inaugural address. "Any vestige of discrimination because of race or religion must be eliminated." A few weeks later Senator Strom Thurmond, the original Dixiecrat-turned-Republican, announced the appointment of a black to his staff.

Besides South Carolina, in five other states with a history of racist politics the gubernatorial elections of 1970, 1971, and early 1972 gave impressive evidence that the Democratic party in the South can retain its solid black core and still win back a substantial portion of the white vote that it lost in the presidential election of 1968. In Florida and Arkansas, where they ousted Republican incumbents, and in Georgia, Mississippi, and Louisiana, moderate Democrats were elected after campaigns remarkably free of racial taint. The Democratic comeback was based, as it had to be, on a return of most of the Wallace voters, as Table 17-1 makes clear.[11] The new governors ex-

10. Kevin P. Phillips, *The Emerging Republican Majority* (Arlington House, 1969), p. 473.

11. Intercounty correlations show that in four of the five states the correlation of the 1970 Democratic gubernatorial vote with the 1968 Wallace (American Independent party) vote was higher than with the 1968 Humphrey vote, and in three of the four much higher. The figures are:

	R	AIP	D
Arkansas	−0.116	0.345	−0.366
Tennessee	−0.808	0.636	0.677
Georgia	−0.855	0.703	−0.054
Florida	−0.699	0.605	−0.157
South Carolina	−0.372	0.238	0.082

Calculations by Gary Greenhalgh.

pressed the same sentiments as West. "Let us now endeavor to make Virginia a model in race relations," Republican Governor Holton said in his inaugural address. "We will have a government based on a partnership of all Virginians, a government in which there will be neither partisanship nor prejudice of any kind." Later he escorted his three children to predominantly black public schools in Richmond, a city then aflame with passion on the issue of school busing. Echoed Democratic Governor Jimmy Carter of Georgia in his inaugural address: "I say to you quite frankly that the time for racial discrimination is over. Our people have already made this major and difficult decision." And Democratic Governor Reubin Askew of Florida: "The law demands, and rightly so, that we put an end to segregation in our society. Only in this way will we put the divisive and self-defeating issue of race behind us once and for all."[12] Observers at the time hailed a new era in the South.

Yet Wallace had no difficulty in reviving the old era when he took his presidential campaign into the region's primaries a few months later. On balance, however, the events of 1972, like those of 1970 and 1971, probably served to check any trend in the South toward a black-white cleavage between the major parties. Wallace's emergence as a major Democratic figure, with a prominent role at the convention and evident aspirations for future national leadership in the party, served to hold his followers to their Democratic identities. While they voted solidly Republican in November, that does not signal a realignment in favor of the GOP any more than did their enthusiastic shift to Goldwater eight years earlier. For the movement to move bodily into the Republican party, the GOP would have to get off the fence on the race issue and accept decisively the views of Wallace and his followers. In the South as well as the North, the Republican party has been moving, if at all, in the opposite direction.

If both the Democratic and Republican parties seem unlikely to fall under the control of the polar forces on the white resistance side of the race issue, there remains the third possible route to realignment—the growth of a third party embodying those forces that would eventually supplant one of the existing major parties in the two-party system. It can be argued that such a prospect might have existed after 1968, subject to a series of ifs—if Governor Wallace had devoted himself to organizing his American Independent party throughout the country, if he had campaigned for its candidates in state and local elections, if he had been elected governor of Alabama in 1970 as an AIP rather than Democratic candidate, and if he had then run for presi-

12. Commencement address, University of Florida, Aug. 28, 1971.

dent in 1972 under its banner. Given all the factors that work against third parties, as evidenced in history—for example, the extent to which the major parties would have adopted his platform in particular localities in state and local politics—it is doubtful that the party would have gained momentum even then. In any case, Wallace did just the opposite of what would have been required. He abandoned the AIP and reentered Democratic politics in Alabama. What momentum had been built was lost. As of 1973, every indication from Governor Wallace was that he was planning to continue his career as a Democrat, and the woeful showing of Congressman John G. Schmitz of California as the AIP candidate for president in 1972 seemed to make clear that a third-party movement without Wallace, as long as he remains an active politician, will amount to nothing.

So the short-term outlook is not for a realignment of the party system on the race issue but rather for continued instability, as the Wallace bloc of voters moves uncertainly from party to party under the particular circumstances of each election. The anti-civil-rights, anti-integration protest movement remains in the position it has occupied since 1948; it is still available to support whichever presidential candidate—Democrat, Republican, or third-party—most nearly approximates its views in each successive election.

THE "NEW BLACK POLITICS"

Whether the continuing realignment crisis on the race issue heightens to the point of actual realignment largely depends on the determination with which the blacks and their liberal allies press their demands for Negro rights. If the blacks heighten and focus their demands, if they unite behind them and present them with militance and determination, it is not impossible that they could bring the country to a new intensity of racial polarization. But that involves another series of large ifs.

Leading blacks have forcefully stated the case for what has been called "the new black politics"—the creation of an independent black political movement at one end of the black-white spectrum comparable to the Wallace forces at the other end, available to throw its weight in one direction or another as circumstances dictated in each election. "In politics, the predictable votes are never rewarded as abundantly as the uncontrollable groups who are ready to change their affiliation," wrote Chuck Stone in 1968. He advocated, therefore, "the political oscillation of fragile loyalties—the negro vote has to swing back and forth periodically between the two parties, shifting its loyalties with the same frequency as the white vote. . . . once the negro vote is taken for granted—as it has been nationally since the New Deal—it loses its bargaining power."[13] Three years later, leading black elected officials were for the first time expressing this view. The Democrats "are going to give us what we are entitled to, or we are going to deny them what they want from us—our votes," declared Representative William Clay of St. Louis, a militant member of the newly organized congressional Black Caucus in the U.S. House of Representatives. "They know the consequences of our taking even 25% of the black vote out of the Democratic column: They wouldn't have a chance in hell to win."[14] "For any black to look upon himself as a Democrat or Republican is ridiculous," said Representative John Conyers of Detroit, another caucus member.[15]

In 1972, an attempt was made to draft a common program and political strategy around which the fourteen million potential black voters could unite. A National Black Political Convention, with 3,300 voting delegates, met at Gary, Indiana, in March and created a National Black Political Assembly as a continuing body to steer a course for the black minority. The congressional Black Caucus published a set of "non-negotiable, minimum" demands as a "Black Bill of Rights" in June. But experience so far suggests that black Americans will encounter just as much difficulty in reaching agreement on a common political strategy to advance their cause as any other group of fourteen million eligible voters of diverse backgrounds, outlook, and interests. Unlike their opponents, the blacks have yet no dominant leader, or even a compact group of leaders, who can make decisions governing the movement. In 1972, their principal spokesmen pursued separate and conflicting strategies after as well as before the Gary conclave.

Those who seek to weld the country's blacks into a powerful, united political force are bound, however, to continue their efforts, and perhaps it is not unreasonable to predict the gradual coalescence of a substantial body of blacks as a polar political force. Their demands will no doubt be radical in content and forcefully presented, and that will serve to strengthen the unity and determination of the opposing polar group.

A scenario could be written sketching how a party realignment might grow from the conflict of the black and white polar groups, on the assumption that the conflict escalates and polarization heightens. The Democratic

13. *Black Political Power in America* (Bobbs-Merrill, 1968), p. 43.
14. *Wall Street Journal*, Oct. 26, 1971.
15. Washington *Star*, Nov. 7, 1971.

party, as Congressman Clay argues, would find it difficult to resist adoption of the black demands. When it embraced them, outraged opponents of the demands would flee to the Republicans, and the national party system would shift on its axis. The Democrats would be at one pole, the Republicans would be forced by the pressure of the polarized community to the other, and voters would make new attachments according to their views about the race issue.

But such a scenario would be predicated on a continued heightening of racial conflict, and the forces for moderation are many and powerful too. Racism as an attitude has been steadily declining in the country as a whole; that the trend of public opinion has been "distinctly and strongly toward increasing approval of integration" is clearly shown in the national polls of the National Opinion Research Center, covering a span of thirty years.[16] Black solidarity around any program so radical as to heighten racial conflict would not be easy to attain. Many black leaders will be contending for position, each with his or her own national or local following, program, and priorities. Many of them have a heavy stake in the continued success of an integrated Democratic party, and will be among the party's centrist elements seeking to moderate the black demands. Some of the younger militants who are now talking "black politics" may themselves be attracted by the security and opportunity of integrated politics—"coopted by the power structure," as the militants would put it. Within the Democratic party as a whole would be a centrist body of white and black leaders striving to prevent the party from taking any position so extreme as to precipitate a realignment that could only convert their majority party into a permanent minority.

Most important of all, if racial tensions heightened, would be the inevitable reaction throughout the society against tension itself. If the country appeared to be on the verge of being torn apart by racial conflict, the weight of the country's nonpolitical leadership and opinion molders would be brought to bear on the politicians to compromise the black demands. What will ultimately save the country from racial realignment, if it appears headed that way, is that the race issue does not directly affect enough people to make it all-pervasive. In individual communities of bitter confrontation, it has reached those proportions. But such conflicts are scattered and local; most Americans are insulated from them, and it is these Americans who form a powerful potential mediating force that has intervened, and would do so again, to support the moderate centrist forces in both parties and bring

16. Andrew M. Greeley and Paul B. Sheatsley, "Attitudes Toward Racial Integration," *Scientific American*, Vol. 225 (December 1971), pp. 13–19.

about some resolution of the issue before the party system as it existed was destroyed.

Yet if realignment on the race issue is not in prospect, neither is stability. The polar forces are unlikely to disappear soon. So the prospect is for a kind of multiparty system for a time. The polar blocs created by the race issue may even organize as formal parties from time to time, as the southern white resistance movement has done in the past. But as equality of rights and opportunities for the black minority is gradually attained, the underlying grievance that gives rise to racial politics will be ameliorated, and the polar forces should eventually decline in strength. In the meantime, of course, the race issue may be overshadowed once again by other issues.

A Rebirth of the New Deal Party System?

The establishment of a new party system and the revitalization of an old one come about in essentially the same way (as was observed in Chapter 13's proposition 16). A new issue (or set of related issues) comes to dominate political discussion and polarize the electorate. The difference is simply that in the first case, the new issue or set of issues cuts across the existing line of party cleavage, while in the second it runs along that line.

If the next set of issues to dominate American politics is in the tradition of the activist-conservative and class conflicts of the last four decades, the New Deal party system can be reborn. Just as the crosscutting issues of the 1960s have blurred that line of cleavage, so issues that run along the line, which may be called "coincident" issues, would redefine and sharpen it. Crosscutting issues weaken the attachment of voters to the existing parties; coincident issues reinforce attachments. If the party system seems meaningless when crosscutting issues dominate political debate ("There is no difference between the parties," "Neither party takes a clear stand," "Neither party represents my point of view"), it takes on meaning when coincident issues dominate.

A number of such issues, which have the potential of arousing intense conflict, either have already entered the political arena or are on the horizon. As the social issue and Vietnam continue to recede from the center of the arena, the new issues will move toward the center. And the dynamics of the two-party system suggest that there will be a genuine confrontation between the major parties on those issues. Depending on the extent to which public and political opinion polarizes, the New Deal party system will be invigorated.

In considering how that confrontation may be brought about, it is instructive to review briefly how a comparable set of coincident issues reinvigorated the New Deal party system during the policy-making cycle that began with the accession of President Eisenhower in 1953 and culminated in President Johnson's Great Society legislation of 1964–65.[17]

THE 1953–68 POLITICAL AND POLICY-MAKING CYCLE

The analogies between the current period and the early stages of the Eisenhower-Kennedy-Johnson policy-making cycle are striking. In 1969 as in 1953, a Republican president came to office after a period of Democratic control. In each case, an unpopular war in Asia and a major domestic issue (communism in government in the first case, the social-racial issue in the second) had contributed to the Democratic defeat. In each case, the new president had promised to extricate the country from its Democratic war and bring Republican peace, and he proceeded to move in that direction. In each case, his mandate on domestic policy was essentially a conservative one—to slow down the pace of change, to separate the wise from the unwise among the reforms of the Democratic years, and to consolidate the former and liquidate the latter. In each case, the crosscutting domestic issue continued to dominate political discussion for a time but then faded as a partisan question.

The early years of the Republican administration, in each case, were a period of quiet on the domestic legislative front. This was due in part to the conservative makeup and mandate of the Republican administration, in part to its preoccupation with reducing the foreign commitments of the Democrats, and in part to the deadlock on domestic policy between the administration and the Congress. In Eisenhower's case, the Democrats controlled the Congress after his first two years; in Nixon's case, from the outset. But the Democrats—defeated, defensive, demoralized, and to some extent discredited—did not immediately offer an affirmative program of their own.

In the second Eisenhower term, however, the Democrats recovered their aggressive spirit and entered into a period of intensive and productive pro-

17. The successive stages of the cycle are traced in James L. Sundquist, *Politics and Policy: The Eisenhower, Kennedy, and Johnson Years* (Brookings Institution, 1968), Chaps. 9–11.

gram-building. Assisted by members of the academic community and by representatives of interest groups, they developed a consensus as to the major problems that demanded action, drafted their remedial measures, circulated and publicized them widely, and refined them through congressional hearings and floor debate, and through a continuing confrontation and dialogue with the Republican administration. By 1960 much of the program that was later enacted as the New Frontier and the Great Society had taken specific form.

Meanwhile, the country had shifted from a conservative to an activist mood. The polls of the period show conclusively that the country wanted action, and Kennedy caught the public mood with his pledge "to get the country moving again." Once the Democrats again controlled the White House as well as the Congress, the program began its slow course toward passage. In the next five years, and particularly in 1964 and 1965, after the assassination of President Kennedy and the landslide election of President Johnson, virtually the whole program was enacted. During the whole of this period, from early 1958 until the summer of 1965, the substance of the party conflict was much like that of the 1930s—a quarrel over the extent and nature of governmental intervention to solve the problems of society, and in particular to improve the lot of the less privileged.

It is especially noteworthy, in support of the thesis of this section, that *during the period when party conflict over activist-conservative issues in the New Deal tradition was at its height, the party attachment of voters apparently strengthened*. The Survey Research Center poll of 1958 (Figure 16-2) showed a significant drop in the proportion of independent voters, all to the benefit of the Democrats. The basic concern that year was unemployment; on that issue the Democrats became aggressively activist and Eisenhower responded with a stubborn conservatism. The difference in party attitudes and programs was clearly limned, and the relevance of the party system was suddenly increased. That fall there was a party landslide, as distinct from the personal landslides achieved by General Eisenhower, and Democrats who had been calling themselves independents told the pollsters they were Democrats again.

As sharp party conflict continued through the 1960 campaign and afterward, the parties retained their significance. The number of independents in the SRC polls remained below the 1956 level until 1965, when the Democrats' activist initiatives had come to an end and the new crosscutting issues had arisen. The Gallup polls show the same decline in the proportion of independents, although the timing is different: their data show the decline as beginning in 1957 and extending through 1962.

PARTY CONFRONTATION IN THE CURRENT CYCLE

As the second Nixon administration began, a set of domestic issues squarely coincident with the line of cleavage of the New Deal party system was rapidly moving back to the center of public and political attention. On the assumption that the country's disengagement in Southeast Asia proved durable, it appeared likely that President Nixon's second term—like President Eisenhower's—would be dominated by the same fundamental dispute over the role of government that defined a new party alignment in the 1930s and has reinforced that alignment on so many occasions since.

In the late 1950s, the issues of the activist-conservative conflict were defined from the activist side, as Democrats in the Congress advanced the measures that later made up much of the New Frontier and the Great Society. They provoked, then, a counteroffensive by the Republican President. In the 1970s, the initiative came at the outset from the other side. It was the Republican President who chose the issues when he set out to liquidate through administrative action, in defiance of the Democratic Congress, not only much of what the New Frontier and the Great Society had created, but even programs that had their origin in the New Deal itself. And it was for the activists to defend, and to counterattack.

Responding to the coincident issues, the parties were taking their familiar stance. Fellow partisans who had been divided by crosscutting issues like Vietnam and busing drew together again. Cohesion within the parties increased, the distance between them widened, party rhetoric renewed old themes. The always difficult problem of the out-party in attaining unity was being eased, in this case, by the fact that the President's attack on Democratic programs appeared also to be an attack on the powers of the Congress as an institution. Conservative senators and representatives who might share the President's disdain for the programs their party colleagues had enacted still had to spring to the defense of Congress's right to determine when and if those programs were to be dismantled.

Certainly there were some within the Democratic party, chastened by the events of 1972, who sought to hold the party back from open conflict with the victorious President over the issues of government spending and economy, but the dynamics of the party system suggest that they could not prevail—not for long, at least. If somewhere near half the electorate is activist by philosophy and temperament (the polls suggest that more than half of it is activist on major domestic problems most of the time),[18] the Democrats, as the party on the activist side of the line of party cleavage, are bound to reflect the attitude of that segment of the population. Party leaders who fail to articulate the activism of the party's rank and file will not remain leaders. Indeed, the prospect was that those who speak for the Democratic party in the Congress would not only resist the President's proposals to cut back the role of government but would also come up with initiatives of their own to expand that role, as they did in the 1950s, to their political gain. So new issues would be added from both sides to the cluster centered on the question of governmental activism, and as the debate progressed the old line of cleavage between the parties would be sharpened and deepened. The New Deal party system would take on a fresh significance as it dealt with the kind of issues for which it was designed.

In the long run, the prospect may well be for a further gradual decomposition of the two-party system. But there is at least as much reason to believe that in the shorter run the headlong march toward decomposition that marked the late 1960s will be checked and even reversed, the New Deal party system will be reinvigorated, and most of those who ceased identifying with one or the other major party in the recent turmoil will reidentify. The parties might not enjoy the degree of voter loyalty that was accorded them in the crisis days of the Great Depression, but the bonds between voter and party would be restored to something like the strength of the late 1950s and the early 1960s—before Goldwater, Vietnam, Watts and Hough, campus riots and draft card burnings, and the Chicago Democratic convention of 1968.

18. For a summary of evidence from the 1950s and the first half of the 1960s bearing on this point, see *Politics and Policy*, Chap. 10; pp. 484–89, 496; and pp. 3–4.

Index